11TH EDITION HAWAII THE BIG ISLAND REVEALED

THE ULTIMATE GUIDEBOOK

P9-BHX-793

ANDREW DOUGHTY

DIRECTOR OF PHOTOGRAPHY LEONA BOYD

R Revealed TRAVEL GUIDES

Altars (called lele hoʻokau), such as this one at the Kuʻemanu Heiau, are still used by some for prayer or meditation.

Hawaii The Big Island Revealed
The Ultimate Guidebook 11th Edition

Published by Wizard Publications, Inc.
Post Office Box 991
Lihu‘e, Hawai‘i 96766–0991

ISBN: 978-1-949678-14-7   1042
Library of Congress Control Number 2022902800
Printed in Korea

Cataloging-in-Publication Data

Doughty, Andrew
   Hawaii the Big Island revealed : the ultimate guidebook / Andrew Doughty. – 11th
ed. Lihue, HI : Wizard Publications, Inc., 2022
      300 p.: col. illus., col. photos, col. maps; 21 cm.
      Includes index.
      Summary : a complete traveler's reference to the island of Hawaii, with full color
photos, maps, directions, and candid advice by an author who resides in Hawaii.
      ISBN 978-1-949678-14-7
      LCCN 2022902800
      1. Hawaii Island (Hawaii) – Guidebooks. 2. Hawaii Island (Hawaii) – Description
and travel. I. Title.

DU 622   919.69__dc21

Cover space imagery courtesy of Earthstar Geographics (terracolor.net).
Cartography by Andrew Doughty.
All artwork and illustrations by Andrew Doughty and Lisa Pollak.

Past and present lava flow information for maps was graciously provided by an over-worked and under-appreciated United States Geological Survey, the silent partner to all mapmakers. Keep up the good work!

We welcome any comments, questions, criticisms or contributions you may have and have incorporated some of your suggestions into this edition. Please send to the address above, or email us at **information@revealedtravelguides.com**.

Check out our website at **RevealedTravelGuides.com** for up-to-the-minute changes. Find us on **Facebook**, **YouTube**, **Instagram** and **Twitter** (@RevealedGuides).

To Harry and Mary—
Their love of travel lives on...

CONTENTS

ABOUT THIS BOOK
9

INTRODUCTION
11

THE BASICS
21

KOHALA SIGHTS
47

KAILUA-KONA SIGHTS
63

SOUTH ISLAND SIGHTS
80

CONTENTS

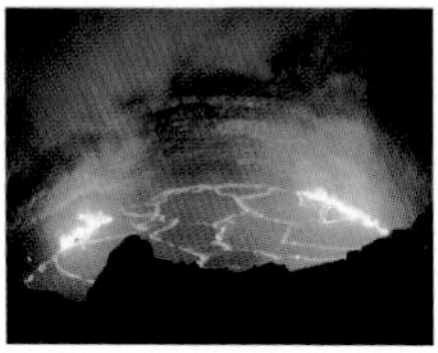

VOLCANO SIGHTS 89

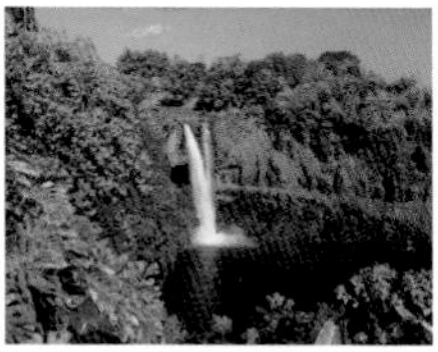

HILO & PUNA SIGHTS 109

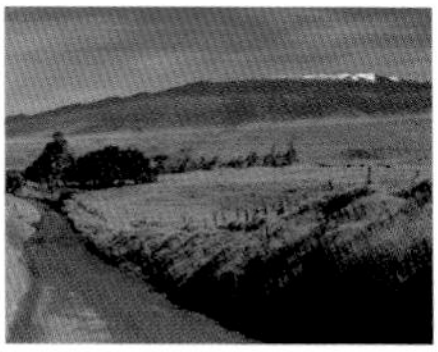

HAMAKUA & WAIMEA SIGHTS 125

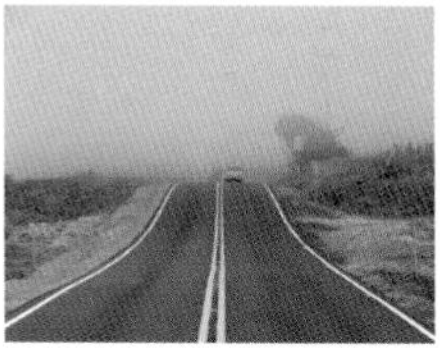

SADDLE ROAD SIGHTS 141

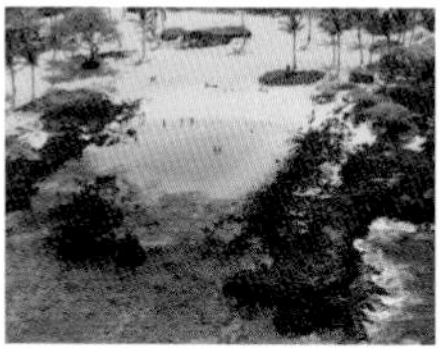

BEACHES 150

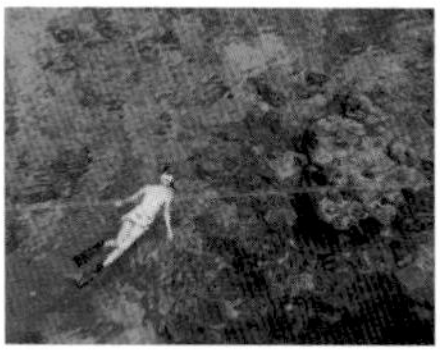

ACTIVITIES 182

(Activities continued...)

The Big Island has it all. Nowhere else in the world will you find the diversity available here. Pristine rain forests, lava deserts, world-class beaches, snow-covered mountains, an active volcano, dazzling sunsets and just about every activity you can think of. The island is huge—about the size of Connecticut. Navigating your way through this maze of opportunity can be daunting.

Most travel publishers send a writer or writers to a given location for a few weeks to become "experts" and to compile in-formation for guidebooks. To our knowledge, we at Wizard Publications are the only ones who actually *live* our books.

We hike the trails, ride the boats, eat in the restaurants, explore the reefs and do the things we write about. It takes us two *years*, full time, to do a first edition book, and we visit places *anonymously*. We marvel at writers who can do it all in a couple of weeks staying in a hotel. Wow, they must be *really* fast. Our method, though it takes much longer, gives us the ability to tell it like it is in a way no one else can. We put in many long hours, and doing all these activities is a burdensome grind. But we do it all for you—only for you. (Feel free to gag at this point.)

We produce brand new editions of our books every year (or so), but in the intervening time we constantly incorporate changes smartphone app, which is a separate product with very different capabilities than a paper book. We also post these changes on our website.

We have found many special places that people born and raised here didn't even know about because that's all *we do*—explore the island.

In this day of easy-to-access online reviews from countless sources, you can get "ratings" for nearly every company out there. What you get from our reviews is a single source, *beholden to none*, and with a comprehensive exposure to all of the companies. There are two critical shortcomings to online reviews. One is that you don't know the source or agenda of the reviewer. Nearly every company that offers a service to the public *thinks* they are doing a good job. (But as you know, not everyone does.) So who can blame a company for trying to rig the system by seeding good reviews of their company at every opportunity or having friends write good reviews? Many also encourage *satisfied* customers to write favorable online reviews (obviously not encouraging *unhappy* customers to do so). But maybe their enemies or competitors retaliate with bad reviews. The point is, you never *really know* where those reviews come from, and it's almost impossible to reconcile terrible reviews right next to glowing ones for the same company. Which do you believe?

The other problem is a lack of a frame of reference. A visitor to Hawai'i goes on a snorkel boat and has a great time. (Hey, he snorkeled in Hawai'i, swam with a turtle—*cool!*) When he goes back home, he posts good reviews all around. That's great. But the problem is, he only went on *one* snorkel boat. We do 'em all. If only he'd known that another company *he didn't even know about* did a much better job, had way better food, and a much nicer boat for the same price.

We are also blessed with hundreds of thousands of readers—from our books as well as our smartphone apps—who alert us to issues with companies and places. *Every single message* from our readers is received, placed in a special database that we constantly have available while we're out and about, and we personally follow up on every observation made by our readers. So when we walk into a business or restaurant, we check to see what our readers say and tips they send us, and we use them to our advantage. (Thanks for the head's up about that incredible coconut cake at so-and-so restaurant—I know what *I'll* be ordering for dessert today.) With such a resource, and after decades reviewing companies in Hawai'i full-time, there ain't much that's gonna get past us.

A quick look at this book will reveal features never before used in other guidebooks. Let's start with the maps. They are more detailed than any other maps you'll find, and yet they omit extraneous information that can sometimes make map reading a chore. We know that people in unfamiliar territory sometimes have a hard time determining where they are on a map, so we include landmarks. Most notable among these are mile markers. At every mile on main roads, the government has erected numbered markers to tell you where you are. Where needed, we've drawn legal public beach access in yellow, so you'll *know* when you're legally entitled to cross someone's land. Most guidebooks have the infuriating habit of mentioning a particular place or sight but then fail to mention how to get there! You won't find that in our book. We tell you exactly how to find the hidden gems and use our own special maps to guide you.

As you read this book, you will also notice that we are very candid in assessing businesses. Unlike some other guidebooks that send out questionnaires asking a business if they are any good (gee, they *all* say they're good), we've had personal contact with the businesses listed in this book. One of the dirty little secrets about guidebook writers is that they sometimes make cozy little deals for good reviews. Well, you won't find that here. We accept no payment for our reviews, we make no deals with businesses for saying nice things, and there are no advertisements in our book. What we've seen and experienced is what you get. If we gush over a certain company, it comes from personal experience. If we rail against a business, it is for the same reason. All businesses mentioned in this book are here by *our* choosing. None has had any input into what we say, and we have not received *a single cent* from any of them for their inclusion. (In fact, there are some who would probably pay to be left out, given our comments.) We always review businesses as anonymous visitors and only later as guidebook writers if we need more information. This ensures that we are treated the same as you. (Amazingly, most travel writers *announce* themselves.) What you get is our opinion on how they operate. Nothing more, nothing less.

Sometimes our candor gets us into trouble. More than once we've had our books pulled from shelves because our comments hit a little too close to home. That's OK, because we don't work for the people who *sell* the book; we work for the people who *read* the book. It's also true that a handful of local residents have become upset because we've told readers about places that they'd rather keep for themselves. Ironically, it's usually not people born and raised here who have this selfish attitude, but rather the newcomers who have read about these places *in our book* (of all things), then adopted the *I'm here now—close the door mentality.*

This book is intended to bring you independence in exploring the Big Island. We don't want to waste any of your precious time by giving you bad advice or bad directions. We want you to experience the best that the island has to offer. Our objective in writing this book is to give you the tools and information necessary to have the greatest Hawaiian experience possible.

We hope we succeeded.

Andrew Doughty
Kailua-Kona, Hawai'i

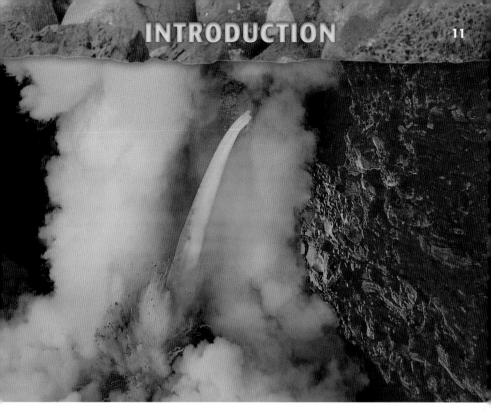

Brand new liquid land flows in a scene as primordial as the island's birth.

As with people, volcanic islands have a life cycle. They emerge from their sea floor womb to be greeted by the warmth of the sun. They grow, mature and eventually die before sinking forever beneath the sea.

HOW IT BEGAN

Sometime around 70 million years ago a cataclysmic rupture occurred in the Earth's mantle, deep below the crust. A hot spot of liquid rock blasted through the Pacific plate like a giant cutting torch, forcing magma to the surface off the coast of Russia, forming the Emperor Seamounts. As the tectonic plate moved slowly over this hot spot, this torch cut a long scar along the plate, piling up mountains of rock, producing island after island.

The oldest of these islands to have survived is Kure. Once a massive island with its own unique eco-system, only its ghost remains in the form of a fringing coral reef, called an atoll.

As soon as the islands were born, a conspiracy of elements proceeded to dismantle them. Ocean waves unmercifully battered the fragile and fractured rock. Abundant rain, especially on the northeastern sides of the mountains, easily carved up the rock surface, seeking faults in the rock and forming rivers and streams. In forming these channels, the water carried away the rock and soil, robbing the islands of their very essence. Additionally, the weight of the islands ensured their doom. Lava flows on top of other lava, and the union of these flows is always weak. This lava also contains countless air pockets and is criss-crossed with hollow lava tubes, making it inherently unstable. As these massive amounts of rock accumulated, their bases were crushed under the weight of subsequent lava flows, causing their summits to sink back into the sea.

What we call the Hawaiian Islands are simply the latest creations from this island-making machine. Someday they will disappear, existing as nothing more than footnotes in the Earth's turbulent geologic history.

Kauaʻi and Niʻihau are the oldest of the eight major islands. Lush and deeply eroded, the last of Kauaʻi's fires died with its volcano a million years ago. Oʻahu, Molokaʻi, Lanaʻi, Kahoʻolawe—their growing days are over as well. Maui is in its twilight days as a growing island. After growing vigorously, Hawaiian volcanoes usually go to sleep for a million years or so before sputtering back to life for one last fling. Maui's volcano Haleakala has entered its final stage and last erupted around 1790.

The latest and newest star in this island chain is Hawaiʻi. Born less than a million years ago, this youngster is still vigorously growing. Though none of its five volcano mountains is considered truly dead, these days Mauna Loa and Kilauea are doing most of the work of making the Big Island bigger. Mauna Loa, the most massive mountain on Earth, consists of 10,000 *cubic miles* of rock. Quieter of the two active volcanoes, it last erupted in 1984. Kilauea is the most boisterous of the volcanoes and is the most active volcano on the planet. Kilauea's most recent eruption began ran from 1983 until 2018, along with a brief hiccup in 2021. Up and coming onto the world stage is Kamaʻehuakanaloa. This new volcano is still 3,200 feet below the ocean's surface, 20 miles off the southeastern coast of the island. Yet in a geologic heartbeat, the Hawaiian Islands will be

The islands were born from the belly of Mother Earth, and the creation has not stopped.

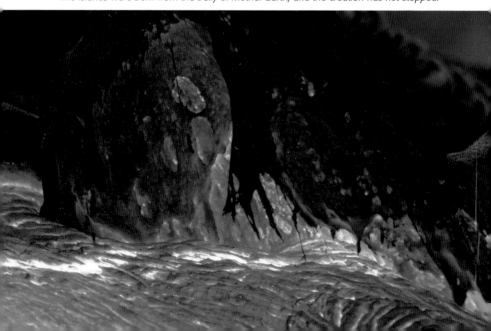

In regions of the island blessed with abundant rains, verdant growth carpets the landscape.

richer with its ascension, sometime in the next 100,000 years.

These virgin islands were barren at birth. Consisting only of volcanic rock, the first life forms to appreciate these new islands were marine creatures. Fish, mammals and microscopic animals discovered this new underwater haven and made homes for themselves. Coral polyps attached themselves to the lava rock and succeeding generations built upon these, creating what would become a coral reef.

Meanwhile, on land, seeds carried by the winds were struggling to colonize the rocky land, eking out a living and breaking down the lava rock. Storms brought the occasional bird, hopelessly blown off course. The lucky ones found the islands. The even luckier ones arrived with mates or had fertilized eggs when they got here. Other animals, stranded on a piece of floating debris, washed ashore against all odds and went on to colonize the islands. These introductions of new species were rare events. It took an extraordinary set of circumstances for a new species to actually make it to the islands. Single specimens were destined to live out their lives in lonely soli-

tude. On average, a new species was successfully deposited here only once every 20,000 years.

When a volcanic island is old, it is a sandy sliver, devoid of mountains. When it's middle-aged, it can be a lush wonderland, a haven for anything green, like Kaua'i. And when it is young, it is dynamic and unpredictable, like the Big Island of Hawai'i. Of all the Hawaiian Islands, none offers a larger range of climates and landscapes than the Big Island. The first people to discover Hawai'i's treasures must have been humbled at their good fortune.

THE FIRST SETTLERS

Sometime around the fifth century A.D. a large, double-hulled voyaging canoe, held together with flexible sennit lashings and propelled by sails made of woven pandanus, slid onto the sand on the Big Island of Hawai'i. These first intrepid adventurers, only a few dozen or so, encountered an island chain of unimaginable beauty.

They had left their home in the Marquesas Islands, 2,500 miles away, for reasons we will never know. Though some say it was because of war, overpopulation

The ancient Polynesians were exceptional navigators. These stones, at the navigational heiau near Mahukona, were aligned to point the way to other Hawaiian islands, Tahiti and other far away places.

or drought, it was more likely part of a purposeful exploration from a culture that had mastered the art of making their way through the featureless seas using celestial navigation and reading subtle signs in the ocean. Their navigational abilities far exceeded all the other "advanced" societies of the time. Whatever their reasons, these initial settlers took a big chance and surely must have been highly motivated. They could not have known that there were islands in these waters since Hawai'i is the most isolated island chain in the world. (Though some speculate that they were led here by the golden plover—see facing page.)

Those settlers who did arrive brought with them food staples from home: taro, breadfruit, pigs, dogs and several types of fowl. This was a pivotal decision. These first settlers found a land that contained almost no edible plants. With no land mammals other than the Hawaiian bat, the first settlers subsisted on fish until their crops matured. From then on, they lived on fish and taro. Although many associate throw-net fishing with Hawai'i,

this practice was introduced by Japanese immigrants much later. The ancient Hawaiians used fishhooks and spears, for the most part, or drove fish into a net already placed in the water. They also had domesticated animals, which were used as ritual foods or reserved for chiefs.

Little is known about the initial culture. Archaeologists believe that a second wave of colonists, probably from Tahiti, may have subdued these initial inhabitants around 1000 A.D. Some may have resisted and fled into the forest, creating the legend of the Menehune.

Today, Menehune are always referred to as being small in stature. Initially referring to their social status, the legend evolved to mean that they were physically short and lived in the woods away from the Hawaiians. (The Hawaiians avoided the woods when possible, fearing that they held evil spirits, and instead stayed on the coastal plains.) The Menehune were purported to build fabulous structures, always in one night. Their numbers were said to be vast, as many as 500,000. It is interesting to note that in a census taken of Kaua'i around 1800, 65 people from a remote valley identified themselves as Menehune.

The second wave probably swept over the island from the south, pushing the first inhabitants ever-north. On a tiny island north of Kaua'i, archeologists have found carvings, clearly not Hawaiian, that closely resemble Marquesan carvings, probably left by the doomed exiles.

This second culture was far more aggressive and developed into a highly class-conscious society. The culture was governed by chiefs, called Ali'i, who established a long list of taboos called kapu. These kapu were designed to keep order, and the penalty for breaking one was usually death by strangulation, club or fire. If the violation was serious enough, the guilty party's entire family might also be killed. It was kapu, for instance, for your shadow to fall across the shadow of the ali'i. It was kapu to interrupt the chief if he was speaking. It was kapu to prepare men's food in the same container used for women's food. It was kapu for women to eat pork or bananas. It was kapu for men and women to eat together. It was kapu not to observe the days designated to the gods. Certain areas were kapu for fishing if they became depleted, allowing the area to replenish itself.

While harsh by our standards today, this system kept the order. Most ali'i were sensitive to the disturbance their presence caused and often ventured outside only at night, or a scout was sent ahead to warn people that an ali'i was on his way. All commoners were required to pay tribute to the ali'i in the form of food and other items. Human sacrifices were common, and war among rival chiefs the norm.

By the 1700s, the Hawaiians had lost all contact with Tahiti, and the Tahitians had lost all memory of Hawai'i. Hawaiian canoes had evolved into fishing, and interisland canoes and were no longer capable of long ocean voyages. The Hawaiians had forgotten how to explore the world.

OUTSIDE WORLD DISCOVERS HAWAI'I

In January 1778 an event occurred that would forever change Hawai'i. Cap-

Hawai'i's First Tour Guide?

Given the remoteness of the Hawaiian Islands relative to the rest of Polynesia (or anywhere else for that matter), you'll be forgiven for wondering how the first settlers

found these islands in the first place. Many scientists think it might have been this little guy here. Called the kolea, or golden plover, this tiny bird flies over 2,500 miles nonstop to Alaska every year for the summer, returning to Hawai'i after mating. Some of these birds continue past Hawai'i and fly another 2,500 miles to Samoa and other South Pacific islands. The early Polynesians surely must have noticed this commute and concluded that there must be land in the direction that the bird was heading. They never would have dreamed that the birds leaving the South Pacific were heading to a land 5,000 miles away, and that Hawai'i was merely a stop in between, where the lazier birds wintered.

tain James Cook, who usually had a genius for predicting where to find islands, stumbled upon Hawai'i. He had not expected the islands to be here. He was on his way to Alaska on his third great voyage of discovery, this time to search for the Northwest Passage linking the Atlantic and Pacific oceans. Cook approached the shores of Waimea, Kaua'i, at night on Jan. 19, 1778. The next morning Kaua'i's inhabitants awoke to a wondrous sight and thought they were being visited by gods. Rushing out to greet their visitors, the Kauaians were fascinated by what they saw: pointy-headed beings (the British wore tri-cornered hats) breathing fire (smoking pipes) and possessing a death-dealing instrument identified as a water squirter (guns). The amount of iron on the ship was incredible. (They had seen iron before in the form of nails on driftwood but never knew where it originated.)

Cook left Kaua'i and briefly explored Ni'ihau before heading north for his mission on Feb. 2, 1778. When Cook returned to the islands in November after failing

It's hard to believe that the Big Island will eventually look like this oldest Hawaiian island, Kure Atoll. One day its last ghostly remains will sink forever beneath the sea.

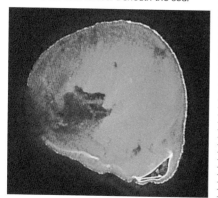

to find the Northwest Passage, he visited the Big Island of Hawai'i.

The Hawaiians had probably seen white men before. Local legend indicates that strange white people washed ashore at Ke'ei Beach sometime around the 1520s and integrated into society. This coincides with Spanish records of two ships lost in this part of the world in 1528. But a few weird-looking stragglers couldn't compare to the arrival of Cook's great ships and instruments.

Despite some recent rewriting of history, all evidence indicates that Cook, unlike some other exploring sea captains of his era, was a thoroughly decent man. Individuals need to be evaluated in the context of their time. Cook knew that his mere presence would have a profound impact on the cultures he encountered, but he also knew that change for these cultures was inevitable, with or without him. He tried, unsuccessfully, to keep the men known to be infected with venereal diseases from mixing with local women, and he frequently flogged infected men who tried to sneak ashore at night. He was greatly distressed when a party he sent to Ni'ihau was forced to stay overnight due to high surf, knowing that his men might transmit diseases to the women (which they did).

Cook arrived on the Big Island at a time of much upheaval. The mo'i, or king, of the Big Island had been badly spanked during an earlier attempt to invade Maui and was now looting and raising hell throughout the islands as retribution. Cook's arrival and his physical appearance (he stood 6 feet, 4 inches) led the Hawaiians to assume that he was the god Lono, who was responsible for fertility of the land. Every year the ruling chiefs and their war god Ku went into abeyance, removing their power so that Lono could return to the land and make it fertile

The Day the Gods Cried...

At the south end of Alii Drive in Kona, when you've past the last resort, there is a lava road leading toward the ocean. This field of lava and an area around the point called Kuamo'o have an extraordinary past. Here occurred an event that forever changed a people. For it was here that the Hawaiians abolished their ancient religion one day in 1820.

The Hawaiian religion was based on the kapu system. A myriad of laws were maintained, with death being the usual punishment for violation. The Hawaiians believed that rigid enforcement for a single violation was necessary, or else the gods would punish the whole community in the form of earthquakes, tsunamis, lava flows and famine. When Captain Cook came, he and his men were unaware of the many laws and inadvertently violated many of them. When natural punishments failed to materialize, many Hawaiians concluded that the gods would not enforce the laws. Since many found the kapu laws burdensome and oppressive, there was pressure to abolish them. While King Kamehameha I was alive, however, none dared challenge the kapu system. Almost as soon as he died, King Kamehameha II, pressured by his stepmother Ka'ahumanu, decided to put an end to the kapu system and destroy the temples around the island. This was before any missionaries ever came to these islands.

It was decided that the action would be consecrated by the simple act of having the king eat with women in public in November 1819. This had heretofore been kapu, and the penalty for breaking this law was death. In breaking this kapu in public, Kamehameha II declared an end to the old ways. One of his cousins, Kekuaokalani, was to be king of the spiritual world and challenged Kamehameha. The ferocious battle took place near here in early 1820. His cousin was hit by Kamehameha II's forces, and the man's grieving wife ran to his side as he fell. She cried out, begging that her wounded husband's life be spared. Instead she and her husband were summarily executed on the spot, with her body falling on top of his. The Hawaiian religion, as a dominant force, died with them on that bloody day. If you look to the south, you can see what look like terraces cut into the side of the mountain. These are the graves of the many hundreds who died in that very battle.

Today there is a resurgence of the Hawaiian religion. Hawaiians are grappling with their role in the world and are reaching back to their roots. The religion that seemingly died on that raw lava field is being reborn in the hearts of some contemporary Hawaiians.

again, bringing back the spring rains. During this time all public works stopped and the land was left alone. At the end of this *Makahiki* season, people would again seize the land from Lono to grow crops and otherwise make a living upon it.

Cook arrived at the beginning of the Makahiki, and the Hawaiians naturally thought *he* was the god Lono, coming to make the land fertile. Cook even sailed into Kealakekua Bay, *exactly* where legend said Lono would arrive.

The Hawaiians went to great lengths to please their "god." All manner of supplies were made available. Eventually, they became suspicious of the visitors. If they were gods, why did they accept Hawaiian women? And if they were gods, why did one of them die?

Cook left at the right time. The British had used up the Hawaiians' hospitality (not to mention their supplies). But shortly after leaving the Big Island, the ship broke a mast, making it necessary to return to Kealakekua Bay for repairs. As they sailed back into the bay, the Hawaiians were nowhere to be seen. A chief had declared the area kapu to help replenish it. When Cook finally found the Hawaiians, they were polite but wary. *Why are you back? Didn't we please you enough already? What do you want now?*

As repair of the mast went along, things began to get tense. Eventually the Hawaiians stole a British rowboat (for the nails), and the normally calm Cook blew his cork. On the morning of Feb. 14, 1779, he went ashore to trick the chief into coming aboard his ship where he would detain him until the rowboat was returned. As Cook and the chief were heading to the water, the chief's wife begged the chief not to go. By now tens of thousands of Hawaiians were crowding around Cook, and he ordered a retreat. A shot was heard from the other side of the bay, and someone shouted that the Englishmen had killed an important chief. A shielded warrior with a dagger came at Cook, who fired his pistol (loaded with non-lethal small shot). The shield stopped the small shot, and the Hawaiians were emboldened. Other shots were fired. Standing in knee-deep water, Cook turned to call for a cease-fire and was struck in the head from behind with a club, then stabbed. Dozens of other Hawaiians pounced on him, stabbing his body repeatedly. The greatest explorer the world had ever known was dead at age 50 in a petty skirmish over a stolen rowboat.

When things calmed down, the Hawaiians were horrified that they had killed a man they had earlier presumed to be a god. See what finally happened to Cook's body on page 76.

KAMEHAMEHA THE GREAT

The most powerful and influential king in Hawaiian history lived during the time of Captain Cook and was born on this island sometime around 1758. Until his rule, the Hawaiian chain had never been ruled by a single person. He was the first to "unite" (i.e., conquer) all the islands.

Kamehameha was an extraordinary man by any standard. He possessed herculean strength, a brilliant mind and boundless ambition. He was marked for death before he was even born. When Kamehameha's mother was pregnant with him, she developed a strange and overpowering craving—she wanted to *eat* the eyeball of a chief. The king of the Big Island, mindful of the rumor that the unborn child's real father was his bitter enemy, the king of Maui, asked his advisors to interpret. Their conclusion was unanimous: The child would grow to be a rebel, a killer of chiefs. The king decided that the child must die as soon as he was born, but the baby was instead whisked away to a remote valley on the northeast coast to be raised.

In ancient Hawaiian society, your role in life was governed by the class you were born into. The Hawaiians believed that breeding among family members produced superior offspring (except for the genetic misfortunes who were killed at birth), and the highest chiefs came from brother/sister combinations. Kamehameha

The Hawaiians built a highly structured society around the needs, desires and demands of their gods. This place of refuge is called Pu'uhonua o Honaunau.

was not of the highest class (his parents were merely cousins), so his future as a chief would not come easily.

As a young man, Kamehameha was impressed by his experience with Captain Cook. He was among the small group that stayed overnight on Cook's ship during Cook's first pass of Maui. (Kamehameha was on Maui valiantly fighting a battle in which his side was getting badly whupped.) Kamehameha recognized that his world had forever changed, and he shrewdly used the knowledge and technology of westerners to his own advantage.

Kamehameha participated in numerous battles. Many of them were lost (by his side), but he learned from his mistakes and developed into a cunning tactician. When he finally consolidated his rule over the Big Island (by luring his enemy to be the inaugural sacrifice at the Pu'ukohola Heiau near Kawaihae), he fixed his sights on the entire chain. In 1795 his large company of troops, armed with some western armaments and advisers, swept across Maui, Moloka'i, Lana'i and O'ahu. After some delays with the last of the holdouts, Kaua'i, their king finally acquiesced to the inevitable, and Kamehameha became the first ruler of all the islands. He spent his final years governing the islands peacefully from his capital at Kailua Bay and died in 1819.

MODERN HAWAI'I

During the 19th century, Hawai'i's character changed dramatically. Businessmen from all over the world came here to exploit Hawai'i's sandalwood, whales, land and people. Hawai'i's leaders, for their part, actively participated in these ventures and took a piece of much of the action for themselves. Workers were brought in from many parts of the world, changing the racial makeup of the islands. Government corruption became the order of the day, and everyone seemed to be profiting, except the Hawaiian commoner. By the time Queen Lili'uokalani lost her throne to a group of American businessmen in 1893, Hawai'i had become directionless, barely resembling the Hawai'i Captain Cook had encountered the previous century. The kapu system had been abolished by the Hawaiians shortly after the death of Kamehameha the Great. The "Great Mahele," begun in 1848, had changed the relationship Hawaiians had with the land. Large tracts of land were sold by the Hawaiian government to royalty, government officials, commoners and foreigners, effectively stripping many Hawaiians of the land they had lived on for generations.

The United States recognized the Republic of Hawai'i in 1894 with Sanford Dole as its president. It was later annexed and became an official territory in 1900. During the 19th and 20th centuries, sugar established itself as king. Pineapple was also a major crop in the islands, with the island of Lana'i purchased in its entirety for the purpose of growing pineapples. As the 20th century rolled on, Hawaiian sugar and pineapple workers found themselves in a lofty position—they became the highest paid workers for these crops in the world. As land prices rose and competition from other parts of the world increased, sugar and pineapple became less and less profitable. Today, these crops no longer hold the position they once had. The "pineapple island" of Lana'i has shifted away from pineapple growing and focuses on luxury tourism, with software mogul Larry Ellison buying the island in 2012. The sugar industry is now dead in Hawai'i, and sugar lands are being converted to other purposes while the workers move into other vocations, often tourist-related.

The story of Hawai'i is not a story of good versus evil. Nearly everyone shares in the blame for what happened to the Hawaiian people and their culture. Westerners certainly saw Hawai'i as a potential bonanza and easily exploitable. They knew what buttons to push and pushed them well. But the Hawaiians, for their part, were in a state of flux. The mere appearance of westerners seemed to reveal a discontent, or at least a weakness, in their system that had been lingering just below the surface. In fact, in 1794, a mere 16 years after first encountering westerners and under no military duress from the West, Kamehameha the Great *volunteered* to cede his island over to Great Britain. He was hungry for western arms so he could defeat his neighbor island opponents. He even declared that, as of that day, they were no longer people of Hawai'i, but rather people of Britain. (Britain declined the offer.) And in 1819, immediately after the death of the strong-willed Kamehameha, the Hawaiians, of their own accord, overthrew their own religion, dumped the kapu system and denied their gods. This was *before* any western missionaries ever came to Hawai'i.

Nonetheless, Hawai'i today is once again seeking guidance from its heritage. The echoes of the past seem to be getting louder with time, rather than diminishing. Interest in the Hawaiian language and culture is at a level not seen in many decades. All who live here are very aware of the issues and the complexities involved, but there is little agreement about where it will lead. As a result, you will be exposed to a more "Hawaiian" Hawai'i than those who might have visited the state a generation ago. This is an interesting time in Hawai'i. Enjoy it as observers, and savor the flavor of Hawai'i.

It might be a simple picnic table, but I'll take it.

In order to get to the islands, you've got to fly here. While this may sound painfully obvious, many people contemplate cruises to the islands. Remember, there isn't a single spec of land between the west coast and Hawai'i. And 2,500 miles of open water is a pretty monotonous stretch to cover.

GETTING HERE

When planning your trip, a travel agent can be helpful. Most online travel agents (OTAs) have consolidated into a couple of big players, but it is worth your time to poke around a bit. If you don't want to go through these sources, there are large wholesalers that can get you airfare, hotel and a rental car, often cheaper than you can get airfare on your own. **Pleasant Holidays** (800-742-9244) is one of the more well-known providers of complete package tours. They are renowned for their impossibly low rates. We've always been amazed that you can sometimes get round trip airfare from the mainland, a hotel, and car for a week for as low as $950 per person, depending on where you fly from, when you fly and where you stay. That's a small price to pay for your little piece of paradise.

If you arrange airline tickets and hotel reservations yourself, you can often count on paying top dollar for each facet of your trip. The prices listed in the *Where to Stay* section of our *Hawaii Revealed* app (and on our website) reflect the Rack rates, meaning the published rates before any discounts. Rates can be significantly lower if you go through a wholesaler.

When you pick your travel source, shop around—the differences can be dramatic.

A good source can make the difference between affording a *one-week* vacation and a *two-week* vacation. It's not always a straightforward process; there is an art to it.

Flight schedules change all the time, but United and others often have *direct* flights to Kona from the mainland. Not having to cool your heels while changing planes on O'ahu is a *big* plus because interisland flights aren't quite as simple and painless as they used to be. Flight attendants zip up and down the aisles hurling juice at you for the short, interisland flight. If you fly to Kona from Honolulu, sit on the left side (seats with an "A") coming in (right side going out) for superb views of several other islands. If you fly into Hilo, sit on the right side coming in. When flying to O'ahu from the mainland, seats on the left side have the best views. Interisland flights are done by **Southwest** (800-435-9792), **Hawaiian** (800-367-5320) and **Mokulele** (866-260-7070). We prefer Mokulele when possible because their smaller planes leave out of the commuter terminal in Kona, avoiding TSA and the rest of the airport system. Arrive 10 minutes early instead of 90.

WHAT TO BRING

This list may assist you in planning what to bring. Obviously you won't bring everything on the list, but it might make you think of a few things you may otherwise overlook:

- Water-resistant, reef-safe sunscreen (SPF 30 or higher, with the ingredients zinc oxide and/or titanium dioxide) or use a rashguard
- Two bathing suits
- Light rain jacket
- Hat or cap for sun protection
- Shorts and other cool clothing
- Warm clothes (for Mauna Kea or other high-altitude activities) and junk clothes for bikes, etc.
- Shoes—flip-flops, trashable sneakers, water shoes, hiking shoes
- Flashlight, if you like caves or for the lava field at night, *if* it's flowing
- Camera with extra batteries
- Mosquito repellent for some hikes
- Cheap, simple backpack or mesh gear bag—you don't need to go hiking to use one; a 10-minute trek to a secluded beach is much easier if you bring a simple pack

GETTING AROUND
Rental Cars

Rental car prices in Hawai'i have *traditionally* been cheaper than almost anywhere else in the country, and the competition is ferocious. (Though the pandemic created havoc with rental car fleet sizes that sometimes results in scarcity and huge price spikes.) Nearly every visitor to the Big Island gets around in a rental car, and for good reason—it's a *big* island. Fortunately, none have mileage charges. Don't forget to check **Turo.com** for car sharing from a basic island car to an exotic one.

This seems like a good place to mention that **Uber** and **Lyft** both have a presence on the island.

At Kona Airport, rental cars are a shuttle bus ride away. It's a good idea to reserve your car in advance since companies can run out of cars during peak times.

Many hotels, condos and rental agents offer excellent room/car packages. Find out from your hotel or travel agent if one is available. You can rent a car in Hilo and return it to Kona (or vice versa). There's usually an extra fee of about $50–$100 (depending on the company and car). And prices overall are usually *much* higher in Hilo than in Kona.

Below is a list of rental car companies. Some have desks at various hotels.

Alamo—(877) 222-9075
Kona: (808) 329-8896
Hilo: (808) 961-3343
Avis—(800) 321-3712
Kona: (808) 327-3000
Hilo: (808) 935-1298
Budget—(800) 527-0700
Kona: (808) 329-8511
Hilo: (808) 935-6878
Discount Hawaii Car Rental—
(800) 292-1930
Local: (808) 292-1930
Dollar—(800) 800-4000
Kona & Hilo: (866) 434-2226
Enterprise—(800) 261-7331
Kona: (808) 334-1810
Hilo: (808) 933-9683
Hertz—(800) 654-3131
Kona: (808) 329-3566
Hilo: (808) 935-2898
National—(877) 222-9058
Kona: (808) 327-3755
Hilo: (808) 935-0891
Thirfty—(800) 367-5238
Kona & Hilo: (877) 283-0898
If you're 21–24 years old, most of the companies will rent to you, but you'll pay about $25 extra *per day* for the crime of being young and reckless. Try **Discount Hawaii Car Rental** first. If you're under 21, rent a bike or moped or take the bus.

4-Wheel Drive

We *strongly* believe that the best vehicle for the island is a four-wheel drive. They come closed (SUV) or open (like a Wrangler). They are more expensive, but there are several roads, beaches and sights that you can't visit without 4WD. Unpaved roads are contractually off limits with most of the rental car companies. That means that if you drive one, the insurance you take out with the rental company is void, so you or your insurance company back home would have to eat it. Different companies have different restrictions, but from a *practical* standpoint, 4WD is the way to go. The drawbacks to *open* Jeeps are more wind and heat and no trunk. Closed 4WDs are best. Expect to pay up to $80–$100 *or more* per day for the privilege of cheating the road builders. For some reason, they usually cost much more in Kona than Hilo.

If a hike or 4WD to Makalawena Beach doesn't sound appealing, you can always kayak to it.

Motorcycles & Scooters

If you really want to ham it up, you can try renting a HOG. (*Disclaimer*—Wizard Publications will not be held liable for bad puns.) Riders-share.com is where locals list their bikes for rent. Prices vary widely (so does your selection), but we've found that you can find Harleys available here and prices for any motorcycle can be quite reasonable. Kona Scooter Rental (808-518-4100) in Kona has scooters for $60 for 24 hours. (These are only useful around Kailua town.) If you want to add a wheel, Aloha Motorsports (808-667-7000) in Waikoloa rents Polaris Slingshots (those sporty, three-wheeled roadsters you see zipping around) for a *just-hurt-me* price of $249 for 4 hours. The hourly prices go down the longer you book them for.

A Few Driving Tips

Gasoline is *obscenely* expensive here. You may want to have some FedExed to you from home to save money. (OK, maybe not *that* expensive.) Kona is said to have among the highest gas prices in the United States (about 15 cents higher than expensive Hilo). Whether that's true or not, prepare to get hammered at the pump. If you're in the Kohala resort area, there's a station off the road to the Waikoloa Resorts at mile marker 76. The cheapest gas on the east side of the island is in Hilo or Pahoa, south of Hilo. The cheapest on the *whole island* is in Kona at Costco (but you have to be a Costco member). It's marked on the map on page 168 and not far from the Kona Airport. Many companies charge a top-off fee due to the airport's distance to town, so fill it to the top. And make sure you check your receipt. On *many* occasions we've topped off the tank to the brim, only to find a $20 "fuel charge" tacked onto our final tab.

Seat belt and child restraint use is required by law, and the police will pull you over for this alone. Wide open roads and frequently changing speed limits make it easy to accidentally speed here. Police usually cruise in their own private, unmarked vehicles with a small blue light on top, so you might not see them coming. And we've noticed a *huge* increase in the number of speed traps on the island in recent years. We strongly recommend using cruise control and paying attention to changes in speed limits if you want to leave the island with the same driving score you arrived with.

Cell phone use is illegal for drivers unless you have a headset or wireless.

It's best not to leave anything valuable in your car. There are teenagers here who pass the time by breaking into cars. Hapuna Beach and several Hilo waterfalls are notorious for car break-ins. When we park at a beach or waterfall, or any other place frequented by visitors, we take all valuables with us, leave the windows up, and leave the doors unlocked. (Just in case someone is curious enough about the inside to smash a window.) There are plenty of stories about someone walking 100 feet to a waterfall in Hilo, coming back to their car, and finding that their brand iPad has walked away. And don't be gullible enough to think that trunks are safe. Someone who sees you put something in your trunk can probably get at it faster than you can with your key.

Kailua-Kona possesses the dry town syndrome: At the first drop of rain, many Kona drivers become vehicularly uncoordinated, driving like a drunken cat on ice, so beware of this.

Traffic has increased *a lot* in the past few years and you should expect to get stuck in it, especially in Kona. Just remember that it could be worse—you could be in traffic back home *and on your way to work.*

2015 was a busy hurricane season, with three threatening Hawai'i at one time, but none nailed us thanks to our normally occurring protective windshear.

A Word About Driving Tours

The Big Island is, to use the scientific term, *one big bugga*. With this in mind, we have decided to describe the various parts of the island in a series of tours. You're not being pigeonholed into seeing the island in this order, but we had to organize the regions in some fashion, and this seemed the logical way to do it rather than a scattershot description. You can take these tours from any place you are staying, but we have described most of them (except the Hilo tour and the Hamakua/Waimea tour) on the assumption that you are starting from the west (Kona) side because the majority of Big Island visitors do just that. The Hamakua/Waimea section is described from the Hilo side first because it's convenient to see it that way after traveling via Saddle Road.

Nearly every guidebook divides the Big Island and its sights by districts. While this land division made perfect sense to the ancients who divvied up the island among themselves, it is not real helpful to the modern traveler who cruises the island by car. So we have divided the island up in a way that makes more sense to today's visitor. It takes into account where most people stay and how they drive. Look at the inside back cover map to see how we have divided the island and on what pages we describe the sights.

Most main roads have mile markers erected every mile. Since Hawai'i is mostly void of other identification signs, these little green signs can be a big help in knowing where you are at a given time. Therefore, we have placed them on the maps represented as a number inside a small box. We will often describe a certain feature or unmarked road as being "0.4 miles past mile marker 22." We hope this helps.

For directions, locals usually describe things as being on the **mauka** (MOW-ka) side of the road—toward the mountains—or **makai** (ma-KIGH)—toward the ocean.

Beaches, activities and adventures are mentioned briefly but described in detail in their own separate chapters.

Buses

Our main island bus is called **Hele-On** (808-961-8744). It was designed for local use, so it doesn't go to all the places that visitors want to go. It's $2. (If you're 60 plus, a student or disabled, it's $1). However, it does go between Hilo and Kona, and they do take luggage (for an extra buck). Call them for a schedule and rates. There are also bus tours from **Roberts Hawai'i** (808-329-1688).

GETTING MARRIED ON BIG ISLAND

A beautiful beach at sunset—many couples dream of such a background for their

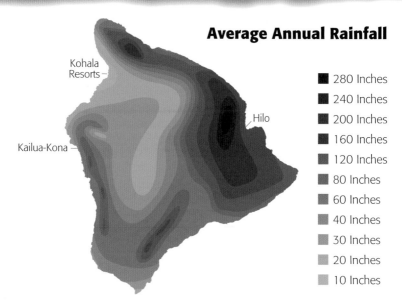

Average Annual Rainfall

Kohala Resorts

Hilo

Kailua-Kona

- 280 Inches
- 240 Inches
- 200 Inches
- 160 Inches
- 120 Inches
- 80 Inches
- 60 Inches
- 40 Inches
- 30 Inches
- 20 Inches
- 10 Inches

special day. 'Anaeho'omalu Beach is one of the more popular spots for sunset weddings. The Big Island offers an almost unlimited selection of wedding, reception and honeymoon possibilities. Although you can set everything up yourself using the internet and email, it's usually easier and *sometimes* less expensive to use a professional who can assist you.

This one's hard for us. Unlike other activities in this book, we can't exactly get married with all the companies and review them. (The flower bills alone would bankrupt us.) Almost all the major resorts have wedding coordinators who can offer help. And there are lots of private wedding coordinators. A good resource is **weddingwire.com**, a wedding network professional exchange.

Expect to pay around $500ish for a minimal wedding package (officiant, flower leis and license assistance). Resorts generally charge a hefty fee to use their grounds whether you are a guest or not. All beaches are public, so it won't be a *private* ceremony. Consider renting a private home or an entire B&B in which to hold the ceremony and reception.

Obtaining a Marriage License

Contact the **State Department of Health** (808-586-4545) on the Big Island (or visit their website) to obtain an application or to get the names of license agents on the Big Island. Both parties must be at least 18. No residency or blood tests are required. The fee is $60 *in cash*, and the license is good for 30 days. Both parties must be present with photo IDs at the time of the appointment with the marriage license agent.

WEATHER

The weather on the Big Island is more diverse than any island or other comparably sized chunk of land *in the world*. You name it, we got it. According to the Köppen Climate Classification System (which is probably *your* favorite system, too, right?), the Big Island has 10 of the 15 types of climatic zones in the world. (Not *climactic* zones, which we accidentally printed in a previous guidebook. Boy, people were *really* anxious to find one of *those*!) Only Cold Continental Climate categories are absent. Here we've got tropical, monsoonal, desert and even *periglacial* climates, among others. So no matter what kind of weather you like, we are sure to have it here. As you ascend the slopes of the volcanoes, you lose about 3 °F for every thousand feet.

Kailua-Kona *traditionally* has had weather that can best be described as eternal springtime. Quite simply, it's almost always warm and wonderful. The average high in February (the coldest month) is 80 °F and the low is 64 °F, whereas in August (the warmest month) the high is 87 °F and the low is 69 °F. Humidity is usually between 50% and 80%. The temperature change between night and day is greater than the temperature change between winter and summer, so it could easily be said that nighttime is the winter of the Big Island. Balmy wraparound onshore breezes usually keep it comfortable. The exception is during Kona winds (so named because they come from the Kona direction, rather than out of the northeast as is usually the case). Kona winds occur about 5% of the time and bring stillness or warm air to Kona, creating uncomfortably humid conditions. Normal conditions in Kona and Kohala mean clear mornings with afternoon clouds created by thermal heating, so morning is usually better for activities such as air tours. During the summer, evening showers often occur as warm moist air is cooled, squeezing rain out of the humidity. Because it is totally protected from the trade winds by Hualalai, Kona is the only place in the state that gets most of its rainfall in the summer afternoons and evenings. The higher up the mountain, the more

rain you get. For 35 years Kona was ravaged by nasty but natural pollutant called *vog* from Kilauea volcano (thanks to airflow patterns), but with the cessation of volcanic activity in 2018, Kona's air is now as clean as any part of the island.

Hilo's weather is almost always described with one word—*rain.* Hilo is the wettest city in the United States. Annual rainfall is rarely less than 100 inches, usually much more. But rain is not a constant here. Hilo has times of drought like anywhere else. (Like when rainfall was a *mere* 70 inches one year, triggering *rationing.*) Most of the rain falls at night. When daytime showers do occur, they are often intense but short-lived. That said, rain or cloudiness *will* be a factor here. One of the reasons that Kailua-Kona is so much more popular than Hilo is that visitors like sunny weather, and Hilo can't compete in that area. Also, all that rain has to go somewhere, which is why the ocean off Hilo is not nearly as clear as Kona's runoff-free waters.

The **Kohala** resort area is the driest part of the island, with rainfall usually around 10 inches per year. Sunshine is almost assured (which is why it is so popular). The weather penalty here is the wind. As the lava fields heat up during the day, the air heats and rises. Air from the ocean rushes in to fill the void, creating strong afternoon convective breezes. The hotter, drier and sunnier it is that day, the breezier it may be that afternoon.

The general rule of thumb is that in wet areas like Hilo, most of the rain falls at night and early morning. Dry areas like Kona and Kohala get their rains in the late afternoon and early evenings.

Water temperatures range from 75 °F at its coldest in February to 82 °F at its warmest in September/October. It's colder in some areas where freshwater springs percolate from the ocean's floor and float to the top, forming a boundary called a *Ghyben-Herzberg lens*.

PLANNING YOUR TRIP

Visitors are usually unprepared for the sheer size and diversity of the Big Island. The island is over 4,000 square miles, and a circular trip around, on Highways 19 and 11, is a hefty 222 miles. During that drive you pass through dozens of different terrains and climates. (And that doesn't even include Saddle Road, Lower Puna, any of North Kohala or scores of other places.) Put simply, this island is too big and too diverse to try to see in a few days. The graphic on page 31 will put it into perspective.

If you are on the island for three days or less, we recommend that you don't try to see the whole island; you'll only end up touring Hawai'i's exotic blacktop. Pick a side. Since one of your days should be spent at the volcano, that leaves you with a scant two days to experience either Hilo's and Puna's beauty or the Kona side's range of activities.

Deciding which side of the island to spend the most time on is a difficult decision, but the numbers are definitely skewed. Most visitors spend most of their time on the western, or Kona, side. There are several reasons for this:

Kona Side

The Kona side has the sunshine. The climate in Kona is as perfect as weather gets, and the Kohala resort area has the highest number of sunny days of anywhere in the state. The Kona side also has *far* more activities available. This leads to another reason—the ocean. Since it's on the leeward side of the island, and because there are no permanent streams on the entire west side of the island (except for the one from Kona to Hilo that's filled with tax money), Kona has the calmest, clearest water in the state. Water sports such as swimming, snorkeling, SCUBA, fishing—you name it—are usually unmatched on the Kona side. This side also has the best beaches on the island, with some, such as Hapuna, consistently rated in the top five in the United States. (With a few notable exceptions, the Hilo side has poor beaches.) All this adds up to a traveler's delight, one of the reasons that the Kona side has such a high visitor repeat ratio.

But stand by for a shock when you fly into Kona Airport for the first time. Kona makes a *rotten* first impression on the uninitiated airborne visitor. Part of the airport sits atop a lava flow from 1801, and the first thing you think when you fly in over all that jet black lava is, "I came all

Only on the Big Island can you experience both conditions on the same day a few dozen miles apart.

this way for *this?*" Don't worry; it gets much better.

Hilo Side

On the other hand, the Kona side is short of what Hilo has in abundance— green. Whereas much of the Kona side is dominated by lava, Hilo is plant heaven. The weather usually comes from the northeast, so Hilo gets around 140 inches of rain per year. This is paradise for anything that grows. Hilo also has breathtaking waterfalls. You won't find *one* on the Kona side unless it's in the lobby of your hotel. Hilo's weather has created beautiful folds and buckles in the terrain. The unweathered Kona side lacks angles—it's mostly gentle slopes. Lastly, Hilo is *much* more convenient for exploring Kilauea volcano.

The Two Sides

The schism between the two sides of the island is wide and deep. Because the two sides are so different and the distances so large (for Hawai'i, that is), many people who live on the west side haven't been to Hilo or Kilauea volcano in years. And lots of Hilo residents haven't been to Kona in years. Both sides tend to playfully badmouth the other. The Kona side creates the tax base, and the Hilo side, the center of county government, spends it (often on Hilo-oriented infrastructure). Hilo has lots of roads that few drive, while Kona drivers curse the traffic on their limited number of roads.

Suggested Itinerary

If you have a week on the Big Island, you might want to spend four to five days on the Kona side and two to three days in Hilo or Puna. The volcano itself can take one to two days, and you're better off exploring it from Hilo or Puna than from Kona. Hilo all but closes down on Sundays,

with most business, even the few tourist-related ones, taking the day off.

WHERE SHOULD I STAY?

Throughout our book we talk about the positives associated with the various areas. In deciding where to stay, here are three negatives for each major location worth considering:

Kohala—Food will cost you more and so will places to stay. You are far from the town of Kailua-Kona and its available resources. You are far from the volcano.

Kailua-Kona—Traffic, while not *nearly* as bad as the mainland, can be troublesome at commute time. There's more noise along Alii Drive.

Hilo—Activities are less numerous. The ocean is less pleasant. Rain will probably be a companion. There are no mega-resorts on this side of the island; choices are fewer and of lesser quality in general.

Kohala

Kohala is famous for its **mega-resorts**. These destination resort hotels have tons to see and do on the premises, pricey restaurants offering superb atmosphere and cuisine, and almost unending sunny weather. The developers have created oases in the lava desert where lava once stretched uninterrupted for miles.

You will notice that accommodation prices are high in Kohala. These snazzy resorts don't come cheap. We leave it up to you to decide if it's in your budget. A lot of them have Real Gem icons next to them. We like to think of ourselves as stingy with these, but facts are facts— these *are* gems. But like the genuine article, these gems come at a price.

Picking the best mega-resort in Kohala is not a straightforward process. All of them have radically different personalities, so *your* personality is key to which one you'll like best. Most of these resorts do a great job at creating an atmosphere. The question is, is it *your* atmosphere? In our view, the Mauna Kea Beach Hotel has the best exotic tropical feel. The Fairmont Orchid has the richest, most luxurious feel. The Hilton Waikoloa Village has the most jaw-dropping, elaborate, yet family-oriented feel. And 10 miles south of the main Kohala resort area, The Four Seasons has some of both Mauna Kea's and the Fairmont Orchid's assets—rich and luxurious, yet also a great tropical feel. Most of these resorts are world class, and we don't say that lightly. Choosing one just depends on what you want.

If it's a cheap **condo** you're looking for, go elsewhere. Kohala only has upscale condos for rent.

Kailua-Kona

The resorts in Kailua-Kona and the surrounding area aren't of the same caliber as the glitzy mega-resorts of Kohala, but neither are the prices. You'll find that you can stay and eat in Kona a lot cheaper than Kohala. Condos are far more numerous here than hotels. Some condos are a downright bargain, while others can only be recommended to in-laws.

Most accommodations in Kailua-Kona are along Alii Drive. This road fronts the shoreline, offering splendid ocean locations and sunsets. The penalty for staying on Alii Drive is auto noise. Cars and motorcycles scoot by, sometimes creating unpleasant reminders in *some* condos that you are still in the real world. (Other condos keep their rooms far enough from the road to keep them blissfully quiet.)

The high season in Kona is December through March, and most condos charge more at that time. Also, most condos have a minimum stay.

Hilo

Your choices in Hilo are much more limited than on the western side of the island. The number of overnight visitors here is a fraction of what the Kona side gets. The hotels are older here, and Hilo's economic woes mean once-grand hotels often have closed wings and shuttered restaurants and spas. But you shouldn't expect Kohala prices either. Hotels can be had quite cheap in Hilo, so even if you are staying on the western side, you should strongly consider staying at least a night here when you are exploring this side or visiting the volcano. That'll keep Hilo from becoming a blur during an around-the-island driving frenzy.

Most of the hotels are located along Banyan Drive. Many have outstanding views of Hilo Bay. There are also a few lovely inns and decent hostels around town, too.

Volcano Village

The town of Volcano Village has a limited number of places to stay, but many of the choices you *do* have are superb. If you are spending a week on the Big Island, at least one night should be spent here. This is the most convenient place to stay when you explore the volcano. You can take your time and do the volcano justice. Remember, it gets chilly here at 4,000 feet, so bring something warm and waterproof. There are lots of B&Bs in Volcano Village, so check online and on our website.

Other Places to Stay

Out of the main areas, accommodations are few and literally far between. Waimea is cool and sometimes chilly at 2,500 feet. There are lots of restaurants to choose from. The northern tip at Hawi has a simple hotel and a nice inn, but your dining choices are fewer. Down at the southern tip you'll find an often-forgotten resort but even fewer dining options to choose from. Lastly, in Honoka'a near Waipi'o Valley is a cheap hotel that also has hostel beds.

Finally, you have B&Bs and vacation rentals. **Airbnb**, **VRBO** and other online resources like our website's links page (revealedtravelguides.com) have lots of choices available to you.

Detailed Resort & Condo Reviews

The Big Island has it all, accommodations-wise, and as you consider where you want to stay—hotel or condo, by the beach or with a mountain view—you might find it intimidating to wade through the vast number of choices.

So here's what we did. We have *personally reviewed* every resort on the island. We have *exhaustively* cataloged all the amenities, formed opinions on what different properties have to offer and created comprehensive reviews. Sure, you can go online and look at reviews by people who have been to one or maybe two resorts. But none of those sources knows them all and can compare one to the other.

Because this information is so exhaustive, there isn't enough room in our book to include it all. So we have put all of our reviews in our smartphone app, *Hawaii Revealed*, and made that portion available *for free* (simply click "free preview"). There you can sort and sift through the resorts in a matter of minutes using our special filters. We also include our own aerial photos, so you'll know if oceanfront really means oceanfront.

For instance, you might say, *I want a hotel in Kohala, on a beach, that's good for families, has an outdoor lanai, a children's pool, and takes service animals. Oh, and a swim-up bar would be nice*. With the filters in our app, you can cut through the 90 or so resorts and get to exactly what you want by

reading our in-depth, brutally honest review. How's that for cutting through the noise?

GEOGRAPHY

The Big Island is made up of five volcanoes. Kohala in the north is the oldest. Next came Mauna Kea, Hualalai, Mauna Loa, and finally Kilauea. None of them are truly dead, but only Mauna Loa and Kilauea make regular appearances, with an occasional walk-on by Hualalai. Nearly the size of Connecticut, the Big Island's 4,000 square miles can easily hold all of the other Hawaiian Islands combined. And it's the only state in the union that can get bigger every year (thanks to Kilauea's land-making machine).

Gentle slopes are the trademark of this young island. It hasn't had time to develop the dramatic, razor-sharp ridges that older islands, such as Kaua'i, possess. The exception is the windward side of Kohala Mountain where erosion and fault collapses have created a series of dramatic valleys. Two of our mountains rise to over 13,000 feet.

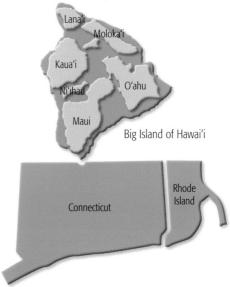

How Big is The Big Island of Hawai'i?

Lana'i
Moloka'i
Kaua'i
O'ahu
Ni'ihau
Maui
Big Island of Hawai'i

Rhode Island
Connecticut

Mauna Kea, at 13,796 feet, is the tallest mountain in the world when measured from its base, eclipsing lightweights such as Mount Everest and K-2. Mauna Loa, though slightly shorter, is much broader, earning it the moniker as the *largest* mountain in the world. It contains a mind-numbing 10,000 cubic *miles* of rock.

Another of our mountains is not really a mountain at all. Kilauea, looking more like a gaping wound on Mauna Loa, is the undisputed volcano show-off of the planet. *When it's erupting*, hundreds of thousands of cubic yards of lava per day create and repave the land.

All this adds up to an exciting and dynamic geographic location. Things change faster here than any place you will ever visit. There have been lots of times that we have gone to a certain beach or area only to find that it has changed beyond recognition. A new black sand beach shifts to another location. Trails become absorbed by a restless and vigorous Mother Nature. Whole roads get covered with lava. Island hopping in this state is like traveling through time. This is an exciting time in the life cycle of this particular island. Enjoy the island in its youth, for like all youths, this, too, shall pass.

SO IS HAWAI'I AN ISLAND OR A STATE?

Both. This island, more than any other in this state, is a bit schizophrenic when it comes to names. This is the biggest island in the state, so it is commonly referred to as (brace yourself) *the Big Island*. Its Hawaiian name is *Hawai'i*. So far, so good. But the whole *state* is called Hawai'i. So you figure the capital must be here, right? Nope, Honolulu is on O'ahu. This must be where most of the people live, right? Uh-uh. O'ahu has 80% of the population. Well, this must be where Pearl Harbor is, correct? Wrong answer—it's on O'ahu, too. So why is the state named after *this* island? Because it's the *biggest* island, and this is where King Kamehameha the Great was from. It was he who brought all the islands under one rule for the first time. His first capital was here at Kailua (another naming headache—see below). When you do all that, you have some historical influence. In this book we will refer to this island as *the Big Island*. When we say Hawai'i, we mean the whole state. (Even my brother, when he came to visit the Big Island, called from Honolulu to have me pick him up, assuming it must be on the "main" island.) In short,

Though tempting, please don't swim in Keanalele Waterhole.

in *Hawai'i* could be anywhere—*on Hawai'i* is on the Big Island.

I won't even get into the name confusion for the town of Waimea. (Or is it Kamuela? See page 137.) Let's tackle a more annoying naming problem. The main town on the west side is called **Kailua-Kona, Kona, Kailua** or sometimes **Kailua Town**. In the old days it was simply Kailua. Though there are also towns named Kailua on O'ahu and Maui, it didn't present much of a problem to anyone until the post office discovered these islands. In order to keep from messing up the mail *(don't say it!)*, they decided to rename the town. (Technically, they renamed their post office, but the subtlety is lost on those who have to address mail.) Since this is the *Kona* side of the island (*Kona* being the name of the less common wind that comes from this direction), they cleverly named the post office *Kailua-Kona*. To complicate matters further, the builders of the airport here named it the *Kona Airport*, so people began to refer to a trip here as "going to Kona." All this leaves you with a quandary. What do you call this place? Well, in keeping with our editorial policy of taking gutsy stands, we'll call it Kailua-Kona...except when we call it Kona or Kailua Town. In fairness, that's because most who live here do the same.

HAZARDS

Just because you're in a tropical paradise doesn't mean there's nothing here that can threaten you. The sun, sea and island critters can all ruin your day. Knowing what to look for is what this section is all about.

The Sun

The hazard that affects by far the most people (excluding the accommodations tax) is the sun. The Big Island, at 19–20 degrees latitude, receives sunlight more directly than anywhere on the mainland. (The more overhead the sunlight is, the less atmosphere it filters through.) If you want to enjoy your *entire* vacation, make sure that you wear a strong sunscreen or cover up, even while snorkeling. We recommend a water-resistant, reef-safe (mineral-based) sunscreen with at least an SPF of 30. Gels work best in the water, lotions on land. Try to avoid the sun between 11 a.m. and 2 p.m. when the sun's rays are particularly strong. If you are fair-skinned or unaccustomed to the sun and want to lay out, 15–20 minutes per side is all you should consider the first day. You can increase it a bit each day. *Beware of the fact that our ever-constant breezes will hide the symptoms of a burn until it's too late.* You might find that trying to get your tan as golden as possible isn't worth it. Tropical suntans are notoriously short lived, whereas you are sure to remember a burned vacation far longer. If, after all of our warnings, you *still* get burned, aloe vera gel works well to relieve the pain. Some come with lidocaine in them. Ask your hotel front desk if they have any aloe plants on the grounds. Peel the skin off a section and make several crisscross cuts in the meat, then rub the plant on your skin. *Oooo,* it'll feel so good!

Water Hazards

The most serious water hazard is the surf. Though more calm in the summer and on the west side, high surf can be found anywhere on the island at any time of the year. The sad fact is that more people drown in Hawai'i each year than anywhere else in the country. This isn't said to keep you from enjoying the ocean, but rather to instill in you a healthy respect for Hawaiian waters. See the *Beaches* chapter for more information on this. Also, water shoes are a good idea if you don't want to step on something sharp and painful.

Ocean Critters

Hawaiian marine life, for the most part, is quite friendly. There are, however, a few notable exceptions. Below is a list of some critters that you should be aware of. This is not mentioned to frighten you out of the water. The odds are overwhelming that you won't have any trouble with any of the beasties listed below. But should you encounter one, this information may be of some help.

Sharks—Hawai'i does have sharks. They are mostly white-tipped reef sharks and the occasional hammerhead or tiger shark. Contrary to what most people think, sharks live in every ocean and don't pose the level of danger people attribute to them. Shark attacks are rare on Big Island, averaging less than one per year, and fatalities are extremely uncommon. When encounters do occur, it's usually a tiger attacking surfers. Considering the number of people who swam in our waters during that time, you are more likely to choke to death on a bone at a lu'au than be attacked by a shark. If you do happen to come upon a shark, however, swim away slowly. This kind of movement doesn't interest them. *Don't* splash about rapidly. By doing this you are imitating a fish in distress, and you don't want to do that. The one kind of ocean water you want to avoid is murky water, such as that found near river mouths. These are not interesting to swim in anyway. Most shark attacks occur in murky water at dawn or dusk since sharks are basically cowards that like to sneak up on their prey. In general, don't go around worrying about sharks. *Any* animal can be threatening. (Even Jessica Alba was once rudely accosted by an overly affectionate male dolphin.)

Portuguese Man-of-War—These are related to jellyfish but are unable to swim. They are instead propelled by a small sail and are at the mercy of the wind. Though small, they are capable of inflicting a painful sting. This occurs when the long, trailing tentacles are touched, triggering hundreds of thousands of spring-loaded stingers, called nematocysts, which inject venom. The resulting burning sensation is usually very unpleasant but not fatal. Fortunately, the Portuguese Man-of-War is very uncommon on the west shore of the island. When they *do* come ashore, they usually do so in great numbers, jostled by a strong storm offshore. If you see them on the beach, don't go in the water. If you do get stung, immediately remove the tentacles with a gloved hand, stick or whatever is handy and rinse thoroughly with vinegar to remove any adhering nematocysts. Then immerse in hot water or apply a hot pack for 45 minutes. If the condition worsens, see a doctor. The old treatments of vinegar or baking soda are no longer recommended. The folk cure is urine (and it comes with a handy applicator for some of us), but you might look pretty silly applying it.

Sea Urchins—These are like living pin cushions. If you step on one or accidentally grab one, remove as much of the spine as possible with tweezers. See a physician if necessary.

Coral—Coral skeletons are very sharp and, since the skeleton is overlaid by millions of living coral polyps, a scrape can leave proteinaceous matter in the wound, causing infection. This is why coral cuts are frustratingly slow to heal. Immediate cleaning and disinfecting of coral cuts should speed up healing time. We don't have fire coral around the Big Island.

Sea Anemones—Related to the jellyfish, these also have stingers and are usually found attached to rocks or coral. It's best not to touch them with your bare hands. Treatment for a sting is similar to that for a Portuguese Man-of-War.

Bugs

Though devoid of the myriad of hideous buggies found in other parts of the world, there are a few evil critters brought here from elsewhere that you should know about.

The worst are **centipedes**. They can get to be 6 or more inches long and are

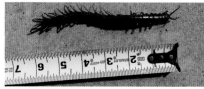

aggressive predators. They shouldn't be messed with. If you get stung, even by a baby, the pain can range from a bad bee sting to a mild gunshot blast. Some local doctors say the only cure is to stay drunk for three days. Others say to use meat tenderizer or a green papaya.

Scorpions are present on the dry, western side of the island. Though not as nasty as the ones you see in the movies, a sting is unpleasant nonetheless. They're usually a couple inches across and mildly aggressive.

Cane spiders are big, dark, and look horrifying, but they're not poisonous. (Though they seem to *think* they are. I've had *them* chase *me* across the room when *I* had the broom in my hand.) We *don't* have no-see-ums, those irritating sand fleas common in the South Pacific and Caribbean. A Hawaiian voyaging canoe that traveled to and from Tahiti on a cultural mission years ago unknowingly brought some back. The crew was forced into quarantine against their will, where the tiny biting insects were discovered and exterminated. No-see-ums would have easily spread here and changed Hawai'i forever.

Mosquitoes were unknown in the islands until the first stowaways arrived on Maui on the *Wellington* in 1826. Since then they have thrived. A good mosquito repellent containing DEET will come in handy, especially if you plan to go hiking. If you find one dive bombing you at night in your room, turn on your overhead fan to help keep them away.

Speaking of mosquitoes, the Big Island *in*frequently suffers through sporadic outbreaks of **Dengue Fever**. The Dengue virus is not endemic to Hawai'i, meaning it doesn't exist here naturally, and it likely won't be a problem during your trip. And during outbreaks, residents get the bug over visitors 4-to-1. Symptoms include sudden onset of high fever, headache and pain behind the eyes, joint and muscle aches, skin rash, and overall fatigue. Try to not fall ill when you see how much stores here charge for a small 4-ounce bottle of repellent—mosquitos aren't the only blood suckers in Hawai'i.

Bees and **yellow jackets** are more common on the drier west side of the island. Usually, the only way you'll get stung is if you run into one. If you rent a scooter, beware; I received my first bee sting while singing *Come Sail Away* on a motorcycle. A bee sting in the mouth can definitely ruin one of your precious vacation days.

Regarding **cockroaches**, there's good news and bad news. The bad news is that here, some are bigger than your thumb and can fly. The good news is that you probably won't see one. One of their predators is the **gecko**. This small, lizard-like creature makes a surprisingly loud chirp at night. They are cute and

OK, that doesn't even look comfortable.

considered good luck in the Islands (probably because they eat mosquitoes and small roaches).

Lastly in the bug hazards, the Big Island has become home to the **little fire ant**. This unwelcome bugger from South America has become established around the island but is worse in the Hilo/Puna area. The bite can be painful and leave a rash that itches for several days. They like to climb trees, and when the winds pick up, can rain down as the worst shower you've ever had. Efforts to keep them at bay haven't been as successful as anyone would like, and they present a huge problem for native ecosystems and agriculture. Make sure to not leave food out overnight, and treat bites with topical creams such as hydrocortisone

Leptospirosis is a bacteria found in some of Hawai'i's freshwater. It is transmitted from animal urine and can enter the body from open cuts, eyes and by drinking. Around 100 people a year in Hawai'i are diagnosed with leptospirosis, which can be treated with antibiotics if caught relatively early. You should avoid crossing streams with open cuts, and treat all water found in nature with treatment pills before drinking. (Many filters are ineffective for lepto.)

Land Critters

One animal you are almost sure to see is the **mongoose**. Think of it as a stealth squirrel with mean-looking red eyes. Mongooses (no, not mongeese) are bold enough to take on cobras in their native India and were brought here to help control rats. Great idea, except mongooses are active during the day and rats work the night shift, so never the twain shall meet. It was a disaster for local birds since mongooses love bird eggs. Kaua'i is the only major island to avoid the mongoose (and vice versa), and the difference between its bird population and the Big Island's is dramatic.

There are no **snakes** in Hawai'i (except for some reporters). There is concern that the brown tree snake *might* have made its way onto the islands from Guam. Although mostly harmless to humans, these snakes can spell extinction to native birds. Government officials aren't allowed to tell you this, but we will: If you ever see one anywhere in Hawai'i, please *kill it* and contact the **Pest Hotline** at (808) 643-7378. At the very least, call them immediately. The entire bird population of Hawai'i will be grateful.

Then there are the **pigs**. We're not referring to your dining choice. We mean the wild ones you may encounter on a hiking trail. Generally, feral pigs will avoid you before you ever see them. If you happen to come upon any piglets and accidentally get between them and their mother, immediately bark like a big dog. Wild pigs are conditioned to run from local dogs (and their hunter masters), and

Momma will leave her kids faster than you can say, "Pass the bacon."

Also, there are some irritating visitors that first arrived on the island a few years back and won't leave. (Well, besides the in-laws.) They're small tree **frogs**, called **coqui**, that emit a whistle all night long. Cute at first, like a bird, but incessant and ultimately irritating. Most of the resorts do their best to deal with them, but there's a chance that some errant froggies may occasionally give you a long night. The Hilo side is froggier (I *swear* that's a real word) than Kona.

Vog

Vog is a mixture of water vapor, carbon dioxide and sulfur dioxide. For decades Kilauea belched 5,000 *tons* of sulfur dioxide *per day*. (During the 1983–2018 eruption it produced enough sulphur dioxide to fill almost a *million* Goodyear blimps.) These gases react with sunlight, oxygen, dust particles and water in the air to form a mixture of sulfate aerosols, sulfuric acid and other oxidized sulfur compounds. Why should *you* care? Because our trade winds usually blow toward the southwest, carrying the vog from its source, down the coast where the winds wrap around Mauna Loa and head up the coast. Then daytime onshore breezes and nighttime offshore breezes rake it back and forth across Kona. Sunsets became events where the sun never seemed to slip below the horizon; it simply sank into a soup of haze and gradually disappeared. In 2018, a brief pause in volcanic activity made Kona once again the land of brilliant sunsets, but the emissions of sulphur dioxide are back (although to a lesser extent) with the new 2020 eruption.

Dehydration

Bring and drink lots of water when you are out and about, especially when you are hiking. Dehydration sneaks up on people. By the time you are thirsty, you're already dehydrated. It's a good idea to take an insulated water jug with you in the car or one of those 1.5 liter bottles of water. Our weather is almost certainly different than what you left behind, and you will probably find yourself thirstier than usual. Just fill it before you leave in the morning and *suck 'em up* (as we say here) all day.

Curses

Legend says that if you remove any lava from the island, bad luck will befall you. *Balderdash!* you say. Hey, we don't know if it's true or not. You don't have to be a believer, but we at Revealed Travel along with resorts and local post offices, get boxes of lava that come in all the time from visitors who brought a souvenir of lava home, only to have their house burn down, have their foot fall off or get audited by the IRS. Coincidence? Maybe. But if you decide to do it anyway, remember… you've been warned.

Also, if the curse isn't enough to dissuade you, the TSA has written us asking us to inform you that they will *confiscate* any large lava rocks, coral or sand found in your luggage.

Grocery Stores

Definitely a hazard. Though restaurants on the Big Island are expensive, don't think you'll get off cheap in grocery stores. You'll certainly save money by cooking your own food, but you'll be amazed, appalled and offended by the prices you see here. If you are staying at a condo, savvy travelers should head over to **Costco** (808-331-4800) just north of Kona (shown on map on page 168) to stock up. If you're not a member of this national warehouse store, you might consider a $55 membership. With one, the savings on food and everything else are incredible, especially for Hawai'i. Otherwise, ask around to see if any residents you are dealing with will let you go with them or have a member get you a Cash Card from there.

There are no large grocery stores in the Kohala resort area, just an upscale market in the **Queens' MarketPlace** in Waikoloa. You'll find a larger store 6 miles up Waikoloa Road (which is across from mile marker 75) in Waikoloa Village. They're easy to find in Kona and Hilo.

TRAVELING WITH CHILDREN (KEIKI)

Should we have put this section under *Hazards*, too? Some Kohala resorts try hard to cater to families. If your keiki (kid) is looking for an adventure, we have a dandy of an adventure just for them on page 242. **All About Babies 'n Beaches** (808-883-3675) has the usual assortment of keiki paraphernalia for rent, such as car seats, strollers, cribs, bathtubs, beach gear, etc., as does **Baby's Away** (800-996-9030).

For swimming, the beach in front of the King Kamehameha's Kona Beach Hotel or the tide-pools at the Natural Energy Lab in Kona, and Onekahakaha in Hilo are probably the safest on the island. (Check them out yourself to be sure.) We don't need to tell you that keiki and surf don't mix. Also check out **Keiki Beach** just north of Kailua Bay. See map on page 65 and park near the gym for the 5-minute walk to this very protected cove.

There's a great playground at **Higashihara Park** just south of Kona past mile marker 115. Another one is at the corner of Kuakini Highway and Makala Boulevard. at the north end of Kona, and **Waimea Park** in Waimea. (See map on page 137.) The **Na Kamalei Toddler Playground** in Kailua Park is an entertaining spot for the youngest visitors. The most

unusual playground is at the **Gilbert Kahele Recreation Area** rest stop on Saddle Road. The equipment there is physics-based and is safer the lighter you are. (Adventurous parents, you have been *warned*.)

'Imiloa Astronomy Center** (808-932-8901) in Hilo has a great hands-on experience for keiki. See page 113 for more. In Hilo Town proper, a free and educational distraction is **Mokupapapa Discovery Center** (808-498-4709). There's a restroom there, too. Closed Sundays and Mondays.

Kids might enjoy the seahorse tour at **Ocean Rider** (see page 62) and if they're old enough, consider **SNUBA**, see page 229.

If you are an animal lover, the **Three Ring Ranch Animal Sanctuary** (808-331-8778) shouldn't be missed. A great excursion with the keiki 6 *and over*, this exotic and native animal rehabilitation facility gives a great hands-on educational experience. You will have to call ahead to set up a tour as time and space are limited. The genuine passion the caretakers have about the animals is contagious. Tours last around 2 hours, and a *minimum* donation of $50 per person is requested.

Lastly, you should know that it's a big fine plus a mandatory safety class if your keiki isn't buckled up in the car.

THE PEOPLE

There's no doubt about it, people really *are* friendlier in Hawai'i. You will notice that people are quick to smile and wave at you here. (Those of us who live in Hawai'i have to remember to pack our "mainland face" when we journey there. Otherwise, we get undesired responses when we smile or wave at complete strangers.) It probably comes down to a matter of happiness. People are happy here, and happy people are friendly people. Some people compare a trip to an outer island in Hawai'i to a trip back in time, when smiles weren't rare, and politeness was the order of the day.

Ethnic Breakdown

The Big Island has an ethnic mix that is as diversified as any you will find. Here, *everyone* is a minority; there are no majorities. The last census revealed the ethnic makeup below:

White	68,604
Asian	42,786
Hispanic	25,999
Hawaiian or Pacific Islander	25,872
Black	1,704
Native American or Alaska Native	1,143
Other	61,404
Total	**201,513**

SOME TERMS

A person of Hawaiian blood is **Hawaiian**. Only people of this race are called by this term. They are also called **Kanaka Maoli**, but only another Hawaiian can use this term. Anybody who was born here, regardless of race (except whites) is called a **local**. If you were born elsewhere but have lived here awhile, you are called a **kama'aina**. If you are white, you are a **haole**. It doesn't matter if you have been here a day or your family has been here for over a century—you will always be a **haole**. The term comes from the time when westerners first encountered these islands. Its precise meaning has been lost, but it is thought to refer to people with no background (since westerners could not chant the kanaenae of their ancestors).

The continental United States is called the **Mainland**. If you are here and are returning, you are not "going back to the states" (we *are* a state). When somebody leaves the island, they are **off-island**.

HAWAIIAN TIME

One aspect of Hawaiian culture you may have heard of is Hawaiian Time. The stereotype is that everyone in Hawai'i moves just a little bit slower than on the mainland. Supposedly, we are more laid-back and don't let things get to us as easily as people on the mainland. This is the stereotype… OK, it's *not* a stereotype. It's real.

The 'ukulele is one of the easiest instruments to learn to play.

Hopefully, during your visit, you will notice that this feeling infects *you* as well. You may find yourself letting another driver cut in front of you in circumstances that would incur your wrath back home. You may find yourself willing to wait for a red light without feeling like you're going to explode. The whole reason for coming to Hawai'i is to experience beauty and a sense of peace, so let it happen. If someone else is moving a bit more slowly than you want, just go with it.

SHAKA

One gesture you will see often and should not be offended by is the *shaka* sign. This is done by extending the pinkie and thumb while curling the three middle fingers. Sometimes visitors think it is some kind of local gesture indicating *up yours* or some similarly unfriendly message. Actually, it is a friendly act used as a sign of greeting or just to say *Hey.* Its origin is thought to date back to the 1930s. A guard at the Kahuku Sugar Plantation on O'ahu used to patrol the plantation railroad to keep local kids from stealing cane from the slow moving trains. This guard had lost his middle fingers in an accident and his manner of waving off the youths became well known. Kids began to warn other kids that he was around by waving their hands in a way that looked like the guard's, and the custom took off.

THE HAWAIIAN LANGUAGE

The Hawaiian language is a beautiful, gentle and melodic language that flows smoothly off the tongue. Just the sounds of the words conjure up trees gently blowing in the breeze and the sound of the surf. Most Polynesian languages share the same roots, and many have common words. Today, Hawaiian is spoken *as an everyday language* only on the privately owned island of Ni'ihau. Visitors are often intimidated by Hawaiian. With a few ground rules you will come to realize that pronunciation is not as hard as you might think.

When missionaries discovered that the Hawaiians had no written language, they sat down and created an alphabet. This Hawaiian alphabet has only twelve letters. Five vowels; a, e i, o and u, as well as seven consonants; h, k, l, m, n, p and w.

The consonants are pronounced just as they are in English with the exception of W. It is often pronounced as a V if it is in the middle of a word and comes after an E or I. Vowels are pronounced as follows:

A—pronounced as in *Ah* if stressed, or *above* if not stressed.

E—pronounced as in *say* if stressed, or *dent* if not stressed.

I—pronounced as in *bee.*

O—pronounced as in *no.*

U—pronounced as in *boo.*

One thing you will notice in this book are glottal stops. These are represented by an upside-down apostrophe ' and are meant to convey a hard stop in the pronunciation. So if we are talking about the type of lava called 'a'a, it is pronounced as two separate As (AH-AH).

Another feature you will encounter are **diphthongs**, where two letters glide together. They are **ae, ai, ao, au, ei, eu, oi,** and **ou.** Unlike many English diphthongs, the second vowel is always pronounced. One word you will read in this book, referring to Hawaiian temples, is *heiau* (HEY-YOW). The e and i flow together as a single sound, then the a and u flow together as a single sound. The Y sound binds the two sounds, making the whole word flow together.

If you examine long Hawaiian words, you will see that most have repeating syllables, making it easier to remember and pronounce.

Let's take a word that might seem impossible to pronounce. When you see how easy this word is, the rest will seem like a snap. The Hawai'i state fish is the **humuhumunukunukuapua'a**. At first glance it seems like a nightmare. But if you read the word slowly, it is pronounced just like it looks and isn't nearly as horrifying as it appears. Try it. **Humu** (hoo-moo) is pronounced twice. **Nuku** (noo-koo) is pronounced twice. **A** (ah) is pronounced once. **Pu** (poo) is pronounced once. **A'a** (ah-ah) is the ah sound pronounced twice, the glottal stop indicating a hard stop between sounds. Now you can try it again. **Humuhumunukunukuapua'a**. Now, wasn't that easy? OK, so it's not easy, but it's not impossible either.

Below are some words that you might hear during your visit.

'Aina (EYE-na)—Land.

Akamai (AH-ka-MY)—Wise or shrewd.

Ali'i (ah-LEE-ee)—A Hawaiian chief; a member of the chiefly class.

Aloha (ah-LO-ha)—Hello, goodbye or a feeling or the spirit of love, affection or kindness.

Hala (HA-la)—Pandanus tree.

Hale (HA-leh)—House or building.

Hana (HA-na)—Work.

Hana hou (HA-na-HO)—To do again.

Haole (HOW-leh)—Originally foreigner, now means Caucasian.

Heiau (HEY-YOW)—Hawaiian temple.

Hula (HOO-la)—The story-telling dance of Hawai'i.

Imu (EE-moo)—An underground oven.

'Iniki (ee-NEE-key)—Sharp and piercing wind (as in Hurricane 'Iniki).

Kahuna (ka-HOO-na)—A priest or minister; someone who is an expert in a profession.

Kai (kigh)—The sea.

Kalua (KA-LOO-ah)—Cooking food underground.

Kama'aina (KA-ma-EYE-na)—Long-time Hawai'i resident.

Kane (KA-neh)—Boy or man.

Kapu (KA-poo)—Forbidden, taboo; keep out.

Keiki (KAY-key)—Child or children.

Kokua (KO-KOO-ah)—Help.

Kona (KO-na)—Leeward side of the island; wind blowing from the south, southwest direction.

Kuleana (KOO-leh-AH-na)—Concern, responsibility or jurisdiction.

Lanai (LA-NIGH)—Porch, veranda, patio.

Lani (LA-nee)—Sky or heaven.

Lei (lay)—Necklace of flowers, shells or feathers. The lehua blossom lei is the lei of the Big Island.

Liliko'i (LEE-lee-KO-ee)—Passion fruit.

Limu (LEE-moo)—Edible seaweed.

Lomi (LOW-me)—To rub or massage; lomi salmon is raw salmon rubbed with salt and spices.

Lu'au (LOO-OW)—Hawaiian feast; literally means taro leaves.

Mahalo (ma-HA-low)—Thank you.

Makai (ma-KIGH)—Toward the sea.

Malihini (MA-lee-HEE-nee)—A newcomer, visitor or guest.

Mauka (MOW-ka)—Toward the mountain.

Moana (mo-AH-na)—Ocean.

Mo'o (MO-oh)—Lizard.

Nani (NA-nee)—Beautiful, pretty.

Nui (NEW-ee)—Big, important, great.

'Ohana (oh-HA-na)—Family.

'Okole (OH-KO-leh)—Derrière.

'Ono (OH-no)—Delicious, the best.

Pakalolo (pa-ka-LO-LO)—Marijuana.

Pali (PA-lee)—A cliff.

Paniolo (PA-nee-OH-lo)—Hawaiian cowboy.

Pau (pow)—Finish, end; *pau hana* means quitting time from work.

Poi (poy)—Pounded kalo (taro) root that forms a paste.

Pono (PO-no)—Goodness, excellence, correct, proper.

Pua (POO-ah)—Flower.

Puka (POO-ka)—Hole.

Pupu (POO-POO)—Appetizer, snacks or finger food.

Wahine (vah-HEE-neh)—Woman.

Wai (why)—Fresh water.

Wikiwiki (WEE-kee-WEE-kee)—To hurry up, very quick.

Quick Pidgin Lesson

Hawaiian pidgin is fun to listen to. It's like ear candy. It's colorful, rhythmic and sways in the wind. Below is a list of some of the words and phrases you might hear on your visit. It's tempting to read some of these and try to use them. If you do, the odds are you will simply look foolish. These words and phrases are used in certain ways and with certain inflections. People who have spent years living in the islands still feel uncomfortable using them. Thick pidgin can be incomprehensible to the untrained ear (that's the idea). If you are someplace and hear two people engaged in a discussion in pidgin, stop and eavesdrop a bit. You won't forget it.

Pidgin Words & Phrases

Ainokea—I no care/I don't care. Try saying it slowly to hear it.

All bus—Drunk.

An' den—And then? So?

Any kine—Anything; any kind.

Ass right—That's right.

Ass why—That's why.

Beef—A problem one has with another.

Brah—Bruddah; friend; brother.

Brok' da mout—Delicious.

Buggah—That's the one; it is difficult.

Bus laugh—To laugh out loud.

Chicken skin kine—Something that gives you goosebumps.

Choke—Plenty; a lot.

Cockaroach—Steal; rip off.

Da kine—A noun or verb used in place of whatever the speaker wishes. Heard constantly.

Das how—That's right.

Fo days—plenty; "He get hair fo days."

Geevum—Go for it! Give 'em hell!

Grind—To eat.

Grinds—Food.

Hold ass—A close call when driving your new car.

How you figga?—How do you figure that? It makes no sense.

Howzit?—How is it going? How are you? Also, Howzit o wot?

I owe you money or wat?—What to say when someone is staring at you.

Lolo—Crazy, stupid.

Lose money—What you say when something bad happens, like if you drop your shave ice.

Mek ass—Make a fool of yourself.

Mek house—Make yourself at home.

Mo' bettah—This is better.

Moke—A large, tough local male. (Don't say it unless you *like scrap*.)

No can—Cannot; I cannot do it.

No mek lidat—Stop doing that.

No, yeah?—No, or is "no" correct?

'Okole squeezer—Something that suddenly frightens you ('okole meaning derrière).

Pau hana—Quit work. (A time of daily, intense celebration in the islands.) Also another name for Happy Hour.

Poi dog—A mutt.

Shahkbait—Shark bait, meaning pale, untanned people or a beach newbie.

Shaka—Great! All right!

Shoots, den—Affirmative/Okay, then. As in "We're meeting for lunch at noon." *Shoots, den.*

Shredding—Riding a gnarly wave.
Slippahs—Flip-flops, thongs, zoris.
Stink eye—Dirty looks; facial expression denoting displeasure.
Suck rocks—Buzz off, or pound sand.
Talk stink—Speak bad about somebody.
Talk story—Shooting the breeze; to rap.
Tanks ah?—Thank you.
Tita—A female moke. Same *scrap* results.
Training brah—A haole trying (unsuccessfully) to speak pidgin.
Yeah?—Used at the end of sentences.

THE HULA

The hula evolved as a means of worship, later becoming a forum for telling a story with chants (called mele), hands and body movement. It can be fascinating to watch. When most people think of the hula, they picture a woman in a grass skirt swinging her hips to the beat of an 'ukulele. But in reality there are two types of hula. The modern hula, or hula 'auana, uses musical instruments and vocals to augment the dancer. It came about after westerners first encountered the islands. Missionaries found the hula distasteful, and the old style was driven underground. The modern type came about as a form of entertainment and was practiced in places where missionaries had no influence. Ancient Hawaiians didn't even use grass skirts. They were later brought by Gilbert Islanders.

The old style of hula is called hula 'olapa or hula kahiko. It consists of chants and is accompanied only by percussion and takes years of training. It can be exciting to watch as performers work together in a synchronous harmony. Both men and women participate, with women's hula being softer (though no less disciplined) and men's hula being more active. This type of hula is physically demanding, requiring strong concentration. Keiki (children's) hula can be charming to watch as well.

The world's best gather each year in Hilo for a week starting the first Thursday after Easter Sunday for the **Merrie Monarch Festival** (named after the 19th-century king credited with reviving the hula). Tickets are often hard to come by if you wait too long. Visit their website for ticket info. Otherwise, check it out on TV. It will utterly dazzle you.

A NOTE ABOUT ACCESS

If a lawful landowner posts a No Trespassing sign on their land, you need to respect their wishes. That seems simple enough. But here's where it gets tricky.

It's common in Hawai'i for someone who doesn't own or control land to erect his own No Trespassing, Keep Out and Road Closed signs. Picture a shoreline fisherman who doesn't want anyone else near his cherished spot, putting up a store-bought sign to protect his solitude. Or a neighbor on a dirt road who hates the dust from cars driving by, so he puts up a sign that he knows locals will ignore, but it might dissuade unwary visitors.

Be alert for subtle signs that you might not be welcome.

In the past we did our best to try to ferret out when No Trespassing signs were valid, and when they were not, and we took *a lot* of heat from residents who thought we were encouraging trespassing when we weren't. But the current environment doesn't permit us to do that anymore. So if you're heading to one of the places we describe, and you encounter a No Trespassing sign, even if you think it's not authorized by the landowner (and even if it's on *public* land), we have to advise you to turn around and heed the sign. All descriptions in our book come with the explicit assumption that you have obtained the permission of the legal landowner, and unfortunately, it'll usually be up to you to determine who that is and how to get it. But please, under no circumstances are we suggesting that you trespass. Plain and clear. Don't trespass… ever…for any reason…period.

A NOTE ON PERSONAL RESPONSIBILITY

In past editions we've had the sad task of removing places that you can no longer visit. The reason, universally cited, is *liability*. Although Hawai'i has a statute indemnifying landowners, the mere threat is often enough to get something closed. Because we, more than any other publication, have exposed heretofore unknown attractions, we feel the need to pass this along.

You need to assess what kind of traveler you are. We've been accused of leaning a bit toward the adventurous side, so you should take that into account when deciding if something's right for you. To paraphrase from the movie *Top Gun*, "Don't let your ego write checks your body can't cash."

You will probably be more physical during your trip, so *train* up for it. If you plan on doing any hiking, snorkeling or other activities, spend the month before

You stay safe by staying smart. You don't need a guidebook to tell you that this is a really bad idea.

coming here pushing yourself. Your body will reward you, we promise.

Please remember that this isn't Disneyland—it's nature. Mother Nature is hard, slippery, sharp and unpredictable. If you go exploring and get into trouble, whether it's your ego that's bruised or something more tangible, please remember that neither the state, the private land owner nor this publication *told* you to go. You *chose* to explore, which is what life, and this book, are all about. And if you complain to or threaten someone controlling land, they'll rarely fix the problem you identified. They'll simply close it… and it will be gone for good.

In the end, nothing can take the place of your own observations and good judgment. If you're doing one of the activities you read about in our book or someplace else and your instinct tells you something is wrong, *trust your judgment* and go do another activity. There are lots of wonderful things to do on the island, and we want you to stay safe and happy.

And also remember to always leave the island the same way you found it.

MISCELLANEOUS INFORMATION

It is customary here for *everyone* to remove their shoes upon entering someone's house (sometimes their office).

If you are going to spend any time at the beach, woven bamboo beach mats can be found all over the island for about $4. Some roll up, some can be folded. The sand comes off these more easily than it comes off towels.

Around the island you'll see signs saying *Visitor Information*, *Volcano Update* or something similar. Allow me to translate. That's usually code for "We want to sell you something."

The **area code** for the state is 808. **Daylight Saving Time** isn't observed here.

If you wear **sunglasses**, *polarized* lenses are highly recommended. Not only are our colors more vivid here, but the lower latitudes of Hawai'i make polarized lenses particularly effective.

Plastic bags are banned on the island, and rather than springing for paper bags, many stores will simply hand you your purchases, no matter how numerous. Consider bringing your own reusable bag.

If you want to arrange a lei greeting for you or your honey when you disembark the airplane, call **LeiGreeting.com** (800) 665-7959. In Kona, you can get a good lei for around $39 and up. (I know where you're going with that—stop it!) Nice way to kick off a romantic trip, huh?

FARMERS MARKETS

Kailua-Kona—The **Kailua Village Farmers Market** (Wednesday–Sunday) at the corner of Hualalai and Alii Drive used to be the biggest in town, but their hours and vendors have been unreliable lately. (Supposedly) open 7 a.m.–4 p.m. The **Alii Gardens Marketplace** near mile marker 2.5 on Alii Drive focuses more on crafts and local handmade items with a few decent food vendors. Open 10 a.m.–5 p.m., closed Mondays. The **Keauhou Farmers Market** (Saturday) at the Keauhou Shopping Center claims to sell only locally grown products, such as coffee and mac nuts. Open 8 a.m.–noon.

Hilo—The **Hilo Farmers Market** on the corner of Mamo Street and Kamehameha Avenue has mostly produce and flowers with a few booths of crafts and gift items. Open every day 7 a.m. *till it's gone* (or 3 p.m.). Wednesdays and Saturdays have the most vendors. **Pana'ewa Farmers Market** is open Saturdays 6 a.m.–10 a.m. and sells mostly plants. Don't go out of your way. "Farmers Market" is a generous term for this small collection of vendors. Across from the Home Depot.

Waimea—The **Waimea Town Market** is has a lot to offer. Among the food, flower and plant vendors, you'll find some great locally made items like goat cheese, chocolate and vanilla beans at Parker School, 65-1224 Lindsey Road. Open Saturdays from 7:30 a.m.–noon. Nearby is the **Waimea Midweek Farmers Market** on Wednesdays 9 a.m.–2 p.m. Some opportunities to dine here in addition to produce. Look for the stand with chocolate bomb bars. At Pukalani Stables.

Pahoa—The **Maku'u Farmers Market** on Sundays, just south of mile marker 7 on Hwy 130, has reached flea market (or possibly bazaar) status. Open Sundays from 7 a.m.–noon.

SMARTPHONE APPS

We love books, which are naturally and instinctively approachable. They convey information in a way that is timeless. But at the same time, new technology allows us to do things with smartphones that can't occur in books. Our app, *Hawaii Revealed*, is unlike *any* travel app you've ever seen. All the information from the books is there, but the app costs extra because we have also harnessed and *invented* features that will blow you away.

For instance, you want to go for a snorkel in Kahalu'u Beach today? You can flip to the page in the book and read all about it. But with our app, you tap to the entry and you can read all about it *and* find out that today isn't a good day to get into the water due to high surf. Want to do a hike near Hilo? Well, the author woke up this morning, saw that the weather was going to be bad on that side of the island, circled a part of the map that he thought might be affected and for how long, and every entry in that area that is weather-sensitive will be updated to reflect the bad weather.

Want to find a restaurant that matches perfectly to your vision? *I want to dine at a place in Kohala, that has a romantic atmosphere, an ocean view, is vegetarian-friendly, full bar, easy parking, outdoor seating, not part of a national chain...oh, and has gluten-free options?* With the filters in our app you can cut through all of the restaurants and get to *exactly* what you want, read our in-depth and brutally honest review and get directions. How's *that* for cutting through the noise? There's more—*a lot* more.

GPS Driving Tour App

When friends and relatives from the mainland come to visit, I often end up tagging along with them in the car showing them the island and expanding on things that I didn't have room for here. I always wished I could do that for all my readers, and now through the magic of smartphone technology, *I can.*

Our *Big Island Revealed Drive Tour* app is just like having me in the backseat showing you the island. (It's actually better, because you don't have to buy me a mai tai at the end of the day.) I have personally narrated all the places we will drive and include lots of additional information, stories and legends along with the occasional personal story associated with a particular place. Your phone's GPS triggers the narrations as you drive over specific points in specific directions and doesn't require a cell signal, so don't worry about being out of range. I absolutely love creating this book you are holding, but creating these audio tours has been one of the most fulfilling things I've ever done. I hope you enjoy using them as much as I did creating them.

You'll find both apps in the Apple or Google Play stores.

Kohala is synonomous with clean water, fancy resorts and condos and bountiful golf.

Kohala is the oldest volcano on the island, having last sputtered 60,000 years ago. It contains lush forest, dry lava desert, windswept grassy plains and outrageous beaches. Some of the most expensive resorts on the island are along the Kohala Coast.

This is a large, diverse area to cover in one chapter, but because of the way the island's resorts are distributed and the roads are laid out, most will see this area in a circular driving tour, so that's how we'll describe it. (See map on page 48.) We're going to start as you leave Kona heading up Hwy 190. If you're staying in Kohala, you can come up Waikoloa Village Road and pick up the description on Hwy 190 heading north. If staying in Hilo, pick it up from Waimea.

UP HIGHWAY 190 FROM KAILUA-KONA

As you leave Kona, you'll take Palani Road, which becomes Mamalahoa Highway (190) heading north. From near sea level, you will be heading up to 3,564 feet then down again into Hawi, so gas up on that cheap *(ha!)* Kona gasoline.

[A] Leaving Kailua-Kona, it's hard to believe that just above the town lies a **DIVERSION** beautiful fern and 'ohi'a **cloud forest** steeped in fog and moss. **ALERT!** Weather here is determined by altitude because the mountain literally creates its own rain through convection. You can see it by taking **Kaloko Drive** just south of the mile marker 34. Follow it for 7 miles as it winds upward into another world. Just before the end of the road, turn left onto Huehue Street that dead ends at 5,000 feet. No expansive views due to overgrown vegetation, but it's cool to see how much lusher things get with altitude. Don't ride your brakes on the way down.

As you leave Kona, you'll get some good views down the coast. Keep an eye out for renegade peacocks (which sound like cats being tortured) from the **Makalei Golf Club** around mile marker 32.

The highway bisects several channels and tubes in the lava between mile markers 28 and 26. Rivers of molten stone coursed down the mountain here during the 1800 Hualalai lava flow. If you look down the coast, you'll get an idea of the scale of a "typical" lava flow. On your right before mile marker 21 is the road to the **Pu'u Wa'awa'a trailhead** described on page 210.

By mile marker 19 you have passed from Hualalai Mountain to the slopes of Mauna Loa. Proof is in the form of a lava flow here that ran for 30 miles in 1859 all the way to Kiholo Bay, destroying Kamehameha's fishpond (see page 207). If clouds are absent, you may see the top of Mauna Kea and its many dome-enclosed telescopes ahead and on your right.

As you continue, you'll notice cactus scattered about, and trees appear again. **Parker Ranch** starts at mile marker 14, part of a colossal 130,000-acre cattle ranch.

At mile marker 11 is the road through **Waikoloa Village**, which leads down to the **Kohala mega-resorts**. It's marked by a giant obelisk shaped like a Hawaiian sail erected by Waikoloa Land Co. in a fit of psychedelic creativity. Waikoloa Village is a relatively stark community. Due to its location, on the leeward side of the saddle between Mauna Loa and Mauna Kea, it's usually pretty windy. (*How consistently windy? When the wind stops, the cows fall down.*) If you are staying at a mega-resort in Kohala, you'll want to know that there is a fairly large **grocery store** here.

Still on Hwy 190 between mile markers 5 and 2 off to your right (up mauka), there's a large hill called **Holoholoku**. Everyone has seen the famous WWII photo and statue of the scene where Marines on Iwo Jima raised the American flag over Mt. Suribachi. Possibly the most dramatic WWII photo ever taken, it puts a lump in your throat every time you see it. What you don't know is that those very guys practiced storming the hill right there on Holoholoku because it was thought to be similar to Suribachi in size and shape.

[B] As you approach the town of **Waimea** (Kamuela), you may decide to check it out now. Since this is the crossroads between the east and west sides of the island, we could have included it here or in the chapter on **Hamakua**. After careful analysis of driving patterns, accommodation indexes and topography…we flipped a coin

Letters **[A]** *correspond to paragraphs in text.*

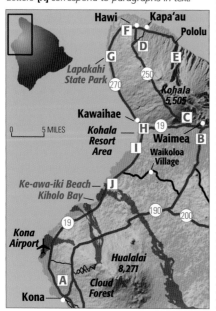

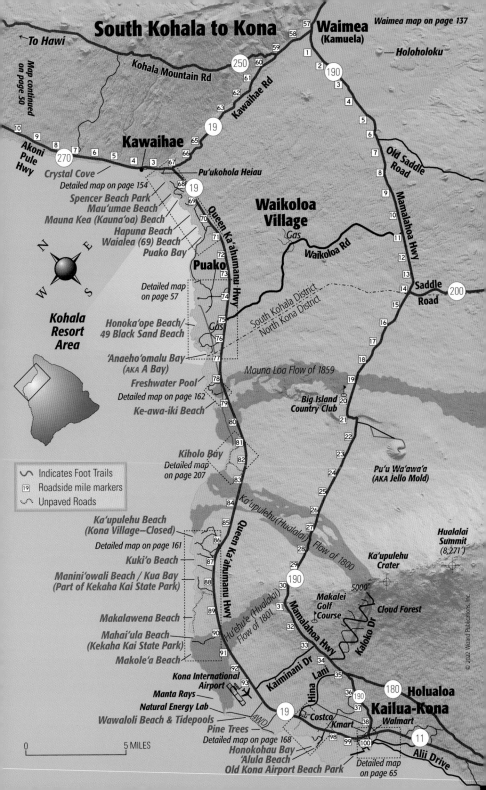

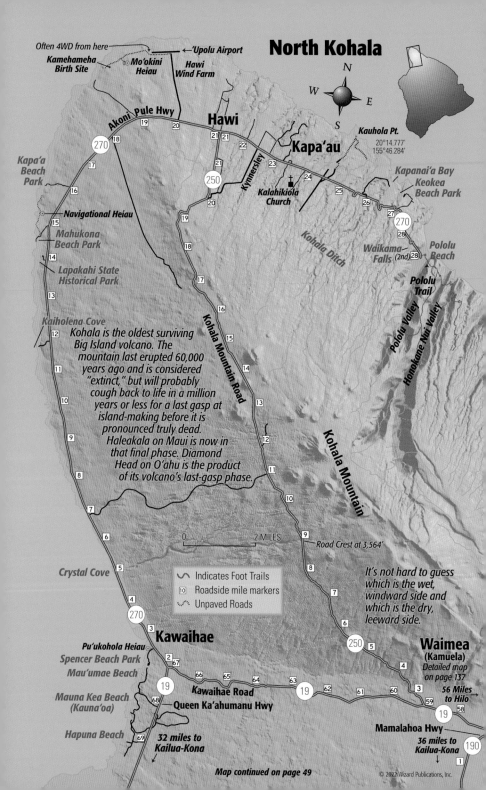

North Kohala

Often 4WD from here
Kamehameha Birth Site
Mo'okini Heiau
←'Upolu Airport
Hawi Wind Farm

Akoni Pule Hwy

19 | 20

Hawi

21 | 21

Kapa'au

Kauhola Pt.
20°14.777'
155°46.284'

22

23

24

25

26

27

270

28

Kymmersley

Kalahikiola Church

Kapanai'a Bay
Keokea Beach Park

28

Waikama Falls (2nd)

Pololu Beach

Pololu Trail

Kohala Ditch

Pololu Valley

Honokane Nui Valley

18

17

270

Kapa'a Beach Park

16

Navigational Heiau

15

Mahukona Beach Park

14

Lapakahi State Historical Park

13

Kaiholena Cove

12

Kohala is the oldest surviving Big Island volcano. The mountain last erupted 60,000 years ago and is considered "extinct," but will probably cough back to life in a million years or less for a last gasp at island-making before it is pronounced truly dead. Haleakala on Maui is now in that final phase. Diamond Head on O'ahu is the product of its volcano's last-gasp phase.

11

10

9

8

7

6

Crystal Cove

5

4

270

3

Kohala Mountain Road

19

18

17

16

15

14

13

12

11

10

9

8

7

6

Kohala Mountain

Road Crest at 3,564'

0   2 MILES

⌒ Indicates Foot Trails
10 Roadside mile markers
⋯ Unpaved Roads

It's not hard to guess which is the wet, windward side and which is the dry, leeward side.

250

5

4

3

Kawaihae

Pu'ukohola Heiau
Spencer Beach Park
Mau'umae Beach

2
67

66   65   64   63   62   61   60

19

19

Kawaihae Road

Waimea
(Kamuela)
Detailed map on page 137

59   58

19

→ 56 Miles to Hilo

Mauna Kea Beach (Kauna'oa)

68

Queen Ka'ahumanu Hwy

69

Hapuna Beach

32 miles to Kailua-Kona

Mamalahoa Hwy

36 miles to Kailua-Kona

190

1

Map continued on page 49

© 2022 Wizard Publications, Inc.

and put it in the *Hamakua & Waimea Sights* chapter. Waimea has an incredibly colorful history and is worth exploring. If you do it now, turn to page 137 before continuing on.

KOHALA MOUNTAIN ROAD

[C] See map on facing page or page 137 to get to Highway 250. (From 190, turn left at the Shell station onto Lindsey Road then right on 250.) You are traveling up the spine of the sleeping Kohala Volcano. (They say you shouldn't honk your horn, or you may wake it up.) You're still on the dry, leeward side and will crest at 3,564 feet before descending to the sea.

Around mile marker 14 you'll start to see a huge mountain looming in front of you. That's not on this island; it's **Maui**, 30 miles across the sea. On clear days, the island of Maui seems to tower over the little town of Hawi even more than the Big Island's own volcanoes. Sometimes it looks gigantic, and sometimes it's less impressive. It's the same reason the moon always looks enormous when it's near a mountain horizon or through trees—it gives your brain some scale to compute its size. Maui looks biggest when you see it *with or through* something other than on the ocean's horizon.

NORTH SHORE OF KOHALA

[D] Be sure to take the left road to **Hawi**, not the right to Kapaʻau (so take the left fork) near mile marker 20. As you pull into Hawi, you're greeted by a couple of old banyan trees on your right. You'll want to head right (east), but if you're hungry for a treat, across the street from **Bamboo Restaurant** on your left is **Kohala Coffee Mill**, which has **Tropical Dreams**, an *outstanding* ice cream made here on the island. We unselfishly review it every time we are on the north shore, just to be thorough.

The sleepy little towns of **Hawi** and **Kapaʻau** lie at this northernmost point of the island. Until the '70s, this was sugar country. When Kohala Sugar pulled out, this area was left high and dry. Rather than let their towns die, residents stuck it

The beautiful ranchlands of North Kohala.

out, opening shops and other small businesses. Today this area is enjoying a comeback of sorts. There are lots of artists who call this area home. A Japanese investment company bought most of Kohala Sugar's land assets (19,000 acres) in 1988 when land here was cheap and has *plans* for a resort and golf course at Mahukona, a restaurant at the end of the road overlooking **Pololu Valley** and more. But they've been *planning* for decades. In the meantime, this is a quiet, peaceful community. It's said that the investor bought all this land after simply flying over it in a helicopter—without ever touching it!

Heading east, you come to the town of **Kapaʻau**. Watch your speed in this area. Police commonly nab people caught by surprise in some of the slower posted areas. On the mauka (mountain) side of the highway in Kapaʻau is a statue of **King Kamehameha the Great**. If you think it looks just like the famous one standing in front of the Judiciary building in Honolulu, that's because it *is* the same…sort of. When the Hawaiian Legislature commissioned the statue in 1878, it was cast in Paris and put on a ship. Unfortunately, the ship and its cargo were lost at sea near the Falkland Islands in the South Atlantic. Since they had shipping insurance, they used the money to order a new one. Meanwhile, the captain of the wrecked ship later spotted the "lost" statue standing in Port Stanley (somebody had salvaged it). He

Though the Pololu Lookout is nice, you'll get a much better vantage point if you go part of the way down the trail.

bought it for $500 and shipped it (this time successfully—must have FedExed it) to Hawai'i where its broken arm was repaired, and it was erected where you see it now. On **King Kamehameha Day** (June 11) the statue is piled high with leis and other decorations and is quite a sight to see. There are public restrooms here behind the building that are *sometimes* open.

Continuing east, just before mile marker 24, is the road to **Kalahikiola Church**, originally built in 1855. It was ravaged by a strong earthquake in 2006. The current building is new, but the stones from the original building, hand-carried from the ocean and rivers of the area in 1850, were used to build the wall around the new church.

If you want to see some raw coastline and have a 4WD vehicle, take a left 0.5 miles past mile marker 24 onto Maulili (which is just after Old Halaula Mill Road). After 0.3 miles it becomes dirt. Turn right when it ends, and the short paved section leads to an unpaved road that goes to **Kauhola Point**. In 1933, they built a lighthouse at this point that was 85 feet away from the edge of the cliff. In 2009 they had to destroy the lighthouse because it was only *20* feet from the shoreline and ready to topple into the sea. If you look at the sides of the cliffs, you can *see* how they're getting munched away by the waves. This area is wild and undeveloped and sports nice views of the sea cliffs that wrap around the north shore. The area a few hundred yards to the right (east) is full of abandoned sugar equipment and cars. Many are actually embedded in the *side* of the cliff, evidence of the rapid pace of cliff erosion. Just a few decades ago the cars were buried in "stable" ground, and the cliffs were farther out.

Back on the highway, look to your left just before mile marker 25. There is a large banyan tree with an **old tree house**. Wouldn't you have *loved* a tree house like that when you were a kid?

There is an **ATV tour** of the coastal cliffs along here as well as other **Land Tours**, described in the *Activities* chapter.

POLOLU VALLEY

[E] The end of the highway (which lacks a turnaround for some reason, so expect vehicular confusion) is the **Pololu**

A REAL GEM

Valley Lookout. This outstanding vista displays the raw, untamed side of the Big Island. (Unfortunately, the state sometimes lets the vegetation block some of the view. The view's *much* nicer halfway down the trail mentioned below.) Nearly vertical cliffs are battered unmercifully by the winter north shore surf. Accessed via a 15–20 minute trail down through lush vegetation, 400 feet below, is **Pololu Beach**. (If you make it back *up* in 15 minutes, we're proud of you. It means you didn't stop once.) If it's been raining much, the trail may be slippery. At the bottom, in several spots, you'll find black sand dunes over 100 feet high, now mostly covered with vegetation. This type of black sand beach is formed as water constantly chips away at the lava river bed. Though the beach is not very swimmable (the surf and current are usually too violent), it's very picturesque and a nice place to observe Mother Nature's force. During the week you may have it nearly to yourself down there. Halfway down the trail is a small natural platform that looks out over the beach—a good photo op.

The beach is prettier from below than above, and there are some rope swings in nearby trees. On the opposite side of the valley, a trail leads up the wall over to the next valley, called **Honokane Nui**. These

Out on a lonely point on the northern tip of the island, Mo'okini Heiau was a place of dread. Thousands of lives were sacrificed on this very rock to the Hawaiian gods.

seven valleys, from Pololu to Waipi'o, are the only part of this new island that show much sign of erosion.

In ancient times Pololu Valley was a bountiful source for waterworn stones. Thousands of tons of stones have been hauled from here to build temples, houses and other structures. The massive **Pu'uko-hola Heiau**, 25 miles away at Kawaihae, was built from stones from this valley. A gigantic chain of men passed stones hand-to-hand all the way. If one was dropped, it was left where it lay (unless it was on his foot) to prevent the cadence from being interrupted. When you're ready, head back west past Hawi.

MO'OKINI HEIAU

[F] Near mile marker 20 is a sign saying simply "'Upolu Airport." This road (unpaved *past* the airport) leads to the northernmost tip of the island and past two important sites. The impressive 10.5 megawatt **Hawi Wind Farm** is just before the airport. Though it looks peaceful, to any pilot who has ever landed at 'Upolu, the location is horrifying. That's because during normal winds, your approach to the airport places

you in the gut-wrenching, scream-for-Mama prop wash from the turbines, turning a previously turbulent runway (before they built the turbines in 2006) into a delightfully terrifying experience.

You head left when you reach the quiet 'Upolu Airport. The county does a *terrible* job maintaining the unpaved portion. If it's dry and they've scraped it lately, you *may* make it in a regular car the 1.5 miles to the heiau described below. Otherwise, it's 4WD on at least *part* of the unpaved section, and the last part might even scare four-wheelers. Puddles last a *long time* here, and some of them are large enough to have nearly spawned their own unique ecosystem. Even during bad weather we've seen rental cars back here, giving legitimacy to the question: *What's the difference between a rental car and a 4WD? A rental car can go anywhere...*

This area is dominated by the legacy of two influential men—an ancient priest named **Pa'ao** and **Kamehameha the Great**. Pa'ao is said to have arrived in the 11th or 12th century and changed the islands. He was born in Tahiti or on one of its neighbor islands. It is said that the Hawaiian islands were in a state of anarchy when Pa'ao arrived. He restructured society, introduced the concept of human sacrifice and brought other similar traditions. Here he built the **Mo'okini Heiau**, where countless people were put to death to please Pa'ao's hungry gods. You'll have to park at the gate and walk 5 minutes to the heiau.

Even before we knew the gory details about Mo'okini Heiau's history, the place gave us the heebie-jeebies. We aren't the only ones who have noticed that the area around the temple is filled with an eerie, ghostly lifelessness, and it's the only place on the island that we like to avoid. Used for human sacrifices, the area feels devoid of a soul. The quiet is not comforting, but rather an empty void. The walls of Mo'okini are extremely tall and thick—oral tradition says that some of the rocks were passed by hand from Pololu Valley, 9 miles away. Just in front of the heiau is a large lava slab with a slight dip in it. It takes little imagination to see that this slab was the *holehole* stone, where unfortunate victims were laid while the flesh was stripped from their bones. These bones were then used to make fishhooks and other objects. The number of Hawaiians sacrificed here ran into the tens of thousands.

There were no signs at this heiau at press time telling the terrible history of what happened at this place. Although people from the **Marquesas Islands** settled on the Big Island around 400 AD, they were eventually overwhelmed by the Tahitians who came with Pa'ao around 1000 AD. It was the Tahitians who built this heiau and became the Hawaiians we know today.

Farther down the road is the **Kamehameha Akahi Aina Hanau Heiau**. This is where Kamehameha the Great, who conquered all the islands, was said to have been born. (Actually, many think he was born nearby, but not right here.) Kamehameha means "the lonely one," which seems ironically fitting given the almost palpable loneliness this area of the island exudes.

After Kamehameha's birthplace, you will come to an old **Coast Guard LORAN station** where you'll probably encounter boulders blocking the road. If so, retrace your route to the highway.

As you pass the tip of Kohala on Hwy 270, take note of how quickly you go from green to lots of dry scrub and an arid feel. That's the rain shadow effect, when the mountain causes it to rain more on one side than on the other.

There are a couple of places along this stretch to swim or snorkel—**Kapa'a Beach Park** and **Mahukona**, both described in the *Beaches* chapter.

Near mile marker 15, look toward the ocean in the distance, and you can see stones sticking up in the air from a fascinating *navigational* heiau where the stones are aligned to point to other Hawaiian islands, Tahiti and more. You can walk to a position below it from **Mahukona Beach Park**. We took a GPS here and were able to verify that the stones *really do* align with Polynesian destinations. Pretty impressive.

By the way, Mahukona is also the name given to the Big Island's first and now-forgotten volcano, located offshore. This volcano started it all but sank beneath the water less than half a million years ago.

On a clear day, you can't miss seeing Maui from here. But on *very* clear late afternoons, in addition to Maui's two mountains, you may see the islands of Lana'i, Kaho'olawe (in front of Lana'i from this angle) and Moloka'i between Lana'i and Maui. Sunsets from this area can be superb.

LAPAKAHI STATE HISTORICAL PARK

[G] At mile marker 14 is **Lapakahi State Historical Park**, which consists of the remains of an old Hawaiian village. There is a trail running through the village, complete with markers noting interesting spots. Open 8 a.m.–4 p.m. (no incoming after 3:30 p.m.), admission is free. This self-guided tour takes around 45 minutes, and the brochure does a reasonable job of explaining what you are seeing. Lapakahi is interesting at times and worthwhile for anyone interested in a taste of how the ancient Hawaiians may have lived in such an inhospitable place. Park rangers have been uncommonly bad here in the past with some of the worst and most inaccurate information we've run across in any park in the state. An example: "This area was once lush rain forest until western man came along and cut it down, causing the rainfall to go from 100 inches to 10 inches annually." (In reality, this was originally a thin, rocky and scrubby *dryland* forest until *the Hawaiians* burned it down to plant crops after they discovered Hawai'i. This area is dry because it is, and always has been, in the rain shadow of Kohala Mountain.) Recent visits have seen much better personnel on site.

One often overlooked aspect to Lapakahi is the fabulous water in **Koai'e Cove** (described on page 155).

The highway between mile marker 14 and Kawaihae (mile marker 4) is replete with dirt roads leading toward the ocean. You may be tempted to explore them, especially if you have 4WD. With that in mind, using a variety of vehicles and on foot, we traversed nearly every inch of all of them, including their branches (and we can cough up the dust-balls to prove it).

Kamehameha was instructed to build Pu'ukohola Heiau in order to conquer all the islands.

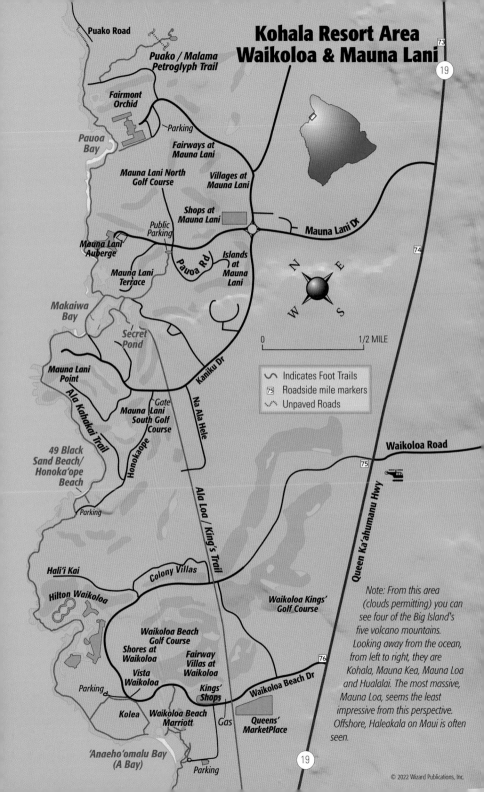

Kohala Resort Area
Waikoloa & Mauna Lani

Puako Road

Puako / Malama
Petroglyph Trail

Fairmont
Orchid

Parking

Pauoa
Bay

Fairways at
Mauna Lani

Mauna Lani North
Golf Course

Villages at
Mauna Lani

Shops at
Mauna Lani

Public
Parking

Mauna Lani Dr

Mauna Lani
Auberge

Pauoa Rd

Islands
at
Mauna
Lani

Mauna Lani
Terrace

Makaiwa
Bay

Secret
Pond

N
W E
S

0   1/2 MILE

Mauna Lani
Point

Kaniku Dr

⌇⌇ Indicates Foot Trails
[75] Roadside mile markers
⋯⋯ Unpaved Roads

Ala Kahakai Trail

Gate

Na Ala Hele

Mauna Lani
South Golf
Course

Waikoloa Road

49 Black
Sand Beach/
Honoka'ope
Beach

Honokaope

[75]

Parking

Ala Loa / King's Trail

Queen Ka'ahumanu Hwy

Hali'i Kai

Colony Villas

Hilton Waikoloa

Waikoloa Kings'
Golf Course

Waikoloa Beach
Golf Course

Shores at
Waikoloa

Fairway
Villas at
Waikoloa

[76]

Vista
Waikoloa

Parking

Kings'
Shops

Waikoloa Beach Dr

Kolea

Waikoloa Beach
Marriott

Gas

Queens'
MarketPlace

'Anaeho'omalu Bay
(A Bay)

Parking

Note: From this area
(clouds permitting) you can
see four of the Big Island's
five volcano mountains.
Looking away from the ocean,
from left to right, they are
Kohala, Mauna Kea, Mauna Loa
and Hualalai. The most massive,
Mauna Loa, seems the least
impressive from this perspective.
Offshore, Haleakala on Maui is often
seen.

[73]
[19]

[74]

[19]

© 2022 Wizard Publications, Inc.

The result? We can say with complete confidence that most of these roads are utterly wretched and lead to absolute squat. The entire coastline in this area is rocky and mostly unprotected. There are *no* beaches. It's pretty but not beautiful, and the land is harsh and unforgiving. (The real beauty of this area is underwater, with lots of extensive coral formations and ultra-clean water.) The only people who bother to make their way to the coast along this stretch are shoreline fishermen or hopeful whale watchers. So don't bother unless you have *way* too much time on your hands. The only exception is **Kaiholena (Sapphire) Cove** between mile markers 11 and 12. The snorkeling is outstanding and *usually* fairly easy to access. (See *Beaches* on page 155 for more.)

Look to the shoreline from this area. Somewhere around here you'll usually find a place where to the left, the ocean looks calm and inviting, whereas to the right it looks choppy and frothing, and the line of demarcation is pretty defined. This is a terrifying place (if you're a pilot). It's the transition zone from waters that are wind-protected to waters that are whipped up from nukin' gales that slither around the tip of North Kohala. The turbulence in this area would make the toughest Ultimate Fighter scream like a little girl if he were flying here. (I've tried taking aerial photos of Kaiholena Cove, but that pesky emotion called *fear of death* keeps turning me away.) So if you see any low flying aircraft around here—salute 'em.

Like an old commercial says, sometimes you feel like a nut. If so, just over 0.5 miles past mile marker 5 is a road that leads to the **Hamakua Macademia Nut Co.** (808-882-1690). They have all things mac nut. Super friendly folks, they'll give you a quickie tour of the processing facilities behind the glass.

KAWAIHAE

[H] The tiny port town of Kawaihae has a few places to eat and shop and is the launching area for some fishing and SCUBA operations. Otherwise, there's not much to see. There's an ice cream place on the back side of Kawaihae Center that has really good ice cream.

This is the driest part of the state, with annual rainfall averaging less than 10 inches. (Contrast that with 240 inches on the slopes northwest of Hilo.)

At the junction of Highways 19 and 270 is the impressive **Pu'ukohola Heiau** (808-882-7218). Entry is free and an interesting visitor center is open 7:30 a.m.–5 p.m. Check out their incredible weapons display. The park also offers a smartphone-guided walking tour to enhance the 0.5 mile paved loop trail. This massive structure was built by King Kamehameha in 1790–91. He had sent his wife's grandmother to visit a kahuna on Kaua'i to ask how he could conquer Hawai'i. The kahuna said that if he built a fabulous heiau (temple) at Kawaihae and dedicated it to his war god, he would prevail. Thousands of "volunteers" worked on the project, carrying boulders from miles away. Workers were routinely sacrificed at different portions of the structure during construction to ensure that the gods would be pleased. When the temple was completed, Kamehameha dedicated it by inviting and then sacrificing his enemy Keoua. During construction Kamehameha himself participated to inspire his workers. When his brother picked up a boulder to help, Kamehameha slapped the rock out of his hand saying, "No, brother, one of us should keep the kapu" (meaning staying pure). Kamehameha then instructed that the rock his brother had touched be taken far out to sea and dumped into deep water. Pu'ukohola Heiau is best viewed from Kawaihae Harbor

Road (the one that leads out to the break-water) in the late afternoon with Mauna Kea in the background. Just offshore are said to be the remains of a shark heiau, called **Hale-o-Kapuni**, where human remains were offered to sharks. Its precise location is unknown, and it has been submerged and buried under silt for decades.

KOHALA RESORT AREA

[I] Continuing *south* onto Highway 19 (called **Queen K** by most locals, short for Ka'ahumanu) toward Kailua-Kona, you will pass the **Kohala mega-resort area**. Ensconced in this desolate sea of lava and scrub, multi-zillion dollar resorts dot the coastline offering the luxury and amenities that have made this region famous. **Golfing** is top notch (and *expensive*) here; see *Activities* chapter. Ocean activities, such as snorkeling and SCUBA, are very good. Though you wouldn't suspect it from the road, some of the best beaches in the state lie between here and Kailua-Kona. Some, such as **Hapuna** and **Mauna**

Even where the land is bone dry and harsh, the exquisitely clear ocean makes up for it.

Kea, are well known. Others, such as **Manini'owali (Kua Bay)** and **Makalawena**, are less known or deliciously secluded. The chapter on *Beaches* describes them all in detail and tells you *exactly* how to get to each one of them.

See that barren lava field on the mauka (mountain) side of the highway? A Japanese company purchased the 3,000 acres in 1990 for a *mere* $45 million. They had big plans for it, including six golf courses and 2,600 homes. After paying taxes on it for nine years, the shrewd investors unloaded it in 1998 for $5 million, and the current owners have built precisely nothing.

Most of the lava you see here flowed thousands of years ago. In other parts of the island it'd be covered with forest. But the very thing that brings visitors here—the utter lack of rain—keeps the lava looking so uninviting.

Hold on to your hat along this stretch. The wind can be fierce in the afternoon. As the lava fields heat up during the day, it causes the air to heat and rise. Air from the ocean rushes in to fill the void, creating strong afternoon breezes.

Hapuna Beach is off the road near mile marker 69. This beach is often featured in travel shows and is a *superb* place to frolic. We like to snorkel from there to **Beach 69** on calm days, or boogie board till we're raw. Otherwise, just gallivant on the fine sand.

The road to the Mauna Lani between mile markers 73 and 74 is worth consideration. See map on page 57. To the north is the **Puako/Malama Petroglyph Trail**. This simple 25-minute walk through kiawe forest leads to a very large field of petroglyphs—or carvings—in the lava. Though not as extensive as the **Pu'u Loa Petroglyph Trail** at Kilauea Volcano, it's one of the largest in the state and worth a stroll if you want to see how ancient Hawaiians expressed themselves through their tenacious carvings.

The **Mauna Lani Auberge** sits adjacent to some of the most fascinating grounds of any Big Island resort. Huge fishponds surrounded by palm trees to the south make for wonder-filled strolling. We like to wander back to **Secret Pond** for a cool, refreshing dip in the crystal clear water. (I know: The other ponds aren't clear—*this* one is.) Park at the public parking area (6:30 a.m.–6:30 p.m.) and wander along the trail toward the fishponds. Allow an hour for this pleasant diversion.

Continuing south, the road at mile marker 76 leads to 'Anaeho'omalu Bay. If you're low on gasoline, there is relief on this road. 'Anaeho'omalu has a gorgeous palm-fronted fishpond behind the beach. If you're looking for the perfect location to take a **sunset photo**, the backside of the fishpond is as good as it gets. When clouds cooperate, even the most photographically challenged (present reader excluded) can take postcard-quality shots.

KOHALA LAVA DESERT AREA

[J] Back on Highway 19 heading south, the large cluster of palms toward the ocean at mile marker 79 surround a large freshwater pond and a pretty but secluded beach called **Ke-awa-iki**. The pond itself is not available to visitors (the barbed wire, half-starved Dobermans, and snipers with night vision glasses see to that), but the beach is accessible via a 15-minute walk, and there is a special freshwater golden pool available to hikers. (See the Golden Pools of Ke-awa-iki hike on page 209).

The scenic turnout at mile marker 82 overlooks **Kiholo Bay**. Down there you will find a saltwater bay with freshwater calmly floating on top, lots of turtles and a lava tube with fresh spring water just 80 feet from the ocean. Intrigued? I hope so. You can drive part of the way during daylight hours and hike around. (See our **Kiholo Bay trail** write-up on page 207 for more.)

Throughout this part of the island you'll occasionally see palm trees along the barren coastline. These are almost always an indication of freshwater spring-fed pools. Since there's no permanent stream on the entire west side of the island, water percolates into the lava and often bubbles to the surface near the shore, forming pools. We look for them when we're hiking along the coast. When you're hot and tired, you can't beat splashing like a fool in a cold, clean freshwater or brackish pool.

If you're looking for a stunning, secluded beach, and don't mind walking for 15–20 minutes, **Makalawena Beach** (described in the *Beaches* chapter) is west of mile marker 89.

You may still see some "Donkey Crossing" signs along here. Until the turn of the century there was a small herd of wild donkeys that crossed the highway at night and early mornings on the older lava north of mile marker 85. They came down out of the mountains to lick the salt off rocks by the shore, drink from springs and occasionally putt on the **Hualalai Golf Club**. (Now *there's* a hazard.) Known locally as **Kona Nightingales**, (because they would call, or "sing" to each other at night), they were the descendants of coffee-hauling pack animals that escaped a century ago. Every so often one got whacked by a passing car, leaving both pretty bent out of shape. They were finally rounded up and hauled away to a corral near Waikoloa Village, but many escaped to terrorize the golf course off Waikoloa Road. They've been rounded up again, and we haven't seen any around these parts for a while, although the signs still memorialize their presence. **Wild goats** still work this area and are fairly easy to spot.

Just north of mile marker 91 is a **large lava tube** from the Hualalai lava flow of 1801 that bisects the highway. On the ocean side of the road it has collapsed, leaving a large chasm in the lava. On the mauka side it forms a cave, which has collapsed in several spots. This cave looks *very* unstable.

Located just south of the Kona airport is the **Natural Energy Laboratory**. This is a classic example of unintended consequences. Started by the government in the 1970s, they monkeyed with making

The Green Flash

Ever heard of the green flash? No, it's not a superhero. We'd heard of the Green Flash for years and assumed that it was an urban myth, or perhaps something seen through the bottom of a beer bottle. But now we know it to be a real phenomenon, complete with a scientific explanation. You may hear other ways to experience the Green Flash— but this is the only true way.

On days when the horizon is crisp and clear with no clouds in the way of the sun as it sets, you stand a reasonable chance of seeing it. Avoid looking directly at the sun until the very last part of the disk is about to slip below the horizon. Looking at it beforehand will burn a greenish image into your retina, creating a "fool's flash" (and possibly wrecking your eyes). The instant before the last part of the sun's disk disappears, a vivid flash of chartreuse is often seen. This is because the sun's rays are passing through the thickest part of the atmosphere, and the light is bent and split into its different components the way it is in a rainbow. The light that is bent the most is the green and blue light, but the blue is less vivid and is overwhelmed by the flash of green, which lingers for the briefest of moments as the very last of the sun sets.

For a variety of reasons, including our latitude, Hawai'i is one of the best places in the world to observe the Green Flash.

If you aren't successful in seeing the real Green Flash, try the beer bottle method—at least it's better than nothing.

electricity using temperature differences between 80 °F surface water and 37 °F deep sea water. Yeah, it worked. But the technology wasn't particularly scalable and was abandoned at this location (though a new company is trying to bring it back). But their three giant pipes (as big as 55 inches) sucking water from as deep as 3,000 feet down has become a magnet for dozens of private companies taking advantage of easy access to cold seawater and year-round sunshine. Industries, such as those raising clams, coral, sea horses, blue green algae, oysters and mushrooms, are thriving out here.

An example is **Kona Cold Lobster**. When the lobsters arrive from the mainland, they have a nasty case of jet lag. (If you flew here from the East coast, you can probably relate.) The beasties are put in the cold water to rejuvenate so that they are bright and alert when you boil them for dinner.

Surprisingly, once you pump seawater out of the ocean, federal environmental laws make it *illegal* to return it, even if it's perfectly clean. So they're forced to pump it into a deep hole (more like a *loop*hole) where it naturally seeps back into the ocean. The energy lab gives tours, but they are pretty dull. Reserve at (808) 329-8073 if you like.

A nice tour here is at **Ocean Rider** (808-329-6840). They have 1-hour weekday tours of their seahorse farm (Hey, shouldn't this be called a ranch?) for $76 ($71 for kids 12 and under, 4 and under free with adult). The price is pretty steep, but there's something undeniably endearing about these critters that have been nearly wiped out in the wild. At the end of the tour you'll get to have one of them wrapped around your finger. (More likely it'll be the other way around.) Good for kids and adults.

A mile offshore is **Blue Ocean Mariculture**. It's an open-sea fish farm that raises a delicious fish called *Hawaiian Kampachi,* which is sometimes available at Roy's and Merriman's restaurants. Normally tasty but inedibly wormy in the wild, these farm-raised kahala fish are worm-free.

An excellent tide-pool is nearby at **Wawaloli Beach.** (See page 168.)

Near mile marker 97 is the parking lot for **Kaloko-Honokohau National Historical Park**. There is a small visitor's center with some interpretive signs and entrance is free. Despite its appearance, this area was once a thriving community, and Hawaiian artifacts are still scattered about the lava field. There's even a holua (stone slide) that was used by chiefs. (See page 71 for more on holua.)

If you are into deep sea fishing, you'll want to check out **Honokohau Harbor** listed in the *Beaches* chapter. Fishing boats leave from here, and weigh-ins take place daily at 10 a.m. and 6 p.m. (You can tell what they caught by the fish flags they hoist.)

KOHALA BEST BETS

Best Sunsets—Behind the fishponds at 'Anaeho'omalu Bay

Best Place to Get the Willies—Mo'okini Heiau in Hawi

Best Treat—Tropical Dream Ice Cream in Hawi

Best Secluded Beach—Makalawena

Best Place to Eat ON the Beach—Lava Lava Beach Club

Best Golf—Mauna Kea Golf Course

Best View of Maui—Coming down Highway 250 into Hawi

Best Overlook— Pololu Valley

Best Boogie-Boarding—Hapuna Beach or Mauna Kea

Best Remnant of Ancient Hawaiian Art—Puako/Malama Petroglyph Trail

For 35 years, good sunsets were hard to come by in Kona. But 2018 changed all that.

Kailua was a tiny fishing village in days gone by. Fishermen would haul in giants from the deep, bountiful waters, while farmers tended their fields up the slopes of Hualalai. Many of the great chiefs of old chose this part of the island as their home. Kona weather and Kona waters were known throughout the islands as the very best, and that hasn't changed. Though no longer the sleepy little village of yesteryear, this is a charming seaside town where the strolling is pleasant, the sunsets are mesmerizing, the food is diverse, and the activities are plentiful. Some people badmouth Kona because it's not the same as it was 20 years ago—what is? Kona is still great; there are simply more people who know it.

The town is alternately referred to as Kailua-Kona, Kona, Kailua, or sometimes Kailua Town. See page 33 for an explanation of this confusing situation.

Kailua-Kona is nestled in the lee of Hualalai Volcano, meaning that it is sheltered from the trade winds coming from the other side of the island. The winds it does get are usually from wraparound sea breezes. The rains from them have already been wrung out.

The heart of Kailua-Kona is the mile-long oceanfront stretch of Alii Drive starting at the Kailua Pier. As with any seaside tourist town, traffic can be heavy. Alii Drive is a particularly good area to take a walk after a meal. There have been times that unsavory-looking characters made night walks intimidating, but shop owners have banded together to hire private patrollers, and it has helped tremendously. Public parking is pretty limited and is shown on the map on the facing page. This part of town has lots of shops and restaurants overlooking the water. If you start strolling from the Kailua Pier, keep an eye out for some of these sights.

AROUND DOWNTOWN KAILUA-KONA

[A] To the right (north) of the pier is the Ahu'ena Heiau. Now wonderfully maintained and very picturesque, this was King Kamehameha the Great's personal heiau (temple) that he had restored in 1812, and it was here that he spent his later years until his death in 1819. Note the bird on top of the tallest ki'i akua (statue of a god). It is a golden plover, the bird that may have guided the first Polynesians here. (See page 15.) Kamehameha dedicated this heiau to the god Lono and filled it with European and Chinese furniture. Nearby

is Hale Nane Mahina 'Ai, where the king went to get away from it all. There was a famous portrait painted here of Kamehameha wearing a red vest, white shirt and a yellow silk necktie. The artist pleaded with him not to wear the fancy sailor's outfit, but Kamehameha insisted.

The tiny beach in front of the heiau is Kamakahonu Beach, one of the calmest beaches on the island. There you can rent kayaks, paddle boats, stand-up paddle boards, snorkel gear, etc. (though at confiscatory prices).

To the left of the pier is the starting gate to end all starting gates. Every year in October an athletic event occurs on the Big Island that draws worldwide attention. The Ironman Triathlon is a profound testimony to the power to challenge, to the ability to reach down to the very core of our spirit and summon the impossible. Three events, any one of which would seem *insurmountable* to most of us mere mortals, are stitched together in a triathlon that seems almost ludicrous. Swim 2.4 miles in the open ocean, then get out and ride a bike 112 miles on a hot road cut through a lava field. Finally, dismount and run a 26.2-mile marathon. All this is done consecutively under the tropical sun. This is the best opportunity you'll ever have to look into the faces of mass excellence, and not just the young. We had a friend who, even in his mid-60s, would blow by most of the 25-year-olds and complete the race in under 12 hours. The Ironman brand, purchased for $3 million in 1989 was sold in 2015 to a Chinese billionaire for $900 million.

The seawall near the pier is usually a great place to fish. During abnormally high seas, water crashes over the wall and is quite a sight to see. Even better fishing is at the wall in front of the Hulihe'e Palace (808-329-1877) farther down.

Letters [A] correspond to paragraphs in text.

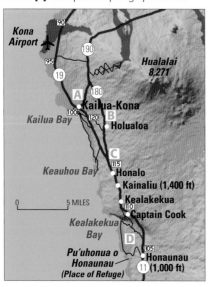

Kona Airport

190

95

19

190

Hualalai
8,271

[A] 180

Kailua-Kona

Kailua Bay

100

120

[B] Holualoa

Keauhou Bay

115

[C]

Honalo

Kainaliu (1,400 ft)

Kealakekua

0   5 MILES   110

Captain Cook

Kealakekua
Bay

Pu'uhonua o
Honaunau
(Place of Refuge)

[D]

105

Honaunau

11 (1,000 ft)

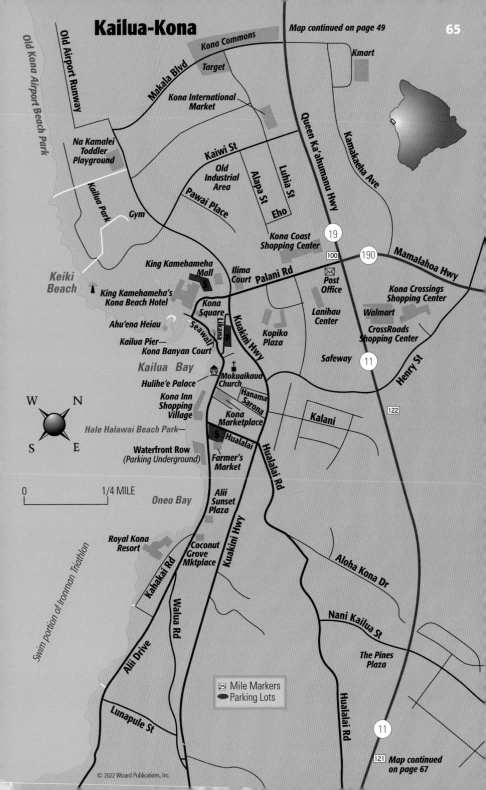

This palace, built in 1838 by Governor Kuakini, quickly became the house of choice for vacationing Hawaiian royalty until 1914. Now a museum lovingly run by the Daughters of Hawai'i, inside you'll find a nice collection of koa furniture, including some stunning armoires, and a 6-foot diameter table cut from a single piece of koa. Most of the furniture was auctioned off in the 1920s but fortunately was cataloged. Later, the buyers were contacted, and many have graciously lent the items to the museum for display. There are many photos of Hawaiian royalty, including Princess Ruth. (History books *never* mention her without mentioning her size, but we're above that…no, we're not. Estimates range from 6-foot-2 to 6-foot-10, 400–450 lbs. She slept in a hut outside.) Spears, fishhooks and other artifacts make this museum a worthwhile stop. Self-guided tours are available by reservation on Saturdays only for $16. (Guided tours on weekdays are $22.) Open 10 a.m.–4 p.m. The Palace Gift Shop next door has interesting items and hard-to-find books and is worth a peek.

A REAL GEM

Outside, on the south side of the Palace *was* a rock with a hole in it. It was the top of a Pohaku Likanaka. This was used for executions out at Kahalu'u Beach Park. People would be forced to stand in front of it while a rope was passed through the hole, around the neck, and back out. The executioner would then pull back for a few minutes…and that was that. Some palace personnel used to grumble that the darkly historic stone shouldn't be there. In 2006 an earthquake damaged the palace, forcing its closure and refurbishment. When they reopened, *whaddayaknow?* The stone had simply vanished. They don't know where it went, and they don't seem too unhappy about it.

Across the street from Hulihe'e Palace is the Mokuaikaua Church. This was the first Christian church built in the islands, in 1820. The initial building was a thatched hut with the current structure erected in 1837. You're welcome inside; admission is free. Built of lava rock and crushed coral with koa hardwood gracing the tall interior, this is a magnificent remnant of the era. Look at the joints inside the building, which were painstakingly attached with pins made from gnarly 'ohi'a trees.

Kamehameha the Great, the first king to rule all the islands, could live anywhere he wanted. He chose Kailua-Kona. This is his Ahu'ena Heiau.

There are exhibits relating to early Hawai'i and the work of the missionaries, along with a model of the *Thaddeus*, which brought the first missionaries here. Sometimes referred to as the Mayflower of Hawai'i, the *Thaddeus* left Boston in October 1819 for a five-month trip to the islands. These men and women left comfortable lives in the United States to come to an alien and mysterious land. Unbeknownst to them, their chances for success were greatly enhanced en route when Kamehameha II and his stepmother Ka'ahumanu orchestrated the overthrow of the Hawaiian religion less than a month into the missionaries' journey to the islands.

There's a large shopping area at Kona Inn, though it looks as though it could use a good sprucing up. If you're looking for a place to watch the sunset or have a picnic, the grass on the ocean side of this center is ideal.

If you want to watch the sunset from a restaurant along here, the best views (from south to north) are: Magics Beach Grill, Don the Beachcomber, and Huggo's. See individual reviews in *Island Dining*. During months around the summer solstice (June 21), the sun may set behind the point from the northernmost restaurants.

ELSEWHERE ALONG ALII DRIVE

As you drive farther south along Alii Drive, keep an eye out for joggers. They trot up and down Alii Drive in large enough numbers to constitute a flock. (Or is it a gaggle?) There are mile markers every half mile here, which we put on the Alii Drive map on this page. Between Kona By The Sea and Kona Isle is a 100-yard access trail that leads to something that even most longtime Alii Drive residents don't know about. It's a public saltwater swimming pool fed by the splashing of waves. It was privately built decades

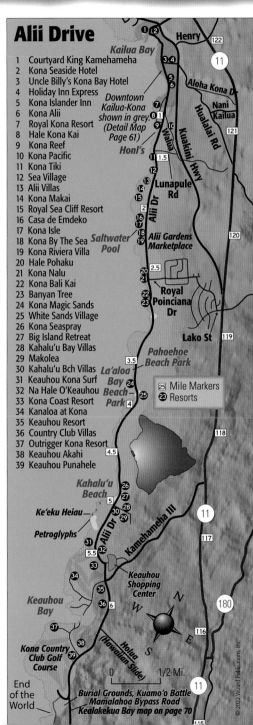

Alii Drive

Kailua Bay

1 Courtyard King Kamehameha
2 Kona Seaside Hotel
3 Uncle Billy's Kona Bay Hotel
4 Holiday Inn Express
5 Kona Islander Inn
6 Kona Alii
7 Royal Kona Resort
8 Hale Kona Kai
9 Kona Reef
10 Kona Pacific
11 Kona Tiki
12 Sea Village
13 Alii Villas
14 Kona Makai
15 Royal Sea Cliff Resort
16 Casa de Emdeko
17 Kona Isle
18 Kona By The Sea
19 Kona Riviera Villa
20 Hale Pohaku
21 Kona Nalu
22 Kona Bali Kai
23 Banyan Tree
24 Kona Magic Sands
25 White Sands Village
26 Kona Seaspray
27 Big Island Retreat
28 Kahalu'u Bay Villas
29 Makolea
30 Kahalu'u Bch Villas
31 Keauhou Kona Surf
32 Na Hale O'Keauhou
33 Kona Coast Resort
34 Kanaloa at Kona
35 Keauhou Resort
36 Country Club Villas
37 Outrigger Kona Resort
38 Keauhou Akahi
39 Keauhou Punahele

Downtown Kailua-Kona shown in grey. (Detail Map Page 61)

Honl's

Saltwater Pool

Alii Gardens Marketplace

Royal Poinciana Dr

Lako St

Pahoehoe Beach Park

La'aloa Bay Beach Park

25 Mile Markers
23 Resorts

Kahalu'u Beach

Ke'eku Heiau

Petroglyphs

Keauhou Shopping Center

Keauhou Bay

Kona Country Club Golf Course

End of the World

Burial Grounds, Kuamo'o Battle
Mamalahoa Bypass Road
Kealakekua Bay map on page 70

Henry

Aloha Kona Dr
Nani Kailua
Huualalai Rd
Kuakini Hwy
Walua
Alii Dr
Lunapule Rd

Kamehameha III
Holua (Hawaiian Slide)

0   1/2 Mi.

N W E S

© 2022 Wizard Publications, Inc.

ago and reverted to the state when the owner died without heirs. The pool directly abuts the ocean and even has some fish in it most of the time. There's a smaller tide-pool to the left. If you want to swim in seawater but are hesitant to go into the ocean, here's your chance. But be fore-warned: The pool is not maintained, so it often gets green and yucky if the surf has been flat for too long.

Keep an eye out on the mauka side of Alii Drive for a farmers market called Ali'i Gardens. Near mile marker 3.5 is Pahoehoe Beach Park. No sand here, but it's a nice place to have a picnic, or to just sit on a bench and watch the surf. White Sands Beach (or as it's known by locals, La'aloa, as the sign says) is a little farther down with good boogie boarding when the sand is in town. (See *Beaches*.)

There are scads of oceanfront condos and apartments along this road. Traffic noise is going to be your penalty for staying on Alii Drive, but it's a penalty most are quite willing to endure.

Soon you'll come to the quaintest little church you've ever seen. St. Peter's Catholic Church is known locally as the "Little Blue Church." This tiny building, with its picturesque location and less than a dozen simple *small* pews, is the most photographed in the islands. Weddings of all denominations take place there. If the doors are unlocked, sunsets through the etched glass can offer dramatic photo opportunities.

To the right of the church is the Ku'emanu Heiau. This is the only heiau (temple) in the state known to be associated solely with surfing. This surf spot was available only to chiefs (commoners caught surfing here were put to death), and they came here to pray for gnarly conditions. (They usually got them, too. Even today this is one of the most dependable breaks in Kona.) To this day, Hawaiians still come here to pay homage to the spirits. The small notch in front was a luapa'u, where discarded bones were tossed—perhaps bones of commoners caught surfing. In-cidentally, surfing in the old days was usually done naked (giving new meaning to the term *hang loose*).

Next to the church is Kahalu'u Beach Park where you'll find some of the easiest access to *usually* (not always) good snokeling

In ancient times Kahalu'u Beach was heavily populated. Today, it is heavily snorkeled.

A Fish Story

Keauhou was dominated by the legacy of a king in the 1600s named Lonoikamakahiki (called Lono by his friends). Lono (not to be confused with the Hawaiian god of the same name) made a series of bets with the king of O'ahu. Each time Lono won. On one occasion, Lono and the O'ahu king were out fishing. Lono's adviser told Lono not to go because he (Lono) didn't know how to fish. They went anyway, and while fishing, Lono got all worked up while the O'ahu king was hauling in a beauty and asked to borrow fishing gear. As Lono's adviser feared, the O'ahu king mocked Lono for not bringing his own gear. Lono's adviser, in order to save his master's honor, volunteered the solution to Lono. He whispered it into his ear and Lono agreed. Lono then shouted, "Hey, I don't need your gear. I'll bet you I can catch a fish on my own." The O'ahu king accepted, knowing that Lono had not brought any fishing gear with him. Then Lono, at his adviser's suggestion, clubbed his adviser to death, ripped open his belly and used his intestines for fishing line. Lono splintered the man's thigh bone for a fishhook. His flesh was used for bait and his head for a sinker. He lowered the gear into the water and immediately caught an ahi. Lono won the bet (a large piece of O'ahu) and later went on to win all of O'ahu in another bet. The moral: If you think you sacrifice a lot for your boss, try working for Lono. (Incidentally, Lono's bones were in the Bishop Museum in Honolulu until 1994 when they were stolen by Hawaiian activists and buried in Waipi'o Valley.)

on the island. See page 171 for more on this gem. It gets crowded on weekends. Kahalu'u had a large population in the old days, and there are very extensive lava tube caves tucked away in the jungle up mauka (toward the mountain).

There used to be a hotel on the other side of Kahalu'u Beach Park and it was the only hotel *in all of Hawai'i* where part of the building was literally over an ocean tidepool. It was a big hotel and part of a chain. We were surprised when the resort chain surrendered the hotel to the landowner, Bishop Estate which owns 11% of all the land in Hawai'i. Even though Bishop was handed the building for free, they ran it a few years and announced they couldn't make any money from it. So they closed it and eventually demolished the building in 2018.

Fronting this parcel on some of the lava at low tide, you can see petroglyphs carved in the rock. They are at the northern end of the salt-and-pepper sand and gravel beach kitty-corner to the heiau described below. In the 16th century, Kamalalawalu, the king of Maui, was impaled alive by Lonoikamakahiki at Ke'eku Heiau for 10 or 11 days. Kamalalawalu was then taken to a flat rock nearby and slain. His body was towed out to sea and fed to the sharks. The petroglyphs on the rock date back to that incident and detail the event. (Lonoikamakahiki had a good reason to be miffed at Kamalalawalu. His general had been captured by invading Maui forces, had his eyes gouged out and his eye sockets pierced with darts *before* being killed. That was considered uncool even by the standards of the time.)

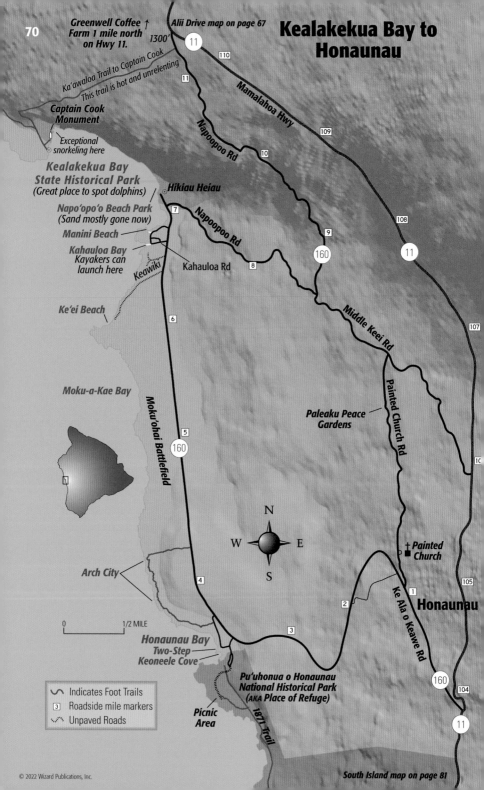

70

Kealakekua Bay to Honaunau

Alii Drive map on page 67

Greenwell Coffee Farm 1 mile north on Hwy 11.

1300'

Ka'awaloa Trail to Captain Cook
This trail is hot and unrelenting

Captain Cook Monument
Exceptional snorkeling here

Kealakekua Bay State Historical Park
(Great place to spot dolphins)

Napo'opo'o Beach Park
(Sand mostly gone now)

Manini Beach

Kahauloa Bay
Kayakers can launch here

Ke'ei Beach

Moku-a-Kae Bay

Moku'ohai Battlefield

Arch City

Hikiau Heiau

Keawiki

Napoopoo Rd

Kahauloa Rd

Kahauloa Rd

Mamalahoa Hwy

Napoopoo Rd

11
110
11
109
10
108
7
9
160
11
8
107
6
5
160

Middle Keei Rd

Painted Church Rd

Paleaku Peace Gardens

Painted Church

Honaunau

Ke Ala o Keawe Rd

1C
105
1
2
4
3
160
104
11

Honaunau Bay
Two-Step
Keoneele Cove

Pu'uhonua o Honaunau National Historical Park
(AKA Place of Refuge)

Picnic Area

1871 Trail

N
W E
S

0   1/2 MILE

⌒ Indicates Foot Trails
3 Roadside mile markers
⋰ Unpaved Roads

© 2022 Wizard Publications, Inc.

South Island map on page 81

The land contains several heiau, including one where thousands of Hawaiians were sacrificed to their gods. Local lore says that any business that operates there is cursed. If you don't believe it, ask the Japanese company that paid millions for the lease to a 454-room hotel here in 1988. They closed the hotel, called the Kona Lagoons, planning extensive renovations. Then they ran out of money. It sat vacant and dilapidated, until they finally gave it up in 1994 to the landowner, Bishop Estate, which bulldozed it a decade later. The re-created heiau you see here are a far cry from the rubble you would have seen at the turn of the century. They are part of a long rebuilding project begun in 2008 by the landowner.

As you ascend Alii Drive toward the Keauhou Shopping Center, keep an eye on your right, in the golf course, for the strangest corkscrew-shaped palm tree we've ever seen. No interesting story here—just weird. There's a flock of imported wild parrots that cruises around these parts. Keep an eye (and ear) out for them.

If you stay on Alii Drive for a moment, pull over at the service entrance to the Kona Country Club golf course and look up mauka. If the vegetation isn't blocking it, you'll see a wide path that looks bulldozed through the lava. That was done *by hand* to create the Keauhou Holua. In ancient times Hawaiians would fill these holua (slides) with dirt and wet grass, then ali'i (Hawaiian royalty) would race down these slides at rippin' speeds on wooden sleds while commoners screamed and cheered them on. These holua remains are 2,500 feet long (not 1,200, which is listed in most references) and at one time extended to Keauhou Bay.

Soon after this, Alii Drive ends near the shoreline. (The road extending south is a bypass used by folks living up in coffee country.) There is a lava road near the dead end. If you walk on the road for a minute (actually you can see it from your car), you'll be able to see, on your left, terraces in the side of the mountain. You are at an extraordinary place. It might not look like much, but this is where the battle between Hawaiians to kill their religion took place one day in 1820. (See page 17 for the amazing story.) The terraces are the graves from that battle.

With a name befitting the area, a cliff-jumping spot past the battlefield called *End of the World* is listed in *Adventures* on page 239.

UP MAUKA OF KAILUA-KONA

[B] Hualalai Volcano erupts sporadically every few hundred years. The last time was in 1801 when it covered part of what is now Kona International Airport. The top of Hualalai is mostly covered with 'ohi'a and eucalyptus forest with occasional koa and pine. The clouds usually roll in around mid-morning, blanketing the 8,271-foot summit in a rich fog that can reduce visibility to zero. Wild goats and pigs scramble about the uninhabited top portion of the mountain. The views of Mauna Kea and Mauna Loa, as well as its own caldera, make Hualalai a hiker's haven. Unfortunately, it's all owned by Bishop Estate, which routinely denies access to the public. (Bishop Estate is a trust set up in the 1800s to help Hawai'i's kids. It has grown to now own 11% of the state and has astonishing power. Many of the houses you see on the island are actually on Bishop land leased for several decades by individuals.)

Hovering above the town of Kailua-Kona is the "artist community" of Holualoa on Highway 180. There are several galleries and a Saturday farmers market. Worth stopping for if you are in the neighborhood.

Kona Coffee

Of all the products produced on the Big Island, none is more well known or has received more accolades than Kona coffee. Though now out-produced in quantity by Kaua'i, Kona

coffee is unmatched in terms of quality. With the possible exception of Jamaican Blue Mountain coffee, Kona coffee is widely considered to be the best in the world. Good Kona coffee lacks the bitterness of coffees from other parts of the world. By the way, contrary to nearly everyone's belief, lighter roasts have more caffeine than darker roasts. (Caffeine cooks away during the roasting process.)

A quality cup of coffee has little resemblance to mass-produced coffee you see on most supermarket shelves. (Of course, you pay more for the good stuff.) Good Kona coffee will set you back $20 or more per pound. Surprisingly little profit is made by the farmer at that price. Most small farmers grow coffee as a labor of love. If you see 100% Kona coffee (not a blend) selling for $12 per pound, it might be poorly chosen, broken or contain poorly roasted beans. You usually get what you pay for. And if you're told in a restaurant that they serve Kona blend because pure Kona is too strong, it's like saying that champagne needs to be blended with gasoline because pure champagne is too strong. Kona blends (which are blended with cheap beans from elsewhere) are less mellow than pure Kona. Blends are usually served because they're cheaper, not better.

Being wretched coffee addicts, we've tried them all. For what it's worth, we like **Kona Amor** (808-322-4160), **Holualoa Kona** (800-334-0348), **Greenwell** (808-323-2295) and **Kona Blue Sky** (808-322-1700). Some aren't available in stores, only by phone or mail order. **Kona Joe** (808-322-2100) grows their trees on a trellis, like grapes, and the Trellis Reserve medium roast is very good. But at about $100 per pound you'll be forgiven if you want to pursue less expensive vices, such as caviar or Cristal champagne.

Coffees that we've tried and didn't like are Royal Aloha, Bad Ass Coffee (owned by the previous), Ferrari Mountain Gold, and Starbuck's Kona coffee. (The last one is surprising.) We are not saying that these companies are bad, just that we didn't like their coffee and didn't think it was worth the money.

Coffee tours are available from many growers, but coffee farms that claim to offer tours are often poorly marked, and owners and employees sometimes seem shocked when you show up to buy coffee. **Greenwell** and **Hula Daddy** (808-327-9744) have good tours. See map on page 70.

Hours can be sporadic. Otherwise, there is not as much to offer the visitor in this quiet, peaceful bedroom community as visitor literature might imply.

Although Kona itself doesn't convey the lushness many associate with Hawai'i, it *does* exist on this side of the island. Kaloko Drive meanders up into a luxuriant cloud forest. See page 47 for more.

SOUTH OF KAILUA-KONA

[C] If you head south out of Kona, you'll come to a series of small towns, all above 1,000 feet. It's usually cool up here, sometimes even foggy. The theme of these towns is often coffee. Free samples are offered at many establishments. Some are mediocre. Others, such as Greenwell, sell very good quality coffee to take with you. Just after the Aloha Theater in Kainaliu, stop at the Donkey Ball Store for some of their namesake treats. (Wonderful chocolate covered mac nuts with thick chocolate.) Available in any quantity. (Not just pairs.)

In Kealakekua (you'll be forgiven if you don't readily see the transition between towns up here) between mile markers 112 and 111 on the ocean side of the road is the Kona Historical Society Museum (808-323-3222). Located in an old general store built during the 1800s, there are lots of old coffee-related photos and other items of historical interest. Worth a stop if you have an interest in the past but call ahead, they're usually open by reservations only.

There are good views down the coast from some spots along here. You've transitioned from Hualalai to Mauna Loa volcano, and up the mountain there are vast ranches that you'd never know existed. After you pass mile marker 111 on Highway 11, you'll see Napoopoo Road on the ocean side of the road—take it. There are lots of coffee farms down here. (See *Kona Coffee* on the facing page for more.) A coffee tour might be worth the effort. You may get to try delicious coffee or meet offbeat characters you'll remember for years to come.

Napoopoo comes to an intersection with Middle Ke'ei Road. Turn right here and head toward the ocean. You'll soon see a sign for Big Island Bees (808-328-1315), which has a *mildly* interesting tour and honey tasting for $20 Mondays to Fridays 10 a.m.–3 p.m. (call ahead as reservations are required). They have you stand behind a screen, but there are still lots of bees in the area. And you can spend up to $59 for a jar of their exotic flower honey, so the bees aren't the only things that can sting you here.

KEALAKEKUA BAY

[D] When you get to the sea, hang a right to Napo'opo'o Beach Park. The stone structure you see in front of you at this southern end of Kealakekua Bay (at the end of the road) is Hikiau Heiau. This

A REAL GEM

was a luakini (a temple where human sacrifices were made). Here Captain Cook was first worshipped as the returning god Lono. During the ceremony, an elder priest named Koa, in the honored tradition of the Hawaiians, chewed the food first before spitting it out and offering it to Cook. (He politely declined.) It was also here that the first Christian ceremony was held in Hawai'i. Ironically it may have contributed to the death of Captain Cook. When one of his men died, Cook ordered him buried near this heiau and personally read the service. This event was proof to some Hawaiians that the strangers were mere mortals, not the gods others felt them to be.

Napo'opo'o Beach used to be a fabulous beach fronting the heiau. It had been

Is there anything more tranquil than coconut trees, like those here at Hōnaunau?

eroding for years, being gradually replaced by boulders. When Hurricane 'Iniki sideswiped the island way back in 1992, its surf removed most of what sand was left. Over the decades very little has returned.

Look a mile across the bay to see a white obelisk, the Captain Cook Monument, which was erected in 1874 by British sailors. It was near this spot in 1779 that Cook was killed by the Hawaiians. (See *Introduction* starting on page 16 for more on this event.) You won't need your passport to go there, even though it is British soil that the monument rests on. The small plot was deeded to the United Kingdom by Princess Likelike. The *actual* spot where Cook died is to the left of the monument (near the kayak tour landing area). A plaque marking the exact spot was swept away during a strong swell a few years ago, but there is still a small "X" carved into the lava rock for interested history buffs to find.

Kealakekua Bay is also popular with dolphins. A large number of spinners reside in the bay, so keep an eye out for them. We see them almost every time we kayak to the monument. Toward the monument side on the bay, up the steep cliff, there is a grayish impression. Local lore says this was made by a cannonball fired from Cook's ship.

These cliffs hold even more secrets. In the past, important chiefs were buried in small caves in the cliff face. After the bones had been separated from the flesh, volunteers were lowered down the face of the cliffs by rope to place the bones in crevices. No one had a long résumé in this line of work. That's because the person doing the burying, once finished with his task, would signal to those above that he was done. The officials on top would promptly cut the rope, sending the burial person, and all knowledge of the location of the bones, crashing to the rocks below. (It was actually considered an honor to be the volunteer at the end of the rope.) All this was to prevent the bones from being desecrated. Bones were often turned into fishhooks and other implements. Skulls were turned into refuse pots or toilets. (*Really* good joke edited out upon further reflection.)

Today, if you hear something fall from the cliff, it won't be a person. Brainless cows from above occasionally wander off the ledge, pleasing the fish below with a refreshing change from their seafood diet.

The waters near the monument are crystal clear and teeming with coral and fish. This is some of the best snorkeling in the state. The local community wants to keep it somewhat difficult to access to prevent it from being overrun with "casual" visitors. If you are wondering how to get there, you have several choices:

You can swim it. This takes us about an hour each way with fins and is guaranteed to tucker you out.

You can walk along the edge of the bay for about 98% of the distance. You'll have to scramble on boulders the whole way and will have to swim for a couple of short patches. You expose yourself to the ocean's whims and falling rocks with this method. Not a great way to get there.

You can kayak over. (See *Kayaking* on page 216.) It's a relatively easy 30-minute paddle across the usually peaceful bay, and you stand a good chance of cruising among dolphins along the way.

Another way to get to the monument is to take the trail near the intersection of Highway 11 and Napoopoo Road. The trailhead is a little over 0.1 miles from the highway across from three large palm trees. (See map on page 70.) You may have to park a short distance

Lawbreakers had one chance to escape the inevitable death penalty: Reach the area's place of refuge before your enemies reached you, and all was forgiven.

up the road as this hike has gotten much more popular since they limited kayaking to the monument. It used to be a road but is now suitable only for hiking, and in spots the tall grasses have made it a one-lane path. It's 2 miles each way with a 1,300-foot constant descent to the water. It's a pretty good puffer coming back up with little shade and some obnoxious footing. It takes most people more than an hour each way. Drink *plenty* of water before and during the ascent, and be careful not to pull your calves during the steady, grueling climb. Along the way you'll pass (but won't see due to brush) the Puhina o Lono Heiau. It was here that Cook's bones were…well, cooked. (See below.)

Lastly, you can take one of the boat trips seen in *Activities* on page 189. They stop for snorkeling near the monument. They also offer SCUBA, SNUBA and all-around fun.

What Finally Happened to Cook?

The Hawaiians traditionally scraped the flesh off the bones of great men. The bones were then bundled together and burned or buried in secret so they wouldn't be desecrated. If the dead person was really loved, the bones were kept in a private home for a while. Because Cook was so respected by the Hawaiians, his body parts were distributed among the chiefs. His head went to the king, his scalp went to a high-ranking chief, his hair went to Kamehameha, etc. Some of his organs, including his heart and liver, were stolen and eaten by some local children who mistook them for dog innards. *(Yuck!)*

Eventually, when two Hawaiians brought a bundle to the ship, the British solemnly unwrapped the bundle and discovered a pile of bloody flesh that had been cut from Cook's body. Even though the Hawaiians were bestowing an honor upon Cook, the British sailors didn't see it that way and were naturally shocked and horrified. The anguished sailors begged Captain Clerke to allow them to go into the village and extract revenge, but he refused, fearing a bloodbath. Some went anyway, killing several villagers. Most of the bones were eventually returned to the British, and Cook was buried at sea in Kealakekua Bay. The ship's surgeon wrote, "In every situation he stood unrivaled and alone. On him all eyes were turned. He was our leading star which, at its setting, left us in darkness and despair."

Moku'ohai Battlefield

The steep cliffs around Kealakekua Bay seem strangely out of place on this otherwise gently sloping mountain. There's a good reason, and it happened in one day. See page 81 for the explanation.

As you leave Napo'opo'o Beach, stay on the ocean-most road heading south. There is a side road leading to Ke'ei Beach. Pretty but not real usable, its historical legacy is a Hawaiian legend, bolstered by Spanish records, which states that white men straggled ashore in the 1520s, 250 years before Cook arrived.

Lots of blood has been spilled on this part of the island. One particularly important battle took place just south of Ke'ei Beach at Moku-a-Kae Bay called the Moku'ohai Battlefield, now overgrown with scrub. It was near here in 1782 that Kamehameha the Great finally became king of this half of the island after defeating Kiwala'o. During a bloody battle, one of Kamehameha's generals, named Ke'eaumoku (call him Ke for short), got tangled in his own spear and tripped, savagely impaling himself. Presuming Ke to be mortally wounded, Kiwala'o ran over to the enemy general to finish him off and seize his prized neck ornament. (Taking it off your enemy's body was symbolic of defeating him.) As he was leaning over Ke's body, Kiwala'o was beaned on the head by a sling stone hurled by one of Kamehameha's warriors, and fell backward. Ke, who wasn't dead from his spear wound, painfully crawled to the unconscious Kiwala'o and slit his throat with a leiomanu (a Hawaiian version of brass knuckles, but with razor-sharp shark's teeth embedded on the outside). Thus Kamehameha was able to defeat his nemesis and rule western Hawai'i.

Battles such as these are a constant throughout Hawaiian history after the 12th century. Rival chiefs or kings were quick to take each other on. Warriors would often congregate on opposite sides of the battlefield and shout insults at each other in an attempt to intimidate. (Insults about lineage were always a real hit.) During battles, spears, sling stones and clubs were used with remarkable efficiency. Shark tooth-studded leiomanus were often given to old men who would go out onto battlefields after the fighting was over to slit the throats of those still alive. Though it may sound harsh (OK, OK—it *is* harsh), this was their way and not considered abhorrent to them.

PU'UHONUA O HONAUNAU (PLACE OF REFUGE)

Soon you come to Pu'uhonua o Honaunau (pronounced Hoe-now-now). Also called Place of Refuge, this is an *awesome* spot to visit. It is a site of great importance and a fun place to explore. In ancient

NOT TO BE

!

MISSED!

Wake me when the mai tais are ready.

times, commoners' lives were governed by the kapu system. There were a dizzying number of laws to observe. Those of lower classes weren't allowed to look at or even walk on the same trails as the upper classes. Men and women were forbidden to eat together, citizens were not allowed to get close to a chief or allow their shadows to fall across them, etc. All manner of laws kept the order. The penalty for breaking any of the laws was usually the same—death by club, strangulation, fire or spear. (Well, it's nice to have choices, at least.) If the offense was severe enough, the offender's *entire family* might be executed. It was believed that the gods retaliated against lawbreakers by sending tidal waves, lava flows, droughts and earthquakes, so communities had a great incentive to dispatch lawbreakers with haste. If a lawbreaker could elude his club or spear-wielding pursuers, however, he had one way out of his mess—the area's pu'uhonua (place of refuge). This pre-designated area offered asylum. If a lawbreaker could make it here, he could perform certain rituals mandated by the kahuna pule (priest). After that, all was forgiven and he could

return home as if nothing had happened, regardless of the violation. Defeated warriors could also come here to await the victor of a battle. They could then pledge their allegiance to whoever won and live out their lives in peace.

Pu'uhonua o Honaunau is such a place. Designated as a national park by Congress in 1961, it is the finest example of a place of refuge in all the islands. Here you will find neatly kept grounds featuring a remarkable stone wall, called the Great Wall. Built in the 1500s, this massive wall is 1,000 feet long, 10 feet high and 17 feet thick in most places. It separated the pu'uhonua from the ali'i's palace grounds. Though the wall has a chiseled appearance, it was made without dressed (cut) stones and without mortar. Also on the grounds you will find reconstructed Hawaiian houses, temples, and a few petroglyphs (rock drawings). There are wood carvings of gods (including one that is anatomically correct, assuming that's how the gods were endowed). The reconstructed thatched structure called Hale-o-Keawe was originally a mausoleum, containing the bones of 23 chiefs. Bones were thought to contain supernatural power, or *mana*, and therefore ensured that the place of refuge would remain sacred.

There are many other sights here as well. Overall, this place is easy to recommend. The walk around the grounds is gentle, and there are facilities, such as drinking water and restrooms. Coconut trees (which have an almost magical, calming effect) are scattered all over. From your phone dial a number to listen to a guided tour around the grounds. It'll take around 30 minutes and is pretty interesting. There is a $20 per-car entrance fee.

Honaunau is particularly enchanting an hour before sunset. Swaying coconut trees have a golden glow as large turtles munch limu in the water near the canoe landing. You won't find a more relaxing or soothing place to finish off the day. Then head over to the middle/southern end of the park where picnic tables and BBQs await. Local families often bring their keiki (kids) to play in the nearby tide-pools, some of which have coral. Drive to that area using the dirt road to the left of the visitor center after you enter the park.

For the less cerebral, you'll find unbeatable snorkeling and SCUBA diving in Honaunau Bay to the right of the boat launch. There are also hiking trails, including the 1871 Trail, so named because area residents paid their taxes in 1871 by fixing up this formerly dilapidated trail. (We have a call in to the IRS to see if the offer's still good.) The trail goes all the way to Hoʻokena Beach, but the portion *outside* of the park is pretty bleak and not worth your time.

Leaving Honaunau, you'll continue up Ke Ala o Keawe Road to Painted Church Road. Hang a left onto it to get to St. Benedict's Catholic Church, known simply as the Painted Church. It's a charming

little building dating back to the 1800s. Between 1899 and 1904, Father John Velge dedicated himself to cre-

ating frescos on the inside walls and ceiling. Everything from hell to the Temptation of Christ is represented in loving detail. There is a sign on the door explaining in detail Father Velge's efforts. Termites and age are starting to take their toll, but this is always worth a stop.

Still on Painted Church Road you'll come to the Paleaku Gardens Peace Sanctuary (808-328-8084). We've never seen someone do so much with only 7 acres. Formerly a Buddhist retreat center, the way the sculpted grounds blend with their indoor settings creates an amazingly tranquil and serene setting. Worth the $10 entrance fee for those looking for a calm, spiritual experience. Closed Sunday and Monday.

Either continue on Painted Church Road to Middle Keei Road, or backtrack to get back up to the highway.

When deciding where to eat in Kailua-Kona, see the *Island Dining* chapter.

KAILUA-KONA BEST BETS

Best Place to Meet Fish for the First Time—Kahaluʻu Beach Park

Best Pizza—Kona Brewing Company

Best Fish Sandwich—Quinn's (cajun)

Best Treat (Despite the Name)—Donkey Balls

Best Snorkeling—Captain Cook Monument or Honaunau

Best Place to Spot Dolphins— Kealakekua Bay

Best Sunset Picnic—The BBQs at Honaunau or the tide-pools of Wawaloli Beach, if the surf's crashing

Best SCUBA Adventure—Manta Ray Night Dive

Best Way to Make Your Lips Numb— Kanaka Kava

Bring your extra-strength hairspray when you visit South Point.

The southern end of the island from Honaunau (near mile marker 104 on Highway 11) to Hawai'i Volcanoes National Park is the least developed part of the Big Island. Long stretches of lava fields on the western side of Mauna Loa's flank give way to green as you round the southern part of the island, where rain is allowed to fall with less interference from Mauna Loa volcano. Along the way you'll pass roads leading to, among other things, a (usually) deserted black sand beach, a lightly inhabited 11,000-plus acre housing subdivision and the southernmost place in the United States. Since most people drive this stretch on their way to the volcano from Kailua-Kona or Kohala, we'll describe it from that direction.

These districts, called **South Kona** and **Ka'u**, are littered with the financial corpses of big businessmen with big plans and big wallets who took a big bath. Most didn't have a clue how business in Hawai'i works and lost their 'okoles as a result. Three examples, all mentioned in detail later, are:

HOVE—*If you build it, they won't come...not for a generation.*

Hawaiian Riviera—*He who underestimates his opponents will ultimately be crushed by them.*

SeaMountain—*How to turn $30 million in cash into $3 million in real estate.*

SOUTH KONA

[A] From Highway 11 heading south from Honaunau, you'll have several opportunities to visit beaches below the road. **Ho'okena** (a decent gray sand beach) and **Pebble Beach** (a violent 'okole kicker) are described in *Beaches*. Distances between gas stations are large, so gas up when you can. Just after Honaunau between mile markers 104 and 103 is the best fruit stand we know of on the west side. **South Kona Fruit Stand** usually has excellent quality friends all organically grown on the adjacent farm.

While driving along the flanks of Mauna Loa here, consider this: Mauna Loa was built from countless thin layers of lava flows, usually less than 15 feet thick. (Flows since 1800 are shown on the map below.) About 120,000 years ago, there was a plain below you where there are now steep hills. At that time, a humongous piece (that's a technical term) of the island, from roughly around mile marker 109 to an area north of Miloli'i (20 miles to the south), broke off and slid into the ocean, creating what is now Kealakekua Bay and the steep hills south of Honaunau. The resulting tsunami (tidal wave) was so huge that it washed completely over the 1,427-foot-high island of Kaho'olawe, continued on and washed almost completely over the 3,370-foot-high island of Lana'i, where it deposited chunks of coral over a thousand feet up the mountain. This area is, geologically speaking, still unstable. Just didn't want you to run out of things to worry about.

Be extra careful driving from mile marker 100 to mile marker 90. Though most of it is wide open, it's also 35 mph and full of speed traps.

Usually referred to as the last remaining fishing village on the island, **Miloli'i** is just past mile marker 89. As a beach destination, it won't offer you much (especially on the weekends—see *Beaches* for more information). From the highway, 2.2 miles into the beach access road, look off to your left, and you will see a narrow a'a lava flow. The nearby village of Ho'opuloa was wiped out when the lava marched down the slopes of Mauna Loa in 1926.

Letters [A] correspond to paragraphs in text.

Miloli'i's residents gained notoriety when they and their lawyer managed to kill the Hawaiian Riviera Resort, 17 miles to the south. (See below.) A 20-minute walk from Miloli'i leads to an exceptionally pictur-esque coconut-lined bay called **Honom-alino**. It got whacked by a tsunami in 2011 and took a few years for nature to restore the sand. See page 175 for more.

The main highway, called the **Hawai'i Belt Road**, follows an old Hawaiian road called the Mamalahoa Highway. If you want to see what driving this area *used* to be like (and why it took so bloody long to circle the island), take the 2-mile stretch of the old road. The intersections are at mile markers 88 and 86 on the mauka (mountain) side of the road.

You'll see lots of macadamia nut trees along this stretch of the island. (By the way, keep the mac nuts away from dogs; they cause paralysis in certain breeds.) The Big Island is a major player in the macadamia nut world though trees in this area show signs of distress from the vog. The inner shell of the macadamia nut is impossibly hard. We've been told by nearly every macadamia farmer we know that if you roll over them with your car, they won't break. So we did it. The result? They all broke. Another myth shot to…

Back on the highway, **Manuka State Park** is near mile marker 81. There's a 2-mile loop trail that wanders through lava flows of several ages, giving you perspective on how things grow over different times. There are restrooms available.

The arrow-straight dirt road 0.7 miles past (south of) mile marker 80 off Highway 11 is a perfect example of why 4WD ve-hicles are so useful here. It's called **Road to the Sea**. (Gee, I wonder where it goes...) Two stark, deserted black sand beaches, unknown even to the vast majority of is-land residents, are at the end. (See *Beaches* on page 177 for an explanation.) It's hard to conceive of a lifeless, arid area being inviting, yet these beaches somehow are. We've even seen plankton-eating whale sharks more than once near the beach. The road is a *public access*, misleading sign notwithstanding.

Another beautiful bay south of here is called **Pohue**, but access to it from the lava road has been scuttled for decades by lawsuits and general bickering. Separately, there was a several *thousand* acre resort called **Hawaiian Riviera** slated to be built from Road to the Sea to Pohue Bay. Even though the developer had big bucks, he was thwarted by a handful of residents from Miloli'i, 17 miles to the north, who protested that a planned marina here (and the resort in general) would interfere with their rich fishing grounds and their way of life. They got a lawyer to take up their cause, and together they successfully killed the project. The 16 *thousand*-acre parcel has changed hands several times since then, the last time for $13 million, and the current owners resurrected giant devel-opment ideas (including an airport) for the area in 2009. But they lost interest and never finished their environmental review, and it's currently back on the market.

Continuing along, **Hawaiian Ocean View Estate** (known locally as HOVE) lies up mauka of the highway along here. They have gas, nice grocery stores (we prefer **Malama Market**) and a few restaurants. HOVE is sort of a new community and an old one at the same time. Look at the map on page 81. Notice all those roads? About 11,000 1-acre parcels on harsh lava are spread among those roads. An oil company built it in the '60s, with the dream of creating a new community. Acre lots originally sold for $995 each, and until the early 2000s you could still pick up lots for $1,500. Prospective buyers were lured by photos of palm tree-backed Pohue Bay (which is distant, private and not reachable) and talk of the HOVE Yacht Club (which never existed). For over 30 years the vast majority of the lots remained unbuilt. They used party line phones until 1998 and around that time they got electricity. Rain catchment has been their lifeline. There's not even a school. Streets have lovely sounding names like *Paradise Parkway* and *Tree Fern Avenue.* But after driving around, you'd expect names like *Lava Lane* and *Rocky Road.* Most of the lots were sold or given away free with a full tank of gas (just teasing). Not to be outdone, another company built a subdivision below the highway (also shown on the map on page 81) with 1,200 3-acre lots. It took the short-lived land boom of around 2005 to finally shake up HOVE real estate values and draw residents.

To be fair, everyone we've met who lives in HOVE loves it there. They have formed a tight-knit community and seem happy as can be with their location. Whenever we drive around here, however, we're reminded that the Big Island is often rumored to be one of the largest repositories of people from the Federal Witness Protection Program. What a perfect place to lose oneself.

SOUTH POINT

[B] Between the 69 and 70 mile markers is the road to South Point (called Ka Lae meaning "the point"). This is the southernmost part of the island, making it the southernmost spot in the entire nation. (Not the Florida Keys, as most trivia books claim.) The road is paved the whole way. The only hazard is that the road is one lane for much of its length. It is mostly straight, and there is space to pull over for on-coming cars. Try to resist the temptation to speed on the seemingly wide open parts of this road; there are some surprise blind hills and turns.

NOT TO BE

MISSED!

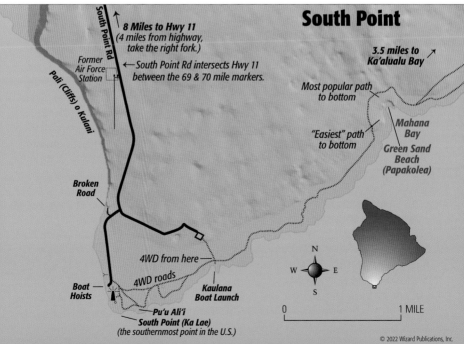

South Point

South Point Rd

8 Miles to Hwy 11
(4 miles from highway,
take the right fork.)

Former
Air Force
Station

← South Point Rd intersects Hwy 11
between the 69 & 70 mile markers.

Pali (Cliffs) o Kulani

3.5 miles to
Ka'alualu Bay

Most popular path
to bottom

"Easiest" path
to bottom

Mahana
Bay

Green Sand
Beach
(Papakolea)

Broken
Road

4WD from here

4WD roads

Boat
Hoists

Kaulana
Boat Launch

N
W   E
S

Pu'u Ali'i
South Point (Ka Lae)
(the southernmost point in the U.S.)

0   1 MILE

© 2022 Wizard Publications, Inc.

Massive turbines are one indication of the ever-present winds in this area.

The wind is always blowing out on this grassy plain, hence this location for the **Pakini Nui Wind Farm** in the distance. The trees here are all wind-blown in the same direction (west), vividly showing what happens to deflected trade winds coming from the northeast. (The inside back cover map puts it in perspective.)

As you get near South Point, turn right at the fork after the Kalae entrance sign. (The sign looked rickety at press time—the fork is a mile south of some abandoned buildings on the right.) South Point is the site of some of the oldest artifacts yet discovered in Hawai'i (as early as 300 A.D.) and was probably the first place the Polynesians came ashore and settled when they discovered these islands. Dry and desolate with no permanent streams, this might seem a surprising place for people to settle. The reason for its settlements, however, lies offshore. The waters off South Point are incredibly rich fishing grounds. Large pelagic game fish, such as tuna, mahimahi and marlin are plentiful. The ancient Hawaiians quickly discovered this but had a problem harvesting the fish. The wind and current together form such a strong offshore force that it would require all the fisherman's attention just

to stay put in a canoe. Those who went out too far were considered lost due to these forces since fishing canoes were not as maneuverable as voyaging canoes, and since the currents are uninterrupted all the way to Antarctica. The bottom drops to great depths quickly, so anchors aren't the answer. Their clever solution was to carve holes into the rock ledge and feed ropes through them so their canoes could be tied to shore while fishing. Some of those holes are still visible near the boat hoists at the cliffs.

Fresh water is very scarce here, even from wells, and what is available is barely potable. In the 1700s a chief named Kalani'opu'u, tired of having to bathe several miles away, asked his kahunas if there was water under the ground. One know-it-all assured him there was water at a certain spot if he dug *really* deep. After much digging, they found nothing. The big-mouth kahuna was promptly executed for his bad advice.

Today, you're likely to see long lines strung from the sea cliffs just to the northwest of the actual South Point. These lines are usually held afloat by empty bleach bottles and are sometimes pulled so taut by the wind and current that you'd swear you could walk on them. Fishermen use toy sailboats or balloons to drag the rope out to sea and dangle 10-foot leaders from the main line at every bleach bottle. When they get a strike, they haul the whole line in.

At the cliffs near South Point are old hoists, used to lower small boats from the low cliffs. A metal cliffside ladder is present, as well. Larger boats use the Kaulana boat launch less than a mile to the east. People lived at Kaulana until the beginning of the 20th century. Most visitors make the mistake of assuming that the cliffs with the boat hoists *are* South Point. The real South Point is past the light beacon to the left of a place where a rock wall trails down into the sea. There is no cliff there. The beacon will be behind you. Next to the beacon is the small Kalaea Heiau.

Since ancient times this entire area has had a reputation for having exceptionally strong currents, and during all but calm seas this is no doubt true. Even so, we know people who love nothing better than to leap into the water from the boat hoist area and come back up via the metal ladder adjacent to a boat hoist. They also jump into the sketchy hole near the cliffs, though I have to confess to not having the stones to do the latter myself. There are also a few spots along the cliffs where you can scramble down to the water. Some people even like to snorkel here at night when fish and clouds of small, beautiful shrimp greet the eye. The water is unbelievably clear and seems quite inviting when calm, especially when you can see lots of fish swimming below.

With this in mind, I've repeatedly snorkeled here below the boat hoists to assess the currents. I was so wary the first time out that I tied myself to the cliff ladder with a long rope—just to be safe. It turned out to be unnecessary. *When calm, I have yet to detect much current below the boat hoist area*, probably because it's protected by the point. The water is teem-

Holding on for dear life as they watch the snorkeler below the cliffs.

ing with life and visibility is usually over 100 feet. But (and I can't stress this enough) I've *never* gone into the water when it's not calm, I don't swim too far, and I don't endorse swimming there. The surge here demonstrates the extreme power of the ocean, and I'm excited and nervous every time I swim at that spot. South of the cliffs at the actual South Point, the water is always violent and unswimmable. I mention all this so you will know what I've experienced here in case you are crazy enough to do it on your own. Check to see that your life insurance policy is in order before you go, and buy a good guidebook to Antarctica—just in case.

South Point was used during WWII for army barracks. Later, the Navy installed a missile tracking station on 33 acres. Not to be left out, the Air Force later took over the facilities and renamed it **South Point Air Force Station**. The station was closed in 1979, and little remains except the shabby buildings on your right as you approach South Point. Look for horses in the buildings' remains.

Just north of the boat hoists (see map on page 83) is a road that leads off a cliff. The road was built in 1955 along with a concrete landing below to service fishing boats. Representing the finest county quality, it lasted less than a year. The surf erased the landing and part of the road. What remains is called (you see this one coming, don't you?) **Broken Road**. The view from the end of Broken Road is spectacular, but the snorkeling isn't as good here as it is below the boat hoists. Off in the distance you see Pali o Kulani, which rises 350 feet from the ocean. At the place where the cliff appears to end, it actually turns inland and runs north to an area just south of Highway 11. The inland cliff was caused by another catastrophic landslide, similar to (but pre-dating) the

one described earlier. It slid to the west and caused a similar splash.

If you had gone left at the aforementioned fork, you'd come to all that remains of former military housing. We were thrilled when state authorities leveled them a while back. Until then, militant squatters had occupied the crumbling buildings for many years, extracting "Green Sand Parking Fees" from visitors and often threatening car break-ins if they didn't comply. It was a well-known problem and generated over 150 police reports in one year alone. Authorities seemed paralyzed until finally 21 officers converged here, brought a BBQ, grilled up burgers for themselves and the squatters, then proceeded to bulldoze all the structures.

When the pavement ends, a dirt road leads to a boat launch 0.25 miles away.

Off to the east of South Point is a strange phenomenon called **Green Sand Beach**. (See page 178.) It features a beautiful mixture of green and black sand and is a fascinating place to visit. If you have 4WD (and insurance) you *might* be able to drive it. It's 2.25 miles each way on the flat but often *deeply* rutted, grassy plain. Sometimes even timid 4WDers can make it. Other times, you'll want to bring along four sumo wrestlers to help you carry your car out of the ruts. Many readers have written us to say we're *way* off on that distance, by the way. We promise, we're not. We've checked it by car odometer and on foot with GPS. It just *seems* longer since the wind is in your face going out. If you're short on time, it's not a *must see*, but it's certainly unusual.

PAST SOUTH POINT

Back on Highway 11, as you continue, you'll wrap around the island and enter the wetter, windward side. Almost instantly,

Don't adjust your book. The sand really is green here.

our old friend green has returned to the scene. This was the edge of sugar country. Big Island sugar died here in 1996 (as a business—some of the cane still lives on), and many of the fields here have been replaced with the more profitable macadamia nut trees. Coffee has also been planted upslope of the highway. It's not in the same league as Kona coffee. We've had some good Ka'u coffee, but a lot of bad cups. (Ka'u growers write to us telling us we're dead wrong and have no taste. *Sorry*, it's just our opinion.) Both coffee and mac nuts can be found at roadside stands and local markets.

Waiohinu and **Na'alehu** are the first towns you come to. Waiohinu's claim to fame was the **Mark Twain Monkeypod Tree**, planted by the author himself. It blew down in the '50s, but its shoots have grown into a respectable new tree. You'll find restrooms down the road at Waiohinu Park.

While in Na'alehu, stop by the best restaurant along this part of the island, **Hana Hou Restaurant & Bakery**.

As you come down the hill near mile marker 62, you'll see **Whittington Park** and the remains of its wharf in the distance. From the vantage point up the hill you truly appreciate the vastness of this Big Island. Whittington is picturesque from a distance and makes a decent restroom pit stop if you're in need.

Just after mile marker 56 is the road to **Punalu'u Black Sand Beach**. This is the **NOT TO BE** easiest volcanic black sand beach to access on the island. The water here is cold due to **MISSED!** the large amounts of fresh water percolating from the floor just offshore. At one time the ancient Hawaiians at Punalu'u (which means *spring dived for*) obtained their fresh water here by diving down with an upside-down, dried, hollow gourd to where the fresh water was streaming out. They would flip the gourd, fill it with fresh water, put their thumbs over it, and come to the surface.

There are scads of turtles in the bay, and it's one of the few areas where we've seen them beach themselves. There is also a picturesque fishpond backed by lots of coconut trees. (Incidentally, there were no coconuts in Hawai'i before the Polynesians came. Though ubiquitous in the South Pacific, Hawai'i is fed by the North Pacific Current, precluding the possibility that a live coconut could have floated here from any place warm. Just thought you needed to know that for your next appearance on *Jeopardy*.) The only eyesore at this exotic black sand beach is the closed and ramshackle restaurant behind the fishpond, whacked by a tsunami in 1975. Fortunately, it's mostly covered over from the beach side, which tells you how long it's been closed—long enough to choke off their lovely view with vegetation. It's been condemned and might be bulldozed by the time you arrive.

When the Japanese attacked Pearl Harbor in 1941, Army troops dynamited the concrete wall over near the boat launch to keep it from being used by the enemy in case of an invasion.

Tour buses sometimes bring groups to Punalu'u, but it *usually* isn't crowded since it is 60 miles from both Hilo and Kona. Forgive us for nagging, but please resist the temptation to take black sand home as a souvenir. Since it is finite, it would eventually deplete the beach for everyone. (Or see *Curses* on page 37.) The sharp edges of the sand grains ensure that swimmers will inadvertently take some home anyway. You will find plenty of stowaways in the lining of your bathing suit, which will stay there for years. The concessionaire at Punalu'u sells black sand and, though they *claim* it's from another beach consumed by the volcano, that certainly can't be said of their green sand, so we hope you won't buy any. OK, end of nag.

This area is sometimes called **SeaMountain**, named by a developer for **Kama'ehuakanaloa** (aka Lo'ihi Seamount). That undersea volcano, 20 miles offshore from here, will be the Big Island's next volcano attraction. It's still 3,200 feet underwater and won't surface for another 100,000 years, but be sure to look for it when we release our 99,000th version of this book. (Call now to reserve your copy early.) The whole property was purchased by a Japanese investment company for more than $30 million at the height of a real estate boom in 1989. After five years and countless challenges to their plans by local residents, they sold it for less than $3 million, not even a *tenth* of what they paid for it. (*Ouch!*) There are older condos here. See *Punalu'u Black Sand Beach* on page 179.

From Punalu'u you'll start your gradual 4,000-foot ascent to Kilauea Volcano. Along the way you pass **Pahala**, a former sugar town. Though friendly, the town is quiet and a little depressing, and the economic harm is, to a certain degree, self-inflicted. Pahala residents were crucial in killing the expansion plan at Punalu'u in the mid-'90s, confident that their sugar plantation jobs were sufficient and fearful of altering their way of life. After that, the coastal land below Pahala was slated to be a spaceport where private satellites would be launched. Again Pahala residents were able to successfully fight the plan, even though it was backed by the state, the governor and the mayor.

Then in the late '90s the last Big Island sugar plantation opened the books and told the workers they either needed to accept a 15% pay cut or the company would have to close down due to ongoing losses. (Every other sugar plantation on the island had failed in the previous years due to a changing marketplace.) The sugar workers voted to reject the pay cut, and the sugar company promptly shut down, putting nearly every resident of this one-industry town out of work. Their way of life changed anyway, but they had nothing to fall back on, and the area has never fully recovered.

[C] A couple miles past the edge of **Hawai'i Volcanoes National Park**, take note of the rugged looking a'a lava. It's hard to believe that barefoot armies marched through this stuff, but they did—sometimes under extraordinary circumstances like those described on page 90.

Nobody knows for certain, but the days of seeing a massive lava lake in Halema'uma'u Crater have been replaced with sporadic minor lava intrusions since the cataclysmic 2018 eruption.

If you had to name the one thing the Big Island is most famous for, it would undoubtedly be **Kilauea Volcano**. In all the world there isn't a more active volcano, and none is as user-friendly as Kilauea. People often refer to it as the drive-in volcano.

Kilauea is an enigma—you can't really see the mountain from anywhere on the island, or even recognize it when you are standing on it. It seems more like a wound on the flanks of Mauna Loa. In the past, everyone thought that it was *part* of Mauna Loa, but today we know that it is separate and distinct, with its own separate (though possibly interrelated) magma chamber. One part of Kilauea, the actual Pu'u 'O'o vent itself, is teasingly inaccessible.

We feel strongly that most people allow far too little time for visiting **Hawai'i Volcanoes National Park**. Many simply blow through on an around-the-island driving frenzy, barely stopping long enough to snap a photo of Kilauea Caldera. There is much more here than meets the eye, and this might be the highlight of your Hawaiian trip. Whether Kilauea is erupting or not, this park may be the most fascinating place you ever visit, and you *surely* don't have anything like this back home. The finest hiking on the island is here. The lushest rainforest you've ever seen is here to stroll through. Vents spewing steam, brand new land, birds-a-plenty, giant chasms, ancient Hawaiian petroglyphs, lava craters, walk-through lava tubes, unrivaled vistas—it's all here. Once you know

Fissure 8 at its peak, with fountains almost 200 feet tall.

what to look for, you will want to spend *at least* a whole day, preferably two. Since driving to the volcano can take 4 hours round trip from Kona or Kohala, consider reserving a place to stay in the town of Volcano. This allows you to experience it at a more leisurely pace and is a nice way to go, if you can swing it. After a long, fulfilling day at the park, the drive back to Kona or Kohala is a drag. If you are staying in Hilo, it's an easy drive back.

WILL I GET TO SEE LAVA FLOWING?

Until 2018 I would have said, probably yes. After that for a couple years, I would have said, probably not. Lava returned to the park after a 28 month absence at Halemaʻumaʻu Crater in the form of an ash explosion and lava lake in the crater in December of 2020 (perhaps as Madame Pele's way of saying *up yours* to that mis-

erable year), but it didn't last long. Then it made an appearance again in the fall of 2021. This eruption has (so far) been confined to Halemaʻumaʻu crater, meaning you'll most likely see volcanic gases billowing out of the crater during the day and an amazing glow to the area at night.

So for your visit the truth is, *I don't know* if you'll get to see lava flowing again. And neither does anyone else. You need to know the history of what happened to get the whole picture.

Historically (meaning since 1778), most Hawaiian eruptions have lasted days or weeks, rarely months. Until 1983, only once—from 1969–1974 at Mauna Ulu—has an eruption outside the crater lasted more than a year. All that changed Jan. 3, 1983, when a fissure opened up in a place later called Puʻu ʻOʻo, shifted to a vent called Kupaianaha from 1986 to 1992,

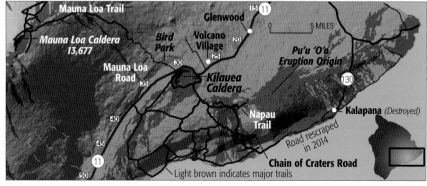

Mauna Loa Trail
Mauna Loa Caldera 13,677
Glenwood
[15] [11]
0   5 MILES
Bird Park
Volcano Village
[20]
Puʻu ʻOʻo Eruption Origin
Mauna Loa Road
[30]
[25]
[35]
Kīlauea Caldera
[130]
[40]
Napau Trail
Kalapana (Destroyed)
[45]
Road rescraped in 2014
[11]
Chain of Craters Road
[50]
Light brown indicates major trails

then shifted back toward Puʻu ʻOʻo until 2018. There was also a lava lake at the summit in Halemaʻumaʻu Crater for the last decade of the eruption.

On April 30, 2018, however, the crater floor collapsed. The lava lake drained all at once, and the crater got deeper and deeper until the magma fell below the water table. The summit is around 4,000 feet in elevation, and the volcano had spent 35 years storing lava for distribution at this higher elevation. Something dramatic was happening.

Like a gopher tunneling underground, the magma worked its way rapidly to the east, outside the park and down the flanks of the mountain. When it got to a quiet residential development called Leilani Estates (elevation 700 feet), scientists sounded the alarm bells. Evacuations were ordered, and on May 3, 2018, fissure after fissure opened up among the houses.

Twenty-two fissures eventually opened until Madame Pele settled in at Fissure 8. And from there came one of the most voluminous lava rivers in modern times. Imagine 40,000 dump trucks of lava—*per hour*—raging down a hellish river in *your* neighborhood. It was as if you had a full water tank located at a high elevation, then ran a hose from it down to a lower elevation. The fluid pressure was enormous, and lava was hotter than any that had previously been measured from Kilauea. The volcano had entered a new phase, and nobody had any idea what would happen or how long it would last.

The lava went due north until it crossed the main street, Leilani Avenue, then pushed its way northeast. It paralleled the ridge down the flank, and some of the lava spilled down the southern flank and made its way to the ocean, but Fissure 8 pushed on. Homes were destroyed. Busi-

nesses were destroyed. At one point the lava broke onto the land where a geothermal power plant existed. This was where the island got 25% of its power, by tapping the heat from a long ago eruption. But this was a geothermal meltdown, forcing the power plant to abandon the wells and flee.

When the massive river made it to a tall cinder cone from a 500-year-old eruption, it slithered around the north end

The massive lava river with Fissure 8 in the background.

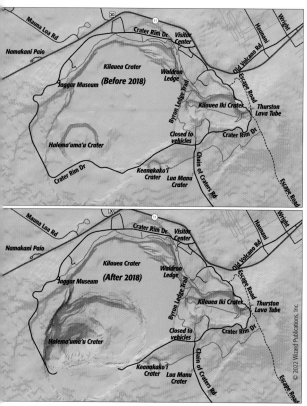

Kilauea Crater before and after 2018.

she'd erupt again. Just goes to show you—never try to predict a volcano.

THE SCENE

If and when lava does return to the park outside the crater, this is what it's like. We've been to the volcano countless times, with and without surface lava. It's always a fantastic experience, though not what people expect.

During a relatively calm flow, pahoehoe lava is silvery coated, red or yellow as it oozes its way toward the sea. It is a humbling experience to stand there and observe earthly creation, like seeing the planet during its fiery adolescence. In most parts of the world, people dread active volcanoes, fearing death and destruction. A huge explosion will send clouds of ash and pumice into air, killing everything in its path. (Or screwing up travel to Europe.) In Hawai'i, people drop whatever they are doing and drive out to see it.

and proceeded to take out some of the most beloved spots in Lower Puna, starting with the one-of-a-kind town and tidepools of Kapoho. See page 121 for more on that.

After fountaining and cascading for a little more than three months, lava from the fissure slowed until it seemed that Fissure 8 was spent. The lava river crusted over. More than 13 square miles of existing land had been covered with lava and 875 acres of *new* land created at the shoreline. Madame Pele, who had been on a massive spending spree in Lower Puna, appeared to have exhausted her savings, and it was *thought* it would be decades before

Rather than apocalyptic explosions, Kilauea mostly drools and dribbles. (In historic times, it has exploded only a few times, and one had astonishing consequences—see page 94.) Though the total volume of lava erupting ranges from 300,000 to more than a million cubic yards *per day,* it is so spread out that it rarely rushes down the mountain in a hellish river of liquid stone. (Well, except for 2018 in Lower Puna, of course.) Usually, it's small rivulets of molten lava separated by large distances from other rivulets. When it hardens (which occurs very quickly), it crunches beneath your feet like shards of glass.

The lava you see around the park came in many flavors and textures.

There are not many places on this planet where you can walk on ground younger than you are, where you can be assured that there is absolutely nothing alive beneath your feet except for the earth itself. We've been there when people from all over the world stood in awe, tears streaming down their cheeks as they tell their children, "You may never see anything like this again in your lifetime."

As freshly hardened pahoehoe lava cools, it stresses the silica coating on the outside. This natural glass then crackles and pops off the rock, creating subtle sounds that bewitch viewers. Heat from the flows can be intense. Many times

The Explosion That Changed History

Mild-mannered Kilauea has exploded on a large scale only twice in recorded history, once in 1790 and once in 1924. (There is evidence that it may have exploded more often in the distant past.) These eruptions are phreatomagmatic, meaning steam-induced (but you knew that).

In 1790, Kamehameha ruled much of the island. While he was distracted with plans to invade Maui, a rival chief named Keoua seized control of this part of the island. Kamehameha sent troops to do battle. Eventually both armies pulled back to their strongholds. As Keoua's troops and their families camped at Kilauea that night, fire and rock spewed from Kilauea Caldera. Keoua thought he had offended Pele, the volcano goddess, by rolling stones into the crater the day before and spent two days trying to appease her. It didn't work. On the third day they tried to leave, organized in three divisions. Right after the first division left, the mountain exploded. Darkness enveloped the area, punctured by volcano-induced thunder and lightning, and streams of red and blue light from the crater. Huge amounts of hot ash rained down, then a suffocating gas belched up from the volcano.

The first division to depart escaped mostly intact. The second division disappeared. When the third division came to the scene, they found their comrades of the second division huddled in circles, some hugging each other with their noses pressed together. Relieved, the third division rushed forward to greet them, only to discover that every last member of the second division—around 400 men and their wives and children—were dead. (Not 85 as the park sign says.) Most had been asphyxiated by the noxious gas. The only survivor was a solitary hog. If you take the Ka'u Desert Trail (see page 108), you can see the faint outline of steps preserved in the ash—steps created by other soldiers at the time of the disaster.

As for Keoua, everyone now knew that Pele was against him and his army. He kept fighting more battles but never turned the tide. Not yet defeated, he was invited by Kamehameha to peacefully dedicate the new Pu'ukohola Heiau in Kawaihae. When Keoua's boat approached the shore of Kawaihae, he was immediately murdered by one of Kamehameha's officers and had the dubious honor of being the temple's first official human sacrifice. Thus was Kamehameha's rule over the island forever solidified.

we've been less than a yard from the molten lava and felt like we would suddenly burst into flames. Other times, the wind has blown from the other direction so we could enjoy the liquid earth in comfort. Sometimes there is unpleasant black smoke and fumes (especially when the volcano is gobbling up more road or forest). Other times it seems to have absolutely no fumes or smoke and no offensive smell. (What smell it does have is hard to describe but never forgotten.)

At night, the lava may glow in numerous spots like a prehistoric scene from yesteryear. Sometimes, as the lava flows into the ocean, brilliant red and orange steam clouds light up the immediate area, creating dazzling light shows as the flow drips or gushes into the ocean. Sometimes, when it burns scrub vegetation at night, the methane emits a blue flame. A night scene might go like this: A crowd of about 50 people on a bluff overlooks a field of fresh pahoehoe. It pops, crackles and glows as the night consumes all. What amazes us is how reverent everybody is. Couples hold each other tight. People speak in soft whispers. They try not to move much for fear of disturbing others as they watch Earth's most primordial show. Nobody wants to leave. Watching the lava enter the sea at night never fails to impress, and we've been told by visitors more times than we can count that it is an unsurpassed highlight.

A FEW BASICS

The park was closed and heavily damaged by relentless earthquakes in the summer of 2018. We were mighty impressed when they reopened their doors a month after the flows were over. Since then most of the park's attractions have been reopened. For more information visit the park website at: nps.gov/havo/index.htm.

The park is open 24 hours, every day of the year. Despite the fact that it is operated by the federal government, the park seems very well run. Much of the staff are friendly and professional. (We've seen other parks where the staff can be real curmudgeons.) The rangers are pretty good at letting you see the action close up. We've been there when they lead people across smoldering lava, the heat coming up through their shoes. They will only keep you away if they *truly* perceive danger, unlike some other parks where they sometimes keep you away from imaginary dangers on orders from the lawyers. Because of this, you should take their cautions seriously. If they say you can't go to a certain area because they expect a lava bench might

The huge plains in the lower part of the park formed from lava rivers charting their own course.

Kilauea Crater

This map is rendered at an angle in order to convey the lay of the land at Kilauea. Visualize it as a solid cast of the land sitting on a table. Each "terraced" contour line represents an elevation change of 20 feet.

Volcano Village

Old Volcano Rd

Gas

27

11

26 miles to Hilo

Thurston Lava Tube

Park Boundary

Escape Rd

Pu'u 'O'o Vent is eight miles this way.

Kilauea Iki Overlook

Park Visitor Center

Park Entrance

28

Crater Rim Dr

Kilauea Iki Trail

Kilauea Iki Crater

Kilauea Iki Trail

Devastation Trail

Crater Rim Trail

Puhimau Crater

Sulphur Banks

Crater Rim Trail

Pu'u Pua'i

Chain of Craters Rd

1

29

Byron Ledge Trail

Keanakako'i Crater (Walkable)

Lua Manu Crater

Walk this part of the road

1 MILE

Volcano House

Old Crater Rim Rd now collapsed & part of Crater Rim Trail

Kilauea Military Camp

'Iliahi (Sandlewood) Trail

Piimauna

Gas

30

Steam Vents

Crater Rim Trail

Kilauea Overlook

Hawaiian Volcano Observatory

Kilauea Caldera

Road Closed

0

Road Closed

Halema'uma'u Crater

Former parking lot

Tree Molds

Volcano Golf & Country Club

Jaggar Museum (Closed)

Kipuka Pua'ulu

Mauna Loa Scenic Rd

31

Crater Rim Dr

Namakanipaio Campgrounds Cabins

11

32

88 miles to Kailua-Kona

Ka'u Desert Trail

Crater Rim Trail

N
E
S
W

Indicates Foot Trails

Roadside mile markers

Closed due to fumes

© 2022 Wizard Publications, Inc.

collapse, don't go there. At least one person has died because he didn't heed this warning. (The ocean drops quickly off the coast of the park, and new lava land is usually destined to break off when it reaches a critical mass.) If rangers say an area is off limits because of the dangers of methane explosions, believe it. Methane from plant matter in older flows can heat up when a new flow covers it. This usually escapes by hissing or by small pops, but sometimes it can be more dramatic. We were there once with many other visitors when a large methane explosion occurred 25 feet from us. It was powerful enough to rip through 12-inch thick lava, pieces of which jumped into the air. Under certain circumstances, these explosions occur 100 yards in advance of a lava flow.

And remember, if there are no accessible surface flows, don't despair. The volcano area is eminently fascinating and exciting, with or without surface flows, and is always worth at least a day of exploration. Below are some of the other delights waiting for you at Hawai'i Volcanoes National Park.

HIKING IN THE PARK

Much of the best hiking on the island is in Hawai'i Volcanoes National Park. See *Hiking* starting on page 201, which lists scads of great hikes in the park. There are also a couple spookier hikes in the *Adventures* chapter. Note that strolls of less than 30 minutes are described in this chapter.

AROUND KILAUEA CRATER

A quick note: We decided not to use our "Real Gem" and "Not To Be Missed" icons in this chapter because they would fill the pages. The entire park is *a real gem* and is *not to be missed.*

In Volcanoes National Park, all roads lead to...sometimes not what you'd expect.

Remember that Kilauea Crater is located at an altitude of 4,000 feet, so make sure you bring your warmies for those days when it's misty and chilly at the summit.

After paying your $30 vehicle entrance fee (it's good for a week) at the gate, stop by the **Visitor Center** on your right. They have up-to-date information, a nice display of books, videos, artifacts, a movie showing and—most important if you've driven a long way—restrooms. Check out the 3-D miniature of the island near the restrooms to get a perspective of the island. Guided hike notices are sometimes posted at the Visitor Center (open 10 a.m.–5 p.m.) if you're interested. Be aware, lines can start forming half an hour before they open. From there, you might want to walk across the street to **Volcano House** for your first peek of Kilauea Caldera from their enviable view.

You'll want to do a counter-clockwise tour of the caldera to start. Take a right from the Visitor Center and the first thing you come to are the **Steam Vents** on your left. Here, rain that has seeped into the ground is heated by Kilauea and issues forth as steam. The amount varies daily depending on the level of rain in the past few days, and it is rarely smelly like Sulphur Banks. In fact, there is usually no smell at all. Make sure you take the trail for 2 to 3 minutes toward the crater rim for a smashing view of the crater, and where additional, more powerful and unobstructed steam vents are present.

From the steam vent parking lot you can follow along the Sulphur Banks Trail. The paved path starts across the street and 800 feet *before* the lot. It leads 5 to 10 minutes through a pretty forest to a boardwalk at the **Sulphur Banks**. This colorful but stinky phenomenon is where hydrogen sulphide gas and steam form deposits of sulphur, gypsum and hematite on the ground. This should be avoided by those with a heart condition, respiratory problems, children or anyone eating lunch.

Continuing on Crater Rim Drive you'll see **Kilauea Military Camp**. Despite the name, if you're a civilian, you can still stay here with active, retired military or DOD sponsorship. They just need an email from your sponsor. No connections? No problem. Visitors are still welcome at their restaurants, game room, lounge and bowling alley (though they reserve the right to bump you from the latter if a *real* guest wants to bowl). The bowling alley (the only one on the east side of the island) has six lanes, a small snack shop, and if you ask *really* nicely, they might even turn on the disco lights.

Small handmade signs asking for military ID may seem at odds with their warm welcome, but the people are friendly, accommodating and seem enthusiastic about visitors.

The general store has a decent selection of sundries and even carries the current edition of our book, *The Big Island Revealed* (just in case you forgot yours at the hotel), which is banned by the park in most places (we gave away a few too many secrets).

There is also a restaurant on site that gets mixed reviews. One of the employees said it used to be great but now just serves cafeteria food.

Rounding the crater, you come to **Kilauea Overlook**. This is a different perspective on Kilauea Crater and its progeny, Halemaʻumaʻu Crater, and is definitely worth a stop. Look for white-tailed tropic birds soaring on the thermals down in the crater.

This is as close as you'll be able to get to **Halemaʻumaʻu Crater**. This crater-within-a-crater is said to be the home to Madame Pele, the Hawaiian volcano goddess. For most of the 19th century this was a boiling lava lake. Mark Twain and other celebrities of his time visited here and described it as viewing the fiery pits of hell. When Isabella Bird saw it in 1873, she wrote:

> Suddenly, just above, and in front of us, gory drops were tossed in air, and springing forwards we stood on the brink of Halemaumau, which was about 35 feet below us. I think we all screamed, I know we all wept, but we were speechless, for a new glory and terror had been added to the Earth. It is the most unutterable of wonderful things. The words of common speech are quite useless. It is unimaginable, indescribable, a sight to remember forever, a sight which at once took possession of every faculty of sense and soul, removing one altogether out of the range of ordinary life. Here was the real "bottomless pit"—the "fire which is not quenched"—"the place of hell"—the "lake which burneth with fire and brimstone"—the "everlasting burnings"—the fiery sea whose waves are never weary. There were groanings, rumblings, and detonations, rushings, hissings, and splashings, and the crashing sound of breakers on the coast, but it was the surging of fiery waves upon a fiery shore.

Halemaʻumaʻu is quieter now. The whole crater has risen and fallen over time—going from 1,335 feet deep to overflowing its top. It was about 3,000 feet across for many decades until the lava retreated in 2018, and once the liquid rock got below the water table, explosions of steam rattled the crater—and the whole region. Strong earthquakes happened daily for months. Today the crater is more than *four times* its previous size and more than 1,000 feet deep. It expanded so much that it swallowed part of the previous viewing area parking lot.

ʻAʻa lava on the right (named by the first Hawaiian to walk on it barefooted?) is rough and clinkery. Pahoehoe on the left is smooth and ropy, like thick cake batter.

Until the road closure, Hawaiians still made offerings here to Pele. It is said that Pele will appear as a beautiful young woman in the mountains and as a very old and ugly woman at the shoreline. (Hence the Hawaiian saying, "Always be nice to an old woman; it might be Pele.")

There may or may not be a lava lake in the crater, but if it's there you probably won't see it because of the depth. At night, however, you'll get to see an orange glow if the crater is active.

Just past the overlook is former **Jaggar Museum** and the **Hawaiian Volcano Observatory**. These structures were built so scientists could observe the erupting volcano up close and personal. They got more than they asked for when Halema'uma'u Crater collapsed in 2018 and the series of earthquakes that followed did so much damage that there are no plans to reopen them.

From the Kilauea Overlook, you're gonna have to backtrack toward, then past, the visitor center, then hang a right before the park entrance to stay on Crater Rim Drive. If you need a break, you could stop by the **Volcano Art Center Gallery** near the visitor center. Built in 1877, this was the original Volcano House before it was moved here to make way for another building. Now an art gallery, they have an exquisite selection from some of the island's top artists, including higher-end wood carvings, glassworks, paintings and more. This is also a good place to check out what's going on in the area in terms of events and demonstrations. Open 9 a.m.–5 p.m.

Now you're going clockwise around the crater. There is a nice hike called the **Earthquake Trail** (see *Hiking* on page 204) that starts near Volcano House. Part of it is on the *old* Crater Rim Drive—before it fell into the crater in 1983—and the results are dramatic.

Watch for the **Kilauea Iki Overlook** on your right. This is definitely worth stopping for. This crater (meaning "little Kilauea") had been asleep for almost a century when it became active in 1959. Then it erupted into gargantuan fountains of lava, some reaching a staggering 1,900 feet—that's more than four times the height of the crater walls and is the highest on record. Scientists had warnings that an eruption was going to occur. Earthquake swarms and a swelling of Kilauea told them it was coming. So they set up their instruments and waited for the inevitable—*at Halema'uma'u*. They were stunned when the lava instead shot from the southwest wall of Kilauea Iki (across from you) 2 miles away from Halema'uma'u. Ground zero was near the Pu'u Pua'i (meaning gushing hill) cinder cone on the other side. It was created as fountains of lava, blown southwest by the trade winds, piled high into a cone. The vent spewed enough lava at one point to bury a football field 15 feet deep in lava—*every minute!* Each time the showers ended, the lava would drain back into the vent opening, only to be shot out again. When it ended, 36 days after it began, the crater floor was a dead zone with a lava bathtub ring above the floor to show how high the lava lake had reached. The lava lake cooled and cracked as sheets of lava buckled and warped, giving the crater the look of dried, crusted-over gravy. Today, steam usually issues from cracks in the crater floor, and the rock is still molten a couple of hundred feet down. There are still vents on the crater, though the main vent was covered by falling cinders. Kilauea Iki offers one of the best hikes on the island. See *Hiking* on page 201.

Kilauea Iki is separated from Kilauea by a narrow shelf of land called **Byron Ledge**. It was on this ledge in 1824 that Princess Kapiolani publicly stood and, to

The 1959 eruption of Kilauea Iki punished this part of the forest when it showered the land with falling bits of gas-frothed lava from the 1,900-foot-high fountains. But it's the forest that will prevail. Take the short Devastation Trail and see for yourself.

the horror and fear of many, denied the volcano goddess Pele and embraced Christianity. She initiated this by eating 'ohelo berries without offering any to Pele first. (It was thought that Pele would strike you dead if you didn't offer her some first by tossing a fruiting branch into the crater.) When the Princess didn't die after snubbing and denying Pele, Christianity was more widely embraced by her people.

Back on Crater Rim Road, you come to a parking lot (probably full of buses). This is **Thurston Lava Tube**. If you are looking for an easy way to see what the inside of natural lava plumbing looks like, Thurston Lava Tube is worth a stop. It is considered one of the "must sees" at the volcano. If you get there between tour buses, it can be an interesting experience. The entrance is a few minutes walk from Crater Rim Drive (see map on page 96). This part of the tube is lit and is the most

widely visited. Most of the lava stalactites have been removed over the decades, but you can still see enough tube detail to get the idea of how the lava travels. Undisturbed tubes often have floors littered with rocks that fall from the ceiling (either from when the tube cooled or from rainwater seeping through the cracks over the years). Thurston has been cleaned up and lighted to make it easy to visit. You exit about halfway through the tube. It's a shame they put up a fence to Thurston's *darker* half. At the stairs at the end of the tube tour and past the gate, Thurston continues for another 1,000 feet (it seems like more) before it ends abruptly. If the park reopens the gate, make sure you bring a good flashlight (or two) for the journey, as you will be in total darkness most of the way. At the end, turn off the light. You've never seen *real* blackness until you've seen *this* blackness.

If you're running tight on time during the day and there are too many other things in the park you want to see, skip Thurston and tour it at night instead, when the crowds will be gone. It's open 24 hours and lit from 8 a.m.–8 p.m., and you may need a flashlight to follow the walkway to the entrance.

The dirt road that leads south of Thurston Lava Tube is an **escape road**. It is well-maintained in case Chain of Craters Road is ever obliterated by a lava flow (again). But in the meanwhile that dirt road is a fun place to ride **mountain bikes**. It goes through very lush forest and is a delight. Just make sure you close all gates behind you. Some areas are fenced off to prevent pig damage. Wild pigs are amazingly destructive, and rangers fight an unending war to minimize their impact.

Lava sometimes bursts from fissures such as this one from the 1970s Mauna Ulu eruption. But life always reclaims the land.

Driving past Thurston Lava Tube, on your right will be a road to the **Pu'u Pua'i Overlook**. The overlook just past the parking lot is great. You're right next to the cinder cone where all the debris from the eruption piled up. From here you can stroll for 10–15 minutes along the **Devastation Trail**. This is where the fallout from the 1959 Kilauea Iki eruption killed the fern and 'ohi'a forest. The line of demarcation is abrupt, going from healthy forest to a field of **tephra** littered with bleached tree trunks. Tephra is airborne gas-frothed lava from fountains, which cools as pumice cinders. The forest is working to come back, and you will see the results along the way. You can either walk back the way you came, loop around on Crater Rim Road, or have someone pick you up at the other end.

Soon you're confronted with the other Crater Rim Drive road closure. If you wanted to walk 0.8 miles on the closed road you'd come to another crater called **Keanakakoʻi**. The Hawaiians used to fetch abnormally hard rock from here until it was covered by subsequent lava flows. Across the road from Keanakakoʻi is a lava fissure. These fissures are usually long cracks where lava erupts in a curtain of fire, as this one did in 1974.

DOWN CHAIN OF CRATERS ROAD

At the road closure you're at **Chain of Craters Road**, which leads 19 miles down to the shore and ends abruptly where the current lava flow cut it off. The road was so named because it passed numerous craters along the rift zone before veering off to the shore. It was rerouted after Madame Pele repaved 12 miles of the road with lava during the 1969–1974 Mauna Ulu flow and now visits fewer craters than it used to. Mile markers are on alternating sides of the road, and we will refer to some of them. There are still some craters along the way you might want to check out, such as Puhimau (but don't bother with Koʻokoʻolau). Remember to check your gas gauge; we've seen people run out of gas coming back up.

A little more than 2 miles into Chain of Craters Road is **Hilina Pali Road**, 8.3 miles long. It may be closed during nene nesting or if there is a perceived fire danger. The drive isn't impressive, but at the end is **Hilina Pali Lookout**. Walk down the path for 100 feet or so, and you are treated to an amazingly expansive view. You're perched above the vast shoreline below, and on a clear day you can see the entire shoreline for over 30 miles south. It's very

The Hawaiians, like people since the dawn of time, were compelled to leave a lasting legacy of themselves to the ages. These ancient petroglyphs are on the short Puʻu Loa trail.

quiet, desolate and peaceful, with the sound of the distant ocean sometimes present. If you take it, please drive very slowly as the endangered nene are usually in the road and aren't afraid of cars. The Kulanaokuaiki backcountry campgrounds are also on Hilina Pali Road.

Less than 0.1 miles past Hilina Pali Road, on the left (east) side is a 60-second walk to **Devil's Throat**. (It's unmarked.) This small collapsed crater is impressively sheer and a genuine heart-stopper. It's *straight* down. Be careful at the edge; it looks pretty fragile.

Along this stretch of Chain of Craters Road, keep an eye to your left. You *might* see steam coming from a hill. This is **Mauna Ulu**, the source of the second longest flank eruption of Kilauea. From 1969–1974 it poured lava and harassed park road builders, forcing Chain of Craters Road to be rerouted. There is a trail off the spur road past Pauahi Crater (another crater worth seeing) that goes near Mauna Ulu. (See *Adventures* on page 236 for more.) In 1997 a couple camping way out

Why You Shouldn't Pick a Lehua Blossom Off an 'Ohi'a Tree

According to legend, 'Ohi'a was a young, handsome Big Island chief. The volcano goddess Pele knew that 'Ohi'a was courting a beautiful young girl named Lehua. Pele became enamored with 'Ohi'a and desired him for a husband. One day as 'Ohi'a went up into the mountains to cut kukui bark to stain his surfboard, Pele appeared to him. She was dressed in her finest clothes and was quite striking. After a time, she announced to 'Ohi'a who she was and asked him to be her husband. Nervously but very diplomatically, he turned her down, professing his eternal love for

Lehua. In her anger, Pele told him he was as gutless as a piece of wood, and changed him into a gnarled tree with grey-green leaves. When the other gods saw what Pele had done, they felt bad and tried to reverse it, but failed. The best they could do to reunite the broken-hearted Lehua with her beloved 'Ohi'a was to turn Lehua into a beautiful blossom on the same tree. To this day, it is said that picking a lehua blossom off an 'ohi'a tree will produce rain. These are the tears from heaven for separated lovers everywhere.

Currently, 'ohi'a trees are under assault from an alien fungus that causes a condition called Rapid 'Ohi'a Death, and it's raising statewide concern.

at Napau Crater Trail (3.5 miles east of Mauna Ulu) was awakened when lava suddenly began gushing from the ground half a mile away.

Just east (to the left) of mile marker 4 is a field of gravel-like tephra. We've walked along here (staying mostly to the left side of the flow) and discovered incredible lava fissures and colorful blobs from five decades ago (such as the one shown in the photo on page 102), with ferns and trees already growing in them. But there is no trail, so you are on virgin, and untested, ground. This is an area where lava fountains shot into the air, and the violence from the event is evident.

Proceeding down the road, you will get an appreciation in several spots of how lava actually flowed down the mountain during the 1969–1974 Mauna Ulu eruption. At the **Alanui Kahakai turnout** (near mile marker 14) you will see a segment of the old, partially covered Chain of Craters Road. At the **Holei Pali Lookout**, just before mile marker 15, there is a great view of the mountain lava flows, where you get a feel for the volume of ʻaʻa and pahoehoe that drooled down the mountain. The newer highway cutting through the lava flow is dramatic.

About 0.3 miles past mile marker 15, you will pass a lava tube on your left. Road crews bisect them every time they cut a new road in this area.

Past mile marker 16 you will see the **Puʻu Loa Petroglyph Trail**. This 15–20 minute walk is over an old pahoehoe lava flow with cairns (mounds of rock) marking the way. (The undulating lava is a bit more tiring than flat ground.) It leads to an area studded with thousands of petroglyphs (rock carvings) representing everything from birth to death. This is the largest petroglyph field in the state. A circular boardwalk has been built near some of them to allow you to view them without walking on them. If you circle the boardwalk from both directions, you notice some you didn't see on the first pass. *Many* more carvings are located past the boardwalk, but they request that you avoid walking around to protect the perishable petroglyphs from wear. The small holes bored in the rock were usually

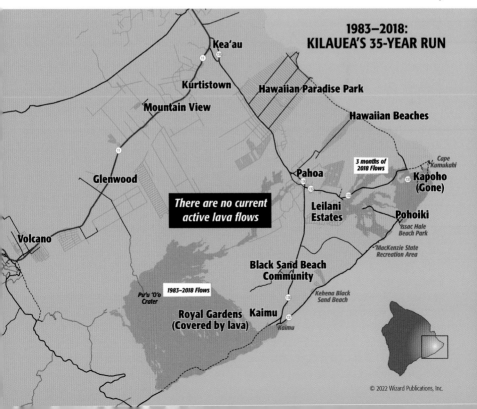

1983–2018:
KILAUEA'S 35-YEAR RUN

© 2022 Wizard Publications, Inc.

cut by parents who placed the umbilical cords from their newborns there for good luck. The area is very peaceful and worth your time if you wish to see a direct expression of ancient Hawaiian life. It's 1.5 miles round trip.

There will be a turn around before the actual pavement ends. At that turnaround, a quick walk to the ocean takes you to the **Holei Sea Arch**, where the ocean has undercut the rock, leaving an arch, but it might be closed due to cliff instability.

Past here is the **end of Chain of Craters Road** and mile after mile of desolate, barren, black lava rock as far as the eye can see. Absolutely incredible. This is where the lava usually flowed during the Pu'u 'Ō'ō eruption when it was heading toward the ocean. Sometimes lava would flow on the surface nearby, other times it would be too far inland to walk, or outside the park boundary altogether. The road you see scraped through the lava goes all the way to the other side of the lava flow. It's blocked. Can you walk or ride on it anyway? See page 120 for an explanation.

Old maps showing Kamoamoa Campgrounds, a visitor center, Waha'ula Heiau, Lae 'Apuki, Waiaka Pond, Queen's Bath, Royal Gardens, Kalapana Gardens and more are all tragically out of date. These were victims of the 1983–2018 eruption. Before you is a newly paved lava wasteland, where liquid rock has poured above and below ground, reaching the ocean and building more land. The park "Visitor Center" at the bottom is now a movable temporary building, which has had to be moved many times to avoid the fate of the last visitor center down here. They may or may not be open (to be safe, assume they won't be). If they are, they may have beverages and souvenirs available; otherwise, there's no place to refill your water bottles, so bring plenty to drink.

OUTSIDE THE PARK ENTRANCE

Just outside the park entrance there are a few sights that are worth checking out, either before or after your park visit.

If you were heading back toward Kona, **Mauna Loa Scenic Road** leads past the **Tree Molds**. These holes are created when a lava flow encounters a sopping wet tree trunk, which resists bursting into flames just long enough to harden the lava around it. They look a little like water wells with the texture of the tree bark that go pretty far down into the ground, giving a good sense of how deep the lava flow that created them must have been. No walking required—the tree molds are right at the parking area.

Farther up the road is **Kipuka Pua'ulu (Bird Park)**. A trail goes through a kipuka, an old growth of forest surrounded by newer lava flows. This kipuka features many native trees and plants, but is less visually dazzling than other hikes nearer the crater. Birds abound in this park—hence its nickname, Bird Park. The entire 1-mile stroll takes only 20–30 minutes plus stopping time. There is a bench partway along the trail, which ascends gently for the first half. If you are feeling adventurous, there is a little-explored cave near to marker No. 6 that you can worm your way into. (It opens up substantially once you get inside.)

Heading farther up Mauna Loa Scenic Road, it's tempting to speed, but the road drops to one lane with several blind turns as it passes through a pretty forest that is different from other forests in the area. No big payoff here (so don't expect an expansive view of the summit), just a lonely road that often ascends into the clouds, usually with lots of pheasants around. At

Creation meets destruction. The ocean begins dismantling the land even before it cools.

the end of the 13-mile road (at 6,650 feet) is the trailhead to **Mauna Loa Trail**. This is where you start your multi-day trek through the cold and altitude to ascend the summit of Mauna Loa. (Maybe another day.) There are picnic tables and a nice view of the park at the road's end. Though pleasant, this road is dispensable if you are budgeting your time.

Off the main highway south of the park entrance near mile marker 38 is the **Ka'u Desert Trail**, which leads less than a mile to **Footprints**. Most of these were created during the explosion of 1790 (plus a few from an earlier explosion in the 1500s). You may read or be told that the footprints are worn away because they were vandalized. The truth is apparently a little more embarrassing. Park sources have told us that park personnel tried to protect the footprints many years ago by placing a glass case over them. Their intentions were good, but when it rained, water condensed on the underside of the cracked glass and dripped onto the prints, wearing them away. That's why the display case is gone, but the vandalism rumor persists. Most personnel believe the vandalism explanation to be true to this day. Regardless, if you look around, you can still find better footprints elsewhere when shifting ash dunes permit.

Just outside the park a mile down Pi-imauna Road, you'll find **Volcano Winery** (808-967-7772). This is a good place to stop for a sip of some locally made wines. They have several unusual wines, including a local favorite, Mac Nut Honey Wine. They also have wines made from fruits— *even grapes*. Hardcore oenophiles might turn up their noses, but less finicky palates might enjoy a snort or two of the exotic. They also offer tea tastings and a few snacks. We like their sign that says "Reserved for Winos."

THE TOWN OF VOLCANO

When you first see the town of **Volcano** on a map, you figure they must spend all their time biting their nails over the active volcano crater less than 2 miles away. In fact, since they're upslope of the crater, they're safer from lava flows than Hilo or even the Kohala Resort area 50 miles away, as far as the geologists are concerned. Though extensive lava flows did cover this area about 500 years ago, the summit has since been reshaped so that today nearly all the lava flows happen on Kilauea's southern flank (away from the village). Their main threat is from falling tephra or ash from the occasional crater explosion like the one in 1790—annoying, but not as bad as a lava flow. And as for volcano smoke, normal trade winds send the smoke around the bottom of the island and up the coast where it harasses Kailua-Kona. It's ironic that this dreamy little community, set in a misty, lush fern-filled forest, can be so snug living on an active volcano.

Volcano is also a convenient place to pick up some supplies and gas (which is *breathtakingly* expensive here). If you enter the loop road from near mile marker 27, you pass by the **Volcano Store** and **Kilauea General Store and Gas Station** farther down. If you're driving back to the west side of the island, you can grab some gas or a snack before the long drive back. It's also amazingly over-represented when it comes to upscale restaurants, so consider dining here.

In addition to the hotels and inns, there are cabins at **Namakanipaio Campground** (844-569-8849). See *Camping* on page 193. Current and retired military can rent cabins at **Kilauea Military Camp** (808-967-8333) right in the park. Higher rank, higher rent.

If you like waterfalls, Rainbow Falls is a perfect example of why you'll want to drive to the Hilo side.

Hilo is a charming mix of old and new Hawai'i. Once a thriving town bolstered by limitless sugar revenues, the demise of the sugar industry has kept Hilo in a time warp. And that's the charm. Though a full-fledged city, things move slower here, and the community is tight. They've been through a lot. Slammed by tsunamis, threatened by lava flows, racked by a changing economy, Hilo has withstood it all. Hilo is also a strikingly beautiful town. Abundant rains give the flora a healthy sheen that soothes the soul. Though the exodus of business has left many of its buildings looking worn and neglected, Hilo's charms lie deeper.

Hilo's Achilles' heel is weather. Only in Hilo would water officials quake in fear and declare a drought, even encouraging water conservation, when they receive *only* 70 inches of rain in a year. (All you Arizona residents can stop laughing now.) This rain translates to an unacceptable gamble for many visitors. People are hesitant to spend precious Big Island days in a soggy place. But they forget that even if it's rain-city here, elsewhere along the eastern side things might be sunnier. Hilo is the logical gateway for exploring Puna, the easternmost part of the island, where you'll find lush rain forests, a black sand beach, and volcano-ravaged towns. Puna is also famous for its outlaws from the 20th century, guerrilla gardeners and bizarre characters.

Hilo has a reputation for being less friendly to visitors than other parts of the island. Sort of a *let da buggahs go to Kona* mentality. Though this reputation is not entirely unearned, it is also not entirely accurate. Some of the friendliest, nicest and most helpful people we've run into have been in Hilo. But we've also gotten more blank expressions and outright nastiness here.

Hilo is a ghost town on Sundays. Don't expect much of anything to be open. We'll describe sights around Hilo in a scattershot manner before heading toward Puna.

AROUND HILO TOWN

[A] Starting at the corner of Kamehameha (which fronts the bay) and Waianuenue (in northern Hilo), head southwest on Waianuenue. (See map on page 112.) When you pass the Hilo Public Library on your right, take a look at that oblong stone out front, six full strides

long. Think you can move it? At age 14 (not his 30s as the official sign claims), Kamehameha risked death (if he failed) and agreed to try to move that Naha Stone (estimated at 7,000 pounds). He did it because legend said that whoever could overturn the stone would be the first king of all the islands. At that time the stone was slightly imbedded in the ground. The ox-like youth, whose strength was unprecedented, squatted and gave a huge push—nothing. He tried and tried but could barely nudge it. As people gathered round and the priest started to come over (to condemn him to death), he summoned a final burst of strength and overturned the boulder, shocking everyone and beginning the fulfillment of his destiny.

Just off Waianuenue Street, on the corner of Haili and Kapiolani, the Lyman Museum (808-935-5021) is worth a stop.

Letters [A] correspond to paragraphs in text.

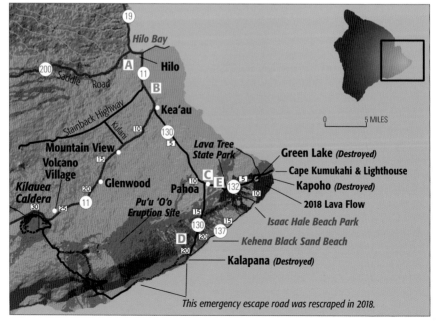

This emergency escape road was rescraped in 2018.

Tranquil parks, such as Wailoa River State Recreation Area, abound in Hilo.

The Earth Heritage exhibit alone justifies the $7 admission (reservations currently required). It has incredible displays of Hawaiian geology, plant, animal and fish life (nicely done), plus an exceptionally beautiful rock and mineral collection from around the world. Elsewhere they have Hawaiian history displays and a few other interesting items. Tours of the Lyman missionary house (built in 1838, it's the oldest framed building on the island) next door are given with a separate advance booking. Closed Saturday and Sunday.

Take the right fork after mile marker 1 and follow the signs to Rainbow Falls. These falls change dramatically depending on water flow. Moderate flow is best. (Too little and the wishbone shape is gone; too much and it's an undefined, roiling mess.) The falls are best seen in the morning when the sun is behind you. (Rainbows can only be seen when the sun is behind you, so if you ever see a photo with the sun and a rainbow in the same frame, it's fake.) The cave below the falls is where Kamehameha is said to have buried the bones of his father.

A mile farther up the road is Wailuku River Boiling Pots State Park. This series of bowl-shaped depressions roil and boil when the water flow is heavy, creating dramatic photo opportunities. From the lookout, odds are you *won't* be able to see the boiling pots because of the state's perpetual lack of vegetation grooming, which *used to mean* you'd have to take the trail to the right of the railing, but access to this trail has been closed.) So while you *can* visit the Boiling Pots State Park, you probably won't be able to see the park's namesake feature...gee, thanks.

To the left of the railings, you will see Pe'epe'e Falls. (No, it's *not* pronounced pee-pee, but rather peh-eh peh-eh, so wipe that smirk off your face.) The trail we mentioned previously used to lead the bottom of the falls, but you'll have to settle for the view from the lookout. While we're nagging, this is probably a good time to

tell you that Boiling Pots and Rainbow Falls are common places for car break-ins. We often see thieving scum casing the lots looking for unsuspecting tourist cars to rob while their drivers are away lost in the beauty.

Less than a mile up Waianuenue the road veers right. From a bridge you can see Wai'ale Falls. The amount of water is considerably more than what you saw downstream at Rainbow Falls, an impressive demonstration of how much actually seeps into the porous lava bed along the way. (It's *not* tapped at the nearby dam.) You can hike there and enjoy some wonderful pools. See *Hiking* on page 211.

Over on Kaumana Drive (see map on facing page) is Kaumana Cave. This lava tube can make for fun exploring and is described in detail in *Saddle Road Sights* on page 149 since it's usually visited by those coming into Hilo from the Saddle.

Off Komohana St. is the 'Imiloa Astronomy Center (808-932-8901), a good hands-on exhibit for kids and a pretty cool planetarium that will make you dizzy. Check their website for a schedule of shows. (They usually have one geared specifically to kids on Saturdays.) $19 for adults, $12 for kids. Closed Monday through Wednesday.

Along the bay, the grassy park fronting the town is the Hilo Bayfront. It used to be the main Japanese district, Hilo's Japan-town. On April Fool's Day 1946 a tsunami (tidal wave) of enormous height was generated by a horrific earthquake off Alaska. The tsunami lashed the entire state, but punished this part of the Big Island the most. In all, 159 people, including 21 schoolchildren in Laupahoehoe, were killed in one of the worst natural disasters in Hawai'i's history. After another tsunami killed 61 more people in 1960, town fathers decided to make this area a park

rather than risk more lives during the next tsunami. (The clock on the side of the road on Kamehameha Street in front of Naniloa Golf Course stands with its hands frozen in time—1:04 a.m.—from the 1960 tsunami. Townsfolk refurbished the clock but refused to rebuild it to working order in honor of those who died.) Tsunamis have unimaginable power. The water first recedes, exposing the ocean's floor, and then bulldozers of water come crashing in. The event can last for hours.

The Pacific Tsunami Museum (808-935-0926) is on Kamehameha and Kalakaua in the old First Hawaiian Bank Building. (You sit in the old bank vault while they show a movie of the tsunami.) It's small and mostly self-guided, though the docents there are helpful. Lots of photos, and you'll leave with a good understanding of what a tsunami is—and why it's not really a wave. Admission is $8.

If you're walking around Hilo town with the kids and need free and educational respite from the heat, stop into Mokupapapa Discovery Center (808-498-4709) on the corner of Kamehameha and Waianuenue. This small learning center has some nice displays about the history, science and marine life of the Northwestern Hawaiian Islands.

Banyan Drive, where most of Hilo's hotels are located, is named after the graceful and stately banyan trees that line the road. If a tree can look wise, then banyan trees definitely qualify. Each tree was named after the person who planted it. Familiar names such as Amelia Earhart, King George V, Babe Ruth, FDR and Richard Nixon. (In one of those ironies of life, the first tree Nixon planted was washed away on election day when he became VP.) Also on Banyan Drive is Lili'uokalani Gardens. This is one of several

A REAL GEM

graceful and serene parks in the area and is our favorite place in Hilo for a great early morning or late afternoon stroll. If you're a bit warm, look for the nearby ice pond. (See map on page 112.) Cold water intruding into this part of the bay (you can sometimes see it percolating to the surface) creates water so cold it'll give you *chicken skin kine.*

If you were to continue east along the shoreline on Kalanianaole, you would pass most of Hilo's beach parks. See *Beaches* chapter for more on these. On your way out to the parks check out a beach access across from Lokoaka Street. It is very jungly and draped with vines. The beach is worthless, but the short walking road is kind of cool as is the trail on the left, which ends at the more desirable Carlsmith Beach Park.

HEADING SOUTH ON HIGHWAY 11

[B] As you head out of town, you will pass by Hilo's biggest shopping area. Prince Kuhio Plaza, Waiakea Center, and Puainako Town Center are where you will find Safeway grocery store, Longs Drugs, Walmart and a zillion fast food restaurants.

On Hinano Street off Kekuanaoa is Big Island Candies (808-935-8890). Their locally made chocolates and cakes are *excellent*, though their prices are confiscatory. (This is a favorite stopping place for tour buses.) Good place for chocolate if you don't mind paying double-extra-super-retail. You can see their impressive operations behind giant glass windows, but refrain from calling their chocolate makers *oompa-loompas*—it irritates 'em.

The road past mile marker 4 heading west leads to Stainback Highway and the Pana'ewa Rain Forest Zoo & Gardens (808-959-7224). We haven't been too warm and fuzzy about this zoo in the past, but they've really put effort into improvements, and it shows. The grounds are lush and beautiful to the point that they have added the word "gardens" to their name. Although small and not overly impressive, it's the only zoo in the U.S. located in a tropical rain-forest, and all the animals featured are able to live comfortably in this hot,

Free energy: In Puna they used to drill for steam, supplying 25% of the island's electricity—until Madame Pele chased them away.

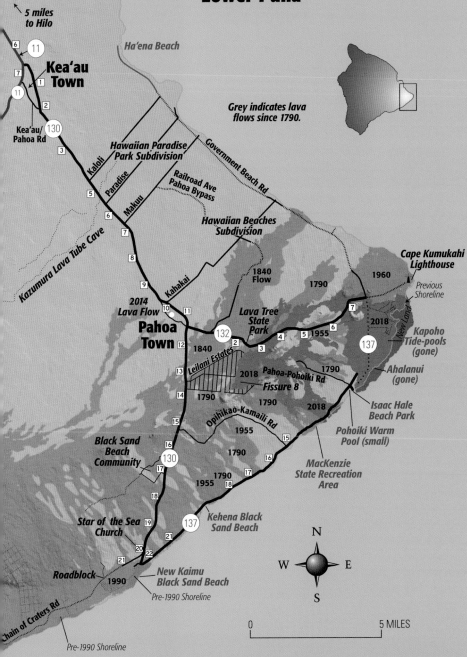

Hilo map on page 112

5 miles to Hilo

Ha'ena Beach

11

6

7

11

Kea'au Town

1

2

Kea'au/ Pahoa Rd

130

3

Kaloli

Paradise

Makuu

Hawaiian Paradise Park Subdivision

Government Beach Rd

Railroad Ave Pahoa Bypass

Hawaiian Beaches Subdivision

Grey indicates lava flows since 1790.

Cape Kumukahi Lighthouse

5

6

7

8

Kahakai

1840 Flow

1790

1960

Previous Shoreline

2018

New Land

Kazumura Lava Tube Cave

9

2014 Lava Flow

10

11

Pahoa Town

12

1840

Lava Tree State Park

132

2

3

4

5

6

7

1955

137

Kapoho Tide-pools (gone)

13

Leilani Estates

2018

Pahoa-Pohoiki Rd

Fissure 8

1790

Ahalanui (gone)

Isaac Hale Beach Park

14

1790

1790

1790

2018

15

Opihikao-Kamaili Rd

1955

15

16

Pohoiki Warm Pool (small)

Black Sand Beach Community

16

130

17

18

17

1790

18

1955

MacKenzie State Recreation Area

Star of the Sea Church

19

21

1955

1790

Kehena Black Sand Beach

20

22

137

N

W   E

S

21

Roadblock

1990

New Kaimu Black Sand Beach

Pre-1990 Shoreline

Chain of Craters Rd

Pre-1990 Shoreline

0   5 MILES

© 2022 Wizard Publications, Inc.

humid environment (so don't expect to find polar bears, but they do have two tigers). Kids should enjoy the zoo as a brief diversion, and parents will enjoy the price—it's free.

Between mile markers 5 and 6 is Macadamia Road and the Mauna Loa Visitor Center (808-966-8618). This is the mac nut giant's main processing plant, popular with tour buses and cruise ships. You can see the process (weekdays only) through the glass or pick up some of their products; otherwise, it's an expendable nut house.

If you're going to explore Puna, your best route is to take Highway 11 to 130, then take 132 to 137, and 137 to Kalapana where you link back up to 130. See map on page 110 or 115. If you want a meaningless diversion, you could continue along Stainback Highway past the zoo until it ends at the Big Island's least popular visitor attraction—our prison. This one-lane road goes for miles through an otherwise impenetrable forest, ending at over 5,000 feet elevation. There are signs saying that it is illegal to drive the road, but they were put up by the prison to cover their 'okole—they told us that it's perfectly OK to drive it as long as you're not planning to spring anyone. Some 13.75 miles into the one-lane (and dead-on straight) road is the Pu'u Maka'ala Forest Reserve. The roads in there are 4WD only, and the trails (if you can find them) are lush and wet.

The Star of the Sea Church had to be pulled from its foundations in Kalapana and moved to avoid being destroyed by an advancing lava flow.

EXPLORING PUNA

[C] Head south on Highway 130 and you come to the town of Pahoa. Known as the Big Island's outlaw town, this is where guerrilla gardeners (pakalolo farmers), dreadlock enthusiasts, FBI fugitives and the never-bathe crowd coexist without stepping on each other's toes—

usually. You'd be surprised to learn how many homes you see are built on vacant land—at least according to the County Tax Assessor's Office. Permit? What's that? To be honest, Pahoa's reputation is a little exaggerated—probably. People-watching here can be a hoot sometimes. There are a couple places to eat here that you may like, reviewed in the *Island Dining* chapter. Pahoa was in the international spotlight in 2014 due to a near-miss with a lava flow. This lava flow started more than 12 miles to the southwest of Pahoa along a vent from Pu'u 'O'o. It was predicted that the flow could reach all the way to the ocean, cutting off Pahoa and lower Puna from the rest of the island in the process.

Forest burned, fences were lost, and one home was claimed by the advancing flow. After burying the town cemetery and part of their refuse station, the flow stopped, sparing the funky town and its relieved residents. There ain't much you can do if a river of lava is coming your way, and the attempt to insulate a couple of power poles can still be seen along Pahoa-Keaau Road.

Turn south onto Hwy 130. Subdivisions in East Hawai'i often have names at odds with reality. Places like *Hawaiian Beaches Subdivision* (there are *no* beaches there), *Hawaiian Paradise Park* (it's not a park, and it sure ain't paradise) and our personal favorite up mauka of mile marker 17 on Hwy 130. It's surrounded by jungle, miles from the ocean, and is called *Black Sand Beach Community*. (The lots were probably easier to sell than if they had named it *Surrounded By Jungle Community*.)

Continuing south on Hwy 130 look for the church on the left (east) side of the road near mile marker 20. Called the Star of the Sea Church, it was built in 1928 by the same priest who created the Painted Church near Honaunau. The building was in the path of an advancing lava flow in 1990. Community members had to wrench it from its foundations to save it just in the nick of time. After sitting on the side of the road for years without a home, it was finally placed on a foundation and can now be visited. Watch for aggressive wasps flying around inside.

[D] Shortly after mile marker 22, you're confronted with the consequences of the previous Kilauea eruption. A rolling sea of hardened lava stretches in front of you. This particular flow occurred in 1990, annihilating the towns of Kalapana, Kaimu and the Royal Gardens Subdivision beyond. (See map on page 105.) Kalapana was a treasured Hawaiian fishing village, richly steeped in the traditions of the past. Its loss was a stunning blow to those wishing to keep the old ways alive.

Until the 1990 lava flow, this was also the site of the most famous black sand beach in the world. A long curving bay of jet black sand with numerous stately palm trees sprinkled about, the black sand beach at Kaimu was universally regarded as the finest. Today, it is gone, forever entombed under 50–75 feet of lava.

When the road stops, get out and walk to the top of the lava and look toward the shore. You'll notice young, sprouting coconut trees in the distance. The campaign to bring the plantings was begun by a local resident. She encouraged others in the community to take trees out to the new black sand beach 0.3 miles in front of you to begin the process of rebuilding their precious beach. Even as she was dying of cancer, residents and school children continued the tradition in her honor. Today, there are vast numbers of sprouting coconuts along the new black sand beach, a testament to the vision of one resident who refused to let her community die, even in the face of her own death.

Like people, black sand beaches have limited life spans. Once the lava flow stops, the source of the sand disappears as well, and the ocean begins robbing the sand. The new Kaimu Beach was born in 1990, but after two decades, it is mostly gone. There is still some black sand that was tossed up beyond the low sea cliffs and a thin padding of sand that's best appreciated at low tide. But the new Kaimu Beach is now mostly a memory. A hundred years from now, when every grain of black sand is gone, visitors may wonder why there are so many coconut trees along a sandless lava shoreline.

Imagine what it must be like to have grown up in Kalapana. Sights that seemed so permanent to you like the freshwater queen's bath you played in as a child, the fishing shrine that your grandfather used every day before he went fishing, that beautiful coconut grove where you had your first kiss. All these things that seemed so timeless, that came before you, and you *knew* would always be there, are now gone, erased without a trace, as if your whole world had been nuked. Kalapana residents didn't just lose their home; they lost all traces to their past and share the unique experience of having outlived their world.

A 5- to 10-minute walk straight out across the lava field on crushed red rocks leads to what's left of the new black sand beach. Don't even consider swimming there—the surf is treacherous. To the right of the trailhead are some perfect impressions of palm trees. Their dying act was to cool and harden the lava around their trunks, forever capturing the bark texture of a vanished Kalapana coconut tree. There are even some hala tree fruit moldings in the lava. A short way out onto the barren, otherwordly field of lava rock there is an "alien landing pad" its builders call the Hawai'i Star Visitor Sanctuary. It's basically a couple of poorly arranged rings of stone. "Junk rocks" as one resident called it. If aliens come all the way for *this,* they'll be mightly disappointed.

If you look at the map on page 105 you'll see another road, Hwy 130, leading toward a demolished neighborhood. For two decades, the Royal Gardens Subdivision was an odd ghost town. Cut off from the rest of the island, most but not all of

This tiny segment of Prince Road is just about all that is left of the once large, thriving community of Royal Gardens at Kalapana. Kilauea Volcano has tragically erased it from the map.

A lonely Puna road.

its homes burned and buried by lava, just a couple of hardy souls stuck around, living a surreal existence in an abandoned neighborhood. But today, all of it is now buried under lava. (Just two tiny road segments are left from the lava flow.) The last resident of Royal Gardens was finally run off by Madame Pele in 2012. During the devastating lava flows, the media and the public focused their sympathy on the people who lost their homes. The *real* people to have felt sorry for were the people who *didn't* lose their homes. You see, insurance covers loss of property, not loss of *access* to property. Imagine an insurance adjuster walking up to your now-worthless house, surrounded but untouched by a sea of hardened lava and saying, "Nothing wrong with this house; claim denied."

The narrow paved access road at the end of Hwy 130 that you drove past is a *public* road, and you *are* allowed to drive on it, despite any misleading "No Trespassing" or "Restricted Area" signs you may see. (The land on *either side* is private,

but not the road.) In about a mile the road is blocked, though it continues into the park. Because it was paid for by FEMA as an emergency bypass when Pahoa was being threatened in 2014, cars aren't allowed past the roadblock. But if you have a mountain bike, it makes for an interesting journey through new land, and we don't know of any restrictions on biking it.

You may be wondering what happens if you own oceanfront property, and the volcano creates new land in front of you (called *accreted land* for the trivia-deprived). Do you now own a larger parcel? No. You don't even own oceanfront any more! Apparently Madame Pele signed a quitclaim deed over to the state, because all newly created land goes to our hungry state government.

At that trailhead to the new Kaimu Beach you'll find some concessions, restrooms and a restaurant. The late and revered patriarch of a local family that remained after the lava flow, Uncle Robert Keli'iho'omalu, has turned his family property here into a farmers market/craft fair/music venue/kava bar (how's *that* for diversification?) Wednesday nights and Saturday mornings. If you're in the Puna area on a Wednesday evening, it is one of the best and more unusual things to do in this remote part of the island.

Leaving the end of Hwy 130, continue onto Hwy 137, which parallels the shoreline. Near where mile marker 19 *should* be (but isn't) is Kehena Beach. This is a powerful testament to the changing nature of the Big Island. This beach wasn't even here until it was created by the 1955 lava flow just past the beach. Officials created stone steps leading down to the western part of the beach. Then an earthquake in 1975 sank the beach 3 feet all at once. The lower portion of the stone steps collapsed. The steps are still there (now blocked by vegetation), ending abruptly 10 feet above the shoreline. The trailhead to the beach itself is to the left of the parking area and has its own shorter dropoff at the end. Swimming is dangerous during high surf, and the beach is often used by nudists (who don't take kindly to cameras on the beach). Be careful not to leave anything in your car here, as we've noticed lots of thieving scum casing cars.

As you drive along this stretch, realize that this is one of the least known parts of the Big Island. The vast majority of island residents and visitors never see this area, and that's a shame. It is mostly untouched and exceptionally beautiful. Take your time here. You will drive through part of the shoreline that was covered by a lava flow in 1790. (See map on page 115.) The flow killed everything in its path, leaving nothing but barren, unforgiving rock for new life to work with. Yet look at what life has managed to accomplish in these two centuries. Remember this natural rejuvenating power when you come to the modern devastation that lies ahead on this road.

About four miles past Kehena you'll come to MacKenzie State Recreation Area. Just past here is where lava from the 2018 eruption veered from the lava river and ran down the south side of Kilauea's flank and hit the ocean here. The highway was recut through the lava months later.

Isaac Hale Beach Park farther down the road is where local fishermen launched their boats for decades. The massive 2018 lava flow came to an end just before overrunning this park. Giant amounts of black sand from the ocean entry piled up in this bay, cutting off the boat ramp and creating the island's newest beach. We were excited when the new black sand beach was created, but already the ocean has erased much of it, leaving a black bouldery beach behind. Pretty, but hard to sink your toes into much of the shoreline. Since the ocean tends to be rough and intimidating here, water-seekers will sometimes take a dip in the pools created where the shore used to be. There are warning signs posted about the dangers of stagnant water, so enter at your own risk. Also, if you take the shoreline trail to the right of the boat launch for two minutes, where it veers inland, you'll come to a surprise. There, set in the vine-covered jungle but only a short walk from the shore, is a small (8-foot by 14-foot) warm water pool (called Pohoiki). The setting is heaven-sent. It's cut off from the ocean, but historically the level follows the tide, so it's deeper and more desirable at high tide if it's being refreshed. You may encounter wild pigs in the jungle here. And being a surprise participant in a notorious pig-licking incident (no, we don't want to talk about it) is a memory that will never leave you.

A wasteland of new lava is all that is past here. Reverse the way you came and read on to find out more about it.

Kapoho was built around a vast area of interconnected tide-pools.

Kapoho & Beyond—What Was Lost

[E] Lava began erupting on May 3, 2018, from Leilani Estates, a residential area below the intersection of Highways 130 and 132 in Puna. It ran for over three months and caused major damage and disruptions. The lava has stopped and Hwy 130 from Pahoa leading to Kaimu, Kalapana is open, along with Hwy 132 which passes Lava Tree State Park and ends near the coast where it intersects with Hwy 137. Highway 137 along the coast is open to Kehena Black Sand Beach, ultimately stopping at Isaac Hale Beach Park. The rest of Hwy 137 has not been cleared at press time.

After Pahoa, turn onto Hwy 132 and you'll soon come to Lava Tree State Park. Lava trees form when fast flowing pahoehoe encounters wet ʻohiʻa trees. As the flow drains away, it leaves a thick coating around the dying tree. Most of these free-standing tubes are moss-covered. You can saunter around the park in 20–60 minutes. Look for the huge chasms created during the explosive eruption of 1790. Even if you don't want to hike (there are better lava trees on the Napau Crater Trail—see page 203), take a minute to drive into the park and gawk at the regal trees that dominate the area.

Across the street from Lava Trees, beyond the treeline is Leilani Estates, the large subdivision that became the center of the volcanic world in May 2018 when an enormous lava river blasted its way to the surface, crossed the main street and wrought havoc in Lower Puna.

Shortly after Lava Trees (once they cut a new road through the lava) take the left fork where Hwy 132 continues toward Kapoho. Ever wonder where people on an island get their electricity? Well, here on the Big Island, 25% of our juice was volcano-powered. They drilled basketball-sized holes a *mile* deep, and when they did, steam shot up at pressures similar to what you'd find inside a SCUBA tank. They used the steam to turn turbines. The underground water source is naturally replaced by the ocean's pressure, so it would have lasted indefinitely—until the 2018 eruption brought lava flows onto their property that forced them to plug their wells and flee until they could make repairs. Interestingly, though the land is private, *all* mineral rights in Hawaiʻi belong to the state government (as all first-time landowners here discover to their shock). This includes "any steam over 150 °F." So, even though the private company returned the water vapor back to the ground, they have to pay the state almost $2 million a year for the steam they temporarily borrowed

The day after Kapoho was taken.

because it's considered *state steam*. (Just thought we'd pass that along, in case you were thinking of opening a gold mine here.) By the way, the cost of steam rose proportionally with the price of oil over the years. But when oil prices dropped, the price the state charged for steam never did. (Gotta be an oversight.)

Across from mile marker 5 on the left (north) side is the lava vent from the 1955 eruption. The vent is interesting to walk on. It's made up of loose and cemented blobs of airborne lava (called tephra) that fountained out of the vent. It's worth a few minutes if you want to poke around. There are opportunities for a good fall, so be careful.

The end of Hwy 132 is on lava flows from 1960. A dirt road leads out to the point. Fountains of lava 1,500 feet high produced enormous amounts of lava that wiped out the town of Kapoho, leaving only two subdivisions. Having hiked through countless lava fields on the island, this wins the prize as the harshest and most difficult to walk through we've ever encountered. (You'd have an easier time walking through the minefields of the de-militarized zone between North and South Korea than hiking through this stuff.) At

the end of the unpaved road leading to the sea is a **light tower**.

Take a deep breath. This is the eastern-most part of the island, and since our winds come from that direction, scientists use it to test "virgin air" that has drifted over the landless Pacific for many weeks. Air from here is considered as pristine as any in the world, and it is analyzed by governments around the globe and used as a benchmark to compare to their air.

While you're out on this point, you'll see a 4WD gray lava road on the right. Until 2018 it was a rough, oil pan-eating road that led 1.2 miles to Kapoho Bay. And it was worth the effort. Why would you want to do that? Simple. A truly awesome experience called **Champagne Pond** awaited.

Imagine a calm, protected ocean inlet filled with *crystal* clear water. A scattering

of fish and sometimes a turtle or two (or *nine,* our personal record here). Fine, you say. There are lots of places with that. Maybe. But how many of them are *heated*? Sparkling clean freshwater heated by the volcano percolated from the ground. It was not Jacuzzi-hot, but rather relax-ing-warm (around 90 °F on top). This was in a gated residential community called Vacationland, and the lava road was the only way to legally access Champagne Pond. Today it's gone, paved over by the massive lava flow described below.

Back at the corner of Hwys 132 and 137, you'll want to head south on 137. But if you feel like a different kind of forest drive, head north first for 5 miles or so. It goes from stark lava to a luxuriant jungle filled with birds almost instantly. One positive result of the lava activity is that some previously very rough roads (such as this one) were improved. This was so residents could evacuate had the flow cut off travel along Hwy 130. It also means that access to some pretty parts of Puna has improved. Here dense jungle and violent, rocky shores (there's no good swimming along this stretch, so don't even try) make for cool scenery. There is even a large grove of mango trees along the road deemed "exceptional" by the county. Turn around when you get to Hawaiian Beaches subdivision at Kahakai Road and return to Hwys 132 and 137 when you're done.

Heading south on Hwy 137 you will see an impressive cinder cone on your right. This cone was the home of a small but 200-foot deep lake called Green Lake. It was created during an eruption 500 years ago. In June 2018 new lava flows from Kilauea did an extraordinary thing. Scientists are normally pretty good about creating maps that show where lava is likely to flow by using slight depressions in the land. When lava coming from a vent 5 miles to the west was approaching the cinder cone, they thought it would go a different direction. What they didn't take into account was the temperature. This flow was the hottest lava that had ever come out of Kilauea. And hotter lava has a thinner viscosity. When it got to the area, it was so thin and of such massive volume, it simply followed the roadbed of Hwy 132. When it slithered around the north side of the cinder cone, it took gravitational advantage of a depression leading into the cone and poured into Green Lake, evaporating the entire body of water in 90 minutes.

After this, the lava flow turned back toward the ocean, widened and set its sights on Kapoho.

There was nothing like Kapoho anywhere in Hawai'i. Dozens and dozens of spring-fed, brackish pools and tide-pools, some volcanically heated, were strewn throughout the area known as the Kapoho Tide-pools. Many of the land-locked pools were incorporated into people's front and back yards as swimming pools. The large pools adjacent to the ocean (called Wai'opae Ponds) were on public property and contained some of the most fascinating snorkeling around. The largest pool snaked its way to the ocean, rising and falling each day with the tide. This created slight currents that were fun to ride. Having lived in Kapoho at one point, I spent many hours in the tide-pools and counted eight kinds of coral. Toward the back (west) a couple of pools were slightly heated by the volcano.

There were hundreds of private homes and vacation rentals available here, and I wept in anguish that terrible day when the broad lava flow literally erased Kapoho from the map, filling in the bay and tide-pools. For me, that was the day the eruption became personal. Lava flows had always been a sense of wonder and delight for me. I must admit I had always felt a certain detachment from the destructive aspect. But not on that June day. I had to struggle to remind myself of this painful but all-too-true reality:

A LOST GEM

No one really owns any of the lands on the flanks of Kilauea. We are merely tenants. And Madame Pele reserves the right to serve an eviction notice any time she wants. This is the way of things and has been for eons.

Farther down Hwy 137 past mile marker 10 was Ahalanui. This delightful gem was a spring- and ocean-fed pool with a manmade wall and an inlet separating it from the ocean. Although the original builders created this spot when the water was *ice cold*, the Kapoho eruptions of 1955 and 1960 reworked the lava plumbing here so that instead of coming out cold, this pool was *volcanically heated* to a toasty 91–95 °F.

With palm trees all around and the sound of the surf over the seawall, this was considered a genuine Pele bath. But that description became all too literal in July 2018 when the eruption swerved to the south and bulldozed this park with lava. And so, Ahalanui is no more.

A LOST GEM

As mapmakers we couldn't help but notice that this area called Puna, which receives *lots* of rain and is the size of Moloka'i, doesn't have a *single* river or stream—not even an intermittent one. The reason? The land's too new. Rain that falls simply seeps into the porous lava. If you get a chance to hike in a lava tube, you'll see it dripping from the ceiling on its way to recharging the vast water table below.

HILO & PUNA BEST BETS

Best Way to Wrench Your Back— Duplicating Kamehameha's Feat of Lifting the Naha Stone
Best Waterfall—Rainbow Falls
Best *Secluded* Waterfall—Wai'ale Falls
Best Shakedown—State Charging for Use of Steam at Puna Geothermal
Best (But Probably Unnecessary) Outdoor Gear—Bear Spray from S. Tokunaga Store
Best Place to Nuke Your Cholesterol Count—Café 100
Best Burger—Hilo Burger Joint

Yeah, so imagine a lava river like this opening up in your neighborhood, the way it did in Leilani Estates.

The lush waterfalls of the Hamakua Coast contrast with this rolling countryside of Waimea, creating one of the best drives on the Big Island.

When local residents speak of driving between Hilo and Kona, they either "drive the saddle" or they "take the upper road." The upper road is the stretch of Highway 19 between Hilo and Waimea. It passes through magnificent country reminiscent of old Hawai'i. Along the way you can check out numerous waterfalls, drive along stunning gorges, gaze over (or go into) an Eden-like valley, or check out Hawai'i's premiere ranch town, home to one of the country's largest private ranches, Parker Ranch. Part of this drive is actually in the districts of North and South Hilo, but that distinction is lost on the driver.

We'll start our description from the Hilo side. (If you're coming the other way, just turn the book upside down.) It's best to start this drive in the morning since the waterfalls and much of the best scenery face east.

Highway 19 was constructed to make it easier and faster to travel this part of the island. Consequently, most people are totally unaware of the almost forgotten stretches of road that make up the old highway. We have a particular fondness for these diversions off the highway and point them out as Diversion Alerts.

LEAVING HILO BEHIND

[A] Heading north (see map on page 127) you will see a cemetery on the mauka side past mile marker 4. Take Nahala Street on the ocean side, then turn left at the T. You pass by **Honoli'i Beach Park.** This is the primo surfing and boogie boarding spot on this side of the island.

DIVERSION

ALERT!

There are stairs leading down to the black sand beach. The road continues around the back of the stream. When it ends, hang a right to go back to the highway, then left. This is probably a good time to mention that, while stopping at scenic spots along here, during certain times of the year, it's a good idea to have mosquito repellent. Sometimes they are absent; other times they are ferocious. Feeling lucky?

Past mile marker 7 is the only part of the old highway that is marked. This 4-mile **scenic route** is breathtaking—do *not* miss it—and leads past the **Hawai'i Tropical Botanical Garden** (808-964-5233). (Consider the 4-mile drive a "Not To Be Missed.") You don't have to be a "garden person" to appreciate this *stunningly* beautiful area that fronts Onomea Bay. For $25 ($12 for kids 6–16 years

A REAL GEM

old), you wander on a self-guided tour for about an hour through over 2,500 exotic types of marked flora. (Umbrellas are thoughtfully provided, but mosquito repellent is extra.) Birds abound in this Eden-like setting. The smell of flowers and fruit (especially mangos) fills the air. **Onomea Falls** is located on the grounds, which makes a nice place to stop and take in the surroundings. Views of the bay are unbeatable. $25 is pretty steep for a garden, but this is the Big Island's best. If you want a free taste of the environment there, a trail on the ocean side just before the HTBG visitor center leads to the shoreline. A guard will politely keep you from accidentally wandering onto garden grounds.

Past the garden on the old highway you'll cross two, one-lane bridges. The second is a historic, wooden bridge that spans **Kawainui Stream**. The stream

Letters **[A]** *correspond to paragraphs in text.*

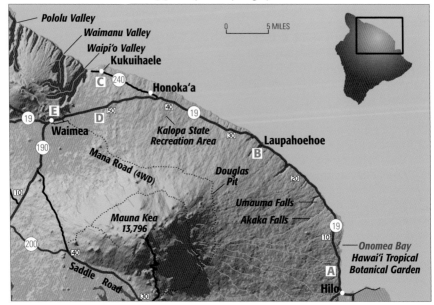

flows through a man-made tunnel (not an old lava tube as local lore tells). If there haven't been heavy rains recently, this is also a great swimming hole. (Lots of rain turns it into a washing machine and you into a rag doll). There's space for two to three cars on the side of the road here. The trail down, next to the parking spot, is steep and requires climbing down tree roots and over rocks. (Not recommended for little ones or those in flip-flops.) There are a couple of large boulders under the bridge here that make for a great place to lounge in the sun and listen to the water rush through the tunnel. Weekends often have a number of people enjoying this spot, but weekdays you'll probably have it to yourself.

A mile past the garden is a food stand called What's Shakin' (808-964-3080) that serves exceptionally good smoothies. (They make 'em the way you're *supposed* to make 'em—starting with frozen bananas, not ice—*oh, yeah...*) They also have a small lunch menu with dependably great food.

Back on the highway between mile markers 13 and 14 is a 3.75-mile road through former sugar land to 'Akaka Falls. This free-fall plunge of 420 feet is best seen in the late morning. It's $10 per car to park in the lot—free outside the parking lot—*and* $5 per person to walk in. They certainly aren't spending the money keeping the views open, and the bottom of the falls might be obscured unless you climb on the railings. If you're in a hurry, walk left 3–5 *beautiful* minutes through lush vegetation and over streams to the lookout for the falls. There you'll find silver/white strands forming as the water hits the rocks on the way down. Otherwise, there is a 0.5-mile, 15–20-minute amble (with *lots* of steps) through the lush bamboo-filled woods along with another waterfall lookout. (Though the latter, Kahuna Falls, is largely blocked by vegetation.) The full loop is recommended if you have the time. Everything's paved. After visiting 'Akaka Falls, consider checking out the shops in Honomu on the way back down the hill. It's a small community, and you can usually find at least a decent cup of coffee and some locally made crafts.

NOT TO BE MISSED!

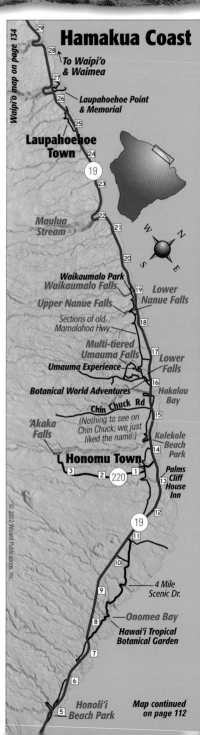

Hamakua Coast

Waipi'o map on page 134

29
28 To Waipi'o & Waimea
27
26 Laupahoehoe Point & Memorial
25
24 Laupahoehoe Town
19
23
22
21 Maulua Stream
20
Waikaumalo Park
Waikaumalo Falls
19 Lower Nanue Falls
Upper Nanue Falls
Sections of old Mamalahoa Hwy
18
Multi-tiered Umauma Falls
17 Lower Falls
Umauma Experience
16
Botanical World Adventures
Hakalau Bay
Chin Chuck Rd
(Nothing to see on Chin Chuck; we just liked the name.)
15
'Akaka Falls
Kolekole Beach Park
14
Honomu Town
3 2 220 1
Palms Cliff House Inn
13
12
19
11
10
4 Mile Scenic Dr.
9
Onomea Bay
8
Hawai'i Tropical Botanical Garden
7
6
5 Honoli'i Beach Park

© 2022 Wizard Publications, Inc.

Map continued on page 112

As you continue on Highway 19, there is another piece of old road to take. It's shortly after mile marker 14 on the mauka (mountain) side. It leads past **DIVERSION** **Kolekole Park**. The massive highway bridge in front of you was part of an old railway. The **ALERT!** great tsunami of 1946 carried away many of the girders, rendering the bridge useless. This was the deathblow for the railway, sparking the construction for the entire highway. This park is currently closed by the state while they assess lead contamination associated with the bridge. This is where the water from 'Akaka Falls ends up, so if you lost something up there, maybe you'll find it here.

If you stay on this road, it crosses the highway, curves left and empties into Hakalau Bay. A rich, vine-filled forest dripping with life ushers you into the bay. The ruins at the mouth on the east bank are from a mill destroyed during the tsunami. The swimming here is poor, but you can't say that about the view. Backtrack to the highway.

The bridge past mile marker 16 boasts nice views of two waterfalls. As impressive as they are, they don't even come close to the multi-tiered beauty of **Umauma Falls** upstream. This may be the most stunning waterfall setting in the state. You can only see it by visiting the **Umauma Experience** (see page 233) and paying $12 or going on one of their zipline tours. (See the photo on page 130 to see if it's worth it to you.)

Whether you want to pay for the falls or not, while you're on the highway, *be sure* to backtrack 0.2 miles from the highway bridge turnout, then take the road on the mauka side across from mile marker 16 and turn right at the T. This 4-mile-long, one-lane country road passes through sugar land before it takes you to a small tree tunnel and several striking gulches. This is the Hawai'i of yesteryear, when life moved a bit slower. You might want to do the same. Stop at one of the old bridges and enjoy the peace. Vine-covered trees and ever-chirping birds give this area an unforgettable feel.

Early into this road is the **Botanical World Adventures** (808-731-

What a drop! 'Akaka Falls tumbles 420 feet.

Hamakua is farm country. Tree farms, that is.

1160). Originally just a garden, they now include (pricey) Segway tours, a zipline course, and a (football field-sized) hedge maze. The grounds are huge and showcase tropical plants from around the world. Kids will like the hedge maze, but you may have some spider webs to dodge. (You'd be amazed how quickly you can find the exit when pulling spiderwebs from your hair.) Entry for self-guided garden tour is $25. Be sure to bring mosquito repellent.

Just past the botanical gardens, across from a sign that says "The Umauma Experience," is a bridge. If you park across from that sign, there is a super-short, steep, treacherous (especially when muddy) trail that leads down to a pretty waterfall and perch from which to observe it. From looking at county TMK maps, it *appears* that the land here is part of a roadway easement, meaning you're allowed to be there, but it's hard to say for certain.

Still on this 4-mile back road, one of the small Depression-era bridges crosses

DIVERSION Nanue Stream (it's stamped into the bridge). The nearside of the bridge has a crude and **ALERT!** *steep* trail that leads down to the stream. From there a person could walk over to the top of the falls (don't fall off), or go upstream where another waterfall awaits. (The upstream falls, though only 900 feet away, require *very* awkward stream hiking. See *Adventures* on page 243.) If you don't have mosquito repellent, be prepared for the bloodletting of a lifetime.

Bypass any opportunities to reconnect with the highway until you pass rarely used Waikaumalo Park near a pretty stream.

Umauma Falls is one waterfall on the island you have to pay to see. Is it worth it? You decide...

When you reacquire the highway just north of mile marker 19, you may want to backtrack less than a mile to see the densely jungled gulch and waterfall visible from the highway that you missed before continuing north.

As you effortlessly cruise these gulches on our modern bridges of today, try to visualize what a nightmare it must have been to cross them in days gone by. It took many days to get from Hilo to **Waipi'o Valley**. When author Isabella Bird toured this area on horseback in 1873, she wrote of the utter dread she felt as she plunged down and then trudged up gulch after harrowing gulch on her way to Waipi'o, fording raging streams on a snorting, terrified horse. Today, the hardest thing about traversing these gulches is resetting the cruise control after a sharp bend.

[B] Just past mile marker 25 is the road leading mauka to the town of **Laupahoehoe**. (The short road on the ocean side sports a nice view of the point mentioned below.) The town itself doesn't offer much. If you're looking for some lunch or just road snacks, the **Papa'aloa Country Store & Café** (808-339-7614) is down a road on the ocean side of the Hwy 0.3 mile past mile marker 24. (See *Island Dining*.)

Also on the highway is the **Laupahoehoe Train Museum** (808-962-6300). This assortment of artifacts and photos of Hamakua's history with trains is somewhat interesting. They have over a dozen volunteers. Some are extremely knowledgeable…and some aren't. It's $10. Monday, Tuesday, Wednesday and Friday. By appointments only other days. 10 a.m.–2 p.m.

Just past mile marker 27 is a road on the ocean side that leads 1 mile down the cliffs to **Laupahoehoe Point**. To many on the Big Island, Laupahoehoe is associated with tragedy. During the April Fool's

DIVERSION

ALERT!

Day tsunami of 1946, 21 schoolchildren and three adults were swept to their deaths. Following this, the village was moved topside. The views from the road down to the rugged point sport dramatic views of the sea cliffs beyond and is well worth the stop. There is a memorial at the bottom to those who lost their lives. From out on the jetty, the ocean's energy feels raw and menacing. Waves come in with powerful anger. You feel (and are) exposed to the ocean's fury on the jetty. Here it's not the calm, soothing ocean of Kona, but rather the unpredictable, hot-tempered ocean of Laupahoehoe. Away from the jetty the surf pounds against the twisted and jagged lava and is spectacular to watch, especially when surf's up, but don't even *think* of swimming here at any time. In 1985 a barge full of brand new Toyotas broke loose from its tug and washed ashore near here, spilling the entire cargo. When an insurance adjuster from Lloyd's of London came to check it out, he insisted on landing on the deck of the wrecked ship in a helicopter. Then a wave knocked the chopper over, drowning the adjuster. Surf is almost always violent here.

This whole area was once dominated by sugar. Over 70,000 acres of the Big Island were under cultivation. Even with generous government subsidies, the last mill shut down in 1996, ending 150 years of sugar production. Today this area has a different look and a different crop. More than 24,000 acres of fast-growing eucalyptus trees were planted. Harvesting is ongoing, so you may see logging trucks carrying their loads to a power plant in Pepe'ekeo to be burned.

Since sugar was king for so many years here, how did they move their crops to boats offshore? The coastline along here is all sea cliffs. One example is still accessible. At 0.75 miles past mile marker 35 there is an abrupt right turn available. The one-lane paved road cuts through the forest toward the ocean. Sometimes it's gated. When it ends, turn right. At .3 miles after a one-lane bridge there's a dirt road on the left. Follow it until it ends. Then take the trail toward the left, which goes through buffalo grass and ultimately takes you to a deep channel cut through the lava, ending at concrete stairs. You're now at sea level, and the dramatic sea cliffs are on both sides. The view is smashing. Avoid on weekends when families use the area for other purposes.

Between mile markers 39 and 40 is the road to Kalopa State Recreation Area, which offers nice hiking and camping.

HONOKA'A

Near mile marker 42 is a road through the town of Honoka'a. Most merely use it to get to Waipi'o Valley, described below. It's got a little touch of old Hawai'i feel and is a good place to shop for antiques. There are also a few places to eat that are mentioned in *Island Dining*.

WAIPI'O VALLEY

[C] Waipio Valley Road down into the valley is currently closed to visitors and island residents who don't live in the valley. The county hired a consulting company which concluded that the road conditions made it unsafe. There has not been an announcement as to when the road will be reopened at press time. The lookout is still open, but you won't be able to drive (or hike) down into the valley for now.

Waipi'o Valley is as beautiful a place as you will ever see. With unimaginably steep walls on all sides, waterfalls etching the perimeter, fields of taro and a luscious mile-long black sand beach, Waipi'o never fails to impress. The instant you arrive at

A REAL GEM

the lookout above this awesome spectacle, you realize why this place was so special to the ancient Hawaiians. Because of its inspiring and tranquilizing effects, Waipi'o was often chosen as the meeting place for chiefs when important decisions, such as the succession of the king, were made. Even the kings who resided in sunny Kona had residences in Waipi'o Valley. According to Hawaiian legend, Waipi'o Valley was gouged out by a powerful warrior with his club to demonstrate his power. (Unfortunately, the warrior was himself clubbed to death by the one he was trying to impress.)

At one time thousands of people lived here, meticulously cultivating the lush valley floor with everything from bananas to taro to coconuts. Even Waipi'o pigs were considered tastier here in the Big Island's breadbasket. During times of famine, you could always count on Waipi'o Valley for much-needed sustenance. Fifty generations of Hawaiians have lived and died here, and they believe that the spiritual mana, or supernatural power left by those departed, is preserved and felt to this day.

The peace of Waipi'o Valley was shattered by the great tsunami of 1946 that washed away nearly everything. Most people moved away, and the valley was left mostly wild for two decades. Then in the '60s and early '70s people started trickling back in. Most were hippies and recently discharged veterans who wanted to "get away from it all." Others soon joined. These days Waipi'o is populated by a colorful assortment of 50 or so characters (including an inordinate number of guys named Dave). Many have turned their backs on traditional society; others simply live there to experience the grace of nature at its grandest. Lots of feuds take place down here, and it's not uncommon for one to result in a building getting torched. Police hesitate to get involved in Waipi'o disputes, so residents usually settle things on their own.

Those who live in the valley have no power, water, sewage, phones, cell or TV coverage. Solar power and generators provide the electricity they need. (A few nearside residents have phones and power courtesy of small lines stretching down into the valley.) They share their valley with two herds of wild horses (the swamp horses and the bush horses) that were left by the departing residents after the tsunami of '46. The horses can get pesky if they want something (such as apples, which they *love*), so don't turn your back on 'em. There are people who live "topside" and come down daily or on weekends to tend their taro patches.

Land ownership is a big issue. Even the biggest, most powerful landowner in Hawai'i, Bishop Estate, has trouble proving how much of the valley they own. Dueling surveyors keep boundaries in flux. When Bishop tried to block access to a beach parcel in 1997, all of their signs were torn down and Bishop gave up.

Until the road closed, the allure of Waipi'o Valley beckoned outsiders. Visitors and residents alike enjoyed the splendor of Waipi'o. Experienced surfers and boogie boarders rode the waves off the black sand beach. Horseback rides were popular. And Waipi'o Valley Shuttle took groups down the steep road. This doesn't mean Waipi'o was ablaze with activity, even before the road closed. To you and me, Waipi'o looks like a quiet, peaceful location. But if you've had the place all to yourself for years, even a few people a week would seem like a crowd. The residents here range from the friendly to the grouchy to the very weird. We've found that we've been less likely to get a smile or a wave in this valley than anywhere else on the island, in sharp contrast to the friendly folks in Kukuihaele and Honoka'a. Stink eye (dirty looks) and overall unfriendliness from some residents is common. Perhaps it's because they see visitors as antithetical to the reason they chose to live in Waipi'o in the first place.

Getting into the Valley

OK, sure, the road is closed for now, but you might as well know what it was like, because honestly, driving into Waipi'o Valley was half the experience.

Back when the valley was open to visitors, it was practically forbidden to even *consider* driving a regular car down Waipi'o Valley Road. The paved one-lane road down into the valley has a ridiculously steep 25% grade. Vehicles with 4WD—*not* AWD or all-wheel drive—and low gears (so you don't burn up your brakes) were able to make it down the 900-foot descent (in less than a mile). Regular cars simply couldn't.

Waipi'o Valley is a lush wonderland where taro farming is still the main occupation.

Waipi'o Valley & Old Mamalahoa Hwy

Next map on page 127

40 Miles to Hilo

Old Mamalahoa Hwy

Hotel Honoka'a Club

Golf

Honoka'a

Lehua

Kalehua

Ahualoa

Kahana Rd

Hamakua Ditch

Old Mamalahoa Hwy

(New) Mamalahoa HWY
(Hawaii Belt Rd)

Hamakua Coast Hwy / Mamane St

Cave #3
20°02.834'
155°32.563'

Dahana Ranch

Indicates Foot Trails
Roadside mile markers
Unpaved Roads
Public Access in Waipi'o
Cave

Barrier

4WD only

Unpaved 2WD usually OK

Kukuihaele

Hamakua Ditch

Waiulili Falls

Kaluahine Falls

Exceptional view from this switchback

Waipi'o Bay

Hi'ilawe Falls

Mud Lane

Old Mamalahoa Hwy

To Waimanu Valley

Muliwai Trail

Waipi'o Valley

Falls

Gate

Note: Dirt roads shown as dashed yellow lines in Waipi'o Valley are county roads. The road to the beach from Waipi'o Valley Road is owned by Kamehameha Schools, which has traditionally allowed access to everyone.

1 Mile To Waimea

Nearly all of the coast in this area is composed of sea cliffs.

2 MILES

© 2022 Wizard Publications, Inc.

Map continued on page 137

(There is a wad of metal that was once a two-wheel drive truck below one of the turns left by someone who thought otherwise. He miraculously survived by jumping from the vehicle just as it started tumbling down the almost vertical plunge.) You would probably be violating your rental car agreement if you brought your SUV down here, meaning that they wouldn't come save your bacon if it broke down. Turnouts were the only way to navigate the one-lane road with other cars around. Downhill traffic yielded to uphill traffic due to the extreme angle. While driving up the road, that steep grade made it feel like your vehicle was about to flip over backward. (Lance Armstrong once biked up the road on a bet in just over *9 minutes*.)

While the overlook sports an unforgettable view of the valley and along the coast, it gives you only a taste of what the valley has to offer. The view from the valley floor with its numerous waterfalls is even better.

Waipi'o Valley Shuttle used to be the best route into the valley for anyone who didn't have a vehicle (or the nerve) fit for the road. They had been operating tours since the '70s, and while we didn't usually do guided tours, they were a good outfit.

Some folks opted to trade horsepower for mule power. **Waipi'o Valley Wagon Tours** would take people down into the valley on a mule-driven wagon, just like they used to do in the olden days. The trip took twice as long, but you got to see the valley in a way that you just couldn't behind a wheel.

Horseback riding was also a popular activity. **Na'alapa Stables–Waipi'o** operated an outstanding Waipi'o tour that would take you deep into the valley for some *excellent* views.

For some people, the best way to get into Waipi'o was on foot. There was a hike that would take you less than a mile to get to the valley floor (though it sure *felt* like 5 miles coming back up).

The wild horses of Waipi'o Valley ain't exactly cute—or patient. This one is saying,"You got an apple and I WANT it!"

At the bottom of the valley is **Waipi'o Beach**. You can still see it from the lookout, but seeing it from the top of the valley doesn't give you the full picture. Sure, it's picturesque from up here, but anyone who went to the bottom of the valley would see that the beach is often treacherous to swim in unless the surf is real calm. Rip currents are a constant problem and the power of the waves is impressive. Legend states that the door to the underworld is near Waipi'o Beach, so Hawaiians were always careful where they camped, lest they should take the one-way trip there themselves.

The back part of Waipi'o Valley is awesome. In the first nook you could see twin falls of staggering heights. One of the falls is periodically shut off by Bishop Estate. (We *assume* that still happens but can't say for certain because we aren't allowed into the valley.) The falls on the right, **Hi'ilawe Falls**, is 1,450 feet high with a free fall of 1,200 feet, the highest on the island. There isn't a good vantage point outside of the valley, but trust us—the falls are there.

Getting Around the Valley

Waipi'o was so idyllic and peaceful that most folks felt compelled to dig in and explore. But the fact is that, other than the roads we show in yellow on the map, the rest of the valley is privately owned and jealously guarded. There are still residents in Waipi'o today, and many of them used to get downright grumpy towards visitors wandering around. This has always been the case with Waipi'o, but we feel some responsibility for steering visitors into the back of the valley. We hope that, if there's any good to come of the road being closed, there's a bit of peace and quiet for Waipi'o residents.

When we did our very first edition, we went down to the county building to diligently research road access in the valley. County personnel took out great big TMK maps and showed us that the roads leading to the back of the valley were "government roads," and we eagerly labeled them as such on our maps. In a later edition, we went back to the county and were shown the same TMK maps. But that time we dug deeper. We looked up ownership of every single parcel that *make up* the road. Lo and behold, most of the "government road" was actually private. What we found is that you could wander down to the bottom of Waipio Valley Road, and about as far back as the second stream crossing, where there used to be an "End of County Road" sign. After that, Waipi'o Valley was pretty much all private parcel.

Visitors traditionally were allowed to use the beach, despite a variety of odd signs over the years. There was also a wonderful hike to the neighboring **Waimanu Valley**, which offered a *far* grander view of Waipi'o than the automobile lookout. You could see the back of the valley, the twin falls, and a whole lot more. **Waimanu** is much farther along the trail, and while the valley is utterly gorgeous, devoid of residents, and *used* to permit camping to those willing to make the trek, there isn't a good way in without getting into Waipi'o first, so it is similarly off limits now. You can still see the zigzagging trail from the lookout if you look to the other side of the valley.

Anyway, even with the road closed, you can see that Waipi'o is an unusually calm valley. It felt wrong to have a guide to the island without at least *describing* the immense beauty of this place. We're anxious to hear more about the road situation, but for now, we're leaving this section in as a love letter to one of the greatest gems on Big Island.

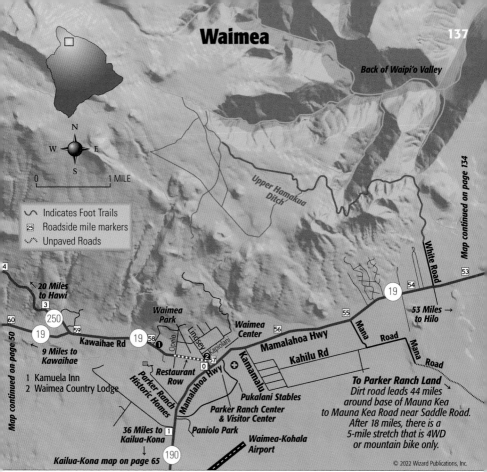

Back of Waipi'o Valley

Map continued on page 134

Upper Hamakua Ditch

White Road

53

54

19

53 Miles → to Hilo

55

Indicates Foot Trails
25 Roadside mile markers
Unpaved Roads

0   1 MILE

4

20 Miles to Hawi
3

60

250

19

59

Kawaihae Rd

19

58

Waimea Park

Waimea Center

56

Mamalahoa Hwy

Kahilu Rd

Mana Road

Mana Road

To Parker Ranch Land
Dirt road leads 44 miles around base of Mauna Kea to Mauna Kea Road near Saddle Road. After 18 miles, there is a 5-mile stretch that is 4WD or mountain bike only.

9 Miles to Kawaihae

1 Kamuela Inn
2 Waimea Country Lodge

Lindsey

Kapiolani

'Opelo

2
57
0

Restaurant Row

Parker Ranch Historic Homes

Mamalahoa Hwy

Kamamalu

Pukalani Stables

Parker Ranch Center & Visitor Center

36 Miles to Kailua-Kona

1

Paniolo Park

Waimea-Kohala Airport

Kailua-Kona map on page 65

190

Map continued on page 50

© 2022 Wizard Publications, Inc.

OLD MAMALAHOA HIGHWAY

[D] Leaving Waipi'o and Honoka'a behind, get back on Hwy 19. Along this stretch of the highway, between mile markers 43 and 52, there is another forgotten piece of the Old Mamalahoa Highway.

DIVERSION
ALERT!

Again the scenery on Old Mamalahoa is much nicer than Hwy 19 and worth the diversion. Lush, green hillsides bracket this old country road. Mist and rain mean that lovers of green will be very happy. If you like caves, there are several along Old Mamalahoa Highway. The best, by far, is labeled on the map as Cave #3. You should bring two flashlights. (There are lots of long chambers snaking pitch black into the mountain and, though tall enough to walk upright in, you'd be groping till the cows come home if you lost your only flashlight toward the back of some of these chambers.) The entrances are often dripping with ferns. Cave #3 has lots of structures inside (such as walls and platforms), presumably built by early Hawaiians, and a few empty drinking bottles, presumably left a bit later. It's 1.5 miles from Dahana Ranch Road or 2.25 miles from where Kahana meets Old Mamalahoa Highway. The other caves labeled are much less impressive. These caves are in old Mauna Kea flows, and it's unusual for lava tube caves to last so long.

WAIMEA

[E] This town is often labeled Kamuela on maps. That's because there are two other Waimeas in the state, so the Post

Office named the local branch Kamuela—Hawaiian for Samuel (as in Samuel Parker; see below). Many locals object to the use of Kamuela, so we will use the original name in deference.

On the surface, Waimea seems like the least Hawaiian town in Hawai'i. In fact, if Scotty beamed you here and asked you where you were, Hawai'i would probably be the last state you'd guess. At 2,600 feet, the air has a cool crispness to it. Clouds slither over the saddle between Kohala and Mauna Loa volcanoes, often bathing Waimea in a cool fog. Evergreen trees and cactus sit side by side, and the trees all seem blown in one direction. (Kind of like your hair if you've rented a convertible.) Rather than seeing surfers in shorts and aloha shirts, you're more apt to see Hawaiian cowboys (called paniolo) wearing blue jeans and driving pickup trucks.

Life runs a little slower here, and families are a bit closer knit. Many people compare its appearance to a Northern California rural town, but prettier. As you drive through town from the east side of the island, note how quickly the terrain changes from lush upland forests and green pastures to dry lava scrubland. If it's raining in Waimea (a common occurrence) and you're heading to Kohala via Hwy 19, it'll stop raining less than 5 minutes after you leave Waimea—*guaranz, brah.*

Don't be lulled into thinking that Waimea is a hick town. It is remarkably over-represented when it comes to fine shopping and has several restaurants that are utterly superb. Some of the homes up in the Waimea Homesteads where the descendants of cattle magnates live are absolutely beautiful.

Be careful if you take the Waimea Bypass. It *looks* wide open, but is a notorious 25 mph speed trap.

PARKER RANCH

The town is dominated by the legacy of John Palmer Parker. When Captain George Vancouver brought long-horned cattle to Kamehameha as a gift in 1793, the king made them kapu (off limits) for 10 years to build up the numbers. By 1815 the wild herds that roamed Kohala were so ferocious that locals steered clear of them. Marauding cattle were known to drive Hawaiians from their homes by munching and goring everything in sight—even the homes themselves. **Kamehameha the Great** hired Massachusetts-born John Palmer Parker to shoot them, salt the meat and bring it to the harbor to sell to passing ships. This was no easy task. Long-horned cattle of that time were not like the tame, mindless morons we know today. They were wily, lean and stealthy. They would charge men on horseback, goring them. They lived in the valleys and canyons as well, making them very difficult to detect. Good horses became the equivalent of hunting dogs—they would smell the wild cattle before they saw them, and their ears would perk up, warning their rider to the danger. Because Parker possessed a musket and good shooting skills, Kamehameha made him the first person ever allowed to kill the

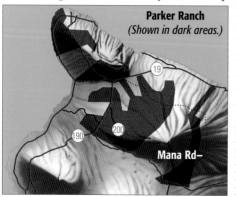

Parker Ranch
(Shown in dark areas.)

19

190   200

Mana Rd—

cattle. Parker took great pains to select cattle with favorable traits and kept them for himself as payment. These he domesticated, starting the Parker herd.

As a totally irrelevant aside, one of the casualties of these cattle was the Scottish botanist David Douglas. He's the guy for whom Douglas fir trees were named. He was walking near Mana Road (see map on facing page) on the slopes of Mauna Kea one day when he fell into one of the covered pits used as a cattle trap. (Some said he was thrown in.) Although he was lucky enough to survive the fall, so was the bull already occupying the pit. The unhappy bovine made his displeasure known by goring Douglas to death. A lonely stone memorial to Douglas by the pit where he died is 28 miles into Mana Road from Waimea (see map on page 126), or 17.7 if coming from Mauna Kea Access Road. Look for the sign and follow the short path.

John Parker himself was a colorful character. A lover of adventure, he was a natural born risk-taker who, though a long-range planner, felt strongly that part of wisdom is to know the value of today. He was well loved and respected by his contemporaries. (But he sure wasn't very photogenic—in his sour photo he makes Ebenezer Scrooge look like Spongbob Squarepants.)

In 1816 John Parker married Kamehameha the Great's granddaughter, forever cementing the bond between him and the royal family. He was eventually allowed to purchase 2 acres of land. His wife, because of her royal blood, was later granted 640 acres, and he bought another 1,000 acres. Thus was born what would become, until the 1990s, the largest privately owned cattle ranch in the entire United States, peaking at over 225,000 acres, 9% of the Big Island. Parker and his descendants would go on to become very powerful on the island.

Later, when Kamehameha III realized that Hawai'i was lacking in people knowledgeable in the ways of cattle ranching, he arranged for three Mexican cowboys to come to the Big Island and teach the locals about ranching. Nearly all Big Island paniolo traditions descend from these three cowboys.

Parker Ranch was severely neglected by subsequent Parkers. John Parker's grandson, Samuel Parker, was a flamboyant playboy who spent money like water and had a genius for making profoundly stupid investments. Unlike King Midas, everything *he* touched turned to manure. As the aging Parker II saw money pouring down Samuel's many ratholes, he began to squirrel away funds as fast as he could. But when the time came to retrieve the money, the old man could not remember where he had hidden most of it. To this day, much of the fortune Parker II hid away has never been found. In 1900 the family hired a Honolulu attorney to manage and rejuvenate the ranch. This he did with a vengeance, turning a dying relic into a powerful and very lucrative operation.

The serenity of Waimea was broken in the 1990s when Richard Smart, the descendent of John Palmer Parker, died, leaving some of his $450 *million* estate to his family, but the bulk of the land (139,000 acres) to a non-profit trust. Lawsuits started flying from disgruntled family members angry about their share, and it was beginning to look as if the ranch might be broken up and fed to the lawyers and tax collectors. Fortunately, the dispute was finally settled, and peace once again returned to sleepy little Waimea.

Most of Parker Ranch is mile after mile of rolling, grassy hills and wide open plains interrupted by rows of trees for windbreaks. Owls, pheasant and wild turkeys crisscross the ranch, while ever-chewing cows wander about. The ranch consists of several non-contiguous segments of land, and its 35,000 cattle are controlled by a mere 12 paniolo (Hawaiian cowboys). The road across from the mile marker 55 (see map on page 137 or graphic on page 138) slices through Parker **DIVERSION** Ranch. Called Mana Road, it goes 45 miles around Mauna Kea mountain to Mauna Kea **ALERT!** Access Road (off Saddle Road). 2WD vehicles can drive it *for the first part* to see what the ranch looks like. After 18 miles there's a *bad* 5-mile segment through forest that requires a 4WD vehicle with high ground clearance, plus there's an area with confusing but *presumably* parallel roads. Choose your route carefully as some of the roads turn into muddy, slanted ruts several feet deep, putting you at risk of tipping and getting stuck against the earth wall, or scraping the heck out of the side of your vehicle. But if you pay attention, it's easy to find alternate ways around the worst sections. Otherwise, you can go as far as your desire takes you. Close any gates that you open (all four of them). According to the county, it is a *public* right of way, despite any signs you may see that *imply* the contrary. Avoid it if it's been too rainy; some of the puddles can be big enough to waterski in. This is a beautiful and adventurous mountain drive through incredible terrain. Allow 3 to 4 hours.

A successful cattle ranch is first and foremost a grass farm. After being raised on sweet Hawaiian range grass for five to six months, most of the cattle are shipped by 747 to the mainland or by boat to Canada, then fattened in various areas before slaughter. (Ironically, cattle class on a 747 has more leg room than what you had in coach.) In the old days, just getting the cows to the ship was a traumatic process. They were driven to Kawaihae,

forced into the ocean, then lashed to the outside of small boats, which ferried them to the main ship where they were belly-hoisted aboard. Now they simply walk onto an old cruise ship, into stalls, and off they go to Canada, where they are then trucked to Texas. Why Canada, which ain't exactly *on the way* to Texas? Because no shipbuilder in the U.S. makes cattle haulers. Yet a government law from 1920 makes it illegal for a foreign-built ship to sail from one U.S. port to another. Hence, they gotta go to Canada.

If you want to get an idea of what Big Island beef tastes like, the best (and most convenient) source is KTA Waikoloa Village (808-883-1088) located in Waikoloa Village at the Waikoloa Highlands Center. The grass-fed beef is darker and stronger than grain-fed beef and is particularly good marinated. Deliveries are usually Tuesdays and Fridays. Expect to pay *double* what you would pay for beef that is flown in by jet from the mainland. For a cheaper (price, not quality) local beef selection, try Honoka'a Country Market (808-775-7744) in Honoka'a and pick up some kiawe wood for grilling, if you're staying someplace with a BBQ.

Past Waimea heading into Kohala, sights are described in the *Kohala Sights* chapter.

HAMAKUA & WAIMEA BEST BETS

Best Garden—Hawai'i Tropical Botanical
  Garden
Best Waterfall—Umauma Falls
Best View—Waipi'o Overlook
Best Place to Wear Down an E-Bike
  Battery—Mana Road E-Biking
  Adventure
Best Hole to Avoid—Douglas Pit
Best Spot to View the Churning Ocean—
  Laupahoehoe Point
Best Place to Find Affordable Local Beef—
  Honoka'a Country Market

Here's one place where you don't want a foggy mountain breakdown.

Saddle Road runs between our largest volcanoes, Mauna Loa and Mauna Kea. The entire area is called the Saddle because of the saddle-shaped valley between the two mountains. It travels through some unpopulated and very surreal-looking country and is the fastest way between the two sides.

The saddle crests at an impressive 6,578 feet. That's some saddle. The 52-mile-long road has a bad and outdated reputation. It was hastily built by the military in 1942 for strategic purposes. This was wartime, and they wanted a road connecting the two sides of the island, and they wanted it fast. They didn't design it with general traffic in mind; it was meant for military vehicles. Until 2013, The Saddle was a bumpy, winding, hilly road with blind turns that weren't banked and had been paved by *Sadists-R-Us*. Driving on it could void your rental agreement. But it's been improved and rerouted in

areas. Today it's probably the smoothest stretch to drive on the island and is the only way to get to Mauna Kea. But there are no lights, and the road is often licked by fog toward the center crest. (We came out here in the middle of the night to watch a comet some years back and *got chicken skin fo days*—i.e., it was spooky. The only sound was a lone birthing cow screaming in the blackness.)

The landscape is otherworldly in places and decidedly different. Even back when it was in horrible shape, we'd take our own personal car on it. (As we all know, *drive it like a rental* is like saying, *drive it like it's stolen*.) And it's a shorter distance than Hwy 19, known locally as *the upper road*. We like to take Saddle Road from the Kona side and return from Hilo on the upper road for variety. In 50 miles the terrain goes from dry lava scrub land to rolling green hills and plains to young lava fields to dripping fern-covered forests.

With this in mind, we'll describe it from west to east. There's no **gas** on this road, so fill up before you go.

Look at the inside back cover map to familiarize yourself with the route and to put it in context. From the intersection of Saddle Road (200) and Hwy 190, you leave lava land behind and enter rolling plains of grasses. Keep an eye out for wild turkey (the bird, not the booze) and pheasant, which are plentiful here.

ASCENDING THE SADDLE

[A] As you ascend to the crest of this saddle, you'll get an idea of the scale of Mauna Kea on your left and Mauna Loa on your right. The military often drives this road in their HUMVEEs and other camouflaged vehicles. If you stop and listen, you'll often hear the booms of artillery from the Pohakuloa Military Training Area. Sometimes you'll see their choppers swooping low like a scene out of *Apocalypse Now*. Tanks and Armored Personnel Carriers also use this road on occasion. (We respectfully suggest that you *always* give armored tanks the right of way.) They have used B2 Stealth Bombers to drop unguided inert bombs from 18,000 feet. If you use the "Historical Imagery" feature on Google Earth, you'll even find a fake airfield and broken jets from bombing practice scattered on part of their lava field.

Gilbert Kahele Recreation Area is near mile marker 34. There are restrooms here. There's also a playground with physics-based equipment if you have kids who are getting antsy in the car. Watch your speed on either side of this park. It's a notorious speed trap when it drops from 55 mph to 45 mph.

You'll find the road up Mauna Kea (on your left) marked by a large mound, called **Pu'u Huluhulu** (hairy hill). This hill is a good place to stretch if you want to walk

Letters **[A]** correspond to paragraphs in text.

One of many telescopes perched high above a sea of clouds during a Mauna Kea sunset.

the 0.7 miles round trip to the top. (If you have kids, this is a good place to let 'em burn off some of that extra energy.) It's an old cinder cone created long ago by Mauna Kea that has been surrounded by more recent lava flows from Mauna Loa. (You can tell by scars on the side that it was once mined for its cinders.) There are several trails on top of this forested mound, but it's kind of hard to get *too* lost. You can go around the top and connect to the trail you took coming up. The splendid view, as well as the birds, makes it a short but worthwhile diversion.

MAUNA KEA

[B] If someone asked you to climb from the base of Mauna Kea to the summit (which is more than 13,000 feet above sea level), you'd have to climb more than 30,000 feet. (The base of Mauna Kea just happens to be 17,000 feet *below* sea level.) Those wimps who climb from the base of Mt. Everest to the summit only have to climb a mere 12,000 feet. (Its base just happens to start at 17,000 feet *above* sea level.) Everest, too, is located in a warm latitude, 28°, as far south as sweltering Orlando, Florida. But people still freeze

to death in the summer on Everest because the summit's high altitude (29,032 feet) offsets the warm latitude.

The second of the five surviving volcanoes to create the island, Mauna Kea (meaning White Mountain) pokes its head 13,803 feet above the ocean. In its prime, half a million years ago, Mauna Kea was 3,500 feet higher. But it gets shorter with age. It shrinks every day, settling under its own weight and bending the ocean floor beneath it. The ancient Hawaiians considered it the home of Poli'ahu, the snow goddess. She and Madame Pele, next door on Mauna Loa, didn't always get along very well, and the saddle between Mauna Loa and Mauna Kea was said to be their battleground. The ancient Hawaiians were uncomfortable in this region, not wishing to get in the middle of this domestic disturbance.

Atop the mountain, the air is dry, thin and incredibly clear. Scientists recognized this spot as possibly the best place in the world to observe stars and have been placing the world's finest telescopes up here for years. (The *twinkle, twinkle* of the little star is caused by air turbulence, and the air above Mauna Kea is some of the least turbulent in the world—windy, but not turbulent.) With little precipitation (except for the occasional blizzard), little in the way of city lights below (those that *do* exist cast a carefully chosen color to make life easier on astronomers), and relatively easy access, Mauna Kea is the pride of the astronomical community. About a dozen of the finest space observatories in the world are sprinkled about the summit or are in the works. Some of these telescopes can look at objects over 12 billion light years away, meaning that the light they are seeing left those objects long before the earth and sun were even born. The mighty **Keck telescope** has a 33-foot wide viewing surface. The moveable part weighs 300 tons but is so perfectly balanced that it can be moved *with one hand.*

Here's a thought for you: Look around at all the infrastructure necessary to look at the stars—the roads, the buildings, the computers, the people, the research, the 'scopes themselves. All of these things and the hundreds of millions of dollars they cost are here for a single purpose: to hold *one tenth of an ounce* of metal in a specific shape. That's how much aluminum coats the giant mirrors that gather all the starlight and where all the information comes from.

Plans to build the most advanced telescope in the world on Mauna Kea came to a grinding halt in 2015 when a large number of protesters physically blocked construction of the massive **Thirty Meter Telescope** (TMT). Although their ancestors were the undisputed masters at navigating by the stars, the protesters, who view Mauna Kea as sacred, succeeded in overturning a permit granted to the TMT by the state. Then when TMT again got permission to proceed in 2019, the same thing happened. A physical stand-off ensued at the corner of Saddle Road and Mauna Kea Access Road. Protesters blocked the road for months and nobody was budging. It took the stay-at-home order at the beginning of the COVID-19 pandemic to break the logjam, and people were once again able to drive up this road.

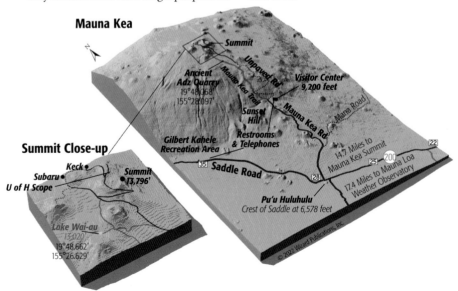

Mauna Kea

Summit

Ancient Adz Quarry
19°48.068'
155°28.097'

Unpaved Rd.

Mauna Kea Trail

Visitor Center
9,200 feet

Sunset Hill

Mauna Kea Rd.

Mana Road

Gilbert Kahele Recreation Area

Restrooms & Telephones

Summit Close-up

Keck
Subaru
U of H Scope

Summit
13,796'

35 Saddle Road

14.7 Miles to Mauna Kea Summit

25 200

28

17.4 Miles to Mauna Loa Weather Observatory

22

Lake Wai-au
13,020
19°48.662'
155°26.629'

Pu'u Huluhulu
Crest of Saddle at 6,578 feet

©2022 Wizard Publications, Inc.

Tours of the **Subaru Telescope** are available 15 days a month, weekdays only. You have to reserve *at least* a week (no more than three months) in advance from their website. Aside from Subaru tours, you won't be able to visit the inside of any of the telescopes except Keck (see map on facing page), which has a visitors' gallery open weekdays 10 a.m.–4 p.m., as well as restrooms. You'll get a glimpse through the window of the telescope itself there. Turn on the light switch by the door for a better view. (As cold as it gets outdoors, it often feels even colder in the temperature-controlled rooms housing the telescopes.)

Before heading to the summit, call (808) 935-6268 for a recorded weather update of Mauna Kea and current road closures (which happens frequently after a snowstorm.) You can also check conditions online at Mauna Kea Weather Center.

The view from atop Mauna Kea can only be described as majestic moonscape. The Apollo astronauts did considerable training up here because it was deemed uniquely moon-like. Looking down on the clouds *below* is mesmerizing. It's a cliché but true—you feel like you're on top of the world! Off in the distance, the still-active volcano of Mauna Loa seems bigger than life, especially from a place about 2 miles down the road from the summit. Ironically, Mauna Loa's massive size makes it appear smaller than Mauna Kea. (*Huh?!*) Because Mauna Loa rises so gently to its 13,679-foot height, you don't get the sense of size that you would if it was steeper, like Mauna Kea. But that very gentle slope hides a volume of rock far greater than Mauna Kea—10,000 *cubic miles* of stone. From atop Mauna Kea, the islands of Maui, Moloka'i and Kaho'olawe can be seen on clear days. From this area people ski down the mountain to link up with the road below.

The *actual* summit is a quick (5–10 short-of-breath minutes) hike from the University of Hawaii Observatory. (You'll see the trail if you look over the railing.) There is a large sign discouraging people from hiking to the summit, but it's not official. It was placed during the fight over the TMT. We checked with authorities and you are still *legally allowed* to go to the true summit, which offers awe-inspiring views in all directions. Consider making the trail a loop hike.

Sunsets from up here when clouds cooperate are an unrivaled splendor of unequaled expansiveness. The summit appears utterly lifeless except for a few unlucky bugs blown up from below and a few flightless native insects that feed on them. No trees, no plants. Just a lifeless void. The mountain last erupted 4,500 years ago and is considered dormant. (If it erupts when you are up there, please disregard this last statement.) Sunset visitors can expect to be rousted 30 minutes after the sun goes down by officials. It's not *you* they hate, it's your headlights that annoy astronomers.

Also located near the top are two oddities. **Lake Wai-au**, at 13,020 feet, sits in the bottom of an old cinder cone and is one of the highest lakes in the United States. The explanation for its unlikely existence goes back to the last ice age, when Mauna Kea was covered by a 20-square-mile glacier that was up to 350 feet thick and extended 3,200 feet below the summit. When the volcano erupted under the ice cap, it formed a dense layer of volcanic ash that prevents water from easily draining through the normally porous lava rock. For a time there was debate over what was feeding the lake, since there are no rivers on top of the mountain, and rain and snow seemed insufficient to replenish it. Many (including us) believed the official answer that *permafrost* left over from the glacier was under the surface, trickle-feeding the area, but that theory went out the door when the lake dried up to a puddle only a few inches deep by the end of 2013, following several years of drought. When heavier rain and snowfall returned, the lake filled back up to the brim. Since then we've even seen a trickle overflowing out the backside, forming what is surely the coldest waterfall in all Hawai'i. Though only 10-15 feet deep, the ancient Hawaiians thought the lake was bottomless, probably because they couldn't find anyone crazy enough to venture into it at this frigid altitude.

Lake Wai-au can be accessed by a 15–30-minute walk from the road. (See map on page 144.) Turn right when the trail intersects another trail. The upper trail, near the hairpin turn on Mauna Kea Road at mile marker 7, is the easier trail.) Many of the gulches you see on the side of Mauna Kea were created when the glacier melted, sending the snowmelt to scour the sides of the mountain.

The other oddity up here is **Keanakako'i**, an ancient Hawaiian adz quarry. (An adz is a stone cutter used for shaping wood.) When Mauna Kea erupted during the last ice age, the glacier cap cooled the lava very quickly. The result is the densest and hardest rock in all the islands (tougher than spring steel) and was the hardest substance in the state. What's impressive is that the ancient Hawaiians discovered this site (at 12,400 feet) and were able to successfully mine it for generations, trading it to other islanders for assorted goodies. The only trail to the adz quarry is near Lake Wai-au. Coming back up involves a grueling 800-foot ascent, a genuine 'okole kicker at this altitude.

DRIVING UP TO MAUNA KEA

From Saddle Road it's 14.7 miles to the summit. About 2 miles into Mauna Kea Access Road is a dirt road on your right called Mana Road. It leads 45 miles *around* Mauna Kea Mountain all the way to Waimea and passes through tranquil forest and pastureland. There's rarely anyone on Mana Road, and you need 4WD (or a mountain bike and legs of steel) to take it. (See *Hamakua & Waimea Sights* for full description of this challenging drive.) The **Onizuka Center for International Astronomy Visitor Information Station** is 6 miles up Mauna Kea Access Road at 9,200 feet. Ellison Onizuka was a native of Kona

NOT TO BE MISSED!

The person standing at the shoreline can thank the last ice age for the existance of Lake Wai-au.

and part of the crew of the Space Shuttle Challenger in 1986 that *"slipped the surly bonds of Earth to touch the face of God."*

The **Visitor Information Station** has a few displays and small telescopes that they break out at night for visitors. They also sell warmies (for those who came in shorts) and brake fluid (for brake-riders coming down the mountain), as well as water and some snacks like freeze-dried ice cream (really weird), sandwiches and instant noodles. There are restrooms available (though heavily used—consider the ones back at the Gilbert Kahele Recreation Area). About 50 people live up here (tending the 'scopes), and they have to bring in their water several times a week by truck.

Across from the visitor center there is a short trail that leads to **Sunset Hill** that offers a nice vantage point for people who don't want to venture all the way to the summit.

While driving up this part of Mauna Kea Road, watch out for mindless, wayward cows occasionally wandering onto the road.

After the visitor center the road is unpaved for 5 miles before it becomes paved again for the last 3.7 miles. 4WD is now *required* to continue past the visitor center and to the summit. The unpaved portion of the somewhat steep road coming down can get a bit slippery at times, especially when wet and it's hard on brakes. 4WD vehicles usually have a gear low enough to deal with this situation. The road is a bit washboardy, and they'll often close it for a short time after a snow until they can plow it. (Finding a good snowplow repairman in Hawai'i must be about as easy as finding a good surfboard shaper in Anchorage, Alaska.)

If you don't want to drive it (there are no shuttles), several companies will pick you up on the west side and take you to the summit for sunset, then come down a bit for some stargazing and hot chocolate sipping. They'll provide warm coats for you, and the total time is 7.5 hours. See *Stargazing* on page 230 for more.

Those who *really* want a challenge can opt to hike the trail from the visitor center to the top. (See map on page 144.) It's 15 miles round trip and a *very* tough day hike, even for the fittest. You need a very early start and should take precautions mentioned in *Hiking* on page 205. Expect blinding headaches, extreme nausea and bewildered looks from anyone who ever finds out that you did it.

If you drive up, drink *plenty* of water before, during and after, as dehydration is a severe problem at that altitude. Children, pregnant women and those with respiratory problems should avoid the summit. The atmosphere is 40% thinner at the summit than sea level, so sunblock and sunglasses are a must to protect against harmful UV rays, which are more intense here. Try to avoid soft drinks and (how do I put this delicately?) foods that produce gas. (You figure it out.) Bring a can of unopened Pringles with you and watch how it explodes when you open it up top. And consider chewing gum on the way down to help with the pressure in your ears. Don't come up here within 24 hours of a SCUBA dive. As far as your nitrogen is concerned, you're flying. Altitude sickness can strike anyone, causing weakness, dizziness and nausea. Some claim that ibuprofen *before* the trip will help this, similar to the way aspirin is said to forestall hangovers, but we won't swear by it. (Well, we'll swear to the *hangover* part.) Go slow and don't exert yourself too much. Acclimating for a half hour or so at the 9,200-foot visitor center can help.

Then there's the cold. Between November and April, snow is not uncommon.

Even summertime brings the occasional freak snowstorm. During the rest of the year, it's often bone-chilling up there. Dress warm. (*Like you packed your parka for your Hawaiian vacation!*) The wind can be exceptionally fierce. It's often warm and calm up there, but you shouldn't *count* on it being this way, especially during sunset. During the winter, you can snow ski short distances. See *Snow Skiing* on page 228. When it snows, local residents often rush up the mountain to frolic. We've seen people dashing down the hill below the summit on every conceivable mode of transportation: skis, snowboards, sleds, boogie boards, surfboards, tarps—we've even seen people sliding down in *ocean kayaks,* complete with paddles!

According to King Kalakaua, the Hawaiians had their own version of the Ironman Triathlon. Here, the objective was to climb Mauna Kea during the winter, grab all the snow you could carry, bolt back down the mountain, and run all the way to the ocean. If you had enough snow for a snowball, you won. (If you didn't, you probably grabbed the winner's snowball and stuck it in his pants.) Ironically, this is still done. Only today people bring the snow back in pickup beds and throw a party when they get home. This may be the only place in the world where you can experience snow less than 30 miles from an 85 °F tropical resort area.

By the way, if you have anything in a watertight case—*keep it closed*. If you open it up here then close it, the lower air pressure trapped inside will seal it shut at sea level. (We learned this the hard way.)

MAUNA LOA

[C] Across the saddle from Mauna Kea is the more active Mauna Loa (long mountain). This is the most difficult volcano

summit on the island to access. You've got two choices, and both are a *buggah.* (See *Hiking* on page 205.) However, off Saddle Road a quarter mile east of the road up Mauna Kea, there is a narrow, paved road leading 17.4 miles up to the **Mauna Loa Weather Observatory**, just above the 11,000-foot level. (It's gated and not open to the public.) From there the view across the saddle to Mauna Kea is stunning, especially if there is snow on top. Otherwise, Mauna Loa Observatory Road offers little for you in exchange for the hour-long drive. Created in 1958, the observatory has the longest record of direct measurement of CO_2 in the world, and their findings are universally cited by climatologists to bolster arguments in favor of global warming. Built near the top of a semi-active volcano, it is protected by a first-of-its-kind lava barrier on the upslope side designed to redirect any lava flows long enough to get the scientists out during an eruption.

This part of Mauna Loa is littered with portions of lava tubes. After telephone pole #138 (then after the lava goes from rough a'a to smoother pahoehoe) there are numerous short sections of a discontiguous lava tube going up the hill for over 0.5 miles. Some are long enough to hike into where you'll get to utter pitch black. Stay on the pahoehoe. Also, you might want to check out the pit crater across the street from telephone pole #200. It's about 50 feet from the road and 50 feet deep where lava drained after overflowing.

APPROACHING HILO

[D] As you continue on Saddle Road, you'll descend toward Hilo. You'll be periodically passing through fields where lava flowed during historic times. (See inside back cover map.)

Ahh, the snows of Hawai'i.

You're on the windward side now, and things will start to get greener. About 1 mile after mile marker 7 (the sixth was missing at press time) you'll have to turn left to stay on Kaumana Drive and Highway 200; look for the sign. (Otherwise, the bypass—Hwy 2000—will take you to Highway 11 if you remember to dog-leg to the right at the end of Highway 2000 onto Puainako—see map on page 112.)

As you approach Hilo, before Hwy 200's mile marker 4, you'll see **Kaumana Cave** on your left. Created by the Mauna Loa lava flow of 1881 that traveled 25 miles and threatened Hilo, this lava tube skylight is saturated with green. Full-grown trees and ferns have taken over the cave and its entrance. It stands in stark contrast to other caves throughout the island. Elsewhere, a century-old lava tube would be little changed from when it was created. But here, in lush, wet Hilo, geologic time marches at a rapid pace. The cave looks old, worn and rickety. You can take the stairs to the bottom and peer in. Once down there, most people are immediately attracted to the large opening to the right, never even noticing the cave entrance to

the left. Remember, this is simply an interruption in a 2-mile long lava tube. If you have a flashlight (make that two—it's so dark you can't tell whether your eyes are open or closed) and sufficient nerve, you can go cave exploring. (Called spelunking—in case that's the only word you forgot in your last crossword puzzle.) The cave to your right has more low overhangs between long stretches of tall ceilings, but the formations are more fascinating. To your left, after an initial low overhang, the cave is more cathedral-like. Tree roots occasionally poke through the ceiling. You could spend hours exploring this lava tube if you wanted.

This flow came within 1.5 miles of Hilo Bay. Princess Ruth was sent from Honolulu to save Hilo. She stood in front of the lava flow beseeching Pele to stop the lava. That night she slept next to the advancing flow, and by morning it had stopped. Today several hundred homes are built on the 1881 flow and can easily be recognized by their rock gardens.

Rainbow Falls and Boiling Pots are off Waianuenue Road in this area. See *Hilo & Puna Sights* for more on these.

In addition to the popular beaches, lesser known gems such as Kikaua Beach are scattered along the west side of the island.

The Big Island has the incorrect reputation of being the island without beaches. That's because in the past, lack of roads and lack of knowledge caused most of its more glorious beaches to go unnoticed. Granted, the island has fewer sand beaches per mile of shoreline than any of the other islands. It's newer, and plentiful beaches are the blessing of older, more mature islands. However, what beaches we *do* have, especially on the west side, are among the very best in the state. The water off the west side of the Big Island is the clearest, warmest and often calmest water in all the islands. There is not one permanent stream on the entire west side, so cloudy river runoff is not a problem. And the shape of the island, along with the pre-vailing current, often gives the west side relatively gentle water. Rough seas usually come from the northeast. Kona and Kohala's calmer waters can be dramatically seen from the air. During normal conditions, the inbound flier will notice that the transition from coarse, choppy channel waters to fine textured leeward waters is almost instantaneous, just south of the northernmost tip of the island. (By the way, flying a small airplane through that wind transition is utterly *nasty*.)

On the Big Island we have white sand, black sand, salt-and-pepper sand and even green sand beaches. As for beach quality, Hapuna Beach is often named the best beach *in the entire country* by travel magazines. Mauna Kea Beach is not far behind.

Kahalu'u and Honaunau offer outrageous snorkeling. And secluded gems like Makalawena and Road to the Sea, along with unusual delights such as Kiholo Bay and Green Sand Beach probably make beach-going on the Big Island the best in the state.

BEACH SAFETY

The biggest danger you will face at the beach is the surf. Though it is calmer on the west side of the Big Island, that's a relative term. Most mainlanders are unprepared for the strength of Hawai'i's surf. We're out in the middle of the biggest ocean in the world, and the surf has lots of room to build up. We have our calm days where the water is like glass. We often have days where the surf is moderate, calling for respect and diligence on the part of the swimmer. And we have the high surf days, perfect for sitting on the beach with a picnic or a mai tai, watching the experienced and the audacious tempt the ocean's patience. Don't make the mistake of underestimating the ocean's power here. Hawai'i is the undisputed drowning capital of the United States, and we don't want you to become a statistic.

Other hazards include rip currents, which can form, cease and form again with no warning. Large "rogue waves" can come ashore with no warning. These usually occur when two or more waves fuse at sea, becoming a larger wave. Even calm seas are no guarantee of safety. Many people have been caught unaware by large waves during ostensibly "calm seas." We've swam and snorkeled most of the beaches described in this book on at least two occasions (usually more than two). But beaches change. The underwater topography changes throughout the year. (White Sands Beach is a dramatic example.) Storms can take a very safe beach and rearrange the sand, turning it into a dangerous beach. Napo'opo'o Beach vanished after a storm in 1992 and never came back. Just because we describe a beach as being a certain way does not mean it will be in that same condition when you visit it.

Consequently, you should take the beach descriptions as a snapshot in calm times. If seas aren't calm, you probably shouldn't go in the water. If you observe a rip current, you probably shouldn't go in the water. If you aren't a comfortable swimmer, you probably shouldn't ever go in the water, except at beaches that have lifeguards. There is no way we can tell you that a certain beach will be swimmable on a certain day, and we claim no such prescience. There is no substitution for your own observations and judgment.

Tell me a lawyer didn't write this beach sign!

If you want to swim in the ocean but fear the power of the surf, Kamakahonu Beach in Kona is about as protected as you can get.

A few standard safety tips: Never turn your back on the ocean. Never swim alone. Never swim in the mouth of a river. Never swim in murky water. Never swim when the seas are not calm. Don't walk too close to the shorebreak; a large wave can come and knock you over and pull you in. Observe ocean conditions carefully. Don't let small children play in the water unsupervised. Fins give you far more power and speed and are a good safety device in addition to being more fun. If you're comfortable in a mask and snorkel, they provide considerable peace of mind, as well as opening up the underwater world. Lastly, don't let Hawai'i's idyllic environment cloud your judgment. Recognize the ocean for what it is—a powerful force that needs to be respected.

If you're going to spend any time at the shoreline or beach, **water shoes** are the best investment you'll ever make. These water-friendly wonders accompany us whenever we go to any beach. Walmart in Kona sells cheap ones, perfect for your short-duration usage. Even on sandy beaches, rocks or sea life seem magnetically attracted to the bottom of feet. With water shoes, you can frolic without the worry.

(Though don't expect them to protect you from everything. Some beaches are backed by kiawe trees, and their thorns could probably penetrate an armored car.)

The ocean here rarely smells fishy since the difference between high and low tide is so small. (In other words, it doesn't strand large amounts of smelly sea plants at low tide like other locations.)

Theft can be a problem when visiting beaches. Visitors like to lock their cars at all beaches, but piles of glass on the ground usually dissuade island residents from doing that at secluded beaches. We usually remove anything we can't bear to have stolen and leave the car with the windows rolled up but unlocked. That way, we're less likely to get our windows broken by a curious thief, though leaving it unlocked *may* leave your insurance company off the hook. Regardless, don't leave anything of value in your car. (Well…maybe the seats can stay.) While in the water, we use a waterproof box or bag for our wallet, phone and keys, and leave everything else on the beach. We don't take a camera to the beach unless we are willing to stay there on the sand and baby-sit it. This way, when we swim, snorkel or just walk, we don't have to constantly watch our things.

Use reef-safe sunscreen (containing zinc oxide and/or titanium dioxide) early and often. Don't pay any attention to the claims from sunscreen makers that their product is waterproof, rubproof, sand blast proof, powerwash proof, etc. Apply 30 minutes prior to exposure and reapply it every couple of hours and after you get out of the ocean. The ocean water will hide sunburn symptoms until after you're toast. Then you can look forward to agony for the rest of your trip. (And yes, you *can* get burned while in the water.) Gel-based sunscreens work best in the water. Lotions work best on land.

People tend to get fatigued while walking in sand. The trick to making it easier is to walk with a very gentle, relaxed stride while lightly striking the sand almost flat-footed.

The Hawai'i Supreme Court ruled in 2006 that all beaches are public to "the upper reaches of the wash of the waves... at high tide during the season of the year in which the highest wash of the waves occurs." This means that if the ocean can touch it, you can be there. The trick, sometimes, can be access. You might have to cross private land to get to a public beach. We've pointed out a legal way in the maps to every beach on the island, and most of the maps have access routes in yellow to show you the way.

In general, surf is higher and stronger during the winter, calmer in the summer, but there are exceptions during all seasons. When we mention that a beach has facilities, it usually includes restrooms, showers, picnic tables and drinking water.

Lastly, remember that just because *you* may be on vacation doesn't mean that residents are. Consequently, beaches are more crowded on weekends.

To get ocean safety information, visit: hawaiibeachsafety.com.

Beaches that are *supposed* to have lifeguards are highlighted with this ⊕ symbol. Those that had year-round lifeguards at press time were:

West—Hapuna, Kahalu'u, Manini'owali / Kua Bay, White Sands
Puna—Isaac Hale Beach Park (Pohoiki)
Hilo—Honoli'i, Richardson's

Those with lifeguards on weekends and holidays:

West—Spencer Beach Park
Hilo—Onekahakaha, Carlsmith

We'll start our descriptions at the end of the road at the top of the island and work our way counter-clockwise. The first few beaches have marginal swimming.

KOHALA BEACHES

❖ Pololu Beach

Located at the end of Highway 270 on the northern end of the island, both this beach and the viewpoint are simply breathtaking. (See *Kohala Sights* on page 53.) High surf and currents usually make this a poor beach for swimming or snorkeling. Access is via a 15–20 minute trail from the Pololu Valley Overlook 400 feet above the beach. Be warned: What goes down must come up, and it won't feel as easy or short. No facilities and parking is minimal.

❖ Keokea Beach Park

Although the swimming is usually poor, the exception is a small cove created by a manmade boulder breakwater. It was constructed as a community project by locals with the help from some heavy equipment donated by a long-gone sugar company. Not worth driving to unless you're in the neighborhood. Access road near mile marker 27 on Highway 270 in North Kohala. Full facilities. Open 6 a.m.–11 p.m.

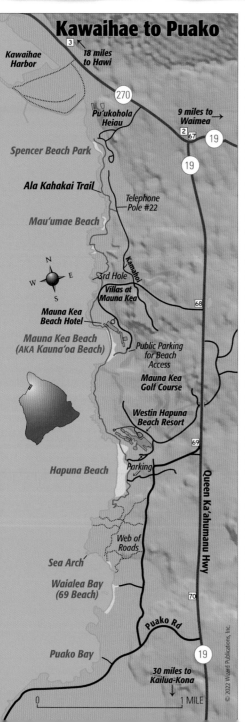

Kawaihae to Puako

Kawaihae Harbor

3 ← 18 miles to Hawi

270

Pu'ukohola Heiau

9 miles to Waimea

2 67 19

Spencer Beach Park

19

Ala Kahakai Trail

Telephone Pole #22

Mau'umae Beach

N W E S

Kamaholi

3rd Hole

Villas at Mauna Kea

68

Mauna Kea Beach Hotel

Mauna Kea Beach (AKA Kauna'oa Beach)

Public Parking for Beach Access

Mauna Kea Golf Course

Westin Hapuna Beach Resort

69

Hapuna Beach Parking

Web of Roads

Sea Arch

Waialea Bay (69 Beach)

70

Queen Ka'ahumanu Hwy

Puako Rd

Puako Bay

19

30 miles to Kailua-Kona

0 _____ 1 MILE

© 2022 Wizard Publications, Inc.

❖ **Kapanai'a Bay**

Tell anyone outside North Kohala that there is a beach below Kapa'au, and they'll look at you like you're crazy. Kapanai'a Bay is one of the best-kept secrets in North Kohala. This small pebble-and-sand beach is backed by trees and was carved out of the cliffs by a small brook. Even during moderate surf, you may see keiki boogie boarding in the back part of the bay. Surfers venture farther out where the waves are completely unobstructed. While there's not much sand and the water is a bit murky, the bay is very picturesque and a wonderful place for a picnic. The catch is that the access road requires a 4WD vehicle and the nerve to punish it between maintenance cycles. See map on page 50.

❖ **Kapa'a Beach Park**

No sand at this beach, just rocks and a little coral rubble. The attractive assets here are the exceptionally clear water for snorkeling and SCUBA, usually abundant fish (sometimes large pelagic fish), coupled with somewhat protected waters except during periods of high surf (which can bring rips and surges). Be careful of surge here. Clear water makes it a good place to take underwater fish pictures. Not much coral but plenty of sea life. Rarely visited during the week, but easy to access just north of mile marker 16 on Highway 270. Facilities include possibly dilapidated restrooms, as well as a BBQ and picnic tables. Excellent view of Maui and a nice place to watch the sunset. Bees and wasps are sometimes a problem here.

❖ **Mahukona Beach Park**

When the seas are calm, it's *really* calm here. Not a beach, but an old abandoned sugar company harbor, Mahukona boasts crystal clear water and ridiculously easy access for snorkeling or swimming. You can practically drive up, open your door and fall in. (But use the ladder at the entrance to the right, OK?) The underwater relief is interesting but sometimes treacherous, so make sure to keep your feet off the bottom or you may end up with a bloody foot (voice of experience). There's usually a large variety of fish, as well as abandoned sugar equipment (giant chains, wheels, etc.) and sparse remains of an old shipwreck. Swimming north along the shoreline brings more coral and more fish. If the surf's up, don't go. When it's calm, check for surginess. During the week you *may* have it all to yourself. Facilities, except drinking water. (Don't drink the shower water!) The dirt road from the other side of the harbor (to the left of the old, giant former sugar building) heading north leads to the navigational heiau shown on page 14. See map on page 50. Afternoon sometimes brings annoying flies that might drive you bonkers.

❖ Lapakahi

We feel kind of funny putting this in the beaches section. Located in Lapakahi State Historical Park near mile marker 14 on Highway 270, this is a reserve and there is no real beach here. (See page 56.) But the *snorkeling* is exceptional. The water is clean and clear in **Koai'e Cove** between site 11 and site 7 near the coconut grove. Not much coral but usually *lots* of fish. Stay inside the cove; the waters get unfriendly outside of its protection. Park personnel used to give bad stink eye to snorkelers accessing the cove, but they've been nothing but nice in recent visits. Open 8 a.m.–4 p.m.

❖ Kaiholena (Sapphire) Cove

There's an unpaved road between mile markers 11 and 12 that leads to a parking area, which is an easy 750-foot walk (because the road's usually too nasty to drive) to a beautiful cove that has inviting waters, lots of fish and sometimes fairly easy

Normally placid, Spencer Beach Park is a popular place for families with keiki (kids).

entry. Make sure you're taking the *right* unpaved road (it's gravel instead of red rocks and dirt). The area itself is hot, harsh and prone to a particularly annoying small fly, especially in the mid to late summer, that may not leave you alone on the land. But the waters here are incredible. Stay in the cove as it gets rougher and more exposed outside. Morning is best, but even afternoons can bring great snorkeling memories. We've seen times when the road gets pretty dilapidated, making 4WD necessary until the craters can be filled in.

⊕ Spencer Beach Park

A great family beach. Located just south of Kawaihae Harbor, the beach is protected by a long offshore reef and the extensive landfill of the harbor to the north.

Luscious Mauna Kea Beach offers some of the best swimming or frolicking on the Big Island.

The beach slope is very gentle, and the swimming is usually quite good. Keiki (kids) enjoy the usually calm waters of Spencer. Though the water is a bit cloudy due to its proximity to the harbor, this shouldn't deter you from enjoying the ocean here. If you snorkel, you will probably see miniature underwater volcanoes from small amounts of cold freshwater seeping from the floor. The amenities include several showers, restrooms, a pavilion, lifeguard, picnic tables, barbecues, a lawn area, lots of shade and basketball/volleyball courts. Camping is permitted by county permit (see *Camping* on page 194). As you approach the park from the access road between mile markers 2 and 3 on Hwy 270, you can go to the right or left side of the park. Whether by design or not, the right (northern) side seems to be used mostly by locals and the left side by visitors. Expect this park to be a little messier than other, more pristine beaches. Open from 6 a.m.–9 p.m.

Just north of here is a small beach in front of the Pu'ukohola Heiau called **Pelekane Beach**. No swimming or sunbathing is allowed there out of deference to the sacred heiau complex. The murky water and frequent black tip reef shark sightings make swimming here a bad idea anyway.

The **Ala Kahakai Trail** between Spencer and **Hapuna Beach** hugs the shoreline. It crosses hole #3 on the golf course but otherwise is easy to follow and passes some pretty shoreline.

❖ Mau'umae Beach

Pretty, secluded, uncrowded during the week and decent swimming when calm. Nice place for a picnic, and you may have it to yourself during the week. Snorkeling is only fair due to slightly cloudy water. Access is through the Mauna Kea Resort entrance, right on Kamahoi, and don't be deterred when it starts looking like an entrance to the maintenance yard. Drive past the building and cross two white bridges. Be sure to come back before 5 p.m. when they close the gate at the second bridge. Park up the road in the dirt lot. Less than a 5-minute trail walk from your car.

You can also get here from Spencer Beach Park by taking the narrow trail by the facilities and following it left. No facilities at *this* beach, though. Usually pronounced Mow-My, this is one of the most underrated and unknown beaches in this part of the island. Winter usually thins out the sand a bit. Sometimes frequented by nudists.

❖ Mauna Kea Beach / Kauna'oa Beach

This is a great beach! Probably the most classically perfect beach on the island. This gorgeous crescent of sand over a quarter-mile long offers *very fine swimming* and boogie boarding during calm seas. On the left side of the beach is a bunch of rocks, creating a linear reef that offers outstanding snorkeling. Don't venture too far out unless calm (the outer portion of this reef is more surgy and unpredictable). The northern (right) side of the beach also offers interesting snorkeling but is more exposed and should only be snorkeled by strong swimmers. There is a big light there that attracts plankton at night, which in turn sometimes attracts large manta rays. Try to resist the urge to swim over to them in the shallow water near the light; it just scares the buggas away. This beach and **Hapuna** are the two best frolicking beaches on the island, if not the state. Mauna Kea is usually less windy than Hapuna. Full facilities. Only 40 cars allowed in the **Mauna Kea Resort** parking lot at a time, which is usually a problem, so try to arrive before 10 a.m. Parking is $20 per car for non-residents (Hawai'i resident parking is free) or you may take the 1-mile shoreline trail from the north end of Hapuna Beach. (A reader compared the trail to the *Bataan death march* but then admitted they had coolers and boogie boards—hey, it's a hike.) Located 32 miles north of Kona in the Kohala resort area off mile marker 68. See map on page 154. The resort's beachside Hau Tree restaurant is open to the public. Open 7 a.m.–6:30 p.m.

⊕ Hapuna Beach

If you close your eyes and picture a perfect beach, there's a good chance you'll see Hapuna in your mind's eye. Half a mile long and 200 feet wide during the summer, beautiful Hapuna is the ultimate frolicking beach. You know how frenzied dogs can get when they go to the beach? That's how most people act when they come to

If Hapuna Beach doesn't ring your wow meter, then maybe you need a new one…

Hapuna or Mauna Kea Beach. It's a beach to savor. Fine golden sand slopes gradually into the ocean. Clean, clear water and excellent swimming conditions during calm seas, full facilities, easy access and gorgeous scenery. The **boogie boarding** here, when the surf's not too high, is exceptional. These are some of the elements that account for the fact that *Condé Nast Traveler* magazine has often voted this beach the best in the entire nation. During the week it usually isn't too crowded, but weekends and holidays bring lots of locals who know a great beach when they see one. Most people who live here bring their guests to Hapuna at least once to gloat. The north lifeguard tower is near the sign saying that there's no lifeguard on duty. Swimming is not safe during periods of high surf, which will kick the living daylights out of you. Also note that the wind sometimes kicks up in the afternoon. We've noticed that the south-

ernmost (left) part of the beach is usually more protected during strong winds, but the north end is usually less crowded. The only shade *on* the beach is a tree at the southern end. (Though there are shaded pavilions behind the beach.)

For more advanced snorkelers on calm days, the area directly south of the sand beach offers superb snorkeling, and it's usually empty during the week because no one knows about it. The waters are usually teeming with fish, and coral is abundant. The sea is unprotected here, so don't go in if it isn't calm, or you'll get beaten up. Check for currents. If it starts to get rough, get out. We often start at the southern end of the beach and snorkel along the rocky coastline all the way to a little black gravel cove half a mile down the coast near a sea arch. Then we walk back along the shore in our water shoes via a poor trail or use the dirt road (don't do it barefooted). Be careful of the wicked kiawe thorns—they can penetrate nearly any shoe and probably most bulletproof vests. If you have some energy left, keep snorkeling past the little gravel cove to

Waialea (Beach 69). The area just past the cove is absolutely heavenly. The north end of the beach can also be awesome.

Hapuna is located 30 miles north of Kailua-Kona in the northern part of the Kohala mega-resort area near mile marker 69 off Highway 19. The restrooms by the parking lot usually look like they're from the third world. Use the ones behind the north lifeguard station. Parking is $10, plus a $5 entrance fee. Open 7 a.m.–6:45 p.m.

❖ Waialea (Beach 69)

A REAL GEM

Sigh! Just another kickin' Kohala beach. This beach slopes gently into the water, giving it nice swimming conditions most of the year when the sea is calm. Not as long or as well known as Hapuna or Mauna Kea, this beach is popular with *akamai* (savvy) residents who sometimes bring their families for a day at the beach on weekends. To the north (right) of the main beach is a secluded little cove, which people sometimes claim for the day, sometimes sans clothing. The snorkeling around the northern part of the beach can be excellent. There's a sea arch at the northern tip, but refrain from walking on it; it looks like it's getting ready to go. Located 30 miles north of Kona near the Kohala resort area off Puako Road. (See map on page 154.) The short road is near telephone pole #71 (it used to be pole #69—hence the name). Facilities include toilets and showers. High surf occasionally strip mines the beach of its sand, which can take months to naturally replenish itself. Parking is $10. Entrance is $5 per person. Open 7 a.m.–7:30 p.m.

❖ Puako

Great snorkeling and SCUBA (see page 223 for directions to best spots, and photo of the reef on page 222), but the swimming is marginal and entry can be tough at low tide. The reef at Puako is *very* extensive. The somewhat cloudy water on entry usually gives way to very clear water at the reef's edge. You stand an excellent chance of sharing the water with multiple turtles. The tops of the reefs are not the most interesting part (and can subject you to the prospect of being raked over them). The best fish and scenic action are at the outer edges of the reef. Check for currents and give the ocean respect. People occasionally bring their dogs to this beach (which end up chasing the catfish, no doubt). Wind often creates chop on the water here, but that doesn't usually affect the underwater experience much. There are 10 legal public accesses along the bay from the boat launch and sometimes the signs *mysteriously* vanish. If that's the case, they are by telephone poles #101, 106, 110/111, 115, 120, 123, 127/128, 131/132 & 137, plus the dirt road at 143. Some of these access points don't have convenient parking.

❖ Mauna Lani

The Mauna Lani Auberge and the Fairmont Orchid both have small, manmade (or enhanced) beaches, such as **Pauoa Bay**, which has lots of fish. The Mauna Lani's beach to the south is usually *very* protected. Access is via the public parking lot shown on the map on page 57. You'll have to walk for about 15 minutes, but the trip through the fishpond area is worth it.

❖ Honoka'ope Beach / 49 Black Sand Beach

This small salt-and-pepper beach is located between the Hilton Waikoloa and the Mauna Lani. Go south from the Mauna Lani roundabout and turn left on Honoka'ope Place. They will sometimes give you a parking pass at the guard station and other times just open the gate for ya;

While not as flashy as some of the other beaches in the area, Honoka'ope Beach is a good place to listen to what's going on under the water.

the lot holds 20 cars. Open 8 a.m.–5 p.m. It's a 2-minute walk from your vehicle following the path past the tennis courts. Like other beaches in this area, it can get windy in the afternoon, and the sand can be lava hot (only a *slight* exaggeration). If you're seeking a hike, the ancient **Ala Kahakai shoreline** lava trail takes 30–60 minutes to reach the beach. (See map on page 57.) This trail segment, which starts near the **Mauna Lani fishponds**, goes through some fabulous lava cliff scenery. When surf's up, waves explode onto the twisted, gnarled lava fragments in the ocean. Facilities.

At the beach the swimming and snorkeling are fair if it's calm, ugly if it's rough. The shape of this beach means there can be some surge; watch out for the little drop off as you enter the water. (Visibility is often poor here.) If the surf's right (not too big, not too small), you can float face down with a mask and snorkel at the surf's edge. As the waves rake you back and forth, listen—the black pebbles mixed with the sand make a great sound as they, too, are raked back and forth.

❖ **'Anaeho'omalu Bay**

A REAL GEM

Another nice Kohala beach. (Even those born and raised here usually call this six-syllable tongue-twister *A Bay*.) This long, curving salt-and-pepper sand beach is popular with both locals and visitors. The swimming is best in the sandy center, whereas the snorkeling (though not great) is best on the right side past the sandy area. The water is not as clear as what you'll find at other nearby beaches, but it's so tranquil here, you won't care. Protected by an offshore reef, this bay is usually safe except during very high surf. Windsurfing is popular here. Say *meow* to the wild cats that live near the restrooms.

'Anaeho'omalu is well known throughout the islands for its two large fishponds. These exceptionally picturesque and placid pools were used by ancient Hawaiians for raising mullet. Hawaiian royalty were the beneficiaries of these ponds—commoners weren't allowed to partake. The beach offers a phenomenal sunset view and a quintessential Instagram op.

There's a pleasant paved path on the mauka side of the fishpond that's worth a stroll. Numerous signs along the way give information about the fishponds and the area in general. Toward the center of the path are the remains of an ancient dwelling, probably a combination of sleeping and eating quarters as well as a shrine. The pond itself contains brackish water; fresh water flows from a natural spring and mixes with ocean tide water. The ancient Hawaiians covered the opening to the fishpond with a grate, which allowed small fry to enter from the ocean. Once inside, they gorged themselves on algae and small shrimp and became too fat to get back through the grate, at which time they were sitting ducks (so to speak) for the Hawaiian pond keepers.

On the right (northern) side of the beach is a hut that rents snorkel gear, kayaks, boogie boards, etc. (at confiscatory rates). If you're hungry, the restaurant at the Waikoloa Beach Marriott behind the beach has pricey but available burgers and hot dogs.

There's a marvelous shoreline trail north between the two Waikoloa hotels that leads through sand, lava and large amounts of brilliant white coral rubble. All along the trail you'll find various tide-pools tucked against the shoreline. Turtles tend to hang out at one particular tide-pool just a few feet from shore. At the north end of this trail is the Hilton Waikoloa. What a way to see this place for the first time! A sunset stroll along this path is unforgettable. Footwear is a must. There is an alternative place to park along this stretch—see map on page 57.

A few minutes walk south of A Bay on a narrow ribbon of sand leads to **Kapalaoa Beach**, a series of sand pockets. There is shade and a pleasant cove for snorkeling at the last pocket. If the surf's not high, the cove is amazingly protected. The short

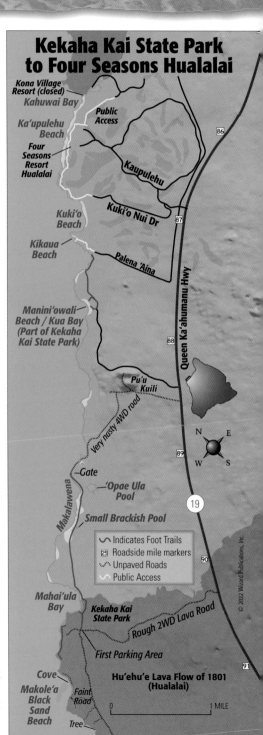

Kekaha Kai State Park to Four Seasons Hualalai

Kona Village Resort (closed)
Kahuwai Bay
Public Access
Ka'upulehu Beach
Four Seasons Resort Hualalai
Kaupulehu
86
Kuki'o Beach
Kuki'o Nui Dr
87
Kikaua Beach
Palena 'Aina
Manini'owali Beach / Kua Bay (Part of Kekaha Kai State Park)
88
Queen Ka'ahumanu Hwy
Pu'u Kuili
Very nasty AWD road
N E W S
89
Gate
'Opae Ula Pool
Makalawena
Small Brackish Pool
Indicates Foot Trails
25 Roadside mile markers
Unpaved Roads
Public Access
19
90
Mahai'ula Bay
Kekaha Kai State Park
Rough 2WD Lava Road
First Parking Area
Cove
Hu'ehu'e Lava Flow of 1801 (Hualalai)
Makole'a Black Sand Beach
Faint Road
Tree
0   1 MILE

© 2022 Wizard Publications, Inc.

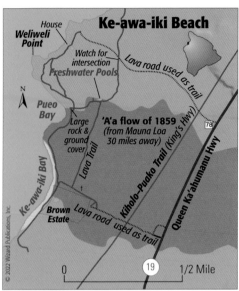

Ke-awa-iki Beach

walk to this beach goes by numerous Hawaiian petroglyphs, some ancient and some modern. The more ambitious will want to take the lava trail farther south for about half an hour until you reach a lone palm tree in the lava, less than a hundred feet from the shore. Here, you are rewarded with an outstanding spring-fed brackish pool with lots of charm. It is very deep in spots and is great for dipping after a hike. You will rarely see anybody else here as it is only accessible by foot, and it's a favorite stopping place of ours. The lava trails in this area offer good hiking, but they can get a bit hot in the middle of the day. The trail leads mostly along the shoreline for miles, all the way to Ke-awa-iki.

To get here from the Highway, take Waikoloa Beach Road, turn left before the Marriott and park in the lot before the end of the road.

❖ **Ke-awa-iki Beach**

This black sand-and-gravel-lined bay is never crowded due to the access—to get there you have to walk on a lava road half the time, and a rougher 'a'a trail to the right of the fence the other half. Few on the island even know it's there. (It takes about 15 minutes to walk to it.) The water off the left (south) is clear and offers good snorkeling when calm, but be wary of currents. There's also some shade there (and sometimes a swing from one of the trees). The best snorkeling is usually in the center of the bay. If you keep walking past the southern edge of the bay, there are lots of tide-pools to explore on an older, smooth pahoehoe lava shelf at low tide. (This is a good place to be wearing water shoes.) Past that are numerous salt deposits from evaporated seawater. These deposits attract goats from the dry scrub inland who warily come and lick the salt off the rocks. Past the right (northern) side of Ke-awa-iki Bay is **Pueo Bay**, lined with black pebbles and semi-protected with nice swimming on calm days. There are off-shore freshwater springs here, causing areas of perturbations in the water, visible as waves of underwater distortion. You will almost certainly have this bay to yourself. No shade here because it's backed by an 'a'a field. If you feel like an extended stroll, you can walk past **Weliweli Point** and take a lava road inland to circle back to the highway. Mauka of Pueo Bay are some beautiful golden pools, described in *Hiking* on page 209.

Both of these beaches were created in 1859 when 'a'a from Mauna Loa drooled down the mountain and exploded when it hit the ocean, creating black sand. The eruption only covered half the bay, and some white sand is still sprinkled at the southern end because there hasn't been enough time to evenly distribute the newer black sand. The entire area has a desolate but pretty character to it and is one of the least known beaches on the west side of the island. The only pockmark is the Brown Estate lining the center part of the beach with its barbed wire fence and its unwelcome feeling. Francis I'i Brown was an influential and beloved Hawaiian businessman in the early 1900s, and in turning his estate into a historical landmark, they seem to have taken away all its charm. They have tours of it for a few hours on the third Tuesday of every month—maybe. (Gee, *that's* convenient!) Located 20 miles north of Kailua-Kona just after mile marker 79.

❖ Kiholo Bay

More of a region than a beach, and there are a few surprises. Access to much of it requires a little hiking. See *Hiking* on page 207. It's certainly worth it. Hours change seasonally. Gates open 7 a.m.–7 p.m., April 1 to Labor Day; 7 a.m.–6 p.m., Labor Day to March 31. Camping available weekends only (Friday–Sunday) at 'Ili'ili (Pebble) beach.

NEAR KONA BEACHES

❖ Ka'upulehu Beach

Most of this long sand beach is fronted by a lava bench, making the swimming poor, but there is a pocket of sand in front of the Kona Village that allows easier access to the water as well as two protected coves (man-made) in front of the Four Seasons. You can access this beach from either of these two resorts. From the Four Seasons it's only 0.1-mile walk, but there are only 10 Beach Access stalls lumped in with employee parking, and the stalls tend to be filled with cars that *don't* look like rentals. From Kona

Village there are plenty of stalls, but it's a half-mile walk from your car to the beach. (Not "1 mile" as we've been told from the guard shack.)

❖ Kuki'o Beach

Near the Four Seasons Resort between Kona and the Kohala Resort area, this is yet another pretty Kohala beach. This long, fringing crescent of white sand is backed in parts by palm, ironwood and kiawe trees offering inviting shade. At the southern end of the bay is a small but very protected sandy cove. The swimming in the bay itself is only fair during calm seas, and the snorkeling offers somewhat murky water. **Turtles** commonly beach themselves here. There is public access from the resort area (see see map on page 161). While Kuki'o Bay might sound like a pretty name, in Hawaiian it means to *stand and defecate* (traditional definition) or *settled dregs* (modern definition). You probably won't be seeing *that* on the back of a postcard. The reason behind the *lovely* name has been lost to the generations, but it's probably safe to say that whoever named it was having a bad hair day. Access is from 6:30 a.m.–6:30 p.m.

❖ Kikaua Beach

One of the things that makes the Big Island so different is its ever-changing nature. Active volcanoes sometimes create new beaches overnight. But in this case, we have modern man—developers, no less—to thank for this one. Kikaua Point was once an isolated area with a pretty, but rocky, cove defining it. A few years ago a private golf and beach club was built behind this point, and it seems obvious that a lot of sand was transported to this cove, whether by man or by nature we can't say. But the result is a dreamy, softly padded sandy bottom and a protected cove that offers easy swimming and wading most of the time. The 27 parking spaces fill up on weekends, but weekdays are usually not bad. To get there, take the Kukiʻo Nui Road just south of mile marker 87. Although this is private property, just tell the nice guards at the gate that you're exercising your beach access rights. It's a 5-minute walk from your car. Full facilities.

✚ Maniniʻowali / Kua Bay

A REAL GEM This is one of our favorite beaches. (Most on the island know it as **Kua Bay**, but the state has been pushing Maniniʻowali Beach as its name.) Off the beaten path, beautiful fine white sand, clear, clean water, gentle slope and a picturesque setting. When the ocean is calm, the swimming is fabulous. The snorkeling off to the right (north) is interesting not for its coral, but for the underwater relief. **Boogie boarding** is excellent during *moderate* surf, but the moderate waves can be strong and deserve respect and have caused more than one spinal injury. There is sand here most of the time, but it is most abundant during the summer months. During the winter, high surf sometimes shifts the sand offshore for a time, leaving the area rocky and undesirable. Many residents consider this one of the best swimming beaches near Kona *when calm*, and on weekends they sometimes make their presence known. Crowds are less common during the week. From Hwy 19 take the paved access road between mile markers 88 and 89. Open 9 a.m.–7 p.m. Note that the waves here have a lot of power, so if the surf's up, don't go in. No shade *at the beach*, but restrooms and barely shaded picnic tables are available behind it.

If want an elevated view of the shoreline, that puʻu (hill) behind you has a trail on the north side (between two speedbumps) that climbs 200 feet, topping off 342 feet above the ocean. You'll be hot, sweaty and dusty. And you'll probably send us a grouchy email saying it's a dumb idea. But the view is grand.

The clean, clear waters of Maniniʻowali/Kua Bay.

Isolated and unknown, Makalawena is one of the finest beaches on the island. Access requires a 15–20 minute walk or a 4WD.

❖ Makalawena Beach

To many, this is the choicest beach on the island…if you don't mind walking to it. In fact, Makalawena is as idyllic a beach as you will find anywhere in the islands. Gobs of superfine, clean white sand, plentiful shade and no crowds during the week. The setting is utterly beautiful. Consisting of a number of coves and rocky points united by a long, curving stretch of beach, the best swimming is in the largest inlet backed by high sand dunes. **Boogie boarding** can be great here (see map on page 161). There's a freshwater pond. A herd of wild goats visits this area often, so keep an eye out for them.

Backed by private (Bishop Estate) land, you get there over the trail from the red houses behind Mahai'ula Beach (about a 20-minute walk). It's a lava trail through an 'a'a field, and the footing is fairly annoying so you'll probably want shoes a little tougher than rubber slippahs. Watch for bees en route. As you walk this trail, try to imagine how ridiculously difficult it would be to walk through the field itself without the trail. Then imagine doing it *barefoot*, as the ancient Hawaiians did. As you approach Makalawena from the Kekaha Kai side, the 'a'a trail suddenly gives way to sand dunes. But if you climb the dunes to the left, rather than finding ocean, you find more 'a'a, indicating that this had been shoreline until a lava flow of 'a'a came along and added more real estate, cutting off the dunes from the sea.

If you have a 4WD (and your fillings are tight), you can take the nasty and intimidating road from the highway between mile markers 88 and 89. Locals do in their stock pick-ups and Jeeps all the time without even blinking, but readers constantly write to us saying it's impassable in their rental Jeeps. It'll take you just north of the beach before a gate forces you to walk like the rest of us dogs. By the way, because it's so isolated, people sometimes travel light to this beach, omitting such extraneous things as their bathing suits. (Yeah, *that* must be the reason.)

❖ Kekaha Kai State Park; Also Mahai'ula Beach / Ka'elehuluhulu

A REAL GEM This beach is outside of Kona town and pretty. It's usually not too crowded. **Mahai'ula Beach** (which you access after a 5-minute walk to the north from the first parking area) offers good swimming and interesting strolling. Just around the southern corner is a pocket of sand called **Ka'elehuluhulu Beach** (park at the second parking area at end of the lava road), not as good as the northern beach. The entire area was once owned by a prominent part-Hawaiian family called the Magoons. They sold the land to a Japanese investor who had visions of a resort. When the state refused permission, the investor sold it to the state, which turned it into a park. The abandoned Magoon house is still located at the northern end of Mahai'ula Beach. This area abounds with freshwater springs that bubble to the surface, occasionally forming ponds. At the farthest northern part of the beach near some palm trees and a rock wall, you may see strange indentations in the sand at low tide. Here, freshwater gurgles right out of the sand and into the ocean. The snorkeling is only fair because the water can be a bit cloudy, especially during spring, and wild goats are common here. This is a good beach to get away from it all, yet still have fairly easy access. There's plenty of shade at the backshore. Access is via a bumpy, but *usually* driveable, semi-paved 1.5-mile road halfway between mile markers 90 and 91 on Queen Ka'ahumanu Highway north of Kailua-Kona. The only negative is the occasional plane overhead as it lands at Kona Airport. Facilities include picnic tables and toilets. Bring your own water. The gate to the beach opens at 9 a.m. Look at the signs to see what time they close it. Note that the closing of the gate is one thing state workers are *guaranteed* to do promptly.

Legend states that before 1801 there was a 3-mile-long fishpond here. That year an old lady came to the village and asked for fish. The village overseer refused, saying that it *all* belonged to the chief. On her way out she was stopped by one villager who gave her food. After eating,

Creamy sand, palm trees, blue sky and clear waters.
Yeah, I guess Mahai'ula Beach will do today.

The quiet tide-pools of Wawaloli Beach at the Natural Energy Lab are an excellent place to go when the surf's pounding.

she told the kind stranger to place kapu (forbidden) sticks outside his house. That night lava from Hualalai roared down the mountain to the village, destroying the great fishpond but sparing the man who fed her. The villagers realized that the old woman was the volcano goddess Pele, avenging the selfishness of the chief.

Check out some of the lava on the road leading to this beach (you'll certainly be driving slowly enough). There are lots of interesting formations where different flows meet. It has patches of gold/rust colored lava, streaks of blue, red and other colors indicating the presence of numerous elements and gases present during cooling.

❖ Makole'a Beach

A REAL GEM

Ask a hundred residents of Kona about a black sand beach just north of town named Makole'a Beach, and you'll get a hundred blank stares. Aside from a handful of shoreline fishermen, few seemed to have known about this beach—until we stumbled upon it for a previous edition. Created during the 1801 lava flow of Hualalai, this small pocket of jet black

sand is the only black sand beach on this part of the island.

To get there you have two options. After driving to Kekaha Kai State Park (see page 166), those with 4WD can take a left at the first parking lot and drive the lava road heading south. Look at the sign to see what time they close and lock the gate and *believe* in their promptness. About 0.6 miles is a faint car path marked by some coral that leads 1,100 feet over lava to the sea. (Though driveable, you can walk this last part if the lava there dissuades you.) The other way is to park at the beach at Kekaha Kai State Park and walk along the shoreline for 15–20 minutes. At one point the sandy trail is interrupted. Best to walk on the smooth pahoehoe lava behind the beach boulders for this part. Just before the black sand beach is a small cove protected at low- to mid-tide during calm seas. It's a perfect place to take a quick dip. The snorkeling and SCUBA diving are great at the black sand beach. Though the visibility is only fair (it's better when you get away from the beach), there is a beautiful field of coral to the north (right) of the beach and to the south farther out. Enter at the sandy

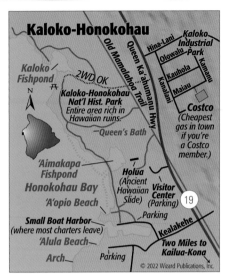

Kaloko-Honokohau

Kaloko Industrial Park
Hina-Lani
Olowalu
Kauhola
Kanalani
Kamanu
Maiau

Old Mamalahoa Trail
Queen Ka'ahumanu Hwy

Kaloko Fishpond
N
2WD OK
Kaloko-Honokohau Nat'l Hist. Park
Entire area rich in Hawaiian ruins.
Queen's Bath

Costco (Cheapest gas in town if you're a Costco member.)

'Aimakapa Fishpond
Honokohau Bay
'A'opio Beach
Holūa (Ancient Hawaiian Slide)
Visitor Center (Parking)
19
Parking

Small Boat Harbor (where most charters leave)
'Alula Beach
Arch
Parking
Kealakehe
Two Miles to Kailua-Kona

© 2022 Wizard Publications, Inc.

part in the center, and beware of unchecked waves. If you walked here, consider cutting across the lava field on your return for different scenery.

❖ **Wawaloli Beach**

A REAL GEM

This is our favorite tide-pool area on the west side of the island (shown on page 167). The instantly accessible sand beach is cut off from the ocean by a large tide-pool that offers warm swimming when the surf is too high elsewhere. There are restrooms and showers here, making it popular with local families who bring their keiki (kids) to play in the mostly protected area. The largest pool (mostly sand-lined) is best near high tide most of the year, only best at low tide if the surf's cranking. The other, less protected tide-pool is better at low tide. A water channel in the lava closer to the restrooms can be fun to wander in. In late afternoon you might want to pick up a pizza on your way out, bring the kids, if you have 'em, and watch the sunset. Take the road to the Natural Energy Lab (near mile marker

94 on the main highway north of Kailua-Kona), and park just as it veers to the right along the shoreline. Some equipment to the south is an eyesore, but try to ignore it, and airplanes sometimes shatter the quiet.

Near here is a 4WD road that leads a mile south to **Pine Trees** (Hawaiian name Kohanaiki), one of the island's premier surf spots. It's so named because of the mangrove in a brackish pool. Surfer dudes thought they were pine trees. The road is fairly poor, but there's a nice paved road from the highway near mile marker 95.

❖ **Kaloko-Honokohau**

Honokohau is an area rich in archaeological treasures. This part of the coast was inhabited for centuries and is filled with relics. Consequently, it was made a national park in 1978 in an effort to preserve what remains (admission is free). At first it might seem surprising that people thrived here. Barren and rocky with particularly harsh 'a'a fields in many areas, the draw here was the freshwater springs. The Hawaiians took advantage of the water to create large fishponds to raise mullet and other fish.

Located just south of the airport (see map above), you can access the park between 8:30 a.m. and 4 p.m. from a parking lot near mile marker 97 on Hwy 19 just north of Kailua-Kona or a gravel road between mile markers 96 and 97 that leads to **Kaloko Fishpond**. You can also access the park from **Honokohau Harbor**, off the paved road between mile markers 97 and 98. From the harbor, a brief walk north will take you to **'Ai'opio Beach**. There are scads of turtles munching on grasses in the cloudy cove water. This was an ocean fish trap in ancient days, where fish entered at high tide and were easily captured. A protected area here is perfect for keiki (kids). An impressive heiau called Hale o Mono rests at the south end. Park at the north end of the harbor (past the restaurant) and take the trail for a minute or two. Turn toward the ocean before you reach the restrooms. This is a nice beach for relaxing. Farther north is **Honokohau Beach**. You may read elsewhere that this is a nude beach, but it is no longer permitted, and they cite violators. This long stretch of salt-and-pepper sand offers reasonable swimming at the center.

At the south end of the Honokohau Harbor is ʻAlula Beach, a small, pleasant crescent of sand, which is fairly protected during calm seas—a good sunning beach. A short walk south of here leads to a large, impressive sea arch. Swimming by the harbor itself is not recommended due to heavy boat traffic and the regular presence of a 16-foot tiger shark named Laverne. Park is open 8 a.m.–5 p.m.

❖ Old Kona Airport Beach Park

This beach park is located at (do we *really* need to say it?) the Old Kona Airport, closed in 1970 because it was unable to accommodate larger aircraft. You park anywhere on the runway (you may taxi as long as you like) and enjoy the patchy beach and full facilities. On the south end are ball fields where Little League parents battle for supremacy. The long beach is an easy one to access, and the sunsets from here are nice. Though you won't be overwhelmed by an abundance of thick sand, it's rarely crowded *during the week*. When low tide combines with the rocky shores, swimming pool-esque areas along the beach get warmed by the sun and often have keiki splashing around in them.

The far end of the runway has a small cove with good snorkeling. Fish counts here can be incredible. Located about 0.5

miles west is the finer **Papawai** or **Pawai Bay**. The **snorkeling** on the way to Papawai Bay is very exciting, especially for the experienced snorkeler. There's a little of everything with crystal clear water, lots of life, caverns, sea arches, drop-offs, small caves and some pinnacles along the shoreline. Here you may see the elusive and extraordinary frog fish (an angler fish) on the coral and Spanish dancers (a contorting nudibranch). During tricky surge, novices should stay away from the more interesting shore. (See *Adventures* on page 237.) The shady backshore of Papawai Bay has plush camping facilities that are private and belong to the Queen Liliʻuokalani Trust, used for Hawaiian children.

❖ Kailua Bay

Located in the heart of downtown Kailua-Kona. (See map on page 65.) Usually areas around piers have nasty water. This one is surprisingly clean due to the daily flushing action of the sea. There are a surprising number of fish in Kailua Bay. We've seen super-schools numbering in the many thousands off Huliheʻe Palace. On calm days we like to snorkel from the pier to the sand pocket across from Kona Islander Inn or the boulder beach across from Bongo Ben's. **Dolphins** often rest in the sandy part of the bay. If you are looking for *exceptionally* calm water and a sandy beach, the very small **Kamakahonu Beach** to the right of the Kailua Pier (in front of

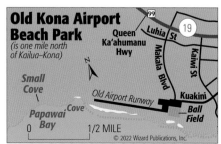

Old Kona Airport Beach Park
(is one mile north of Kailua–Kona)

Small Cove

Papawai Bay

Cove

Queen Kaʻahumanu Hwy

Luhia St

99

19

Makala Blvd

Kaiwi St

Old Airport Runway

Kuakini

Ball Field

0   1/2 MILE

© 2022 Wizard Publications, Inc.

the Courtyard King Kamehameha's Kona Beach Hotel) is perhaps the gentlest and safest water on the island (with the *possible* exception of your hotel bathtub). Children love frolicking in the water here, though freshwater springs sometimes make it cold. This is where King Kamehameha chose to spend the last years of his extraordinary life, so you gotta figure it has something going for it. His personal **Ahuʻena Heiau** is right in front of you. The sand at the beach doesn't extend very far into the water, but it is shallow the whole way. If you swim out from the beach, you'll notice a private ocean entrance to the right. It leads to a house once owned by billionaire Paul Allen, the less famous co-founder of Microsoft. He bought this gloriously located house back in the 1990s for $11 million. (Don't worry, it was probably a mere rounding error in his checkbook.) After he passed away, it sold in 2021 for $43 million. A recently discovered map hints that this might be the location of Kamehameha's tomb, but if so, it was probably destroyed when the shoreline was rearranged in the 1950s.

There is a concessionaire at Kamakahonu renting various beach accouterments at the usual confiscatory prices—but it's convenient. Large schools and many species of fish sometimes congregate on the far side of the heiau. It's about 300 yards from the public parking lot to the beach, so you may want to drop off your stuff (and a person) at the pier first.

To the left (south) of the pier is another pocket of sand, sometimes called **Dig Me Beach**. (They sometimes do scuba intros there.) It's a bit less protected but still relatively calm. Boogie boarders like to ride the normally small but long lasting swells. The grueling Ironman Triathlon starts here. They swim 2.4 miles before starting their 112-mile bike ride and 26.2-mile marathon run—*all in the same day!* (Makes

you sore just thinking about it, huh?) If it's rained recently, snorkelers should look for little calderas of what looks like boiling sand, like mini volcanoes. They're caused by small amounts of cold freshwater bubbling to the surface.

South of the Royal Kona Resort is a small sand pocket called **Honl's** that has good boogie boarding if you have fins.

❖ **Pahoehoe Beach Park**
Though there's little sand here to speak of, this is a nice place to have a picnic and enjoy the surf and sunset from the benches. We've never seen it crowded. Backed by pretty trees and a lawn, there is a small gravel entrance to the water, but swimmers are discouraged from entering unless equipped with snorkeling gear. Even then, advanced snorkelers only need apply. That's because there are numerous holes, arches and pockets on the lava shelf offshore, making exploration very exciting. But surf can sometimes rake you over and even under the reef, making it *too* exciting. Lots of fish here, as well. Located north of mile marker 4 on Alii Drive in Kailua (just north of **White Sands Beach**).

➕ **Laʻaloa Bay Beach Park**
Also known as **White Sands**, **Magic Sands** and **Disappearing Sands**. Located just north of mile marker 4 on Alii Drive in Kailua, this small beach has particularly nomadic sand that retreats at the first sign of a surf assault, settling in a repository just offshore. Once the surf subsides, the sand slowly drifts back onto the shoreline until the next high surf. This occasional flushing of the sand tends to keep it clean and white. Those who live here can tell you of countless instances where the entire beach washes away in less than a day. Much of the time there is a shallow sandbar just offshore, making the swimming and

Good reef protected by a boulder breakwater have made Kahalu'u the most popular snorkel site in Kona.

boogie boarding quite good. (The best wave break is on the left [south] side of the beach.) Watch for undertow and some rocks at the end of the ride. When the sand's thick, the frolicking is good. (But water shoes are recommended in case you step on a rock.) When there's no sand or it's in the process of disappearing (i.e., when the surf's high), there is a strong rip current, making water activities hazardous. This small beach tends to be pretty crowded. Lifeguard and facilities are here along with some shade trees. On calm days, the snorkeler will want to check out the area to the right (north), in front of Kona Magic Sands condominiums. Especially large schools of fish sometimes hang out there. We've also seen more moray eels here than at any other place on the island. (*If an eel bites your hand, and you bleed in the sand...that's a'moray.*)

Just south of here right at **mile marker 4** is a **small cove** where the SCUBA diving is excellent, offering short, easy access and good underwater relief and caves. The snorkeling is not bad either. Just offshore from this location we often see a pod of dolphins patrolling the waters. Why they hang out there, we don't know, but whatever the reason, keep an eye out for them. Open 7 a.m.–8 p.m.

➕ Kahalu'u Beach Park

This is one of the nicer snorkeling spots on the Big Island. It is often teeming with fish and offers more variety of sea life than any other easily accessible spot in Kona. Among the many fish present are wrasses, parrotfish, convict tang, porcupinefish, needlefish and puffers, as well as the occasional lobster, eel and octopus.

Outside the reef you may occasionally see deep sea life, such as tuna, marlin and dolphin jumping about. When you first enter the water you might think, "What's all the hubbub about?" Well…it's about 100 feet offshore. The perimeter of this small, sheltered bay has numerous fresh-water springs, making the near-shore water cold and cloudy. But once you swim out toward the middle, it gets warmer and clearer, and life is abundant. One reason is the Menehune breakwater offshore. Built in ancient times, it has been partially disassembled by countless waves, creating an excellent fish environment. Almost across the street is **Kahalu'u Bay Surf & Sea**. They rent pretty much anything you could want including snorkel gear, boogie boards (but the boogie boarding here is not good—just surfing), rash guards, paddle boards and more. They'll usually offer surfing lessons at the beach if you book ahead and conditions are friendly. There is a full range of facilities. A family of turtles calls Kahalu'u home, and they usually won't dart away from you if you don't harass them. (We've noticed that near high tide, they often work the grasses that are otherwise exposed on the left/southern side of the bay.) Your odds of swimming with turtles are probably greater here than anywhere else on the island, with the possible exception of remote **Punalu'u Beach**. The best way to keep a turtle from fleeing is to act disinterested—like you don't give a flying fish. (*Ooo*, sorry.) If you scope him out, he'll run off. If you pretend to eat the same grasses he eats, you aren't a threat. The more intrepid might venture around the breakwater on very calm days where life is also abundant. Exceptionally large mixed schools of fish sometimes congregate just outside the reef, but you expose yourself to the possibility of being strained through the reef—better stay inside unless it is real calm or you are real confident.

Crowds accumulate at Kahalu'u, but it's *usually* less crowded than White Sands Beach. One nice benefit of the crowds is that the fish here are used to humans, so they will let you get super close. During periods of high surf, large waves can wash over the reef and form a rip current flowing out of the reef opening at the north end of the bay, making it unsafe.

Though this has traditionally been a popular place to feed fish, conservationists are making a concerted effort to end the practice here. See Snorkeling in the Activities chapter for more.

To the left is a **tide-pool**. The water there is sometimes as warm as bathwater as it gets heated by the sun, a natural black-bottom pool. Cruise around in the shallows and look for eels.

Eight hundred feet to the left (south) of Kahalu'u is **Makole'a Beach**. (Not to be confused with the beach described on page 167 with the same name.) There are several heiau along this beach that are

Kahalu'u Beach Park

Excellent surf break ↗

N ↑

Menehune Breakwater

Alii Drive

Strong rip current when surf's high

Best snorkeling is in this area

Kahalu'u Beach Park Parking

5 Makolea

Between low & high tide on calm days, **Tide-pool Area** is excellent for the timid snorkeler. Do not walk on the fragile coral.

0 ——— 1000 Feet

Petroglyphs (at low tide) ⊙   ⊙ Ke'eku Heiau

© 2022 Wizard Publications, Inc.

They say the fish are really friendly at Pu'uhonua o Honaunau's Two-Step.

under restoration. Because of this, the access to this beach is currently closed off. But if you *do* happen to catch it at a time when it's open, then you'll find a salt-and-pepper sand and gravel beach that's usually empty and has a lonely, forgotten feel. The swimming is poor since you are facing large tide-pools. Look for the gory petroglyphs mentioned on page 69. Kahalu'u is open 6 a.m.–11 p.m.

❖ Napo'opo'o Beach

Jumping all the way down to Captain Cook is Napo'opo'o Beach. Well, it *used* to be a beach. It disappeared when Hurricane 'Iniki sideswiped the island *way* back in 1992, and the surf wiped the beach clean, depositing boulders there. You'll find little more than a small patch of sand. This beach will probably never return to its former glory—part of the ever-changing nature of the Big Island. Across the Kealakekua Bay is the Captain Cook Monument, described on page 75. The view ain't bad, but the beach isn't worth a stop unless you're in the area. You stand a reasonably good chance of seeing **dolphins** in the middle of the bay during the very

early morning. Slightly south is **Manini Beach** (shown on the map on page 70). Coral rubble sprinkled with 'a'a lava and poor swimming make this another must-miss beach.

In the small neighborhood to the south, **Kahauloa Bay** (formerly Grandma's Little Beach) is where you can launch kayaks to use in Kealakekua Bay.

❖ Ke'ei Beach

Between Kealakekua and Honaunau (see map on page 70), this pretty but small stretch of sand is backed by numerous coconut trees. Though it's picturesque, poor swimming and difficult parking mean that it is used almost solely by the small, adjacent community; you probably won't feel very welcome. The road is bumpy and narrow; watch out for semi-feral animals that act like they own the place. You'll see parking to your right before the end of the gravel road. This area seems to have been a magnet for historical events. Local legend (bolstered by old Spanish records) says that foreigners washed ashore here during the 1520s. Several big battles took place nearby, including the one where Kamehameha became king. (See page 77.)

❖ Pu'uhonua o Honaunau (Two-Step)

A REAL GEM This is a popular place to visit for reasons other than its water. It was the Place of Refuge in ancient times. See detailed description on page 77. For ocean lovers, the snorkeling and SCUBA just north of the boat launch (at a place commonly called Two-Step because of its easy entry) are incredible. Perhaps even as good as the more difficult-to-reach Captain Cook Monument at Kealakekua Bay, making it some of the best in the state when conditions are good, though it's deeper. *Lots* of coral. Offshore from Place of Refuge, there is a small cave where a 6-foot reef shark often rests. Don't worry, he's not a man-eater—*yet.* Very little sand here, but people lie on the hot black lava rock to warm up between rounds of snorkeling. It's outside the park so you don't have to pay. Parking can get full, but there are some lots that charge $5 if you're desperate. There are also picnic tables near the shoreline at the southern half of the park that make for absolutely splendid late afternoon picnics. We've made good use of the BBQs there and can recommend them highly. But the park closes 15 minutes *before* sunset. (How thoughtful of them…)

SOUTH ISLAND BEACHES

❖ Ho'okena Beach Park

South of Kona between mile markers 101 and 102 is a paved road leading 2.3 miles to Ho'okena Beach Park, which is nestled at the base of a cliff and lined with palm trees. Unlike other beach parks, the local community gathered together and petitioned the county to turn park operations over to them, and they have transformed this into a *(usually)* family-friendly gathering place for locals and visitors alike. You can tent camp (808-328-7321) for $21 per person per night, rent kayaks, snorkel gear or boogie boards, purchase food, and the facilities include showers, restrooms, picnic tables and shade. This pocket of fine salt-and-pepper sand is hot on your feet. Keiki (kids) ride the waves on calm days and splash about in a few tide-pools adjacent to the sandy beach. Decent snorkeling is to the left. Dolphins often enter the bay. If you walk 250 yards along the shoreline to the north, you'll come to a small inlet, the size of a swimming pool, that is *sometimes* protected from the stronger ocean.

❖ Pebble Beach

Located down a *very* steep road. (You lose 1,050 feet of elevation in 6,000 feet of driving—that's almost as steep as the notorious road into Waipi'o Valley.) It's at the bottom of Kona Paradise (off Highway 11 between mile markers 96 and 97, 20 miles south of Kona) and is one of the most violent beaches we know of. Even when calm, it will kick your 'okole. We've seen fish tossed out of the water on calm days. (*Seriously!*) The "beach" is actually countless large water-worn pebbles, which

Pu'uhonua o Honaunau

160

Less experienced
snorkelers

N

Back Entrance

Honaunau Bay

Most snorkelers enter
here at "2-Step"

Main Entrance

Excellent SCUBA →
More experienced
snorkelers here

Surgy

Boat Ramp

Visitor Center

To Picnic Tables

Hale-o-Keawe Heiau

© 2022 Wizard Publications, Inc.

Honomalino Beach on a crowded day.

make a great sound when the surf's up. If you've got the nerve, it's fun to let the surge pull you up and down the steep beach (but stay away from the shore break).

A 5-minute walk to your right (go through the rocks and find the path back through the brush) leads to a small cove with smaller pebbles and black and green sand beneath them. Not good swimming but secluded and private. Unlike the Pebble Beach rumble, this one fizzes like a glass of soda.

❖ Miloliʻi Beach Park

Located 30 miles south of Kailua-Kona, this is considered a very local beach, meaning that on *weekends* it's best to leave it to them. There is a very tight local community here, and, though Hawaiʻi is as friendly a place as you will find, you may get a little stink eye if you visit during "their time"—like crashing someone's family barbeque. This community beach sports a pavilion used by local bands playing outstanding Hawaiian music on weekends and holidays. There's not much sand, but the surfing is good, and the facilities are well-developed. (The sand was removed by a storm in the 1970s. The same storm also removed many houses. Some homeowners made the mistake of bulldozing their crumpled houses and were not allowed to rebuild. Shrewd owners knew that to stay that close to the water, they were required to keep and repair the *original* structure.)

Follow the road sign towards Miloliʻi and take the winding, one-lane paved road just south of mile marker 89 (do not take Ohana Road). Drive slowly at the end of the road, and watch for local kids.

❖ Honomalino Bay

Ask most people who live here where Honomalino is, and they'll probably tell you it's on Maui. This lovely black-and-white

Sure, you can 4WD right up to the second Road to the Sea beach. But only if you're willing to beat your vehicle like a rented mule (as the driver in the photo apparently did). Best to walk the last mile.

sand beach is 150 yards or so long, backed by scads of coconut trees, decent swimming when calm (which is often), and it's usually deserted. It's a 20-minute walk from your car. The Japanese tsunami of 2011 badly damaged this bay, killing trees and vegetation and generally roughing it up, washing away our gem rating in the process. But we're pleased to report the sand is back, along with our Real Gem rating.

To get there, start at Miloliʻi Beach Park. Go to the end of the road, and you'll see bathrooms and a yellow church. The public access is between them. (A left fork is private property; the right fork is yours.) If tide is up, you may get your feet wet. About 3 to 4 minutes into the trail after some tide-pools and a palm-backed spit of sand, follow the fenceline on your left up and over the black rock at the back of the beach and continue south for 15 min-

utes. There may be a few fallen trees to hop over. The snorkeling on the right side of the bay in the cluster of rocks is interesting when calm. If you plunge your hand into the sand at the water's edge at the south end of the beach, the sand's cold. That's freshwater (called a basal spring) percolating into the sand from below.

One of Honomalino's little-known joys is the pod of **dolphins** that sometimes cruises the sand-lined bay in the morning. Scientists think that, while resting, dolphins are able to turn off half their brain (including the half that runs their echolocation abilities). They do a sort of snooze and cruise, counting on the fact that the shallow water and light bottom will alert them to predators in the absence of their sonars. This means that, in the morning, dolphins are literally operating on half a brain. (Come to think of it, so am I before my coffee.) Open 6 a.m.–11 p.m.

From Honomalino, it's possible to find another, even more secluded black sand beach 1.5 miles south at **Okoe Bay**, but getting there requires a long hike through a hot field of lava rock, and the swimming is less protected. There are ruins of a house here. It was lifted off its foundation in the trees by the 2011 Japanese tsunami, sucked out to the shore and thrown back inland by another tsunami wave. The bay was named after a notorious serial killer from ancient times who, along with her husband, would kill *and bake* any travelers unlucky enough to come near their home.

❖ Road to the Sea Beach

This is one of Ka'u district's best-kept secrets. In Basics we mentioned that having a 4WD can come in handy. Here's a perfect example why. First, if you don't have a 4WD, you won't make it. Even some SUVs might have issues, depending on the level of cruelty you normally inflict on rental cars. This is a lava rock road, so drive slow or you risk tearing a hole in your tire. Make sure you have a spare. (Yeah, that was us changing a flat on an uneven road while you drove by and waved. Thanks for the help—*not*.) The access road is 0.7 miles past (south of) mile marker 80 on Hwy 11. The first of two beaches is at the end of this 6-mile long dirt road. Remember, you're far from Kona. If you get stuck, the first thing the tow truck driver will ask is, "Do you own your own home?" County maps show this as a *public* access, though we've seen hand-made Keep Out signs in years past.

Anyway, these two beautiful black-and-green sand beaches are nearly always deserted, especially during the week. The first beach is at the end of the road. Swimming *during calm seas* is fair, and the beach is inviting; enter it from the left (south) side. Harmless plankton-eating whale sharks are sometimes seen in the area. To the right of the end of the road is a *deep* tide-pool—7 to 9 feet in spots. It

makes a *great* wading pool *when calm*, and there's even some coral in it—unusual for a tide-pool.

The second beach is reached via a one-mile long *rough* 4WD road 0.3 miles back up from the *very* end of the road. Don't take the first Fool's Road to the left (which only leads to sorrow). Take the one with the yellow gate. If you find it too rough for your driving tastes (which you probably will), walk the mile to the second beach. It's worth it. The road leads to a much longer and finer black-and-green sand beach. (See **Green Sand Beach** on page 178 for an explanation of green sand.) At the end to the right is a freshwater pool. This one is saltier than most, but is great for dipping. There is some shade at the back part of the beach. Stay close to shore; the water can get tricky farther out.

This is a great beach to get away from it all, and you *may* have it all to yourself except during times it gets claimed for weeks at a time by…campers.

The entire area out here is lifeless, arid and desolate. It was utterly assaulted by savage lava flows 250 years ago and on paper isn't worth a hill of beans. Yet despite this (or perhaps because of it), it's alluring. The lava field looks young and raw, and the beaches are desirable. If you

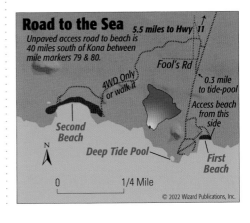

Road to the Sea 5.5 miles to Hwy 11
Unpaved access road to beach is 40 miles south of Kona between mile markers 79 & 80.
Fool's Rd
4WD Only or walk it
0.3 mile to tide-pool
Access beach from this side
Second Beach
N
Deep Tide Pool
First Beach
0   1/4 Mile
© 2022 Wizard Publications, Inc.

You won't have to walk far, but you will have to drive far to find Punalu'u Black Sand Beach.

have 4WD, it's a recommended trip. Located 40 miles south of Kona; see map on page 177.

By the way, shade is provided courtesy of the way winds wrap around Mauna Loa. Almost every day during normal tradewinds between 10 and 11 a.m., a shearline cloud forms about 5,000 feet above the beach, creating shade for the rest of the day.

❖ Green Sand (Papakolea) Beach

A REAL GEM

So you say you've seen white sand beaches. You've seen plenty of golden sand beaches. Maybe you've even seen a black sand beach. But when is the last time you frolicked on a *green* sand beach? This unusual beach owes its name and color to a large deposit of a semi-precious gem called olivine liberally mixed with black sand. After ancient volcanic eruptions created Pu'u o Mahana, a small littoral cone containing gobs of the stuff, the ocean went to work dismantling it. It has already broken through one side, and when the surf is up, each wave rakes at the back side, revealing more and more olivine. Though most of the gemstones are in the form of sand particles, people occasionally find large nuggets. (Actually, your best chance of finding a nugget is at the rarely visited adjacent cove on the far side of Green Sand Beach. Access is from the far [northeast] side). See map on page 83.

Located near South Point, which (this will stun you) is at the southernmost point on the island, access to the beach requires a 2.25-mile (each way) walk or 4WD from Kaulana Boat Launch. (The four-wheeling is sometimes pretty rough, depending on road conditions during your visit.) There are more dirt roads than we showed on the map because people are constantly creating new ones. They all go to the beach and beyond. You'd have to try real hard to get lost since you always stay within sight of the shore. Drivers will want to take the high road (near the fenceline), while walkers will want to stay closer to the shore, where they might find cool pockets of stranded white and green sand before reaching the actual Green Sand Beach. Keep an eye out for the remains of several Hawaiian structures dotting the area. During extended dry times the government often prohibits 4WD vehicles in the name of fire safety, though local residents seem to ignore the prohibition and have created a cottage industry by driving people to and from the beach for a fee. Hey, beats walking it. (They do especially brisk business with hikers who decide they don't want to walk the return trip.)

Once at the cone, most people walk down a path from about the middle of the cone, which can be slippery due to sand particles on the hard surface. Some stairs at the steepest part helps. We prefer the "path" on the closest (southwest) side (see map on page 83), which requires a short hop off a rock at one point. Unfortunately, the path is more evident from the beach than from the top and might be tough to spot. Use your best judgment. Everyone from small keiki to the elderly goes to the beach, but you are on your own in evaluating it. Check to see that the waves are not inundating the entire beach before you go down. The ocean is unprotected, so the waves are at full strength. Many books tell you that you will drown if you even *think* about swimming there. We swam there plenty of times, and if the surf's not up, it's not bad. The sand bottom is thick and there are few exposed rocks. We have yet to encounter nasty currents *in the bay,* but we're not stupid enough to venture out of the bay where the prevailing current will give you a splendid tour of Antarctica.

Again, use your best judgment. There is a shorebreak, and the undertow can be harsh. You might see plenty of local kids (or us) playing in the surf, but this is not Waikiki. And if the surf is high, definitely stay out. Those same large waves that expose the olivine could pull you in. There's no shade here, and the wind, which has beautifully sculpted the eastern side of the bay, is also the same wind that might get on your nerves if it is blowing hard, particularly in the late afternoon. Go earlier if you can. No facilities. Please resist the urge to take any of the sand with you. We've seen people taking large amounts, and the supply is finite.

The spooky snorkeling at **South Point** itself is described on page 85.

❖ Whittington Park Beach
Located off the road between mile markers 61 and 62 on the southern part of the island. Very pretty from a distance but not much of a destination. Think of it as a pit stop with restrooms and picnic tables.

❖ Punalu'u **Black Sand Beach**

This is the most easily accessible black sand beach on the island. Backed by palm trees and a freshwater pond, the sand is

Kua Bay White Sand	Green Sand Beach	New Black Sand Beach	White Powder Sand from Florida

genuine black sand—the kind created when a chunky 'a'a lava flow meets the ocean and shatters into small pieces on contact with the water. These small chunks are quickly pulverized by the ocean, forming a delicious black sand. This differs from older black sand beaches where the sand is made up of lava chipped from a river bed by coursing water. Genuine black sand beaches are relatively fleeting since the source of the sand ends as soon as the lava flow stops. This contrasts with white and golden sand beaches, which have organic sources (coral or shells) that continue to build up sand over time. (In fact, one large, coral-munching parrotfish can produce 3 *tons* of white sand per year by himself!) That's why you don't see genuine black sand on old islands—the black sand erodes into the ocean over time and cannot be recovered.

The swimming is a bit different here than at many other island beaches. Cold freshwater springs bubble up from just offshore. Consequently, the top 8 to 12 inches of the water is guaranteed to freeze your 'okole off. You can usually see the floating freshwater while swimming and will be tempted to swim below to get a semblance of warmth. The visibility here is only fair, and you need to be conscious of rip currents. Generally, you want to stay fairly close to shore and be aware of currents during all but the calmest seas. Past the boat launch on the left (north) side of the beach, the rips can be a problem. Check with the lifeguards before swimming that area.

So why swim Punalu'u at all? Well, one of this beach's lesser-known treats is its **turtles**. The waters can get almost *crowded* with them. We've been here when you

Meet Isaac Hale Black Sand Beach—born August 2018.

could see small groups of turtles every couple of minutes. They munch on limu that clings to rocks on the sea floor. Please remember not to disturb or play with them. In addition to the possible harm, it might cause them to find a less accessible beach to frolic.

Near the southern tip of the island between mile markers 56 and 55 on Hwy 11. The facilities at the southwest end parking lot get heavy use from the local community as well as tour buses. The less-used northeast lot is much more convenient.

EAST SIDE BEACHES

Past Punalu'u your choices for beaches diminish along with their caliber. Put simply, the east shore, which is exposed to more hazardous surf and lots of river runoff, has fewer and mostly poorer beaches. Therefore, we are breaking them up into regions and deviating from our usual organization by describing many in the tours of the various regions.

❖ Puna Beaches

Located near the extreme eastern part of the island, **Kehena Black Sand Beach** and ✚ **Isaac Hale Beach Park** survived the 2018 volcanic eruption. **Ahalanui Warm Springs**, and **Kapoho Tide-pools** were victims of the lava flows and no longer exist. All are described in *Hilo & Puna Sights*. **Ha'ena Beach** is described in *Hiking* on page 213.

❖ Hilo Beach Parks

To the east on Kalanianaole (where highways 11 and 19 meet) are Hilo's most popular beach parks starting with **Keaukaha**. During summer months it's a tent and tarp city with long-term campers. The rest of the year it's simply a great park to avoid. ✚ **Onekahakaha Beach Park** has a boulder-enclosed pool

that is popular with local keiki (kids). The sand-lined pool is utterly protected except during very high seas. The pool to the left is rockier and has lots of urchins on the floor. Past Onekahakaha is **(James) Kealoha Beach Park**. Though picturesque, the swimming is poor, and you're likely to share it with young toughs drinking too much and giving you stink eye. Best to move on to ✚ **Carlsmith Beach Park** just across the bay. There are full facilities and a nice lawn area. The swimming is marginal around the lifeguard tower. Go to the far right side where the water is more protected, and keep an eye out for turtles. If you drive past the Mauna Loa Shores condo to an unmarked parking lot, you can access the park from a short but *very* cool jungle trail. (Bring bug spray for it.) Farther east is **Wai'olena** and **Wai'uli Beach Parks**. This last area contains ✚ **Richardson's Ocean Center** at the far end and is particularly attractive with freshwater pools sprinkled about. The county Aquatics Division is located here. This is an excellent place for a picnic, though sometimes the (James) Kealoha crowd spills over to here. There's a small black sand cove where you can enter the water. It'll be cold from freshwater intruding into the area. Some of Hilo's better snorkeling is here. Dolphins often frequent the area, and turtles usually congregate a little farther down the coast toward Hilo. Check with lifeguards because this area is subject to strong surf.

Other beach parks north of Hilo are ✚ **Honoli'i, Kolekole Beach, Hakalau Bay, Waikaumalo Park**, and **Laupahoehoe Point**. Farther north is the difficult to access but beautiful black sand beach of **Waipi'o Bay**. All are described in the *Hamakua & Waimea Sights* chapter.

The Big Island is a snorkeler's paradise. This is at the Captain Cook Monument in Kealakekua Bay.

Take a deep breath and do some stretching before you read this chapter, because the Big Island has so much to see and do that you're likely to pull something just reading about it all. Among the more popular activities are fishing, golfing, snorkeling, SCUBA, hiking, horseback riding, kayaking, helicopter tours, boat trips, submarine rides and whale watching. Whatever you're into—even snow skiing!—you're likely to find it here on the Big Island.

It's sometimes less expensive to book an activity directly with the individual provider (most offer discounts for making reservations online), but not always. Many resorts have activity directors and booths, sometimes run by the activity providers themselves, so be aware that their "recommendations" may be biased. Many of the booths spread around the island are actually forums for selling timeshares. That's not a dig at timeshares; it's just that you need to know the real purpose of some of these booths. They can be very aggressive. (Don't get skewered by one of the long metal hooks.) Free breakfasts and "island orientations" are often similar to activity booths. So if you are steered to XYZ helicopter company and assured that they are the best, that's fine, but consider the source. We walk up to these booths frequently. Some are reputable and honest, and some are outrageous. We have no stake in *any* company we recommend; we just want to steer you in the best direction we can.

And speaking of our smartphone app (OK, we weren't speaking of it—this is just our clumsy way of talking about it here), we've GPSed all the companies in this and every other section. Not necessarily their home office (which Google might take you to) but the actual location where you are expected to check in, as well as all of our trails, all the roads, etc. You can even see where you are on our maps at all times. Can't do that in a book or eBook. But our *Hawaii Revealed* smartphone app does just that, even when you're out of cell phone range. It does a bunch of other cool stuff, too.

If you've been on a helicopter or airplane flight on another island, especially Kaua'i, you've been treated to wall-to-wall, tongue-wagging sights. The Big Island, however, has lots of fantastic areas spread about with less interesting areas connecting them. The northeast side is a lush wonderland, the southeast side is where the volcano is, and the west side is dominated by mostly bare lava. That's why limited tours are so different on each side of the island.

Here, more than most islands, your tour is affected by the passion (or lack thereof) of the pilot. A boring pilot will sound something like this: "On your left is such and such valley, and on your right is such and such hill, and in front is the such and such lava flow." *So what?!* What you really want is a knowledgeable pilot with a command of the island who also knows to speak only when it improves the silence. We prefer companies that let you ask the pilot questions through a microphone, as opposed to those where the pilots tells you "everything you need to know."

Caution—Before spending the money to see the erupting volcano at Halema-'uma'u Crater, make sure that what is happening in the crater is visually worth the price of a flight. There is sometimes a TFR (temporary flight restriction) over the crater up to the 9,000-foot level, and when there

is you won't be getting anywhere near the eruption crater, regardless of what the helicopter companies tell you. Even when there's no TFR, it might not be visually compelling enough (especially compared to the shamelessly out of date photos some companies promote) to justify the cost.

HELICOPTER TOURS

Years ago helicopters were allowed to skim the ground. Now, air tour operators are restricted to flying 500 feet or higher over unpopulated areas. That doesn't mean that you won't walk off the aircraft with drool running down your shirt from the mesmerizing experience. It can still happen; you just aren't *assured* of it. When the music, helicopter, pilot and sights all come together, it'll still blow you away. We've flown with pilots who have an undisguised passion for the island and those who may as well be driving a flying bus. Unfortunately, most companies don't use the same pilots all the time, so it's sometimes hard to steer you toward the good ones.

With Kilauea volcano putting on a lava show from 1983 until 2018, a whole industry was created and matured to showcase the lava and the national park from the air. But that all changed in the summer of 2018 when the lava flows increased in fury in Lower Puna before fizzling out altogether. You will doubtless see countless photos on brochures and websites showing dramatic reasons to take a volcano tour from Hilo. But odds are you won't see that. Consequently, we recommend tours of the valleys of Hamakua to get the most bang for your helicopter buck, and only two companies do that from Kohala. (Hilo is too far with too much uninteresting aerial terrain in between.) Yeah, the park is still interesting from the air, and you'll see the devastating consequences of the 2018 flow, but it's harder to justify the money you'll put out for a volcano flight. Like exotic life that forms ecosystems at undersea volcanic vents, when the volcano stops, the ecosystem loses its source of energy. The same seems to have happened for Hilo-based flights.

In general, we recommend that helicopter tours be taken from Kohala. Tours that leave from Kona bound for the volcano spend too much time over less interesting areas, and you'll pay through the nose. Hilo flights suffer from the issues described above. But Blue Hawaiian leaves from Waikoloa, and Sunshine leaves from Hapuna, so the Hamakua coast (described below) is close by.

A-Star helicopters are the most popular. They hold six passengers, with four in back and two beside the pilot up front. The middle seats in the back are so-so; the others are good. Think of the A-Star as a pleasant tour bus. Blue Hawaiian and Sunshine use **Eco-Stars** (aka Whisper-Stars), a much larger, quieter and cushier cousin to the A-Star. Windows are larger, so you'll have better views, and it's noticeably roomier inside. The downside is the price. Since these birds are so expensive (more than $3 million a pop), you may pay a hefty premium of around 20% more for the comfort. **MD 500s** have two passengers in the somewhat cramped back and two *outstanding* front seats next to the pilot. This copter feels like a sports car, and the side views from the back are excellent. Windows come off, if you want. They are less popular because they are less profitable for the operators. Some companies, like Tropical, have them but use them more often for non-tour business. **Bell Jet Rangers** are less comfortable with three in back and one passenger up front. The back middle seat is a poor seat indeed. The **Bell 407** carries two unlucky passengers facing backward (which is charitably called *limousine* seating). It's a terrible configuration for a tour helicopter. We like the MD 500s, Eco-Stars and A-Stars much better.

Afternoon tours are sometimes bumpier. I can tell you that as a pilot myself, I do most of my flying on the Big Island in the morning when conditions are usually best. You may want to also.

If you want to get around the altitude restrictions, think about *chartering* the aircraft. It's worth considering if you have a group, or if you strike up a friendship with other travelers. It might not cost any more than a regular tour, and *you* get to call the shots. (And you can leave the doors off, if you want, on the MDs.)

The Companies

Blue Hawaiian (800-745-2583) flies nice A-Stars and Eco-Stars out of Waikoloa, near the Kohala resort area, and out of Hilo. They use the expensive Bose Acoustic Noise-Canceling headphones and offer a recording of your trip on USB for an extra $60. (Pretty poor quality, though.) The 2-hour volcano and Hamakua Coast tour (called the Big Island Spectacular), which leaves from Waikoloa and briefly lands in Hilo, is $649 and uses roomy **Eco-Stars**. For an extra $225 they'll land at Punalulu Falls on the Hamakua Coast and let you roam around for a bit. This 800-foot falls (not 1,200 feet, as they claim) is truly spectacular. They also have a Kohala Coast Adventure for $359. It goes from Waikoloa to Waipi'o Valley, but misses the beautiful Hamakua Coast. Overall, the most tightly run outfit of the bunch. Their online discounts can be pretty decent.

Sunshine (808-270-3999) must be mighty glad they secured a departure point at the Hapuna Heliport in Kohala years ago, because now their tours of the

Hamakua coast stand out as a good product, while their volcano flights from this distant departure point should be avoided. (By the way, the photos on their website show the volcano in its boisterous heyday, not like it is now.) They use Eco-Stars (which they call Whisper-Stars), and it's $324 ($399 for the front seat) for the 40-minute trips. A recording of your trip on USB is an extra $60. Try to book online if you can—doing so usually rewards you with a sizable discount.

There's much less reason to go with **Paradise Helicopters** (808-969–7392). For a whopping $869 you fly from Kona to the volcano, then up the whole windward side to the Hamakua Coast for a brief landing. Yeah, the landing is cool, but you're paying for a lot less compelling scenery between all that. Also, they use a Bell 407 that includes two unfortunate rear-facing seats. Paradise also has a doors-off MD 500 trip out of Waimea, which is a sporty way to see waterfalls for around $380. (For $520 they'll also land in the mountains for a 0.5-mile hike.) If price is everything, they have some of the cheapest flights from Hilo in the Bell. They also go by the old name **Tropical Helicopters**, and if you call them that on the phone, you get a discount. (Seriously.)

Safari Helicopters (808-969-1259) leaves from Hilo. We've always been a bit lukewarm about their product and still are. Their prices seem unjustifiably steep. The 55-minute tour is around $300 over Volcanoes National Park, as well as several

Beware of helicopter companies that use photos such as this to lure your business. This isn't happening anymore.

186

waterfalls, to the new black sand beach. Their website rates (where you may see lots of photos of how the volcano *used* to be, but isn't now) can be dramatically cheaper. They do offer discounts if you have a larger group, so if you think you'll be filling out one (or more) of these helicopters, it may be worth contacting them in advance and asking what the best rate is. Otherwise, you can always book a private tour for $1,450.

Mauna Loa Helicopters (808-329-4422) is a little different. These are private charters. They don't sell tickets individually, and you can expect the costs to reflect that. They offer 30-minute R44 flights out of Kona for their Kona Coast Experience and their Kona Sunset Experience. Both of these are $190 per person, with a minimum of two people and a maximum of three. If money's no object, you can spring for their R66 tours—the Magical Waterfalls Tour (a 75-minute showcase of some of Big Island's waterfalls for $380 per person) or the Big Island Experience (a 2-hour amalgam of all of their other tours, plus an aerial view of the volcano for $515 per person). You can choose doors on or off for their R44 tours, which is pretty nifty. The Magical Waterfalls tour lets you fly with the doors off if you don't have any passengers under 12. The Big Island Experience is exclusively a doors-on tour. (They say it's for passenger comfort, and we believe them—2 hours of brisk winds is a bit much.) These are not turbine-driven choppers like the other guys. They are cheaper-to-operate Robinsons, and they have tighter weight restrictions for the group.

AIRPLANE TOURS

Because of its size and relative flatness, the Big Island makes airplane tours an acceptable alternative. The Hamakua Coast experience is diminished a bit (because planes aren't as nimble in the valleys as helicopters), but if you insist on leaving from Kona, the price and quantity of terrain shown is tempting.

Big Island Air (808-329-4868) flies a four-passenger Cessna P337H Skymaster from Kona on round-the-island tours (well…*mostly* around) for around $558. (Plus, shorter tours of waterfalls and valleys for around $398.) They do a pretty good job, the routes are interesting, and the pilot does his narrating well. It's bumpy at times, so consider motion sickness medicine. (Morning is definitely best.) Though the plane is very old (they stopped making these in 1982) the pusher/puller twin engine design is considered one of the safest twins if properly maintained.

Tropicbird (808-895-4753) is a more traditional flight school with a Cessna 172, 182 and much newer Diamond Eclipse. Pilots will enjoy taking the controls, and students will find the Big Island a cool place to take lessons. Check their website for complicated pricing.

Company	Phone	Departure	Helicopter Type	2-Way*
Blue Hawaiian	(800) 745-2583	Waikoloa, Hilo	A-Star, Eco-Star	Yes
Sunshine	(808) 270-3999	Hapuna	Eco-Star	Yes
Paradise Helicopters	(808) 969-7392	Waimea, Kona	Bell 407, Hughes	Yes
Safari Helicopters	(808) 969-1259	Hilo	A-Star	Yes
Mauna Loa Helicopters	(808) 329-4422	Kona	Robinson R44, R66	Yes

Companies toward the top are recommended more than the ones toward the bottom.
*Indicates whether craft has a microphone for you to talk to the pilot.

The only thing better than seeing the many falls along the Hamakua Coast is to land at one, as one helicopter company does.

Ahh, those four-wheeled things that look like Tonka Toys on steroids with knobby tires. They are often used by ranchers to chase cows these days and are quite a bit of fun to ride.

All About the View (808-775-7291) also conducts tours on their working livestock ranch. Tours are $150 and 2.5 hours long. Note that drivers must be 18 or up with a valid driver's license.

Another company, **Aloha Adventure Farms** (808-796-0110), includes an educational aspect to their tours. The 2-hour tour travels through different "villages" that represent various islands throughout Polynesia, each with its own cultural activity—you can even add on a wood carving lesson. $189 per person for the standard tour where you can either be a driver on an ATV, or a passenger with a guide on a UTV (which stands for Utility Terrain Vehicles and just means there's seating for more than one person).

Umauma Experience (808-930-9477) has the most expensive ATV/UTV tour at $212 for a 1.5-hour ride. Here you also get the option of taking a quick dip in a waterfall during the snack break.

With a moniker like the Big Island, you would expect an endless variety of biking choices. Sure enough, many of the highways, such as Queen K where they run the Ironman, have nice bike lanes so you can cruise long distances.

But be prepared for strong crosswinds in Kohala.

MOUNTAIN BIKING

If it's **mountain biking** that you prefer, and you are willing to transport a bike somewhere, these four rides can be fun:

South Point—Check out the map on page 83 and the description of the area in the *South Island Sights* chapter. You can ride from South Point past Green Sand Beach on the 4WD roads—lots of fun. The wind is usually with you coming back. This is wide-open country with good mountain bike roads.

Hawai'i Volcanoes National Park—There are always a number of riding possibilities here, but it's a good idea to check with them to see what's open. This park has gone through enormous geological shifts recently resulting in closures (and some reopenings). Volcanoes can be unpredictable and this park changes quickly. Check out our app for more current information on what trails are ridable.

Our favorite current path is a dirt "escape" road that leads through beautiful rainforest from Thurston Lava Tube to Chain of Craters Road and the Mauna Ulu Trailhead. (See maps on pages 96 and 203.) It's a 4-mile well maintained and very scenic road, with green assaulting your eyes from both directions. Return on the escape road, or take Chain of Craters road back up (right) 1.5 miles, then turn left onto Hilina Pali Road (before mile marker 3 on Chain of Craters Road) as far as you want to go before returning.

Mana Road—This road leads through Parker Ranch and winds around the makai (ocean) side of Mauna Kea. It starts near mile marker 55 on the main highway in Waimea. See maps on page 126 and 137, as well as the inside back cover map of the route. It's a 45-mile dirt road that leads to Mauna Kea Access Road, which then connects to Saddle Road. Unless you are very motivated/insane and arrange for transportation from Saddle Road, you'll probably just want to take Mana Road as far as you like, then turn around and come back. If you decide you want to bike the whole road, you can read more on this in *Adventures* on page 245.

Kona and Hilo—If you are staying in Kona and want to ride on the street, cruise down Alii Drive along the coast. If you're staying in Hilo, Stainback Highway (see page 116) is a great road to sail down on a mountain bike. You could then take North Kulani to Highway 11 where the shoulders coming back to Hilo are usually wide.

GUIDED BIKE TOURS

Several companies offer a variety of guided tours. **Big Island Bike Tours** (808-769-1308) has day and multi-day tours including lodging. Prices vary. And **Bike Volcano** (808-934-9199) does tours of Volcanoes National Park starting at $230. Their advertising photos—showing Pu'u 'O'o from the air and surface flows and fountaining lava—are unrealistic now (since there is no lava). This company seems to have random block-off dates for their tours.

BIKE SHOPS

Most bike shops offer discounts on multi-day rentals. In Kona, the best bike shop we know is **Bike Works** (808-326-2453), visible from the highway, off Kaiwi Street. Excellent selection of bikes and bike accessories. Full suspension mountain bikes (the best you'll find on the island) rent for $75 per day. $55 for a hardtail. They also offer electric-assisted e-bikes for $100 per day. (Prices drop if you rent for longer.) In Kohala, **Bike Works Beach & Sports** (808-886-5000) in the Queens' MarketPlace has specialized road bikes and e-bikes for $80–$95; hybrids and cruisers are $40 per day. **Bike Works Mauka** (808-885-7943) in Waimea on Hwy 19 near Kamamalu has hardtail and full-suspension mountain bikes, as well as gravel bikes and e-bikes, for $80–$95 per day. If you're a serious biker and want to bring your own from home, **Hilo Bike Hub** (808-961-4452) will receive and assemble it, then pack it back up for you for about $120. Adjustments are extra, as are shipping cartons. **Bike Works** has a similar service.

Boat Tours

Aspen has its ski slopes, Washington has its monuments, Orlando has Disney World, and the Big Island has the Kona Coast waters. Quite simply, if you visit the Big Island and don't ply the Kona waters, you haven't *really* been to the Big Island.

The waters off the Kona Coast are the finest in all the islands. Calmer, clearer and teeming with fish, Big Island waters make residents of other islands turn *blue* with envy. A popular way to see these waters is on an ocean tour. If you take one of the many tours along the coast, you *may* see turtles. You are *likely* to see dolphins, flying fish off the bow and whales during whale season. You *will* see smiles from fellow passengers.

You're less likely to get **seasick** on Kona's calm waters than anywhere else we can think of. Nonetheless, if you take seasickness medication, do it *before* you leave. (The night before and morning of are best. It's useless to take it once you're on the boat.) Also, avoid any alcohol the night before. No greasy foods before or during the trip. And some think that citrus is a no-no. Ginger is a very good preventative/treatment. Below deck is a bad place to be if you're worried about getting seasick. Without a reference point,

Though it's possible to encounter dolphins on a traditional snorkel tour, your best bet is a dedicated dolphin encounter mentioned in Adventures.

you're much more likely to let 'er rip down there. Scopolamine patches work but have side effects, including (occasionally) blurred vision that can last a week. (Been there, done that, on a 10-day California–Hawai'i trip.)

Boats are usually less crowded on weekends since that's when visitors usually arrive and depart the island. And remember, most single-hull power boats ride smoothest in the back.

KEALAKEKUA BAY

The Captain Cook Monument in Kealakekua Bay is a favorite destination. Snorkeling near the monument is perhaps the best you will find anywhere in the state. If you've never snorkeled before, this is the place to start. Experienced snorkelers will be dazzled. A large number of spinner dolphins reside in the bay, and you're likely to see them—perhaps even swim near them, if you're *real* lucky. (They are called spinners because they are the only untrained dolphins that routinely leap clear of the water and spin on their longitudinal axis.) Companies sometimes offer a choice of morning or afternoon tours. Take the morning; it's calmer and the water is usually clearer. Prices may be lower for children; check to see if there is a discount for booking online.

THE BIG BOATS

Fair Wind II (808-322-2788) uses a 60-foot power catamaran to bring 100 or so people. They leave from Keauhou Bay, 7.5 miles north and stay tied to their mooring for a couple hours. While they're moored, people make good use of the short waterslide, high dive platform and cash bar. You motor along at a leisurely 10 mph the whole way, which is great, but the boat trolls most of the way, far enough from shore that you won't see many coastal features. This is a good tour overall, especially for families with young kids and those wary about the ocean. $159 for the 4.5-hour morning tour, $115 for the 3.5-hour afternoon tour. SNUBA is available for an extra charge. Overall, this is a great tour, and most guests seem to really love it.

One gripe, though. The owners must have become vegans, and that is certainly their choice. But they apparently insist

The last one in the water is buying the mai tais.

that you do the same onboard, too, because they ditched the awesome BBQ burgers and serve only vegan food. If you're an omnivore, the food won't seem quite as hearty after your snorkel, during which we usually work up an appetite. It's also worth mentioning that sodas are only free during lunch; they charge the rest of the time. Oh, and no dessert. Alcohol only available the last hour of your trip.

Hula Kai (808-322-2788) is from the same company that runs Fair Wind II, and it also leaves from Keauhou Bay. But this power cat smokes along at 25 knots and visits two snorkel spots. They market this as a more upscale trip with a bit more personal attention, smaller crowds and no one under age 7. They also have paddle boards for the snorkel-shy. There isn't a bad seat on the boat (though not all seats have shade), and they're very comfortable. Two bathrooms on board. Cash bar limited to beer and wine. Overall, a very nice 5-hour morning for $165. SNUBA and underwater scooters available for an extra charge.

Sea Paradise (808-322-2500) is a 45-foot sailing trimaran that leaves from Keauhou Bay. They attempt to sail on every trip if there's wind. With juices and muffins in the morning, sandwiches, soft drinks and cash bar at lunch, a friendly staff and good boat, this is an easy trip to recommend. $137 for this less-crowded alternative to the Fair Wind II. The morning trip includes two snorkel spots; the afternoon cruise goes to Kealakekua Bay for $82 but does not include lunch.

THE SMALL KINE BOATS

Sea Quest (808-329-7238) is a totally different experience from the big boats. They take up to 14 passengers on their rigid-hull inflatables (which is a good design because it absorbs bumps better than a regular rubber raft) to the Captain Cook Monument and beyond to Honaunau (Place of Refuge) for snorkeling. It's bumpier than the Fair Wind II, and there's no shade unless you're on the boat they use for the 5-hour tours. (Bumpier means more thrilling though potentially more seasick.) You won't have all that wandering room that you have on the Fair Wind II, and it's snacks instead of a meal, but these guys give an entertaining tour. They travel out as far as 2 miles away from the shore and then get up close and personal with the coastline, doing a great job of narrating what you are seeing the whole time. Along the way they poke the boat into several "sea caves," and show you how they are formed. We like them better than Captain Zodiac below because they snorkel in two spots and take their time on the way back. (They can afford to because they depart from Keauhou Bay, 10 miles closer to the monument than Captain Zodiac.) $142 for the more recommended 4.5-hour morning trip, $105 for the 3-hour trip, which omits Honaunau. And it's $155 if you want three snorkel spots (and shade) over the course of 5 hours with a deli lunch.

Dolphin Discoveries (808-322-8000) uses a rigid-hull inflatable boat like Sea Quest, offering a very similar product for similar prices. They do a pretty good job as well. Their boats have a touch of shade—seems to be more for the captain, really. They take 14 people at most. Their 4-hour, morning snorkel cruise is $130 and includes two snorkel spots, gear, snacks and drinks. The afternoon snorkel tour is 3 hours and only one snorkel stop for $104. The Dolphin Discovery Adventure has changed to become more of a dolphin watching tour with three stops for snorkeling. The tour is $149 but not different enough from the morning snorkel cruise to justify the higher price.

Captain Zodiac (808-329-3199) leaves from Honokohau Harbor. Though the crew does well, they suffer from their location. Honokohau adds 20 miles (round trip) of relatively uninteresting Kona shoreline compared to rafts that leave from Keauhou Bay. Perhaps this is why they only snorkel at one spot. The good news is that one and a half of the 4 hours is spent at the monument area with snacks provided. $125 per person. They have a 5-hour tour for $140 that includes one or two snorkeling spots and lunch. This is an adequate tour, but we recommend Sea Quest or the Fair Wind II over Captain Zodiac. They also have a contract with the cruise ships, so on cruise ship days, boats are packed to the max.

OTHER BOAT DESTINATIONS

Body Glove (808-326-7122) leaves from Kailua Pier and usually cruises to Red Hill 10 miles to the south (which has fairly good snorkeling, but not as good as Kealakekua Bay). The Kanoa II is a 65-foot catamaran that carries 105 passengers. They have continental breakfast at boarding and BBQ lunch at the site. In addition to snorkeling, they have SCUBA (for an extra fee). Good boats, crew and location make this a good deal, and we recommend it wholeheartedly when they're not at max capacity—105 or less. (When they're full, expect lines getting in and out of the water.) Lots of shade, waterslide, restrooms and a full cash bar on board. Fun noodles and see-thru boogie boards for the timid. Their 4.5-hour morning tour is $158. What they do best is their dinner cruise, see page 292.

Kamanu Charters (808-329-2021) leaves Honokohau Harbor in their 36-foot *sailing* catamaran and heads 2.25 miles south to Pawai Bay. $99, 24 passengers at most,

good snorkeling, light lunch along with beer and wine. Only a little shade for this 3-hour tour (like Gilligan's Island?). It's an acceptable trip, but unless you really want to *sail*, you're better off on the Body Glove—better boat, longer trip.

Kailua Bay Charter (808-324-1749) has quickie tours (less than an hour) of Kailua Bay with a glass-bottom boat for $58. No food, just a quick jaunt through the water. Leaves from Kailua Pier. Not overly compelling.

Ocean Sports (808-886-6666) has several boats but generally picks up their customers from the beach at ʻAnaehoʻomalu Bay in Waikoloa. Morning snorkel trips from their 58-foot catamaran Sea Smoke go south to the Ke-awa-iki Beach area or north to the Mauna Lani area. The 3.5-hour trip includes fruit and juice in the morning, deli lunch and open bar that includes two local beers on tap. They'll usually sail for half the trip, and overall, the crew does a good job. (Avoid the pricey parking at the Marriott in favor of the free public beach parking.) Usually 30–40 people. $159.

Boogie boarding (riders are derisively referred to as *spongers* by surfers) is where you ride a wave on what is essentially a sawed-off surfboard. It can be a real blast. You need short, stubby fins to catch bigger waves (which break in deeper water), but small waves can be snared by simply standing in shallow water and lurching forward as the wave is breaking. If you've never done it before, stay away from big waves; they can drill you. Surf is usually highest in winter months. Smooth-bottom boards work best. Men who don't do this often should—*this is important*—wear shirts, oth-

A boogie boarder rides his first...and last wave of the day.

erwise you can rub your *da kines* raw. (Women will already have their *da kines* covered, except at Kehena Beach.)

The chapter on **Beaches** describes whether a beach is good for boogie boarding. Our favorite is **Hapuna** in Kohala. Conditions are usually excellent. We also like Mauna Kea, Maniniʻowali/Kua Bay and White Sands Beach. You won't have any trouble finding places to rent boards, so we won't bother mentioning them individually. Just keep an eye out for signs. Expect to pay $5–$8 per day, $15–$20 per week. Or you can buy them at Costco, Walmart, etc., for $30 plus. The bigger you are, the bigger the board you need.

CAMPING

From jungles to beaches and everything in between, the Big Island has a plethora of camping opportunities (some even include the cabin—no tents required).

VOLCANO CAMPING

There's a drive-up campground at the Kilauea Volcano called **Namakanipaio** **Campground**, just outside the park entrance at 4,000 feet. (See map on page 96.) They have 10 simple cabins for $92 each. Each has multiple beds, community showers (good thing it's not the other way around) and a BBQ and firepit. Call (808) 756-9625 for reservations. Plan plenty far in advance; the cabins fill up quickly, and we've noticed the campground is sometimes closed for months at a time. Tents are also permitted for $15, and there's almost always plenty of space. For an *additional* $40, they will provide and set up a tent for you. Inside the park there's a $10 per night backcountry campsite (pit toilet only) called **Kulanaokuaiki** on Hilina Pali Road.

Also in the park are several campsites that require *long* hikes. (The lagoon at **Halape** is awesome.) Contact the park directly at (808) 985-6178 to see which ones are open. You can pick up your $10 permits when you get there, and there's usually no problem getting them.

MOUNTAIN CAMPING

Along the Hamakua Coast but not on the ocean, **Kalopa State Recreation Area**

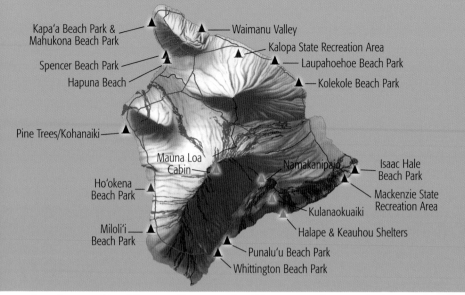

Campsites–County Sites in Black, State Sites in Red, National Park Sites in Green

Kapa'a Beach Park & Mahukona Beach Park

Waimanu Valley

Kalopa State Recreation Area

Spencer Beach Park

Laupahoehoe Beach Park

Hapuna Beach

Kolekole Beach Park

Pine Trees/Kohanaiki

Mauna Loa Cabin

Namakanipaio

Isaac Hale Beach Park

Ho'okena Beach Park

Mackenzie State Recreation Area

Kulanaokuaiki

Miloli'i Beach Park

Halape & Keauhou Shelters

Punalu'u Beach Park

Whittington Beach Park

---

has decent cabins (plus a well-equipped kitchen/dining hall) for $100 and covered campsites for tents for $30. The limited hiking is good (but *muddy*), and the park is in beautiful shape.

BEACH CAMPING

Many of the beach parks around the island are available for camping with a permit. The best near Kona is **Pine Trees (Kohanaiki Beach Park)**, just slightly south of the airport. Fall out of your car and pitch your tent in the sand. Full bathroom and shower facilities.

South of Kona, **Ho'okena** (see the beach description on page 174) stands out. They're privately run, so you'll have to book through their website.

In Kohala, **Hapuna State Park** has A-frame shelters available, but they're $70 per night and pretty bleak. There were other sites at press time that weren't recommendable, so we left them off the map. **Spencer Beach Park** is OK.

Waimanu Valley is utterly remote and stunningly beautiful, but it'll take most of a day to go down into Waipi'o Valley, up the trail on the cliff, then down into Waimanu. Unfortunately, due to Waipi'o's road closure, camping in Waimanu Valley is not an option, and probably won't be for the foreseeable future.

CAMPSITE RESERVATIONS

For state campsite reservations, visit **camping.ehawaii.gov**. For county campsites, visit **hawaiicounty.ehawaii.gov**. Tent camping at state parks is $30 per site per night. The county charges an outrageous price of $21 *per person* per night. And you thought camping on the beach would be a good way to save money.

OK, so technically we should have put this under *spelunking*, but we had a sneaking suspicion that it might get overlooked there.

The Big Island is the land of lava tubes. The other islands had them, too, but most have collapsed over time. Lava tubes are a characteristic of young, growing islands. And they don't get any younger than the Big Island.

In the *Sights* and *Adventures* chapters we've identified some lava tubes that you can hike through *on your own*. If that prospect seems too much trouble or too risky for you, there are guided lava tube hikes that you may want to consider. They are in the southern or eastern part of the island since it's the most geologically active. We list them in order of our preference. Contemplate bringing your own bright light since the one provided might not be that great.

Kazumura Cave Tours (808-967-7208) takes you along part of Kazumura Cave near Glenwood, one of the longest lava tubes known in the world. The guide's knowledge of geology is good, and he reminds us of our favorite teacher from high school. The walking is pretty easy (with a few ladders), and you'll learn a lot. $45 per person. Their 4-hour tour—more physical with some rock scrambling—is $90 and well worth it. Closed Sundays. You have to wear long pants and closed shoes.

Kula Kai Caverns (808-929-9725) in Ka'u is a different experience. They have a 1-hour tour for $28. The portion of the cave for this tour is lighted. It's less physically demanding but lacks the punch of the longer tours. For $95, they take you to a harder-to-reach portion where you get to walk in the footsteps of the ancients. In days of old, living in Ka'u was hard, and finding freshwater was even harder. Hawaiians used to place hollowed-out gourds to catch water from the dripping ceilings, and some of their remains, including burned-out torches, gourds and spent kukui nuts

(for lamp oil), are still evident. There is nothing else like this in Hawai'i, and the owners are serious cavers who have a passion for conservation.

Volcano Cave Adventures (808-960-5664) has an unusual cave from a Mauna Loa flow in Glenwood. Though their knowledge of geology is poor, the tube is a bit more interesting. It's unusual in that there's lots of mud and some water flowing through it. The footing is much more awkward here (and the lights are weak, too), but it's fun and they're friendly, if a bit disorganized. $25 per person—two-person minimum. No preset tour times; try to call the owner after 5 p.m. to schedule something.

Our last choice would be **Kilauea Caverns of Fire** (808-217-2363). It's 10 miles

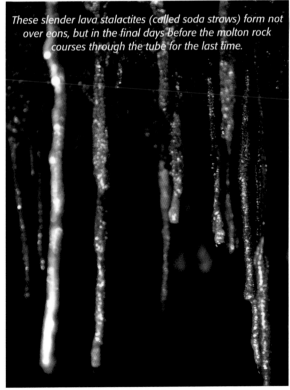

These slender lava stalactites (called soda straws) form not over eons, but in the final days before the molton rock courses through the tube for the last time.

south of Hilo. Their stretch of lava tube is less interesting than the others, and their command of geology is highly suspect. They really need to work on their light situation. (On one visit, our dim flashlight was the only one working when the guide's light died.) It's $29 for the 1-hour tour. Their $89 3-hour "adventure tour" is even less recommended. They also offer a "Day in the Cave" for $279, which explores miles of the cave.

If you had to pick the one sport Kona is most famous for, it would probably be its big game fishing. The waters off the Kona coast drop to great depths quickly and are teeming with big game fish. When there's a strike, the adrenaline level of everyone on board shoots through the roof. Most talked about are the marlin *(very hard fighters known for multiple runs)*, including blue, stripers and the occasional black. These goliaths can tip the scales at over 1,000 pounds. (Virtually all marlin above 300 pounds are female.) Also in abundance are ono, also called wahoo (one of the fastest fish in the ocean and indescribably delicious—they strike very hard but tire quicker), mahimahi (vigorous fighters—excellent on light tackle), ahi (delicious yellowfin tuna) and spearfish. With calm sunny conditions 300 days per year, quick access to the fishing areas, and strong competition among more than 100 fishing companies, Kona has become a magnet for first-timers wishing to try their hand at catching the big one.

FISHING BASICS

A marine fishing license is required as of 2021 for all non-residents...but the system to book it isn't up and running as of press time. When it is up, a license will be $20 per day or $40 per week. For now, you only need a license for freshwater fishing, which is $11 per week or $21 per month. Visit: **dlnr.hawaii.gov/dar/** for updates.

Fish are plentiful year-round but more numerous in the summer.

The largest blue marlin ever caught in the state was a hull-popping 1,805 lbs.

Most boats leave out of **Honokohau Harbor**, just north of Kona. A surprising number of the thousand-pounders (granders) have been caught just outside the harbor. This is probably because the harbor is flushed clean every day by freshwater springs, expelling the contents of the harbor. Perhaps passing fish like to hang around the harbor entrance to scoop up the results of that day's fish cleaning.

Most boats troll nonstop. They don't target a particular fish—they just troll for whatever they can get. You will probably have to bring your own food and beverages.

Most passengers on Kona fishing boats are novices, so don't feel self-conscious if you have no idea what you are doing. Deck hands will handle all of the arrangements; just sit back and relax.

You should know in advance that in Hawai'i, the fish belongs to the boat. What happens to the fish is entirely up to the captains, and they usually keep it. You may catch a 1,000-pound marlin and be told that you can't have as much as a steak from it. If this bothers you, you're out of luck. If the ono or another small fish are striking a lot and there is a glut of them, you might be allowed to keep it—or half of it. You *may* be able to make arrangements in advance to the contrary, but I doubt it.

You will go on a shared charter (with other folks) or a private charter. Nearly all charter boats are licensed for six people. Since boats range from 26–60 feet, how big a boat you charter will determine how roomy it feels. The fewer people on your boat, the greater the chance that *you* will be the one reeling in the fish since you share the lines with fewer people.

There are half-day (morning or afternoon) charters, full-day, and overnighters. If it's your first time, do a half day to see if boat travel agrees with you. Mornings offer best conditions. Shared charters are getting harder to find. *Usually,* the bigger the boat, the higher the price. Individual boat rates can change often depending on the season, fishing conditions and whims of the owners. Consequently, we'll forgo listing individual boat rates since this information is so perishable and instead list a few companies that we recommend. Call them directly to get current rates.

If you're easy-queasy, take an anti-seasickness medication. Some people never get sick regardless of conditions, and others turn green just watching *Deadliest Catch*. Nothing can ruin an ocean outing quicker than being hunched over the stern feeding the fish. Scopolamine patches prescribed by doctors can have side effects, including (occasionally) blurred vision that can last a week. Dramamine or Bonine taken the night before and the morning of a trip also seems to work well for many, though some drowsiness may occur. Ginger is a mild preventative. Try powdered ginger, ginger pills or even *real* ginger ale—can't hurt, right?

Tipping: 15–20% split between the captain and deck hand is customary, but if the captain is a jerk and the deck hand throws up on you, you're not obligated to give 'em diddly.

If you want to catch and release, or tag and release, make sure in advance that your boat will accommodate you. Most will, but some don't. If you do, use lures—live bait usually results in the fish coughing up its stomach, which kills it.

You might want to go down to the fuel dock at Honokohau Harbor around 11 a.m. or 3:30 p.m. for fish weigh-ins to see what's being caught and by whom. The boats hoist flags on their way back, each one representing a different species of fish caught on that trip.

If you fish from Kawaihae, expect ono and mahimahi rather than bigger stuff.

Popular boats can get booked up in advance. Make arrangements before you arrive to maximize your chances of getting a good boat.

FISHING BOATS

Captains and deckhands come and go. Below are some boats that we've had good experiences with or that have good reputations as of press time. If you have a contrary experience with any one of them or have an experience with any company that you'd like to share with us, please send us feedback via email so we can stay on top of these boats. The number after each name is the boat length.

For the big stuff, try:

Camelot (34-ft) (808) 936-9515

Strong Persuader (43-ft) (808) 896-3111

Hooked on Kona (40- & 45-ft) (808) 960-1424

Sea Genie II (39-ft) (808) 640-8302

Sea Strike (31-ft) (808) 895-1972

Many company reservations default to a booking company called **Charter Locker** (808-326-2553).

Kona's famous **International Billfish Tournament** is held each year in July or August. Fishermen from all over the world come to compete for prizes, so boats tend to fill up faster during this time.

Whether you catch fish or not, it's great being out on the Kona Coast.

SHORELINE FISHING

The entire shoreline is available to you. If you want, you can find a secluded spot off any ugly-looking lava road on the island. Otherwise, on Hilo side, Hilo Bay, especially near the mouth of the Wailuku River, is good. Get supplies from **S. Tokunaga Store** (808-935-6965) for fishing near Hilo. South Point is excellent. In Kailua-Kona, the seawall in front of Hulihe'e Palace is a great place and easy to access. As snorkelers, we've seen schools numbering in the many thousands congregate off this area.

And remember: Never say, "I'm going fishing." Say, "I am going to the woods." Hawaiian legend holds that the fish will hear and avoid you if you warn them.

The Big Island is known as *the* island to visit if you want to golf till you drop. This presented a problem for us while evaluating individual courses. It would have been easy to froth at the mouth over most of them because compared to courses elsewhere, most are outstanding. But that would have missed the point. So with elevated expectations in mind, we reviewed the courses *relative to each other*. This is important because if we get less than excited about a particular course, it doesn't mean it's a dump. It just means that you can do better elsewhere on the island.

Prices at the top courses are higher than many are used to. If you stay at a resort near the course, you'll probably be eligible for much cheaper rates.

GOLFING TIPS

Wind is often a factor at Kohala courses and is usually stronger in the afternoon. Sunshine is *almost* guaranteed in Kohala. Conditions are usually best in the mornings at all courses around the island.

Greens tend to break to the ocean, even when they look uphill.

Some courses offer big discounts after noon or 3 p.m. Check with individual courses for these or other discounts.

All the courses rent clubs, but only Mauna Kea and Hapuna currently rent shoes (for $15).

THE COURSES

The best courses, by far, are in Kohala. According to local lore, in the early 1960s Laurance Rockefeller flew Robert Trent Jones, Sr., to an isolated, barren, mostly unknown place on the Big Island. He took him out to an 'a'a lava field, pointed to the rock, and asked, "Can you build me a golf course out of that?" Jones knelt down, picked up two pieces of 'a'a and ground them together. They crumbled. He then said, "Mr. Rockefeller—you've got yourself a golf course."

The **Mauna Kea Golf Course** (808-882-5400) opened in 1964 and is still the course by which all others are compared. Fairly open and forgiving rolling terrain, this course epitomizes what a Big Island course can be. The layout is brilliant, the location is dazzling, and the course is just plain fun.

Hapuna Golf Course (808-880-3000) is the other course at the Mauna Kea/Hapuna Beach Resort complex. It features narrower fairways, but don't expect to be overwhelmed with hazards. The narrowness is your challenge.

Mauna Lani Resort (808-885-6655) has two courses. The **South Course** is by far the most popular. It is closer to the

Course	Phone	Par	Yards	Fees
Hamakua Country Club (X2)	(808) 775-7244	66	4,980	$25
Hapuna Golf Course	(808) 880-3000	72	6,535	$195*
Hilo Municipal Golf Course	(808) 959-7711	71	6,325	$44
Hualalai Golf Club	(808) 325-8480	72	6,632	$350*
Kona Country Club	(808) 322-2595	72	6,613	$180*
Makalei Golf Club	(808) 325-6625	72	6,698	$109*
Makani Golf Club	(808) 325-5044	72	6,510	$119*
Mauna Kea	(808) 882-5400	72	6,806	$295*
Mauna Lani North	(808) 885-6655	72	6,601	$251*
Mauna Lani South	(808) 885-6655	72	6,436	$251*
Naniloa Golf Course (X2)	(808) 935-3000	70	5,750	$18
Volcano Golf & Country Club	(808) 319-4745	72	6,503	$60*
Waikoloa Beach Nine	(808) 886-7888	35	3,281	$185* **
Waikoloa Kings' Nine	(808) 886-7888	36	3,286	$185* **
Waikoloa Lakes Nine	(808) 886-7888	35	3,285	$185* **
Waikoloa Vllage	(808) 883-9621	72	6,791	$96*

*Indicates golf cart included in price. Yards are from the men's regular tees.
** Price is based on mix and match 18 holes between Waikoloa Beach, Kings' and Lakes.

ocean and is nicely incorporated into the stark lava. The less used **North Course** has more trees and a more "traditional" use of lava boundaries. Mauna Lani courses are the best-maintained courses on the island. If you can only play one, make it the South.

The **Waikoloa Beach Resort** (808-886-7888) south of Mauna Lani does things a little differently. They have three 9-hole courses—the **Beach Nine**, **Lakes Nine** and **Kings' Nine**—and you get to mix and match two of them for an 18-hole experience. The Beach Nine is popular due to its proximity to the ocean. The Lakes Nine adds several hazards, including lakes (in case you haven't lost your ball to the Pacific yet) and large tracts of dried lava. We think the Kings' Nine is a better course overall (though it is tougher than the others). The courses are in a nice location near the ocean, but they aren't in the same league as Mauna Lani or Mauna Kea.

Hualalai Golf Club (808-325-8480) is private, only available to guests of the Four Seasons Resort between Kona and Kohala. This Jack Nicklaus course is more player-friendly than most of his designs.

Up Mauka of the Kohala resort area, **Waikoloa Village** (808-883-9621) brings three words to mind—cheaper, windy and walking. Play *early* if you want to avoid the wind. Overall, underwhelming.

South of Waikoloa Village on Highway 190 at an elevation of 2,200 feet is **Makani Golf Club** (808-325-5044). You would expect more expansive views. But the pleasing rolling terrain keeps you a bit boxed in. What you will get, however, are lots of close encounters with birds. The number of wild turkey, nene, pheasant and small colorful birds is impressive. As for the golf, fairways are in decent shape but can be a bit narrow, and the course is not well marked. Frequent visitors will recognize this as the old Big Island Country Club. The new owners may turn this into a private club at some point in the future, so if

Over the water and onto the green. Mauna Kea's hole No. 3 is vintage Hawaiian golf.

you want to hit the links, now is the time to do it.

One of the lesser-known Big Island courses is **Makalei Golf Club** (808-325-6625) just north of Kona on Hwy 190. Located 2,100–2,900 feet upslope, it's cooler and less windy than at the Kohala courses. There are beautiful views down the coast, and bougainvilleas dot the cart paths.

In Kona, they only game in town is **Kona Country Club** (808-322-2595). Even on a breezy day there is less wind than the Kohala-area courses, and it's not as hot. But it also lacks the ubiquitous lava rock hazards that make playing up north such a unique-to-Hawaii experience. A few holes offer knockout ocean views, but most are away from the shoreline.

Who would ever think that you could have a lush course just 1 mile from the main crater of the most active volcano on earth? Bring your warmies to play at the **Volcano Golf & Country Club** (808-319-4745)—the 4,000-foot altitude

brings a chill to the air. The play is straightforward with few hazards. The clubhouse, restaurant and grounds all show signs of neglect.

In Hilo, at **Naniloa Golf Course** (808-935-3000), much of the infrastructure is rundown and dilapidated, but the course, aided by the fertile Hilo climate, is in fairly nice shape. Guests of the Grand Naniloa Hotel get cheap 9-hole rounds and club rentals.

Hilo Municipal (808-959-7711) is a fairly flat layout with no sand traps (too much rain). The play is not overly hard, and the setting is quite pretty, especially given the lower rates.

Near Waipi'o Valley, **Hamakua Country Club** (808-775-7244) was built as a community course in the formerly sugar-rich area of Hamakua. It's a *small* nine-hole course, popular with locals who come to play and talk story in the "clubhouse." Greens fees are one of the cheapest on the island. The holes are very close together and amazingly well tended.

The Big Island has plenty of hiking to keep you happy. You can wander through a lush rainforest, walk on a volcano crater floor, puff up a frigid, possibly snow-covered mountain, hike along an empty tropical beach, teeter on the edge of steep valleys, or saunter along an old Hawaiian lava trail. The possibilities and diversity are incredible.

Footwear—Hiking sandals or light trail shoes work fine for most trails here. Hiking boots are best for muddy conditions and hiking over rough lava rock (make sure they are already well broken in). And for walking through streams, nothing beats tabis. These look like green fuzzy mittens for your feet and stick to wet, slippery rocks better than any other kind of footwear and they are legal here. (Because they're not very stiff, tabis may leave the bottoms of your feet feeling a bit sore.) You'll find tabis for about $18–$40 at Walmart in Kona and Hilo.

Hawai'i Forest & Trail (808-331-8505) on Olowalu Street (see map on page 168) has hiking sticks and other supplies. In addition to helping ease the difficulty of long hikes, hiking sticks can also save you from a nasty fall on sharp lava rock.

Lastly, it's nice to be able to visually see *where* you are on a trail and know you're going in the right direction. But many of the trails on the island do not show up on a typical GPS or Google maps. *Well,* it just so happens that we GPSed every trail in our apps. The best part is you don't need a cell signal for the GPS function to work.

KILAUEA VOLCANO HIKES

Much of the best hiking on the island is found in and around Hawai'i Volcanoes National Park. In *Volcano Sights* we've described lots of strolls of 30 minutes or less. They include **Bird Park** (a nice 30-minute walk through the forest), **Devastation Trail** (see how the volcano wiped out part of a forest with flying, frothed lava and how it is coming back), **Pu'u Loa Petroglyph Trail** (less than 2 miles round trip, it heads to a massive field of ancient rock carvings—this one takes a bit more than 30 minutes), **Thurston Lava Tube** (see what lava sees as it travels underground) and a few others. We've also described a trek to the edge of the smoldering **Mauna Ulu Crater** in *Adventures* on page 236.

Kilauea Iki (3 Mile Loop)

This is a great hike! If you only have time to do one hike while you are on the Big Island, this is one we'd recommend. It goes from ancient rain forest to a newly lava-paved crater and back through rain forest. At a little over 3 miles, it can take anywhere from 2 hours if you hoof it without distractions, to 4 hours if you stop and gawk as much as we do and enjoy lunch on the crater floor. It is a *reasonably* easy hike (well…maybe moderate) with only about 15 minutes of gentle but constant incline toward the end when you ascend about 450 feet. Before hiking, read some background on this crater and its attention-grabbing past in here.

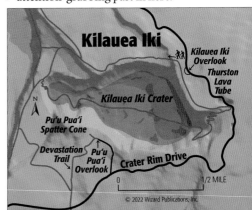

© 2022 Wizard Publications, Inc.

We like to start this hike at the Kilauea Iki Overlook and go counterclockwise, through the forest first. The trip is gentler this way and is preferable to going into the crater first. (You could also start from the Visitor Center and get there via the Earthquake Trail and Byron Ledge—see page 204.) You will go through a gorgeous, ancient fern and ʻohiʻa forest as the trail skirts the edge of Kilauea Iki Crater. Take your time here, and enjoy the beauty and grace of the forest and birds. All along are short spur trails offering magnificent views of the crater. Judging size and distance is surprisingly difficult here until you see people walking on the crater floor. The abrupt contrast between the ancient fern forest and the newly created maw of the crater floor couldn't be greater. Though the forest is lush and cool, the 4,000-foot altitude seems to prevent mosquito problems here (though it's always a good idea to bring repellent, just in case). Before the trail veers away from the crater for a bit, take a look across at Puʻu Puaʻi, and you will appreciate the scale of the eruptive event. Just keep to the left whenever you encounter a trail intersection. The descent into the crater is somewhat

steep, but there are steps carved into the trail in spots and a few railings to help ease the way.

In a heartbeat you go from lush forest to barren lava. The trail bears to your left for a bit, then goes right. Cairns (piles of rock) mark the path across the floor. The lava here is more jagged since it contains remnants of lava spatters rather than the smooth lava farther ahead. Keep an eye out for a small sign pointing to the actual vent, where lava fragments are accumulating. Where you see steam escaping from cracks, you will notice minerals leaching from the rock. The steam seems inoffensive compared to the nasty stuff that used to come out of parts of Halemaʻumaʻu. We like to have lunch near a steam vent about a third of the way across the crater floor.

The crater floor is quiet and peaceful. You may be hot, cold, wet or dry here, depending on the weather. (Gee, *that's* a useful piece of insight.) Sounds bounce around the crater in an unpredictable way. You may hear the crunching of footsteps when no one is nearby. Plants and trees are already starting to make themselves at home in cracks on the lava floor. It's amazing to stand in this near-dead crater and to see and hear the profusion of life all around you just beyond this hostile field of Pele's destruction.

After you ascend the crater wall, keep to your left along the edge of the crater, and you are back at the overlook. Outstanding!

Napau Crater Trail
(2 or 13 Miles Round Trip)

Another nice hike is the Napau Crater Trail to **Pu'u Huluhulu**. The trail (occasionally called the **Mauna Ulu Trail**) is the only place in the park where you can see Pu'u 'O'o, the heart of the previous eruption. This is a *long* day hike if you do the whole thing. Mauna Ulu (meaning growing mountain) erupted between 1969 and 1974, adding more than 200 acres of new land to Hawai'i's coastline, and its effects are dramatically seen on this trail. It was Kilauea's second longest flank eruption in recorded history. This trail starts on an old segment of Chain of Craters Road. (Twelve miles of this road were buried by the Mauna Ulu flow, and we've shown it on the inside back cover map as a stippled line.) This fairly easy trek wanders over the young Mauna Ulu flow, as well as through old forest. You'll notice stone sentries along the way, strangely shaped columns of rock. These are called **lava trees**. When lava from the Mauna Ulu flow coursed its way through here, it occasionally encountered exceptionally wet trees. These resisted the flow and the temperatures long enough for the lava to harden around the tree. When the lava level lowered, these piles remained. You will often see a circle in the middle of **lava trees**, the outline of the now-dead tree. Sometimes, there are half-circle outlines of the tree. These are on the upstream side of the lava, showing you which way the lava flowed.

At about 30 minutes, you come to Pu'u Huluhulu (shaggy hill), a heavily forested mound. There is a 5-minute spur trail leading up to the top. From there you get an awesome view of Mauna Ulu, a third of a mile in front of you. Be sure to look down into the pristine, fern-filled rain forest below you in the crater. It's utterly untouched, looking much like it did a thousand years ago. Unfortunately, during our last visit, the park had let the vegetation grow, blocking your view of the crater floor. Looking off in the distance, you can see how the Mauna Ulu flow cut into the heart of the forest, going from green to black in a single footstep.

The view of Mauna Ulu is gorgeous. Looking over at it, you might be tempted to walk over to the top and peer into **Mauna Ulu Crater**. If so, check your insurance and see *Adventures* on page 236.

Most people turn around from here. Past this point the trail footing gets more difficult and goes to the massive Makaopuhi Crater, then to Napau Crater, where camping is allowed. (Technically, you need

Napau Crater Trail

Forests ruled by ferns and 'ohi'a trees make volcano hiking a time of wonder and magic.

a permit to go that far.) That's 6.7 miles one way. Just before Napau, you will pass the remains of an old pulu factory. Pulu is the soft, down-like fuzz that covers the stems of some ferns. Someone thought it would make a great stuffing for pillows and mattresses, so they built a factory out here. Unfortunately, pulu turns to dust after a few years. Consequently, so did their business.

Another 2 miles past Napau is **Pu'u 'O'o**. The heart of the 1983–2018 volcano eruption looms ahead of you the whole way, reminding you why you've started this 17-mile round trip hike. The trail goes nearly to the base, but it may be closed if park personnel deem it unsafe because of stability issues. Check with the visitor center if you have your heart set on this last part.

On the way back, you might choose to detour south onto the **Naulu Trail**. Parts of the trail are along the old road, so you go from lava to road segments spared from an eruption, eventually through a beautiful forest before the trail encounters Chain of Craters Road. (You'd have to hitch a ride 6 miles back up to your car.)

Earthquake Trail/Byron Ledge (3.5 Mile Loop)

There is a cluster of trails around and below Volcano House. One of our favorite combinations is described below. It sounds more complicated than it is—use map on page 96. All told, it takes 90–120 minutes and is moderately difficult (if that). You descend, then ascend about 400 feet. This is a good hike to take on a clear day because the views of the crater can be spectacular.

From the Visitor Center, you can walk around the right side of Volcano House, eventually heading to your left as you pass in front of Volcano House. Parts of the old trail and Crater Rim Road *fell into the crater* after an earthquake in 1983. This part of the road has become part of the **Crater Rim Trail**. It is eerie to see the road split in half, with guardrails dangling into nothingness. Large, gaping chasms in the old road dispel any notions you may have that ground is inherently stable. Parts of the trail detour from the old road for safety reasons, but it is fascinating to try to safely glimpse as much of the crumbling road as you can, even if through the bushes at times. The best part shows the guardrail and split road. Watch for this part as it's off the main trail. When the road forks, you'll usually take the right fork whenever you can. See map on page 96. The trail will eventually leave the road and descend through 'ohi'a forest. You'll turn right onto Kilauea Iki Trail, then right onto Byron Ledge Trail and continue to the Kilauea Crater floor. (The map and trail intersection signs make it much clearer.) On the crater floor, you'll get an idea of the texture of a skimmed-over lava lake. You are only on the crater floor for a few minutes before you head back up. It's not overly steep. On the way back up, you will pass the remains of a landslide. Look up from the big rock. You are at eye level and can almost feel the slide coming at you.

At the intersection with the **Sandalwood ('Iliahi) Trail**, you have the choice of continuing up to the right (which is a little steeper) or taking the Sandalwood Trail. We recommend the latter. It straddles the crater for a while, featuring great views and several steam vents. Then take the **Sulphur Banks Trail** back to the Visitor Center.

You might want to add the **Kilauea Iki Trail** (see page 201) to this hike. You can access it early on from the Byron Ledge Trail.

Also in the Park

Consider **Crater Rim Drive**. It used to circle the entire Kilauea Caldera, but after the earthquake swarms of 2018 much of the road was heavily damaged. Closed to cars but open to pedestrians, the short 0.7 mile walk from the intersection of Crater Rim and Chain of Craters Road shows the severity of the damage. (Keep your eyes peeled for the section of road that was consumed by the expanding crater on your right as you head out.)

Currently there are no active lava flows to hike to, but we have a section in the *Adventures* on page 250 that addresses this. Volcanoes are nothing if not unpredictable, and our app will be updated the moment this changes.

There are also long overnight trails (with camping) at **Halape**, **Keauhou** and **Ka'aha**. (Halape is *incredible*.) Hikes are down the mountain or along the coast and go for many miles. Contact the Park Service at (808) 985-6178 for more information.

Mauna Loa Summit
(13 or 38 Miles Round Trip)

Getting to the top of Mauna Loa is tough, no matter which way you slice it. It's 13,677 feet high, and there are no roads to the summit. You can do it the hard way or the *very* hard way—it's your choice. The first is a three- to five-day hike from the Kilauea side up the Mauna Loa Trail. The trail starts at the end of the Mauna Loa Scenic Road. This hike has been known to humble even the most conditioned athlete. Though the gradient rarely exceeds 12 degrees, it's 38 miles round trip through lava with mediocre footing, constant exposure to the sun and wind, and you gain 6,500 feet. **Red Hill Cabin** is 7.5 miles into the hike at 10,035 feet, and **Mauna Loa Summit Cabin** is near the crater rim at 13,250 feet—another 11.5 miles. This trail is in Hawai'i Volcanoes National Park, and you need a permit from them to camp. There's no cooking gear at the cabin and no trash cans anywhere on the trail, so pack it out.

The other way up is a *tough* 13-mile round-trip day hike from the **Mauna Loa Weather Observatory** off Saddle Road. (See page 148 for directions.) You start at 11,000 feet, so you won't have a chance to get acclimated—count on altitude sickness from starting so high. (Savvy hikers often car-camp at the weather observatory the night before to acclimate.) This trail is steeper than the **Mauna Loa Trail** and over rougher terrain, but you can do it in a day if you're into punishment, and the views across the saddle will be superb. Make sure you get an early start.

It's always cold up there, and snow can come at any time of the year without warning. Altitude sickness is common, even among the fittest. For either of these hikes, thorough preparation is the key. Just because you are in the tropics doesn't mean you can take this mountain lightly. The *base* may be in the tropics, but the *summit* is in Alaska. And make note: The park can tell you if there's water at the cabins, but don't you dare *rely* on it. We've hiked to the top dreaming of (and *counting* on) water at Mauna Loa Summit Cabin,

only to turn tail and hoof it back down after finding nothing but dry tanks and utter disappointment up there.

MAUNA KEA HIKES

The cold hike to Lake Wai-au on top of Mauna Kea and the challenging climb from the visitor center to the summit are described in *Saddle Road Sights*.

The 0.8-mile **Mauna Kea Summit Loop Trail** takes you to the true summit. Start at mile marker 8 and go behind the guardrail, then follow the rim of the cinder cone in a counterclockwise direction. You'll only gain a couple hundred feet of elevation going to the top, but you'll definitely notice the thinner air at this altitude.

The slightly shorter hike up the **Puʻu Poliʻahu** cinder cone (on the opposite side of the observatories) offers a totally different vantage point.

If you don't want to head all the way up to the summit, **Sunset Hill** usually offers a clear line of sight for watching the sun dip below the clouds. The 0.4-mile trail starts across from the Visitor

Information Station at the 9,200-foot elevation level. You'll gain more than 300 feet during the 15-minute walk. Bring a flashlight for the way back down.

KOHALA AREA HIKES

Puakamo/Malama Petroglyph Trail
(1.25 Miles Round Trip)

Located near the **Mauna Lani Resort** area in Kohala, this 10- to 15-minute-long trail (each way) through a kiawe forest has a few petroglyphs sprinkled along the way. (Kiawe thorns are evil, wicked and hateful; be careful not to let them penetrate your shoe.) The real payoff is at the end (just past a dirt road intersection) with hundreds and hundreds of lava carvings adjacent to each other in this field in the middle of nowhere. The reasons for the Hawaiians' selection of this site has been lost to the ages. Perhaps the most obvious reason is that the slabs in this area make nice canvases. Regardless, some Hawaiians say that if you close your eyes and listen to the breeze, you can hear the sound of rock scraping against rock.

Kiholo Bay (2 to 3 Miles Round Trip)

This is a fabulous place. You can catch a nice glimpse of the bay from the scenic turnout near mile marker 82 on Highway 19. (See map at right.) Between mile markers 82 and 83 a gravel road leads almost to the shore. The gate is open from 7 a.m.–7 p.m. (6 p.m. during winter.) When the road forks, take the right. This last short patch is rough, and some 2WD drivers may want to park the car here and walk to the water. From there you could walk 300 yards to the right along the shoreline to **Queen's Bath**. Porta potties, but no water.

There's also a trail from the main highway just south of mile marker 81. If you take the latter trail, park at the north end of the guardrail and take the trail toward the ocean. The trail from the highway to Kiholo Bay takes about 25 minutes but can feel longer with the heat. To find the correct trailhead, take the gravel road straight down through the wooden posts until you come to a well-marked trailhead. The trail begins as a slight clearing through gravel and rocks but very shortly becomes a wide road. Follow the beach access signs, avoiding the two well-labeled private gates along the way.

Kiholo Bay is a beautiful and uniquely shaped ocean inlet. It has several points of interest that make it great for exploring. First, the lagoon offers waters that are usually dead calm (but cold and fairly cloudy due to freshwater springs leaking into the bay, kicking up fine silt). Turtles *abound* here, grazing on limu in the bay. The fishponds inland, called **Wainanali'i Pond**, are on private property. Turtles swim through the manmade channel to the fishponds at night, perhaps to sleep unmolested. Walking around this part of the bay offers magnificent scenery. You can usually look right into the lagoon water and see the fish.

This whole area was once a gigantic freshwater/brackish fishpond, built by Kamehameha the Great in 1810 after another fishpond (where the airport is now)

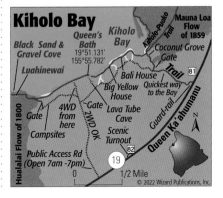

Kiholo Bay

Black Sand & Gravel Cove
Luahinewai
Queen's Bath
19°51.131'
155°55.782'
Kiholo Bay
Kiholo-Puako Trail
Mauna Loa Flow of 1859
Coconut Grove Gate
Bali House
Big Yellow House
Quickest way to the Bay
Lava Tube Cave
Scenic Turnout
4WD from here
Gate
2WD OK
Gate
Campsites
Hualalai Flow of 1800
Guard-rail
Queen Ka'ahumanu
Public Access Rd (Open 7am -7pm)
0   1/2 Mile
© 2022 Wizard Publications, Inc.

Kiholo Bay is a fabulous place to wander around.

was destroyed by lava from the 1801 Hualalai flow. Enormous stone walls up to 6 feet tall and 20 feet wide were laboriously erected, creating a deep pool 2 miles in circumference where all manner of deep sea fish were stocked. It was said that half the population worked to complete it, and it was considered one of the "artificial wonders of Hawai'i" at the time. The lagoon now composing the farthest reaches of Kiholo Bay was once part of that pond, and the waterworn stones were part of the wall. The Mauna Loa lava flow of 1859 traveled *30 miles* to fill in most of the pond and breach the southern wall, creating the lagoon. Fresh water, which initially fed the pond, still intrudes into the bay from springs. Since the water in the back part of the bay is usually as calm as a swimming pool, the snorkeling there, though the visibility is poor, can be surreal. If nobody has been there to disturb the water (except for the ubiquitous turtles), the swimmer or snorkeler might encounter what appears to be a pane of glass suspended horizontally in the water about a foot down. That's the lighter freshwater floating on top of the heavier seawater. Left undisturbed, the dividing line between the two can be straight, razor thin and very visible. If you swim slowly with your hand extended vertically in the middle of where these two layers join, the top of

your hand will be cold (from the freshwater) and the bottom will be warm (from the seawater).

Walking along the gravel shoreline from the bay heading southwest, you pass several houses. One is called the **Bali House**. It was built by the guy you see on TV who runs Paul Mitchell hair care products. He paid 200 Balinese workers $1.50 a day for two years to create the intricate carvings and assemble the house. All was then disassembled and shipped to Kiholo Bay, where American and Balinese workers reassembled it. To the shock of many, they used large green logs from the *Borneo rainforest*, which shrank and split in less-humid Hawai'i, and much effort went into responding to the shrinking structure. While being built, the owner was amazingly gracious about letting people tour the house, so many on the island have gotten to see the inside. The Bali House is about midway between the row of houses on the beach, and you *will* know it when you see it.

Continuing south, you'll pass a big yellow house with security cameras, tennis courts and guards. (We used to quip that they were "guards named Bruiser." The owner of the house at the time—the guy who invented the battery-powered pacemaker—wrote to us good naturedly and said that "Bruiser is no longer on the staff.") About 300 yards southwest of the house, only 80 feet from the ocean and *on state land* is a delight often referred to as **Queen's Bath**. (Its *actual* name is **Keanalele Waterhole**.) It's just off the mauka (mountain) side of the gravel road and easy to miss. There you are, spitting distance from the ocean, above a fabulous crystal clear, spring-fed lava tube pool, open to the sky in two spots. It is attached to a dry lava tube cave, shown on the map on page 207. (By the way, the dry part of the lava tube has numerous petroglyphs carved into it). Though filled with freshwater, its level rises and falls each day with the tides. Our thermometer says this water is 71 °F, but it sure *feels* colder.

When you go to Keanalele, you may notice an abundance of signs urging you not to swim in the water. Although visitors and locals alike used to take a dip in the waterhole, many organizations are urging everyone to help preserve Keanalele by refraining from swimming in it. The pool was historically used seasonally as a place for Hawaiians to gather freshwater from, and people in recent years have introduced sunscreen, bug spray and detergents into the previously pristine waters. These chemicals ruin the waterhole's potability and eventually flow into nearshore estuaries, which negatively impacts the ecosystems surrounding the pool.

Though swimming isn't advisable, the pool is a beautiful sight, and the petroglyphs are evidence of the cultural and historical significance of this area.

There occasionally may be some yellowjackets flying around the area. Try not to make them mad.

Golden Pools of Ke-awa-iki
(4 Miles Round Trip)

How about a hike that leads to a deserted beach with white sand on one end and black sand on the other? A trail that leads over harsh 'a'a, along the beach, past a jewel-like freshwater pool and back to your car in 4 miles. We've taken friends on this hike, and they love it. It displays the raw nature of the Kohala coast, has a variety of sights you'll never forget, and rewards you with a cool dip if you get warm.

Slightly north of mile marker 79 on Queen K (Hwy 19) there are boulders blocking a road on the fresh (150-year-old) lava leading to the sea. (See map on page 162.) Take the road-turned-trail toward the ocean and go around the right side of the fence.

The beach was created when lava from the 1859 Mauna Loa eruption flowed 30 miles, landing at the north end of the beach. The black sand created hasn't had a chance to mix with the previous white beach sand at the southern end, resulting in a nice blend from black to white along the stretch. Just past the south end there are tide-pools to explore if you have water shoes.

Continuing north (right) you'll come to **Pueo Bay**. Large amounts of freshwater enter this tiny bay from underground, creating some strange snorkeling conditions. From Pueo Bay you can either take the trail toward the highway (to the right of a very large lava rock) to the pools, or take the other trail to **Weliweli Point** and link up with another trail. Look for the latter to Weliweli marked with pieces of coral. (The map on page 162 makes these trails easier to visualize.) The pools (there are two of them) can be seen from far away because they are marked by hala trees. (The ends of their branches look like palm tree-inspired pompoms.) Once at the pools, take a moment to savor the scene. Here in the middle of all this raw harshness is a magnificent oasis—freshwater (no hint of seawater at all) lined with golden-coated lava. (The gold comes from a growth on the rocks and makes the ponds too fragile to swim in.) If you want a quick, cool dip, walk just beyond the golden pools to the pool under the hala trees. It's sand- and gravel-lined and makes a good place to cool off your legs before taking the trail back to your car.

Puʻu Waʻawaʻa (6.5 Miles Round Trip)

About 100,000 years ago, an explosion under Hualalai Volcano created the largest cinder cone on the island—Puʻu Waʻawaʻa. Meaning "many-furrowed hill," it is known by locals as the "Jello Mold." Big hill— gotta climb it, right? Luckily there's a trail to the top, but the cone is bigger than it looks, and you can easily be humbled by the steep grade. The 3.2-mile trail ascends 1,800 feet from your car to the summit and will literally take your breath away. Equally breathtaking is the view from atop the puʻu. On a clear day, expect to see Hualalai, Mauna Loa, Mauna Kea, Kohala and possibly Haleakala on Maui. Your best chance for clear skies is early in the

morning, and a picnic lunch up top can be spectacular if the weather cooperates.

The road to the trailhead on Hwy 190 is 0.6 mile past mile marker 22 when heading north from Kona. (See map on page 49.) You'll turn off at a gate that will open and close for you (so give it some room) unlocked 6 a.m.–6 p.m., Mon.–Fri. Go left at the fork and park at the hunter parking station. There's a box here for hikers with a sign-in sheet and pamphlets describing the hike. You have two options. Walk the road all the way up or detour on the ʻOhiʻa Trail, adding a nature lesson and 0.4 miles. While not very inspiring, it's a bit more scenic and less steep than the pavement. You'll go left when it reaches a gravel road called Miki's Road. After a long climb, you come out of the forest at the base of Puʻu Waʻawaʻa. If you use the Porta-Potty, you should know that we've seen it knocked over by the wind, so get 'er done quick.

Continue on the road until it reaches a rusty gate. Take the grassy path to the right. It will meander along the side of the hill, passing through a pedestrian gate,

Inland of Keʻawaʻiki you'll find a golden jewel ensconsed in a harsh lava desert.

until it reaches the backside. Horses are often grazing around here, and you'll walk through a century-old corral. The grassy road curls into the crater and up the steepest climb yet to the rim.

Follow the grassy road to the left on the rim. This takes you to the highest point and offers a commanding view of the island. The grass is really soft up here, so take a seat and revel in your accomplishment. Hiking back down is hard on the knees. Add the sweat you expended on the way up, and you have a strenuous 7 miles round trip. Give yourself 4 hours for this hike, and start early for best viewing conditions.

KONA AREA HIKE

Makahi Trail Through a Cloud Forest (1.5 Miles Round Trip)

There aren't many hiking opportunities in the Kona area, but the short Makahi Trail through the cloud forest is a delight. Bright green ferns. Lots of bird sounds. Lots of roots. Lots of opportunities to roll your ankle. Starting on the side of Hualalai Volcano at more than 3,000 feet of elevation, this lush rainforest is often covered in clouds, adding an air of mystery to this hike.

From Kona, head up-mountain to Mamalahoa Highway (Hwy 190) and then head up Kaloko Drive, between mile markers 34 and 35. (See map on page 49.) Turn left onto Makahi Road and park at the end. Don't leave any valuables in your car. Head straight down the trail ignoring the many turnoffs. Turn around when you hit the dirt road, or continue on that for as long as you like. Coming back, you'll pick up the 400 feet of elevation you lost on the way down.

For an easier stroll, you can also start from Hoa Street instead. A brief walk from the parking area will take you to the flat dirt road, which is now closed to vehicles.

HILO & PUNA HIKES

Wai'ale Falls (0.5 Miles Round Trip)

Many people come to Hawai'i looking for an idyllic pool or waterfall to frolic in. Well, here it is, and it's only a 10-minute hike to get there.

Wai'ale Falls itself is a pretty and fairly high-volume waterfall. Above the falls lie several beautiful pools and some small falls that can be a delight to play in (if the flow's not too high).

You start on Waianuenue Avenue past Boiling Pots. You'll see the falls (700 feet away) from the bridge that crosses the river. (See map on page 137.) The trailhead is just past the bridge; park on the shoulder. The trail itself is plagued with mosquitoes, but once at the water we've haven't found them to be a big problem. Bring bug juice just in case. Follow the narrow trail up through the strawberry guava lining the north bank of the **Wailuku River**. There are several offshoots that allow you to visit the large pool below the falls (if you wish) and some false trails that can be confusing. The trail ends at the *top* of those falls. Remember that spot for your return.

At the top, rocks make little swimming pools or (*cold*) bath tubs for soakin' and splashin'. We've always found this area to feel secluded even though the road is still visible. The footing is much less slippery than many other stream banks around the islands, thanks to the consolidated lava here.

INSTRUCTIONS FOR WATERFALL USE: Prance, frolic and have fun. Repeat if necessary.

Stay out of pools that have a fast moving exit. Other pools lie farther upstream.

Wai'ale Falls is a short hike but rewards you with the opportunity to frolic next to a waterfall.

And, of course, always be aware that a flash flood can occur anywhere in nature. So if you see a large wall of water coming your way...well, you're already screwed, so what does it matter?

Leleiwi Tide-pool (0.6 Miles Round Trip)

At the end of Kalanianaole Avenue in Hilo, past all the beach parks, you'll find a large gravel cul-de-sac near the shore. Beyond this is a unique coastline that hides a gem of a tide-pool. The Leleiwi Tide-pool (in undeveloped Lehia Park) has a sandy bottom with an easy entry and is perfect for a dip. Plus it has a surreal backdrop of pine trees growing on large tilted slabs of volcanic rock with everything covered in pine needles. Although it's only 0.25 miles away from the end of the road, it will take you 20 minutes or more to get there.

What makes this hike different is that if you time it right, you're walking in the water most of the way. (That's good, not bad.) A couple hours before high tide the water is snaking its way inland. Wear water shoes and hike up your shorts when necessary, then embrace the tide. You could mess around trying to stay dry in the jungle, but that misses the point. The tide-pools and the tide itself are the real jewels here.

Don't leave anything valuable in your car here—we've seen the place empty and we've seen shady characters. From the parking area at the end of the road, walk ahead slightly toward the ocean. Almost immediately you'll encounter a tide-caused stream. Get your feet wet and slowly slosh your way along the tide-pool. Take your time—Leleiwi ain't far. The water is usually clean, and you might see disturbances where freshwater is percolating from the ground, mixing with seawater. Try to notice if you can see the tidal changes or the slight currents in the shallow pools.

Once at Leleiwi (look at the photo below to orient yourself), you can take a cool dip in the sand-lined pool. Waves crash violently on the outer rocks that protect the pool, but inside, the waters should be perfectly still. You may see local families already swimming here, but the main pool is big enough to share. Bring a lunch and enjoy an afternoon of pristine relaxation here. There's no need to venture past the pools since it's only stark lava shoreline.

Ironically, this serene area, *Leleiwi Point*, refers to an altar on which the bodies of human sacrifices were left on display.

Puna Trail to Ha'ena Beach
(5 Miles Round Trip)

The east side of the Big Island isn't known for its beaches. The best one, however, can be found at the end of this hike. Bring some bug spray (we're not kidding) and wear sturdy shoes that can get muddy. The Puna Trail itself isn't the star—it doesn't have sweeping views or dramatic sea cliffs, it's often muddy, and the uneven terrain can be difficult on little ones or the less nimble. But besides the payoff of the beach, the setting of the trail can be captivating. Rusted-out derby racers, ruins of a 19th-century schoolhouse and stacked rock walls of an ancient village are barely visible through the vegetation along the trail's margins. The remains of a WWII pillbox are supposed to lie somewhere along the trail, but we haven't been able to locate it. (Let us know if *you* do.) About a mile into the hike you come to some large banyan trees and the opening of a collapsed lava tube. There's not much to the tube, but the setting of banyans, vines and jungle flora makes for striking scene.

Throughout the hike you'll probably be able to hear the waves crashing on the nearby rocky shoreline. This sound becomes all the more noticeable as you near the end of the trail. Around 2 miles in, the trail splits (a gate to your left is the landmark to look for). You can either continue straight ahead or go right to travel near the shore. For convenience (and especially if the surf is high), we recommend continuing straight, though you will need to

Leleiwi is a calm tide-pool protected from the restless ocean.

cross a small stream just before you reach the beach. If you go along the shoreline, the trail becomes less defined, and you may need to boulder hop if fallen trees are blocking the way. Your payoff for the hike is only another quarter mile or so from here.

The small inlet is protected from normal surf conditions by boulders except during high surf and at its best at low tide. The bottom is shallow, gently sloping and sandy (especially toward the left/north side of the beach), making it great for keiki. There's another surprise here—there are several freshwater springs feeding into the north side of the beach that rival Ice Pond in briskness. You can see it gushing out of the bank below some large trees just past where the sand ends. The land, buildings and nicely manicured lawn directly behind the beach is owned by the Shipman family, and there are plenty of signs indicating where the private property line is.

OTHER BEACH HIKES

For other beach hikes, often to secluded spots, check out **Honomalino, Makalawena, Green Sand, 'Anaeho'omalu** (going south to the freshwater pool), and **Road to the Sea** (the second beach), all described in the *Beaches* chapter. Also consider the trail between **Spencer Beach Park** and **Hapuna**. It's along the shoreline and is vague only where it crosses the golf course at hole number 3.

HIKES DESCRIBED ELSEWHERE

The hike to the **Captain Cook Monument** is on page 75. We describe how to

Ha'ena Beach is reserved exclusively to those willing to hike 5 miles round trip...and to the lucky landowners behind it.

get to a **lava tube** in the *Adventures* chapter on page 244.

HORSEBACK RIDING

If you want to let someone else do the walking, consider horseback riding. The Big Island has quite a tradition when it comes to horses, and we've noticed that, of all the Hawaiian islands, companies here tend to be of a higher caliber. There are lots of companies offering wildly different kinds of rides. It just depends on the type of riding and terrain you want to see.

Most stables provide a small saddle bag and rain gear, suggest long pants, require reservations, closed-toe shoes and need a minimum number of riders before they'll go. Dress in layers, wear a hat and sunscreen. Most have 230-pound weight limits.

HORSEBACK TOURS

Naʻalapa Stables–Kahua Ranch (808-889-0022) on the uphill side of Kohala Mountain Road, runs a 1.5-hour ride for $100 and a 2.5-hour ride for $120. The meeting spot for this is at their ranch north of Waimea. Not super compelling. 230 pound weight limit.

Despite the closure of the Waipiʻo Valley, **Waipiʻo on Horseback** (808-775-7291) is still conducting tours. You'll start at their ranch and ride uphill into the mountains for a 2 to 2.5-hour tour. While the experience isn't the same as exploring the valley, their 500-acre ranch covers diverse terrain and has some nice ocean views. $150 for both the morning and afternoon tours. If you're a single rider and others who were supposed to go cancel, they'll buck you off as well. 200 pound weight limit.

Paniolo Adventures (808-889-5354) has nice quality, well cared-for horses and gear. Their 2.5-hour trips are $119 and take you across a wide-open working ranch featuring beautiful views. This is not one of those nose-to-tail rides. You go across open country, and you can canter if you like. (That means to go faster than a trot, for all you city slickers.) The guides aren't patronizing; they genuinely seem to want you to experience the peace of the Hawaiian countryside. Rides have between two and 14 people and aren't at all gimmicky. This is a working ranch, and if it's calving season, you might get to see a calf being born. Thick dusters and the like are available for free, but it's a good idea to bring a sweatshirt and long pants. Located 0.2 miles north of the mile marker 13 on Hwy 250 in Kohala. Easy to recommend. They also have a sunset ride that's an hour shorter and $10 cheaper (which we highly recommend if you're in it for the scenery) and a 4-hour "Wrangler Ride" for experienced horsemen where they'll give you free rein to trot and canter for $185. 230 pound weight limit.

4d Quarter Horses (808-987-4872) has several tours of their 2,500-acre ranch off the Old Mamalahoa Highway (ask for directions) in southern Waimea. You see lush, rolling pastures from open country, not from a trail. Bring warm clothes; it's sometimes misty or rainy in this part of Waimea. (You might want to call them for a weather check.) It's $110 for their 1.5-hour tour and $150 for the 2-hour tour. For experienced riders, they offer a cattle drive ride for $200. This is not the kind where you sit there while they do all the work. For at least 2.5 hours, your group will do all the hard work from horseback while they bark out orders, and you'll probably have a great time doing it. Four people are necessary for this. (Call them to see if any others have signed up.) There's a 300-pound weight limit, and kids age 3 and up are welcome (except on the round-up ride). Well run by good folks.

Jet Skiing

Call them Jet Skis, Wave Runners (which are brand names) or personal watercraft—whatever your name for them, these motorcycles of the sea can currently *only* be rented in Kona.

Make reservations in advance and **Big Island Watersports** (808-240-1993) will shuttle you out to their floating island in the middle of Kailua Bay from the pier so that you can go tearing around on their smallish track.

Early morning is usually very smooth, late afternoon choppy. Late morning seems a good balance to give the water some texture. It's around $120 for 1 hour, $80 for half an hour. Even 30 minutes will tucker out most people, especially if you're like us and you drive it like it's stolen. Experiment with different ways to hold your feet while you sit. Extra riders are allowed for around $50 (up to three, with 350 pound weight limit), but we recommend one person per craft. Use the complementary goggles; your eyes will be grateful. Doubling or tripling up seems to increase the risk of the passengers flying off, from what we observed. Some people seem to feel that these craft are hazardous to the ocean; others say modern jet skis are no different than regular boats. We honestly don't know which is the case; we're just saying what it's like to rent one. Unlike Jet Ski operations on Maui, these guys are allowed to operate during whale season.

KAYAKING

On the Big Island, kayaking is mostly an ocean affair. Although other islands, such as Kaua'i, have rivers to kayak, the Big Island lacks navigable rivers. But there are several areas on the normally calm Kona coast where ocean kayaking is excellent. Our favorite is across **Kealakekua Bay** to the **Captain Cook Monument**. (See page 73 for a complete description of the bay.) The 1-mile (each way) trip often features fairly calm waters, spinner dolphins and outrageous snorkeling at the monument. Other kayak trips are from Kailua Pier to the north or south, or from Kohala beaches such as 'Anaeho'omalu. Old Kona Airport or Honokohau Harbor to Makalawena is a long, pleasant voyage. (See *Beaches* for descriptions and locations of landings.) The area south of Keauhou Bay has numerous cavities (called "sea caves" by the more optimistic companies) that can be fun to paddle by.

Kealakekua Bay has been the source of *lots* of drama and government regulation in recent years, and the state has been slow in making their final decisions. At press time there were a few companies with permits to rent you a kayak to go on your own, and a few that could do guided trips. But check our website for updates since this is a moving target.

Remember that the ocean, even in Kona, can be treacherous and unforgiving, especially during periods of high surf. We don't want to rain on anybody's parade, but if you don't give the ocean the respect it deserves, it can humble

The crazy beautiful waters at the far end of Kealakekua Bay.

you quickly. Only paddle when it's calm, and always be wary near the shore where a rogue wave can beach (or rock) you.

RENTING A KAYAK FOR KEALAKEKUA BAY

As mentioned, if you want to rent a kayak to paddle Kealakekua Bay, these companies can rent to you. You won't be able to *land* your kayak, you'll have to drag it around by rope as you snorkel. Since permits are limited, it's a good idea to reserve in advance. You will *probably* launch your kayak at an old boat launch at **Kahauloa Bay**, aka Grandma's Little Beach. Prices are higher for this location because the permits are like gold.

Bayside Adventures (808-896-0610) charges $40 for singles, $60 for doubles, and they operate down at the bay. No lugging kayaks from afar.

If you call in advance, **Ehu & Kai** (808-328-8775) will have a kayak (or stand up paddle board) ready for you right at the boat launch. They're friendly and knowledgeable. $45 for a single, $65 for a double, $85 for a triple. Paddle board rentals and lessons also available.

Kona Boys Kayaks (808-328-1234) prices are a bit too high. It's $64 for a single, $89 for a double (prices are for all day), and you'll have to transport the kayak from their shop on Hwy 11 past mile marker 113.

You will likely encounter others at **Napoʻopoʻo Beach** who are willing to rent you a kayak, but they may or *cough* may not have permits.

KAYAK RENTALS ELSEWHERE

At Keauhou Bay, **Ocean Safaris** (808-326-4699) has singles for $30, doubles at $50.

Kona Boys Kayaks (808-329-2345) also has a more convenient concession to the right of the pier in Kona that rents kayaks by the (expensive) hour for use in that area. Kohala companies rent them by the minute (OK, OK…by the hour). $19–$29 hourly.

Among them are **Ocean Sports** which rents kayaks at ʻAnaehoʻomalu Bay as **Hypr Nalu Hawaiʻi** (808-990-7776) for $40–$65 per hour. (And they'll only rent between 8:15 a.m. and 1 p.m.) You'll have to cash in your IRA for the cost of Kohala rentals.

Rudders make it easier to stay on track in any ocean water, but it's virtually impossible to rent a kayak with one here. Their absence is particularly felt in Kohala where winds tend to annoyingly weathercock you sideways.

GUIDED KAYAK TOURS

If you want a guided trip and want to *land* at the Captain Cook Monument for snorkeling, **Adventures in Paradise** (808-447-0080), **Aloha Kayak Co.** (808-322-2868) and **Kona Boys Kayaks** (808-328-1234) have the proper permits. Adventures in Paradise and Aloha Kayak charge $100 for their 3.5-hour tours and include water and snacks. **Kona Boys** is $200 but is closer to 5 hours and includes lunch and a take home, aluminum water bottle. Be forewarned, readers upon readers have written to tell us about some scheduling and refund issues with **Aloha Kayak Co.**, so we suggest booking elsewhere. You'll get 90 minutes or so at the monument for snorkeling and eating. Ask about discounts for kids.

Other guided kayak trips in Kona are less desirable.

PADDLING CANOE TRIPS

We'd love to point you to a good paddling canoe trip, but we haven't found one we liked. **Eka Canoe Adventures** (808-756-3335) takes people in a twin-hulled canoe with a Hawaiian sail, but they motor most of the time, which kills the experience. Currently they only offer private tours during the day, or a nighttime manta ray snorkel tour for $100. **Ehu & Kai** (808-328-8775) will take you out for a permitted tour of Kealekekua Bay, but they need six people to go for $110 per person.

Parasailing is where you get pulled by a boat while attached to a parachute and a long line. We've done it, and to many people (including us), it *looks* more fun and thrilling than it really is. But if you have your heart set on it, then you have your heart set on it.

UFO Parasail (808-359-4836) in Kona will drag you around for $136 per person using a 1,200-foot line. Rides are 8 minutes long for a single rider (so you better enjoy it—that's about $17 *per minute* you are in the air) and 10 minutes for double and triple riders. The combined weight of all riders must be between 160–450 pounds.

One tip (*especially* for guys): Don't wear any slippery shorts, or you may cinch forward in your harness, resulting in…the longest 8 minutes of your life.

Whether you're already a certified SCUBA diver or are interested in trying it out, you've found paradise on the west side of the Big Island. Whereas the east (windward) side of the island has poorer diving due to river runoff and rough waters, the Kona side offers some of the best in the state. There are no permanent streams on the *entire* west side (from the northern tip to the southern tip), so runoff is not a problem.

Kona waters are mostly shielded from winds and the ocean's prevailing northeast swell, so calmness is the norm. Fish, coral and divers appreciate the warmer water of the Big Island, the southernmost of all Hawaiian Islands. It's 75 °F at its coldest in February, 82 °F at its warmest in October. 100-plus-foot visibility is common.

You have your choice of boat dives or shore dives. Boats mostly leave from **Kailua Pier**, **Honokohau Harbor** and **Kawaihae Harbor**. Typical dives here are two tanks at two different sites. The price range in the table refers to those who have their own gear vs. those who need to rent it.

The island doesn't have a decompression chamber. Everyone knows not to fly after a dive, but don't forget that the heights of some of our mountains simulate flying as far as your body tissues are concerned. Just the saddle *between* Mauna Loa and Mauna Kea reaches 6,600 feet. And if you decide to drive to Place of Refuge from Kona, you'll reach 1,400 feet on the way—probably too high if you dove deep.

So you'll know our perspective when we review companies, here is what we like and don't like on a dive. Good outfits will give you a briefing, tell you about some of the endemic species here, what to look for and will point out various things on the dives, keeping it moving but not too fast. Bad outfits take you on a non-stop excursion that keeps you kicking the whole time instead of letting you stop to explore the nooks and crannies. Good outfits explain the unique qualities of Hawai'i's environment. Bad dive masters may tell you what *they* saw (but *you* missed). Good companies work around your needs, wishes and desires. Bad companies keep everyone on a short leash. Good dive masters know their stuff and share it with you. Bad dive masters don't know squat but imply they know it all in order to impress you. As divers, we tend to like companies that wander toward the boat for the latter part of the dive and allow you to go up when you are near the end of your tank, as opposed to everyone going up when the heaviest breather has burned through his/ her bottle. We define bad dive shop attitude as what you experience when you walk into a shop (or onto a boat), and the crew does nothing but convey the attitude, *I'm so cool; don't you wish you were as cool as me?*

During times when we feel the diving conditions are bad (poor visibility or big swells), we like to call around and ask about conditions. We appreciate the companies who admit it's bad, and we hold it against those who tell us how wonderful conditions are.

THE TOPS IN KONA

There are lots of dive outfits on the island—some good, some bad. Some of them stand apart from the rest. Any of them would make a good choice. If we had to pick one, it would probably be Pacific Rim Divers.

Pacific Rim Divers (808-987-6113) is a small, dedicated team headed by a husband/wife duo. Wife Patrice is deeply knowledgeable about marine life and has a great talent for spotting sea critters. On one of our recent dives, we noticed that the vast majority of other visitors have been diving with Pacific Rim for years. (They boast an 85% repeat customer rate, and we can absolutely see why.) With their warm attitude, comfortable 34-foot boat and reasonable price, we're as happy and relaxed as can be at the end of a dive. (Their killer homemade brownies don't hurt either.) The boat is also equipped with a sling and davit for divers with disabilities.

Kona Diving Company (808-331-1858) is another top-notch company. They have two boats, and their 34-foot catamaran has plenty of shade, a bathroom and hot shower. With smaller dive groups, the knowledgeable dive masters make sure you see things you could miss with a larger group. All the gear is in excellent condition, and they give you lunch between dives (but we'll be honest, the food is pretty mediocre). No prescription masks.

Big Island Divers (808-329-6068) is also a good company. We like how they pace the dives (not too fast, not too slow) and how they'll rinse your own gear if you like.

We've noticed a certain fondness on their part for deep dives, and they have a pretty good black water dive. There's shade and snacks on the boat. They do a good manta dive. They use 29-, 35- and 36-foot boats. Biggest gripe is that you need to check in at the shop before heading to the harbor.

Jack's Diving Locker (808-329-7585) is a good shop with five boats ranging from a 23-foot tin can to a 46-foot double-decker that holds 18 divers. Good ascent policy, hot shower on most, and dive masters carry slates. They do a lot of work with novices, but experienced divers will also be pleased. They are also careful with

Dive Operator	Services Available	Price of 2 Tank Boat	Rent Gear Shore Dive	Camera Rental	Dive Computer	Manta Ray Night Dive	Dive Certification
Aquatic Life Divers (808)345-4411	Boat Dives	$169–$214	No	Yes	Yes	$149–$234 (1 or 2 tank)	Yes
Big Island Divers (808)329-6068	Dive Shop & Boat Dives	$189–$303	$90	Yes	Yes	$159–$249 (1 or 2 tank)	Yes
Blue Wilderness (808)886-0980	Dive Shop & Boat Dives	$175–$220	$60	Yes	Yes	$165–$210 (1 tank)	Yes
Jack's Diving Locker (808)329-7585	Dive Shop, Boat & Shore Dives	$199–$259	$100	Yes	Yes	$229–$289 (2 tank dusk dive)	Yes
Kohala Divers (808)882-7774	Dive Shop & Boat Dives	$179–$314	$87	Yes	Yes	No	Yes
Kona Diving Company (808)331-1858	Boat Dives	$180–$220	$60	No	Yes	$200–$240 (2 tank)	Yes
Kona Diving EcoAdvent. (808)325-1687	Boat Dives	$155–$195	No	Yes	Yes	$145–$185 (1 tank)	Yes
Kona Honu Divers (808)324-4668	Dive Shop, Boat & Shore Dives	$209–$333	$79	No	Yes	$239–$302 (2 tank dusk dive)	Yes
Mauna Lani Sea Advent. (808)885-7883	Boat Dives & Shore Dives	$180–$230	No	No	No	No	Yes
Pacific Rim Divers (808)987-6113	Boat Dives	$180–$325	No	No	Yes	$210–$260 (1 or 2 tank)	Yes

the ocean's critters. They're a *big* outfit and have had a few growing pains recently, but overall, they're still a good company with an excellent attitude.

Others in Kona

Kona Honu Divers (808-324-4668) has a beautiful 46-foot boat with plenty of shade. The big boat is comfortable and easy to get around on. Two dive steps into the water and two showers on board. Their guides are professional. Good briefing and snacks between dives and a relaxed pace. Our concern is that they may let their equipment get a bit long in the tooth between replacement cycles. Get it new, and you'll be happy. Otherwise, maybe not. They tend to have larger groups per dive master than other companies. They also do shore dives, blackwater dives and manta dives. A decent company, but there are better options.

Kona Diving EcoAdventures (808-325-1687) is a smaller outfit. They have a 40-foot Newton called The Manta that holds 32 people, and though it doesn't have all the bells and whistles of its competitors, it's a nice ship with shade and hot showers. The crew here is passionate about reef life and does a good job providing info on the dive spots before going in. On our dives, we were split into groups based on skill level and what we wanted to see underwater. Overall, they do a nice job. Food is a standard selection of sandwiches, chips, brownies and canned drinks, plus water as needed.

Aquatic Life Divers (808-345-4411) is an eco-conscious dive shop that focuses heavily on educating divers about marine ecosystems and reef health. They offer a few different types of dives, including their conservation-focused dive and regular dives, as well as black water and manta ray night dives. Most of their crew is trained in marine biology (either through college or a program offered by Reef Check, a global organization that monitors reef health), and the information is very good. The dives themselves are thorough and easy, and the crew does all the grunt work so you can spend all of your time in the water appreciating the marine life. Snacks includes chips, granola bars and some fruit, plus beverages. They leave from Honokohau Harbor.

Hawaiian SCUBA Shack (808-217-2044) offers pretty cheap rental gear if you're looking to dive on your own. They also have a few dive tours along with lessons in other water activities.

IN KOHALA

The diving in Kohala is often richer in coral than Kona. Lush finger coral gardens are plentiful. It's a bit less protected than Kona and sometimes a little bumpy, especially December through April (though less bumpy than most of the other Hawaiian Islands during those months). There are only a few operators there.

Your best bet is **Kohala Divers** (808-882-7774), which has a 46-foot Newton Dive Special that leaves from Kawaihae Harbor. Decent equipment, bathroom, warm shower, plentiful snacks and professional captain and crew.

Mauna Lani Sea Adventures (808-885-7883) has exclusive use of a boat dock right at Mauna Lani. It's so handy and they love their dock so much that they don't stray too far from it during their boat dive and return you to it for minimal snacks between dives. Crew is good, but if they have an afternoon dive scheduled, morning dives feel a little rushed.

Last on our list is **Blue Wilderness** (808-886-0980). On the positive side, they usually dive the beautiful Puako Reef, and the boat ride is short. On the negative side, they seem a bit disorganized and lack focus on their customers. For instance,

You could dive Puako every day of your trip and still not see it all.

they might bring along snorkelers, who gobble up the snacks while you are under. And your divemaster may spend the entire trip taking photos—not of your group, but for himself. The boat's on the small side. In short, you can do better.

IN HILO

Yes, they *do* dive the Hilo side. Though the visibility and calmness are *much* better on the Kona side, life is abundant here and often overlooked. You may see more turtles in some spots here than Kona.

Hilo Ocean Adventures (808-934-8344) is the only dive *shop* on the east shore, and they offer a lot more than just diving. Besides offering some of the only diving for this side of the island (both boat and shore dives), they have snorkel tours, sightseeing tours, fishing charters and a variety of gear for rent. (They even have a swim school at their own indoor pool.) The SCUBA equiment selection isn't huge, but it's quality and they usually have a number of kid-sized fins, masks and wetsuits that are higher quality than you find at the box stores.

The other option for the area, **East Hawai'i Divers** (808-965-7840) gives guided two-tank shore dives for $100 (add gear for around $20 more). Private groups, and there is a good chance you won't see any other divers at the lesser-known locations that the owner takes you. (But that depends on ocean conditions and your skill level.) He dives all over the east side, with a focus on Hilo and Puna sites, and has over 30 years experience. A good resource.

MANTA RAY NIGHT DIVE

This dive is *so* good, we put it in the *Adventures* chapter. If you are a diver or want to be, check out that chapter and make plans for the dive of a lifetime.

BLACKWATER DIVE

If you're looking for something other than reef, consider this dive. You go out into 7,000 feet of water, and they lower you on a tether to 40 feet—*at night*. Just hang there and see what kind of exotic pelagic life wanders by. Lots of light-emitting bioluminescence, alien-like gelatinous creatures, schools of squid and perhaps even the elusive Hawaiian seahorse. **Jack's Diving Locker** takes small groups for around $230 per person (one tank, but it's big). **Big Island Divers** also does this after their manta dive for $210. **Kona Honu Divers** is $230. **Aquatic Life Divers** will run you about $200.

IF YOU'VE NEVER DIVED BEFORE

Several companies will introduce you to SCUBA by giving instructions, then taking you down on a supervised dive. That's how we started, and we were smitten enough to get certified. **Jack's Diving Locker** does good intros, though the pricing may be a little misleading. All intros require a pre-dive in their glass-walled pool for $75. It's $175 for a one-tank shore dive and $300 for a two-tank boat intro ($250 and $375 respectively when you factor in the required pool time).

DIVE SITES

Mentioning specific boat dive spots isn't particularly helpful because different companies sometimes use different names for the same spots, and you will usually go where the boat goes. As far as *shore* dive spots are concerned, here are some beauties you may want to check out on the Kona side. For Hilo side, see **Hilo Ocean Adventures**.

Puako—Virtually every dive shop and book tells you to go to the end of the road where the pavement becomes dirt. (You actually turn right *just before* the end.) They'll say go about 25 yards on the dirt, park and swim out about 50–75 yards. Turn right (north), and you should see several large vertical holes in the reef to drop through to the bottom. Exit the tunnel on the ocean side.

That's fine, but those sources don't know about the far better area. There are several public accesses along here, but the *best* is at telephone pole number 120 (kitty-corner from a church 2 miles from the highway). If the Public Access

sign is missing, we can confirm that it *is* a public access. Park near the road, and the water is a 175-foot walk away. Entry is easy. You can see the reef edge from the shore (polarized sunglasses really enhance it), so during the normally calm seas, kick almost straight out (slightly to the left) over the fairly shallow reef shelf so you'll end up seaward of a house with a corrugated metal roof. (Remember where you entered; other entry/exit points are harder on the diver.) Once at the reef wall (150 feet or so from shore), work your way northwest along the wall where countless chasms, arches and small caves, coupled with boundless coral, fish and the occasional turtle, create a delightful (though shallow 30–40 feet) dive. If you want to go deep, simply leave the coral behind and continue a short way farther offshore where the sand slopes relentlessly toward the abyss, broken only by vast fields of garden eels. (Approach them slowly, or they'll disappear into their holes.) If you're not too narc'd, return to the heavenly reef edge and make your way back. This is one of the few dives where you can go to 135 feet, yet still stay wet for an hour and be within your profile. Snorkelers, too, will enjoy the reef edge.

South Point—If you're a junkyard dog in search of a thrill, South Point has *lots* of fishing relics strewn about the ocean floor. Currents and surf can be unforgiving, so go only when calm. (Winter is sometimes best.) Not-so-easy entry is from rocks to the left (southeast) of the boat hoists. See page 83 for more information on this area. Stay away from the point.

The *Beaches* chapter describes nearly all the beaches around the island. Divers should read the descriptions of Kohala beaches, such as **Kapaʻa Beach Park**,

If you don't want to shoot photos of fish with your waterproof camera, use it to goof off, like we did with our friends here.

Mahukona and Hapuna (the southern end). In Kona, try the Alii Drive **Mile Marker 4** just south of **White Sands Beach** (from the cove head slightly south), **Kahalu'u Beach Park** (outside the breakwater) and **Pu'uhonua o Honaunau** (Place of Refuge).

Shopping

The Big Island isn't necessarily known for its shopping scene. That being said, if you know where to look there are a plethora of both local and chain shops that offer an incredible variety. Wandering through the smaller towns you'll be rewarded with unique finds or island antiques. Stroll the main strips for souvenirs and forgotten trip must-haves (reef-safe sunscreen anyone?). Each area of this island holds a different shopping experience.

KOHALA SHOPPING

The main shopping area in Kohala consists of the King's Shops located at the Waikoloa Beach Resort. Just about anything can be found here from high-priced clothing to high-priced jewelry and collectibles. (Because it's so near the posh resorts, stores and restaurants here are a little pricey.) Directly across the street is Queens' MarketPlace. Here there's a food court as well as Island Gourmet Markets if you're hungry. The

Shops at Mauna Lani is another resort shopping area with a similar feel.

Farther north is the quaint town of **Hawi**. Although it's small, it is easy to spend a day meandering through the interesting shops and stopping at the various restaurants. This area is more or less the antithesis of Kohala shopping. Stores here are very local and welcoming, and the short strip is definitely worth a walk through.

KAILUA-KONA SHOPPING

Kailua-Kona offers many small shopping areas to keep your stomach filled and wallet emptied. Kona Commons is a shopping center north of Kona on Makala Blvd. off Hwy 19. The main store is Target, but you'll find a collection of not-so-local stores here as well. The Kona International Market in the old industrial area north of Kona on Kaiwi and Luhia has small vendor stalls.

Continuing south on Kuakini is the King Kamehameha Mall where you'll find more island-inspired shops. This is also a good area to pick up any sandals or clothing you might need, as is Alii Drive. Other shopping areas include Kona Marketplace, Kona Inn Shopping Village, Keauhou Shopping Center and Walmart (the cheapest and, unfortunately, easiest place to pick up a bunch of souvenirs at once). Above Kona in **Holualoa** is a must-stop for art lovers. Here, you'll find some of the most original galleries on the island.

HAMAKUA & WAIMEA SHOPPING

Moving to Waimea, the Parker Ranch Center has some local and mainland shops, including a Foodland grocery store, a natural food store called Healthways II and Starbucks. Across the street is Waimea Center with a few more shops and good restaurants. You should also plan to wander along Kawaihae Road at Parker Square

where you'll find many outstanding shops and boutiques.

The **Honoka'a** historic main drag has been going through a revitalization. It is an early-day town as most shops shut down by 5 or 6 p.m., but it's *the* place for antiques and vintage finds. Malama Market also in Honoka'a, is a fine supermarket for foodstuffs and supplies (and your only choice for groceries for miles in either direction).

Although this area is pretty sparse, there are also some good stops on the way to 'Akaka Falls in Honomu.

HILO SHOPPING

Hilo's shopping gives you easy and abundant access to local and Hawai'i-made products. The historic richness and friendly ease of the shop owners allows you to take your time. Allow a day for exploring.

Kamehameha Avenue is where you will find the bulk of the shopping, but Kilauea Avenue is also fast becoming a hip strip, especially for foodies. Before you put yourself in a food coma, stroll through the antiques shops for unique and interesting finds. Check our *Island Dining* chapter for a range of culinary suggestions from around the globe that will have you loosening your belt. For a take-home treat (like our favorite: macnut shortbread dipped in caramel and chocolate) head over to Big Island Candies on Hinano Street.

On Hwy. 11 heading south, Prince Kuhio Plaza has popular mainland chain stores, such as Macy's.

Across Makaala Street is Walmart (with cheap souvenirs—you don't have to tell friends and family you got 'em here) and Ross (which has umbrellas at good prices). Farther down the same road is a Safeway grocery store and Target.

If you've ever gazed into an aquarium and wondered what it was like to see colorful fish in their natural environment, complete with coral, lava tubes and strange ocean creatures, you've come to the right Hawaiian island. Hawai'i features a dazzling variety of fish. Over 600 species are found in our waters. Here's our dilemma: If we blather on and on again about how good the water can be on the west side of the island, you're probably going to get sick. But we *have* to! Because this is where Kona really pays off. Usually calm, clear and teeming with fish, the Kona side offers some of the best snorkeling in the state.

We'll admit that we're snorkeling junkies and never tire of experiencing the water here. If you snorkel often, you can go right to our list below of recommended areas. But it you're completely or relatively inexperienced, you should read on.

For identifying ocean critters, the best books we've seen are *Shore Fishes of Hawai'i* by John Randall and *Hawaiian Reef Fish* by Casey Mahaney. They're what we use. You should see plenty of butterflyfish, wrasse, convict tang, Achilles tang, parrotfish, angelfish, damselfish, Moorish idol, pufferfish, trumpetfish, moray eel, and humuhumunukunukuapua'a, or Picasso triggerfish—a beautiful but very skittish fish. (It's as if they somehow *know* how good they look in aquariums.)

We know people who have a fear of putting on a mask and snorkel. Gives 'em the willies. For them, we recommend boogie boards with clear windows on them to observe the life below.

A FEW TIPS

- Use Sea Drops or another brand of anti-fog goop. Spread a thin layer on the inside of a dry mask, then do a quick rinse.
- Feeding the fish is generally not recommended since it introduces unnatural behavior to the reef, and it actually

Fish and clear water are the two best reasons to visit Kealakekua Bay.

causes the variety of fish to dwindle since bolder species do well and soon crowd out meeker ones. In the past it was a common practice at Kahalu'u Beach Park, but today conservationists are making a concerted effort to dissuade fish feeding.

- Most damage to coral comes when people grab it or stand on it. Even touching the coral lightly can transfer your oils to the polyps, killing them. If your mask starts to leak or you get water in your snorkel, be careful not to stand on the coral to clear them. Find a spot where you won't damage coral or drift into it. Fish and future snorkelers (not to mention the coral) will thank you.

- Don't use your arms much, or you will spook the fish—just gentle fin motion. Any rapid motion can cause the little critters to scatter. Be patient, fish are naturally curious and they'll want to check you out, too.

- Try to keep your hair out of the mask, because it will let water leak in. Don't over-tighten your mask either.

- If you have a mustache and have trouble with a leaking mask, try a little Vaseline. Don't get any on the glass—it can get *really* ugly.

- We prefer using divers' fins (the kind that slip over water shoes) so that we can walk easily into and out of the water without tearing up our feet. (If you wear socks or nylons under the shoes, they'll keep you from rubbing the tops of your toes raw.)

- Try to snorkel in calm areas. If you're in rougher water and a large wave comes and churns up the water with bubbles, put your arms in front of you to protect your head. You won't sense motion, and may get slammed into a rock before you know it.

SNORKEL GEAR

You'll find the least expensive gear in Kailua-Kona. The business can be cutthroat, so look for coupons in the free magazines scattered around the island. If you're going to snorkel more than once, it's nice to rent gear for a week, leave it in the trunk, and go whenever you have the desire.

The snorkel gear at **Jack's Diving Locker** (808-329-7585) is $9 per day, $49 per week. Divers' fins are available for an additional fee.

Snorkel Bob's (808-329-0770) near Huggo's restaurant on Alii Drive in Kona has gear for $4–$15 per day, $10–$52 per week. Expect to get talked into the expensive stuff here. You can also rent gear from a truck at **Kahalu'u Beach Park** for use there or at the concessionaire to the right of Kailua Pier.

You won't find inexpensive gear in Kohala, but you can try **Ocean Sports** (808-886-6666), which has a shack at 'Anaeho'omalu Beach. Convenient, but they rent snorkel gear for (hold onto your wallet) $30 *per day*. They rent all kinds of other goodies there at rates that aren't *quite* as confiscatory.

Boss Frog (808-331-1880) in the heart of the Alii Drive tourist area is more reasonable at $2–$14 per day, $10–$84 per week. They usually have some deals posted on their website, so we suggest checking there and coming in prepared.

At a certain point, it makes sense to just buy a cheap set instead of renting. You can get a decent snorkel, mask and fins for $30–$50 at Walmart.

SNORKEL BOAT TOURS

These can be fun. They'll take you to a good spot, provide gear and show you how to use it, and sometimes provide lunch. *Boat Tours* on page 189 includes reviews, prices and where they take you.

Our favorites are **Fair Wind II**, **Hula Kai**, **Body Glove** and **Sea Quest**.

NIGHT SNORKELING WITH MANTA RAYS

Though not as adventurous as a night manta SCUBA (see page 235 for more), this has become a big attraction on the Big Island. Lots of companies will take you out to snorkel with the mantas. You have three options: You can swim out on your own. (From the back of Keauhou Bay it's 0.25 miles each way unless you take a shortcut through the Sheraton.) You can go with a kayak company for the short paddle. We prefer **Aloha Kayak Co.** (808-322-2868). Though pricey ($89), they leave in the dark, usually after the others are gone. You don't get in the water until they see mantas (because you get cold faster at night). And you get to roam around as much as you want.

Lastly, you can take a boat out there. If you go on a SCUBA boat, you'll probably go to the airport manta site. You'll get a good briefing on mantas and get more freedom of movement, but as a snorkeler you're a tag-along. You'll be out there for hours while the divers complete two dives. **Big Island Divers** (808-329-6068) is $139, and **Jack's Diving Locker** (808-329-7585) is $199. Both do a good job. You can also take a larger snorkel boat, such as **Hula Kai** (808-322-2788) for the 2-minute ride to the Sheraton site. The 1.5-hour experience includes snacks, warm soup and a cash bar for $129–$149. **Sea Paradise** (808-322-2500) does this in a smaller boat for $122.

Boats going to the more reliable airport site on dedicated snorkel trips are **Ocean Encounters** (808-494-9150), which runs $102 on their 46-foot fishing boat, and **Kamanu Charters** (808-329-2021) for $115 from their 36-foot power cat.

SNORKEL SITES

The *Beaches* chapter has complete descriptions of all beaches. Our usual bias toward west Hawai'i for water activities applies here. Clarity and calmness just can't compare on the Hilo side, but sea life can be just as abundant there.

On the west side, be sure to check out some of these beaches:

Kahalu'u—Easy access and lots of life.

Kealakekua Bay near Captain Cook Monument—Some of the best snorkeling in the state.

Pu'uhonua o Honaunau—Easy access, excellent area, lots of turtles and coral make it almost as good as the Captain Cook Monument.

Papawai Bay—Very interesting underwater relief.

Hapuna to Waialea Beach—Great stretch of reef.

Mahukona—Good underwater junk.

Puako—Very extensive reef.

Kiholo Bay—Strange conditions.

Kapa'a Beach Park—Interesting underwater sights.

Lapakahi—Sometimes exceptional amounts of fish.

On the east side check out:

Punalu'u—Cold black sand conditions but *lots* of turtles.

Is this a misprint? Nope. Mauna Kea is 13,796 feet high, and in the winter it gets snow—sometimes a lot of it.

Ski Guides Hawai'i (808-885-4188) rents gear for $50 on the off chance you somehow *forgot* to bring your own. Mauna Kea snow (called pineapple powder) is not reliable and neither is the company, so call them when you arrive to see if skiing is available. (It's usually tough to get them

Hey, follow me. I'll show you where the turtle cleaning station is.

on the phone.) Granted, the conditions will be better at Aspen. But you can't go straight from the snow to the beach there, now can you? You'll need to take a 4WD to the observatory area where everyone but the driver can slide down the mountain on boogie boards or anything you think will do, while the driver takes the vehicle to the bottom to act as a ski lift.

If you're a little hesitant about trying SCUBA, consider SNUBA. That's where you swim below a raft with tanks and a 20-foot hose, regulator in mouth and an instructor by your side.

Big Island Watersports (808-240-1993) takes you on a shore dive near King Kamehameha Hotel in Kona for $89. Groups of two to six per instructor. Expect about 30–45 minutes of bottom time. You must be at least 8 years of age and be able to

swim. Children ages 4–7 can check out their SNUBA-Doo. Check-in is at the Kailua Pier.

If you feel the need to lose yourself in the blissfulness of a decadent overall body massage and treatment, the two best (and most expensive) spas on the island are the Fairmont Orchid and the Mauna Lani, both in the Kohala resort area.

The Fairmont Orchid (808-887-7540) and their "Spa Without Walls" is the best *tropical* experience. We love their outdoor cabanas located at manmade waterfalls. Cabanas 4 and 5 are directly over the water with a small glass panel under your head to watch the koi fish while you're lying on your stomach. Couples can enjoy an outdoor sunset massage right at the shoreline. Scrubs and facials take place inside. The only downside is that non-guests of the hotel won't have access to the fitness facilities or Jacuzzis.

Auberge Spa at Mauna Lani Resort (808-796-3954) is a great second choice only for guests of the hotel. It's much smaller than the old spa at the same property with only five treatment rooms, but you will be well-pampered. It features Goop products.

A weaker choice is the **Mandara Spa** (808-886-8191) at the Waikoloa Beach Marriott. You might get good treatments, but it is all indoors and not as luxurious as the first two. Schedule in advance.

In Kona, the **Ho'ola Spa** (808-930-4848) at the Sheraton is a slightly more affordable alternative to the pricier Kohala resort-area spas, but don't expect the same level of pampering. Massage indoors or outdoors on an oceanfront lanai. They automatically add a 20% tip to your bill "for your convenience." Gee, thanks for thinking of me, Sheraton.

STARGAZING

The Big Island has some of the best stargazing in the world. It's so good in fact, that NASA built telescopes at the peak of Mauna Kea. With or without telescopes, the view from this island is sure to impress.

If you want to go stargazing on Mauna Kea, home to the world's finest and most coveted telescopes, you can drive to the visitor center on Mauna Kea Access Road and look through their telescopes for free and listen to their star talk. If you want more pampering (and don't want to drive) **Hawai'i Forest & Trail** (808-331-8505) does the best job. They'll pick you up in Waikoloa or near Honokohau Harbor in Kona. Then they drive you to an old sheep-shearing station at the lower altitudes of Mauna Kea for a pretty good catered dinner, take you to the summit for sunset, then bring you back down to the visitor center for stargazing from their own telescope. While you sip hot chocolate and eat cookies, their knowledgeable guides do a good job pointing out—with lasers—the night sky. It's 7.5 hours altogether for $255.

Another company, **Mauna Kea Summit Adventures** (808-322-2366), has a similar product, but it's not executed nearly as well. It's up to $290 (depending on time of year and if you opt for a hot meal).

Star Gaze Hawai'i (808-323-3481) will let you peek through their scopes at the Westin Hapuna Beach Resort for $50. Kind of hard to get excited about that one, and their claim that you'll get better views at sea level than atop Mauna Kea is pretty laughable. But you sure won't be as cold. Check with them about their hours since they change seasonally.

submarine

You won't *Run Silent, Run Deep*. There won't be the sound of sonar pinging away in the background. And it's unlikely that anyone will shoot torpedoes at you. But if you want to see the undersea world and *refuse* to get wet, *dis is da buggah.*

Atlantis Adventures (808-326-7939) has a 48-passenger sub that ambles over a very healthy reef in Kailua Bay. This is the opposite of an aquarium—this is *their* world, and *you* are the oddity. This 45-minute, $134 ride is a kick. Kids ($58) like it. Adults like it. Even certified divers like us like it. Claustrophobics will probably be too busy staring through the windows to be nervous. Photographers will want to use fast (at least 400 speed) ISO, and turn off the flash. Mornings are usually best. Wear a bright red shirt, and watch what happens to its color on the way down. Also, you have to descend (and later ascend) a ladder to get into the sub with other people standing below you. Why am I mentioning this? Let's just say that ladies should leave their skirts back at the hotel. Kids need to be 36 inches tall.

SURFING

Ho, da shreddin's da kine, brah. (Just trying to get you in the mood.) Surfing is synonymous with Hawai'i. And why not? Hawaiians invented da buggah. Lessons aren't as difficult as you may think. They put you on a large, soft board the size of a garage door (well...almost), so it's fairly easy to master, at least at this level.

SURFING HOTSPOTS

Dudes, the most gnarly surfing on the west side is at **Pine Trees** just north of Kailua-Kona. (See page 168 for directions.) The breaks are outstanding. In Kona, the break off the "little blue church" near **Kahalu'u** is one of the most dependable. **Banyans** on Alii Drive just south of Kona Bali Kai has excellent waves. Other great surf spots are **Ke'ei** and **Old Kona Airport**, are both described in *Beaches* chapter. You should know that Banyans and Lyman's (just around the bend) are notorious for surfers with bad attitudes. Outsiders will be as welcome as reef rash. (By the way, a collection of surfboards is known in surfing lingo here as a *quiver.* A little kid surfer who doesn't have a job or a car yet is called a *grommet.* Double *overhead* is when the waves are huge, and if you get good

enough, you might get a chance to visit the *green room.* If someone says your girlfriend is *filthy,* it's a compliment. And a *landshark* is someone who says he surfs… but doesn't.)

SURFBOARD RENTALS

In Kona, **Pacific Vibrations** (808-329-4140) rents boards for $15 per day. For lessons, **Hawai'i Lifeguard Surf Instructors** (808-324-0442) does an excellent job at Kahalu'u Beach Park. It's $149 for a private lesson for about 2 hours, though that price seems to vary *a lot.* It's usually cheaper. Also for group lessons consider **Ocean Eco Tours** (808-960-8174) for around $119, and **Kona Surf Company** (808-333-7375) for $99 per person.

STAND UP PADDLING

Stand Up Paddling, or **SUP**, is extremely popular with residents and visitors. The hardest part about learning to surf is standing up on the board while it's moving. This sport has made things easier by giving you a board big enough to dance on. SUP boards are wider, thicker and longer than the biggest longboards people commonly learn to surf on. SUP instruction focuses on keeping your balance while using a tall paddle to move you into the waves. (This provides an excellent central core workout, with your feet—of all things—hurting the most.) The sight of people standing and dipping long paddles in the water has earned SUP surfers the derogatory title "janitors" or "moppers" from traditional surfers. The size of the board, as well as the fact that you are already standing up, gives you an advantage in catching waves early. You don't have to drop in exactly where the wave is breaking. Moppers can catch waves behind the lineup, but all surfing rules apply once you've caught the wave. Traditional surfers will

A male humpback whale doing his best to show off to a nearby female.

be more inclined to drop in on your wave since they'll feel that you didn't work as hard to get it as they did.

SUP in the open ocean is one area where it really pays to take a lesson to learn proper techniques. For rates, call the surfing guys listed earlier. For several reasons, surfing companies seem less interested in giving SUP lessons and will make you jump through more hoops. **Hypr Nalu Hawai'i** (808-960-4667) in Waikoloa does a good job. It's $50 per hour. **Pacific Vibrations** (808-329-4140) has the cheapest rental prices. In Kohala at the Mauna Lani, **Hulakai** (808-896-3141) charges a little over a buck a minute for 90-minute lessons, but their SUP location isn't as good. **Mauna Lani Sea Adventures** (808-885-7883) has better prices and a better location at Makaiwa Bay, but the parking police won't let you in. You'll have to leave your car at Mauna Lani's public parking and walk 0.7 miles to the sand beach at the south end.

Humpback whales are common in Hawai'i between December and March or April. Humpbacks don't eat while they're here and may lose a third of their body weight during their Hawaiian vacation. (I doubt that many *human* visitors can make that same claim.) They're here to take advantage of Hawai'i's romantic atmosphere and mate in our waters (so don't stare), returning the following year to give birth. Though whales are more numerous off Maui, the Big Island is still a splendid place to see them blow and breach. From shore, you may see humpback whales causing a ruckus or just generally frolicking. But out on a boat, you can sometimes get up close and personal. Additionally, there are several other species—including giant sperm whales, pilot whales, false killer whales, beaked whales, pygmy killer whales and melon-headed whales—that reside here and require boats to see.

WHALE WATCHING TOURS

Captain Dan McSweeney's Whale Watch (808-322-0028) is our resident expert. He has spent approximately 8 zillion hours studying whales off Kona. For $120 you'll take their 40-foot boat offshore for hours of whale watching and education. Snacks provided, restrooms on board.

They claim a 90% success rate in finding whales, and guarantee a sighting or you can come back for free.

Several other boat companies listed under *Boat Tours* (see page 189) provide whale watching during humpback season, but this company has more experience.

HUMPBACK WHALE HOTSPOTS

From the shoreline, elevated vantage points are hard to come by. Near Kua Bay, **Pu'u Kuili** is a 342-foot high cinder cone that can be a good place to spot whales.

Lastly, during humpback season, we like to swim out beyond the sound of the breakers (say, 100 feet past the breakwater at **Kahalu'u Beach**) and listen to those soulful giants sing the blues. You certainly won't get to *see* them underwater, but their concert is often the best in town. (But I sometimes wonder if the fish all around me are thinking, "I *hate* it when the humpbacks come to town. They make such a racket when we're trying to sleep!") You can hear whales from much farther distances if your ears are a few feet underwater. (Hint: Hang upside down.) Some years, the whale crowd is pretty raucous, constantly breaching, blowing and singing. Other years the behemoths may be strangely quiet.

Ever seen movies where military commandos don a harness, hook a pulley onto a steel cable and zip down into the action? This is similar—without the hostile fire at the end.

Ziplining has become a big business on this island, but not all zips are created equal. We zipped all the companies and found three that do a great job and two that are pretty avoidable. By the way, don't

wear too-short shorts, or the harness will get under your skin (so to speak). Minimum age is *usually* 10.

The best overall is the **Umauma Experience** (808-930-9477). They zip along and over the spectacularly beautiful Umauma Falls and gulch 15 miles north of Hilo. (See photo on page 234.) No. 2 and 4 zips are probably the most dramatic ziplines in the state. After No. 4 (which had us zipping around 40 mph over a distance of 2,000 feet) you cross a suspension bridge, then you'll have four anticlimactic zips before ending it on impressive No. 9 for $209. They say there are 14 waterfalls along the zip, but don't bother counting (many are multi-tiered)—just enjoy the expansive beauty. It takes 1.5–3 hours, depending on the size of the group, and the van ride to the ziplines is very short. Their harnesses are good, and they are the only zip on the island that *encourages* you to try tricks and go *upside down*. The first four of the lines are dual side-by-side. They will take kids as young as 4 years or 35 pounds, but they *may* be tethered to an instructor. With fun zips, lively guides and a stunning backdrop, this should definitely be your first choice. For about $90 extra you get to go down to the river to swim, kayak and frolic. Only ding here is they charge $45 to borrow a GoPro camera. Weight restriction is 35–275 pounds.

Hawaii Zipline Tours (808-963-6353) north of Hilo in Honomu has seven zips. They also market it as Akaka Falls Zipline, which is misleading because you'll never see those falls. It's also unnecessary, because their final zip *is* across a beautiful waterfall, just not 'Akaka. The first four are fairly short (the first one *embarrassingly* so), but they win the arms race with their final zip, at 3,350 feet, and it's a (literal) scream that will probably have you zipping at 40-

plus mph. No pampering here—they will lend you a jacket if it rains and give you water refills, but that's it. The guides are smart, friendly and efficient. Even though this tour can fill up, the line moves quickly. $180 for 2.5 hours. Weight restriction is 80–260 pounds. Ages 10 and up.

Up north past Hawi is **Kohala Zipline** (808-331-3620). The forest and gulches are pretty, but there are downsides here. They have a self-braking system using gloves, and the tour includes a rappel, which adds to the gear you have to carry (plus the anxiety of getting your fingers caught). Though they market it as a challenge course, the rappel is underwhelmingly slow and short. It takes about 3 hours to complete the nine zips for $205. Don't let the pictures on their website fool ya. You will *not* be zipping over a waterfall. But they do offer a "Zip & Dip" for $295 where they drive you to a waterfall after the course. Most of the zips are less than 500 feet.

Weight restriction is 70–270 pounds. Ages 8 and up.

Right next to Umauma Experience (but a million miles away in terms of quality) is **Zip Isle** (808-963-5427). To be blunt, we can't think of anything we liked about this product. Their terrain is boring (it's *not* over Umauma), groups have up to 16 people (with longer waits between zips), their harnesses feel less reassuring than others, and the first six zips average a ridiculously short 300 feet at 13 mph. Number 7 is 1,100 feet, but by that time you're getting restless. We've zipped these guys right after zipping Umauma, and the contrast is staggering. The guides are knowledgeable about the area, however, so entertain yourself by asking questions since you probably won't be entertained much on the ziplines. $187. At the Botanical World Adventures 15 miles north of Hilo. Weight range is 35–275 pounds, but anyone under 70 pounds will ride with a guide. Ages 4 (*sometimes* younger) and up.

If you don't scream at some point on this one, you gotta check your pulse.

The manta ray night dive is one of those few adventures that is even better with a crowd.

The adventures described below (except for the resort dolphin encounter) are for the serious adventurer. They can be experiences of a lifetime. We are assuming that, if you consider attempting any of them, you are a person of sound judgment, capable of assessing risks. All adventures carry potential dangers of one kind or another. Our descriptions below do not attempt to convey all risks associated with an activity. These activities are not for everyone. Preparation is essential. In the end, it comes down to your own good judgment.

MANTA RAY NIGHT DIVE

Imagine the following scene: You take a boat to a dark piece of shoreline, leaving just before sunset. When you arrive, perhaps another dive boat is already there. *Damn,* you think. They'll ruin it. As you slip into the water and approach what is affectionately called *the campfire,* numerous lights beckon to you, like a porch light calling to moths. Then gigantic shadows blot out the lights. *Mantas!* As you approach, one zooms over your head, missing you by an inch. There you sit, with all the other divers, mesmerized by the performance before you. One, two, maybe three stinger-less manta rays, 6–10 feet across their wings, slowly swirling, looping and soaring all about you. Like an extraterrestrial dance performed by alien beings, these filter-feeding leviathans are more graceful than you could possibly imagine. They seem to understand that they are on stage, and they rarely disappoint. When you think you have gotten used to their size, a goliath 14 feet across may swoop in, its enormous maw scooping up thousands of the tiny, darting shrimp that cloud the water along with the bubbles. You struggle to resist the urge to reach up and touch them—it's best to let them initiate any touching. Above the fray, a sea of needlefish gobbles up what they can. Nearby, a friendly eel might slither over to give you a kiss.

It all started back in the '70s when the Kona Surf Hotel (now a Sheraton) started flooding the shoreline with light, attracting tiny brine shrimp, a form of plankton. This plankton brought large manta rays, which gobble them by the millions. Then in 2000 the resort closed (and turned off their light), and the mantas vanished. By luck they were discovered to be congregating at a spot near the Kona Airport (perplexing dive operators since there are no lights there to attract their food source). When the resort reopened five years later, some returned, but there are times that they seem to take a vacation and don't show up at all. The airport location tends to be the most manta-laden.

You will likely have plenty of air left since the dive takes place at about 35 feet, and you move very little. Diver etiquette dictates that you leave your snorkel on the boat; the protruding tube can scratch the mantas' belly. This is one of those rare dives where a crowd, as long as it's not *too* big, actually makes it better. More lights and more wide eyes. Snorkelers who try to dive down or those who use scooters can scare them off. Ask for a hood to help keep you warmer.

If you started diving because you wanted to feel like you were floating in space, night dives provide that feeling. But for this dive, weight yourself a bit heavy; it'll make it easier to stay put. (Don't assume that if the surf is up, boats won't go. Though usually calm, we see boats out there when the surf is high enough to make us grateful *we're* not there.) Some companies use one-third to one-half of the 50- to 60-minute dive for roaming around. Others, like **Kona Honu Divers** (808-324-4668), spend nearly all their time with the mantas. We've had good luck with **Jack's Diving Locker** (808-329-7585) and **Big Island Divers** (808-329-6068). Boats that leave from Keauhou Bay have a convenient 600-*yard* cruise out to the Sheraton site.

Lastly, if the mantas *don't* show, the night dive at the Sheraton is fairly boring. (Sorry, but it's true.) And no-shows seem more common around the full moon. (Perhaps more light everywhere makes this site less compelling to the mantas.)

If you've night dived before, do this one! If you've never night dived before, consider doing it now! Expect to spend about $145–$302 for this dive—the best money you will ever spend underwater, if they show.

If you only want to **snorkel** with the mantas, see page 228 for more.

MAUNA ULU CRATER HIKE

This short hike is not for the easily frightened or the faint at heart. Mauna Ulu erupted between 1969 and 1974, at times shooting fountains of lava more than 1,770 feet into the air—that's as high as the One World Trade Center building in New York. When it was all over, the event left a smoldering maw 400 feet deep and 500 feet across. (That's a guess—it gets bigger all the time.) This sheer drop is accessible via a 45-minute hike from Chain of Craters Road in Hawai'i Volcanoes National Park. From there, you just walk up to Mauna Ulu Crater.

We need to stress that this is new land. The part of the hill adjacent to Pu'u Huluhulu *seems* to be the most stable, but that is a relative term. There are several areas where thin, shelly lava breaks beneath your feet. You may only drop an inch or two, but your adrenaline tells you otherwise. The rim of the crater is nearly straight down and crumbling all the time. If you get too close, it may break off, you may fall in, and then you're *really* out of luck. If all this doesn't dissuade you, you'll get to see a view that is beyond belief. The crater is raw, like an open wound on Kilauea. It usually steams from several spots. There are empty lava river banks around it where huge quantities of lava coursed their

The Mauna Ulu hike is an 'okole squeezer, not an average stroll.

way down the mountain. There are blobs where lava spattered where it fell, large cracks with heat still escaping. This is as close as you may ever get to experiencing an erupting vent—while it's not erupting. But remember, this hike is what we call an 'okole squeezer, so be smart about the edge. A selfie stick may help extend your reach if you want to take a picture peeking over the edge to look at the bottom. Permits are only required if you plan to overnight at the Napau backcountry campsite, so you *are* allowed to do a day hike to Mauna Ulu without a permit or permission. That's official from the park, but some park personnel sometimes erroneously tell visitors otherwise. Morning is usually best for this hike.

MARATHON SNORKEL TO PAPAWAI BAY

Snorkeling at a beach such as Kahalu'u can be a great way to see the ocean. You can also snorkel with manta rays from a boat. But for those with an adventurous streak, the shoreline between the end of Old Airport and Papawai Bay (aka Pawai Bay) can be a real thrill.

First things first. You only do this when the ocean's calm—period. If it looks even remotely like our photo on page 238, you shouldn't be anywhere near this spot. It's almost a half mile to your turnaround point. So if you can't swim a mile with fins, this ain't the time to try. Once at Papawai, you can venture into the protected cove, but the land surrounding it is private, and you are not welcome ashore. Legally, you're only allowed to stand on the sandy shoreline to the high water mark. From a practical standpoint, you should stay in the water unless you're having some kind of emergency.

The swim features lots of cool underwater relief, fairly deep nearshore water and nice coral in the beginning. Fish life here can be exceptional. Expert snorkelers may not consider this an adventure, but the distance from the shore coupled with the narrow entry to Papawai Bay and the sometimes tricky water exit at the end all combine to make this challenging.

Park at the far end of the old runway, and you'll see a somewhat sandy cove. If you go at low tide, expect a shallow exit with plenty of urchins on all sides. We like to wear scuba gloves and carry a set of reef shoes tucked into the back of our board shorts to make the final water exit injury free. Enter the water from the sand and head out until you're away from any breakers. If you get beat up on the way out, the ocean's telling you to do something

else that day. Because it faces south, it *tends* to get calmer seas in the winter than summer. Follow the shoreline west and notice the remarkable water clarity early on. It will come and go. The shoreline is an extended underwater cliff with lots of holes, chasms and arches. Don't get lulled into getting raked over the top of the reef by the surf.

Depending on how fast you swim, Papawai Bay may come quicker than you think. You'll see some underwater debris (pipes or wiring, it looks like) at the entrance. Don't go in if you think the surf will chew you up. The entrance is pretty narrow at the surface. The whole trip *can* be done in an hour, but will certainly take longer. Use your best judgment on how far out to sea you travel, but always roughly follow the coastline and come back to your starting point alert to the water hazards. Expect to be jostled by surge the entire way. If you're feeling halfway to tired, turn around regardless of your progress. Because there's nowhere to exit the ocean until you get all the way back to your starting point, you need to constantly

It's almost a half mile from Old Airport to Papawai Bay. But if the ocean looks anything like it does in this photo, don't go anywhere near the water.

assess if this whole thing feels right to you. You are committed, so don't let your excitement for adventure get ahead of your abilities.

JUMP OFF THE END OF THE WORLD

Cliff jumpers, rejoice. There's a place for you just past the south end of Alii Drive. (See map on page 67.) Drive to the end of the road and take the lava road by foot toward the ocean, veer left, and just before the road begins to ascend (next to a short paved section), take the trail to the right to the ocean. It's only a 5–10 minute walk altogether. There at the cliff you are confronted by a 35-foot drop to the water. You have your choices—there are several elevations above the water. And beneath you is clean, clear water up to 15 feet deep. If you *want* to hit bottom, you probably can if you do your best impression of a pencil, but it's better to spread 'em as soon as you strike water. This is your cliff-jumping opportunity, where countless locals (who named this spot) have dared the ocean. Use your best judgment in deciding whether to jump. Judgment is what adventures are all about. The surf can rearrange the bottom, bringing in shallower boulders, so you'll have to evaluate all conditions for yourself. And there could be a critter near the surface that you might collide with. After you've jumped, do you have a nice, easy

Don't like heights or falling? Not to worry; it won't last long.

path to climb back up? No, sorry. After you hit the water in a shockingly abrupt fashion, you'll look to the left of the cave you just plummeted in front of and begin the daunting task of climbing the cliff face so you can do it all over again. Don't like those options? Then don't jump off the end of the world.

You probably won't be gettin' this up close and personal.

One final word of warning: Don't even *think* about jumping when the surf is up, or you may find yourself slammed against the cliff and unable to climb out.

Another popular cliff-jumping place is from the boat hoist area at South Point. See page 85 for directions to that. People jump and then climb the ladder back up, or they climb the rocks to the right (looking from the water).

CLOSE ENCOUNTER WITH DOLPHINS

To start, we have to point out that dolphin encounters have become a victim of their own success. The popularity of these tours exploded in the past few years, and there have been lots of companies offering increasingly closer encounters with dolphins. Though Hawaiian spinner dolphins are *not* endangered, they are protected under the Marine Mammal Protection Act, and NOAA Fisheries implemented stricter rules at the end of 2021 to enhance protection and prevent disturbance of the dolphins. The rules prohibit swimming with, approaching or remaining within 50 yards of a Hawaiian spinner dolphin. This means swimming with wild dolphins is against the rules whether you're on your own or with a tour operator. The only time you can be close to a dolphin is if one approaches you, and even then you're supposed to take immediate action to put distance between you and dolphin (which seems kind of rude to the inquisitive mammal, if you ask me). Hefty fines await those who don't abide by the new rules.

Even with the stricter rules in place, there are a few ways to still have an amazing dolphin experience. The first is to head to one of the bays where dolphins like to hang out and then swim or kayak out into the bay. In the Kona area, from north to south, your best bets are Kealakekua Bay (Captain Cook), Honaunau (Two-Step), and Hoʻokena Beach. But whether or not the dolphins show is a total gamble. We've had good luck at Kealakekua Bay. (There is almost always someone at Napoʻopoʻo Beach willing to rent you a kayak to make it easier to get out to them.) Go early in the morning, when the dolphins are still active.

If you want an easier way to do this, booking a boat tour is the way to go. There is still no guarantee you'll see dolphins, but these small cetaceans often play in the waves cut by the bow of the boats. (Apparently they didn't get the memo that *they* should stay 50 yards away.)

Dolphins hunt during the night and then come into shallower water to sleep, where they rely on the light reflecting off the bottom of protected bays to help alert them to predators. But they never fall completely asleep; half their brain stays awake so they can still surface and breathe. (You can tell when they are in this resting state because one eye will be closed, and they move more slowly and tend to swim deeper along the bottom.)

Good companies take time to observe how the dolphins are behaving before allowing swimmers to get in the water with them. Bad operators (which have ruined this experience for everyone) aggressively chase them down, encircle them and dump swimmers right on top of them. Their only focus is on getting their guests up close, regardless of whether the dolphins want to play. Dolphins are curious about

us, just like we are curious about them. Treating them with respect makes for a better experience for all involved.

Almost all companies offer a discount for booking online, and some offer cheaper rates for kids. A few have surprisingly low age restrictions, but we've found that children under 9 generally don't have as good a time, since you need to be a decently good swimmer.

When booking (see *Boat Tours* on page 189), you'll likely have the option of doing just a dolphin watch or a combo tour that includes snorkeling, *usually* at Kealakekua Bay. A combo tour gives you the best bang for your buck. The majority of tours leave from Honokohau Harbor (south of the Kona airport), but we prefer the operators that depart from the Keauhou boat launch because it is closer to Kealakekua Bay, meaning you get more time to snorkel there after the dolphin watch.

Bring a towel, reef-safe sunscreen, light cover-up and sunglasses. The tour guide will provide a snorkel, mask and fins (or you can bring your own). One word of warning: Lots of boat tour brochures still *imply* you will swim with dolphins on these tours, but now you know what the rules *really* are.

Dolphin Quest Dolphin Encounter

A much more structured way to get facetime with a dolphin is at Dolphin Quest at the Hilton Waikoloa Village. They have several Atlantic bottle-nosed dolphins in their lagoon where children and adults can get in the water and interact with them. (Our own local spinner dolphins need deeper water and wouldn't successfully adapt to the program.) You stand on a shallow sandy shore with three or four other folks while the dolphins come up to you. It really is an experience that you will remember for life. It's hard to express the enthusiasm people have when they get up close and personal with these ocean-going mammals. But it's undeniable that the encounter is incredibly enriching. You also can't help but notice that the dolphins seem to love their contact with humans as well.

The water in their lagoon is replaced with fresh seawater every few hours by massive pumps, keeping it very clean for them and you. The dolphins are very active and playful, reproduce when they get to the right age (wink, wink), and the trainers seem to show them extraordinary love and affection.

If you're interested, call them at (808) 987-3434. It's not always easy to get in on this. Kids are the most desired customers here. Personnel love to introduce kids, not only to the dolphins, but also to various issues regarding the dolphins' environment (without becoming too heavy-handed). Make reservations 60 days in advance to ensure access. Their most popular option is $269 per person, which includes 30 minutes with the dolphins. They also offer a program for kids 2–4 years, which is $210 per adult/toddler pair, but you only spend about 10 minutes with the dolphins. Other programs are available as well. If you don't want to pay a dime, you can watch the whole process from the nearby lawn separating the lagoon from the ocean.

BOULDER-HOP TO A WATERFALL

If you spend any time in Hilo or along the Hamakua Coast, you'll see lots of waterfalls. But let's be honest—you didn't really *earn* them, did you? (Well, except for paying to come to Hawai'i, I guess.) But let's face it: You usually drive up to a parking area, walk over to a viewpoint

You didn't drive to Nanue Falls. You didn't really even hike here. You just sort of…groped your way to this lovely waterfall.

and take a picture. Maybe you'll take a short trail, like Wai'ale Falls. But to see *these* falls, you're gonna have to get wet and risk falling and breaking your 'okole. Because although they're only 900 feet from your car, you can't see 'em, and there is no trail. You'll have to get *in* the river and scramble upstream on big old boulders. And if you slip and fall, you probably can't even use your cell phone to call for help, so be careful.

This is not an all-day adventure (unless you drove here from Kona). It'll take most people up to an hour to struggle through the river. (Though well-balanced trail gods could probably sprint their way in 10 minutes.) Once at the falls, the beautiful, multi-tiered falls tumble into a deep pool. Take your time here; you *earned* it.

The falls are north of Hilo. Just north of mile marker 18, turn mauka off the highway and hang a right. The next bridge is stamped NANUE. A so-called trail on the nearside leads down to the stream. From here, head upstream as carefully as you can until there's a waterfall on your head. Flip-flops are *not* a good way to go on these rocks. Serious gear junkies would want canyoning shoes and a pair of carbide-tipped hiking sticks. Most people, however, will do fine with some local fishing tabis (available from

Walmart) or some hiking shoes with fairly soft rubber.

An alternative is **Waikaumalo Falls** farther down the same road. It's a bit farther upstream (1,250 feet). Starting at Waikaumalo Park, ignore the teaser trail behind the facilities (it only leads to frustration and despair), and instead head upstream on the nearshore bank. The boulders aren't as difficult (most of the time) as Nanue, but there's a place two-thirds of the way in where you'll have to swim across a pool to continue, and the end just before the falls is pretty clumsy. This stream doesn't seem quite as clean as Nanue, but the waterfall at the end is still rewarding.

Avoid when the streams are raging, and read up on **leptospirosis**, listed under *Hazards* on page 36.

Though rare, **flash floods** can occur in any freshwater stream anywhere in the world, and it can happen when it's sunny where you are but raining up the mountain. Be alert for them.

EXPLORE UNTAMED LAVA TUBES

One of the cool things about being on a volcano is exploring lava tubes, the plumbing that Madame Pele uses to move magma from one place to another. At the national park you can see a well-trampled one (Thurston). But what about exploring

The back of the lava tube when your flashlight fails.

a wild lava tube on your own? *That's* not so easy. Most are either inaccessible or on private property. For a previous edition we found one in a forest, near a highway, on state land. Then someone bought the parcel next door and brought a snarling dog, which scared everybody (including us) away. Then we found one on Saddle Road that was awesome—until the state came along and shut it down. So we searched high and low (*quite literally*) and found these two—in the middle of nowhere—a long drive from wherever you are staying. They're on state land, legally accessible and only 3 miles round trip from your car. And you'll be able to hike your way into *utter* darkness (which is more rare than most people realize).

Being an adventure, these caves ain't paved, they're not lit, have no hand railings and there's no good entrance. The only way to see the first one is to drop through a skylight in the ceiling and grope your way through a tunnel darker than Vantablack. (You'll have to Google that one.) You have to be strong enough to be able to lower yourself down boulders and ledges, then climb back up. (Definitely not for kids.) The only way to find these tubes is to either follow faint lines on the ground, or use our smartphone app, which is GPS-aware. (We *swear* we're not shamelessly pushing the app, but facts are facts.) Lastly, all lava tubes eventually collapse (and the island will eventually sink into the sea), so if you're unlucky enough to be there when that happens, then it wasn't your day. (You should've stayed in bed.)

Once inside the first cave, a chamber opens, and you'll see another skylight. Start exploring. Frozen lava icicles cling to the ceiling like stalactites. The walls are melted smooth—a reminder that liquid rock once flowed through here. Because it's a single tube, you can't get lost. (Unless you lose your lights—then you're screwed.) Make sure to stop and marvel at the formations along the way; that's what you came for. Turn around when you get to a part where you need to crawl (it leads to a collapsed section that is impassible), and head back to the entrance point.

At the second cave, a tree grows in the middle of the collapsed ceiling where you enter the tube. The rubble here from the collapse is sharp, so take time negotiating the best way down. To the left is a fairly short segment, but the cathedral-like chamber is nice to gawk at. Head to the right (toward the ocean if you could see it) to access the chamber that leads deeper into the tube. This side is hot and humid. You can even see the moisture escaping from the cave—moss and ferns cling to the polished, exposed surfaces here, soaking it up. This tube is home to an owl that may give you a surprise as it swoops silently out of its lair. There are numerous small chambers that branch off from the main tube here, all of which dead end quickly.

The nuts and bolts: On Highway 11 between Pahala and Hawai'i Volcanoes National Park, halfway between mile markers 48 and 49, there is a gravel pull-out on the ocean (south) side of the road and a utility pole. With few wide shoulder areas along this stretch, this spot should be obvious. Park here and head toward the ocean.

The path quickly veers to the left and parallels the highway for a short distance. There are white lines spraypainted on the exposed lava rock. (Which is how we stumbled onto this the first time.) This is the path you'll follow for the entirety of this hike. You'll generally never go more than 50 feet without seeing one of these white lines. Always follow the general direction the last one was trending. The first cave is 0.4 miles into the hike. Look for orange paint on the exposed lava veering off to the left. Follow this trail a short distance to a small, silk oak tree and go to the right of it. An orange X marks the spot. The best access to this tube is on the left.

The second cave is 0.8 miles farther along the trail. (Look for the stacked-stone cairns to help navigate through the high grass.) The opening is difficult to see until you are almost right on top of it, so don't fall in. There is a tree growing through the center of the hole. When you are done exploring, return the way you came.

Start this hike early in the day, as finding your way back to the highway in fading light is no fun at all. And promise—come on, raise your hand and *promise*—not to take anything from the caves other than memories.

PEDAL THROUGH BIG ISLAND'S BACKCOUNTRY

If you've ever looked at the Tour de France and thought *I can do that*, well, now's your chance to put your money where your mouth is…well, kind of. This is an approximately 46-mile bike trip that takes you along Big Island's famous Mana Road, with a bit of a twist—you get to do it all on an electric bike.

First, you should know that this trip might take a little logistical finesse. You'll want two vehicles—one to drop you off, and one waiting for you at the end. You'll start off near Saddle Road and end up in Waimea. Don't do it the other way because the Saddle Road start is at 7,000 feet elevation and Waimea is at 2,700 feet. The whole 46-mile trip will probably take a *minimum* of five hours (we tried to limit our stops, and it took us over six, so if you do it in under five hours, you're a beast).

Even with electric power, this still isn't an easy trip. When you think you're halfway done, you're only a few miles in. When

*Mana Road is uneven and rocky most of the trip…
but hey, that's what makes it an adventure.*

you start to feel like Evel Knievel's got nothin' on you and that you should be the next Red Bull spokesman, you'll flip over a rogue rock and swear you've dislocated your shoulder. (Turns out it was just a bruise, but thank you for your concern.) The more you stop and rest, the harder it will be to get back on the bike, and apart from those of you who are insane horseback riding or cycling enthusiasts, what starts out feeling bad ass will ultimately lead to a very sore one.

All that being said, the trip is worth it. Mana Road is a beautiful way to see some of Big Island's more remote scenery, with unparalleled views of the mountains and lush grasslands. If that isn't enough, anyone who bikes all of Mana Road is entitled to major bragging rights and a great story to tell. As much a mental feat as a physical one, we took some kind of warped solace in the fact that we HAD to finish (ain't no one coming to pick us up if we decide we're tired). When we told people we were sore from e-biking, they scoffed but, trust us, even with a little electric help, this is a tough and arduous journey (though ultimately a worthwhile one).

Before you start on this odyssey, there are a few basics you should know.

We suggest renting your bike from **Bike Works Mauka** (808-885-7943) in Waimea. Bike rentals are around $100 for 24 hours (prices go down if you choose to hold onto yours longer) and come with a helmet. (We absolutely recommend wearing a helmet for this one; Mana Road has a penchant for tipping over your bike when you least expect it.) The shop is open 9 a.m.–5 p.m. Tuesday–Saturday (closed Sunday and Monday), and, again, we recommend starting as early in the day as possible.

Weather in this area can be wet, so be prepared for at least a thick (but refreshing) mist, and at most…a torrential downpour. Bring more water than you think you'll need (yes, even if it's raining), a rain jacket, a dry sweater/light fleece and a first aid kit. The long downhill slopes can be slick and scary, and chances are you'll crash early on and learn your lesson.

You might be worried about your e-bike running out of battery. The bike shop we rented our e-bikes from assured us that the batteries would last the whole ride—and they did—but by the end they were super low. You should know that an e-bike doesn't do all the pedaling for you. It just uses electricity to make pedaling a bit easier. To avoid draining the whole thing, we suggest setting your bike on the lowest level you can stand to make sure you can keep that boost for when you need it most. It's a bit of a balancing act getting the setting just right: If you overuse the electricity, you'll be near the end doing all the pedaling yourself, but if you conserve all the electricity, then you'll be the one who runs out of juice. Find a low-power setting that's comfortable for you.

Don't worry too much about where you need to go. Mana Road is pretty easy to follow, leaving all your energy for pedaling. See our write-up on Mana Road on page 140 for more details about this part of the island and the gates you'll pass through. You know you're at the last (and easiest) section when the road changes from rough rocks to more of a dirt-and-gravel path with houses scattered about. You'll follow Mana Road until it turns into Kahilu Road. Then hang a right on Hale Alii where it curves into Kamanawa Street, and take your final right on Kamanalu Street, following it all the way back to Bike Works Mauka. If that sounds

like a lot of street names to remember, you may want to keep your phone handy. Although there is hardly any cell service during the majority of your ride, service returns miles before the end of the road.

Finally, you need to have a plan about vehicles. If you have two cars, park one near Bike Works Mauka in Waimea. That's the car where you'll finish your journey. Then take the other car up to the **Pu'u Huluhulu Trail** parking lot, leave it there, and start pedaling up Mauna Kea Access Road, taking a right onto Mana Road when it splits. If you've managed to bribe someone into hauling you and your e-bikes, they may be able to drop you off right at the Mana Road gate, saving you a bit of pedaling. By the end of this trip, you'll be thankful for it.

COMMAND YOUR OWN BOAT

There are lots of charter boats plying the waters off Kona. But what if you want to do things your *own* way? At press time, only one company rented power boats. **Kona Boat Rentals (808-326-9155)** at

This black sand beach was created by a lava flow in 1950. It's not accessible by land and has no official name. The only way you'll ever get to it is to command your own boat.

Though the sand often disappears at Honokane Nui Beach, the hike still offers a great place to get away from it all.

Honokohau Harbor rents 20- to 23-foot, single-hull boats. They're made using an amazingly tough material/process called Roplene. With their 115- to 150-horsepower outboards, they'll cut through the water at 25-plus mph. Best of all, you *don't* need prior experience. (Though they will screen you to make sure you're not a moron.) Take it as far north as Kawaihae, as far south as Miloli'i. (Check out the otherwise-inaccessible black sand beach at N19°20.512' by W155°53.168'.) They'll outfit you with fishing or snorkel gear (SCUBA is extra). Their GPS is preprogrammed with numerous moorings, and they'll show you how to tie up to them. They'll give you some instructions, bring the boat to the harbor, and off you go.

The catch? *Price.* A 4-hour rental is $385–$450; it's $495–$595 for 6 hours, plus gas. That's a big chunk of money. If you have four to six people, it's not quite as painful when you split it. Seeing the area this way is a real hoot. But nobody ever said hoots were cheap. Nevertheless, it's a great way to scuba, snorkel or fish *where* and *how* you want.

HONOKANE NUI HIKE

At the north end of the island where Hwy 270 ends, you'll find Pololu Valley. (See page 53.) Though the trek into Pololu takes only 15–20 minutes, the more adventurous might want to venture beyond this beautiful valley to the more secluded **Honokane Nui Valley** and its accompanying stream. From the car lookout, it takes most people 90–120 minutes each way to hike into Honokane Nui. On the far side of Pololu, the trail goes up the 600-foot-high ridge, then drops down into Honokane. The view of Honokane Nui from the ridge top is breathtaking. Be prepared for a wet, sloppy trail going up the ridge from Pololu if it's been raining recently. (It's drier going down into Honokane.) Horseback riders occasionally take this trail and leave a few…gifts along the way. (Technically speaking, the *riders* probably aren't leaving those gifts; their *horses* are.) Usually winter is wetter.

Descending into Honokane Nui, there is a section of trail that was wiped out during the earthquake of 2006. People have forged a new way down (the easy-to-miss turnoff is just before the landslide section) and put ropes in place to help. (Trust them at your own risk.) This new path is steep and features loose dirt and rocks. This is the most difficult part of the trail and one that may turn you back. Once in Honokane Nui the trail gets vague as it goes toward the rocky beach. Don't disturb any of the rock walls here. They are ruins in the valley from days gone by when it was populated. There is a large deposit of black sand offshore, but it doesn't do *you* a lot of good. Stay out of the ocean here; it'll hurt you. On the far side of the valley is a nice stream and pool except during dry times—a perfect place to have lunch.

Although the trail continues into the next valley (Honokane Iki), it's got a number of residents (despite its remoteness), and you are less welcome there.

All in all, this is a nice hike when conditions are good. If you are tired, you might be tempted to skirt the water's edge back to Pololu, thereby avoiding the trip up and down the ridge. If it's calm and low tide, you *might* get away with it, or you might get slammed by a rogue wave and washed out to sea, so we don't recommend it unless you're feeling lucky.

Some of the valley trail intersections can get confusing, so be observant. Bring bug juice just in case. Hiking boots are recommended. Don't cross Pololu Stream when it's raging. Leave for this hike early. Theoretically, you could walk all the way to Waipi'o Valley from here, but the trail disappears in spots, and only those with mountain goat in their lineage will want to try it.

SPEARFISHING

Usually when you go fishing, you do it blind. You dip a lure or bait in the water and hope a hungry fish swims past. You don't get to choose what you catch; it chooses you. Spearfishing is like going to a restaurant with an aquarium full of critters to choose from for your dinner entrée. Only the tank is much larger, and you swim around in it trying to nab your dinner. Spearfishing is widely done in Hawai'i, but it's usually reserved for experienced spearos with their own gear. **Topshot Spearfishing** (808-205-8585) offers a 5-hour intro course for $199.

The price includes use of their nice rental gear. The small classes (four people max) are done well, and the owner (who will be your guide) has more than two

Pololu Valley & Honokane Nui Hike

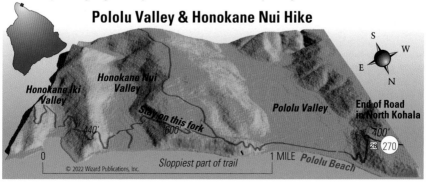

decades' experience spearfishing. He does a good job making sure you're comfortable in the water before the hunt begins. You won't be kept on a tight leash, but you'll be more successful if you stay close. (He'll point out fish for you, and show you where to dive.) We liked his patient, laid-back teaching style and his ethical approach to spearfishing. The first part of the course is done on land, where you'll become familiar with the speargun and learn the techniques, fish identification, laws and emergency procedures. During the second part of the day you enter the water from the shore and hunt for dinner. Unlike local charter boats, you get to *keep* the fish you spear. Overall, this is an excellent value and an adventure that you'll never forget.

HIKE TO FLOWING LAVA

Since the very first edition of this book, we've always had a section on how to hike to flowing lava and we know our existing readers will be looking for this. But Kilauea ended its 35-year flow in 2018 with great fanfare and there is no telling when Madame Pele

will reappear. While it's true that a new eruption began in 2021, it was short lived, mostly isolated to the lower part of Halemaʻumaʻu crater, and you couldn't even *see the lava* from the boardwalk, much less *hike* to it. We're always watching to see if the lava really begins to flow again, but we have no idea on when—or if—it will. So we'll show a few cuts from Madame Pele's *Best of* album and hope that she will pop back into our lives one day (away from structures) and allow us mere mortals to gaze upon her greatness again.

Yeah, this table will do...

By their very nature, restaurant reviews are the most subjective part of any guidebook. Nothing strains the credibility of a guidebook more. No matter what we say, if you eat at enough restaurants here, you will eventually have a dining experience directly in conflict with what this book leads you to believe. All it takes is one person to wreck what is usually a good meal. Many of us have had the experience when a friend referred us to a restaurant using reverent terms, indicating that they were about to experience dining ecstasy. And, of course, when you go there, the food is awful and the waiter is a jerk. There are many variables involved in getting a good or bad meal. Is the chef new? Was the place sold last month? Was the waitress just released from prison for mauling a customer? We truly hope that our reviews match your experience. If they don't, please drop us a line. We read every restaurant comment readers send, and they help us decide which restaurant to re-evaluate on a given day.

Unlike some travel writers who announce themselves to restaurants (to cop a free meal, if the truth be told), we always review *anonymously* and only expose ourselves after a meal (not literally, of course) by phone if we need additional information. By their reviews, many guidebooks lead you to believe that every meal you eat in Hawai'i will be a feast, the best food in the free world. Frankly, that's not our style. Like anywhere else, there's ample opportunity to have lousy food served with a rotten ambiance by uncaring waiters. In the interest of space, we've left out *some* of the dives. We did, however, leave in a few of these turkeys just to demonstrate that we know we live the real world. Restaurants that stand out from the others in some way are highlighted with an **ono** symbol.

ono

For each restaurant, we list the price *per person* you can expect to pay. It ranges from the least expensive entrées alone, to the most expensive plus a beverage and usually appetizers. You can spend more if you try, but this is a good guideline. *The price excludes alcoholic beverages since this component of a meal can be so variable.* Obviously, everyone's ordering pattern is different, but we thought that it would be easier to compare various restaurants using dollar amounts than if we used different numbers of dollar signs or drawings of forks or whatever to differentiate prices between various restaurants. All take credit cards unless otherwise noted. When we mention that prices are reasonable, please take it in context. We mean reasonable *for Hawai'i.* (We *know* you pay less back home.) Food in Hawai'i is expensive, even if it's grown here. (You probably pay less for our fruit on the mainland than *we* do here.)

When we give directions to a restaurant, *mauka side* of highway means "toward the mountain" (or away from the ocean). The shopping centers we mention are on the maps to that area.

The difference between local and Hawaiian food can be difficult to classify. Basically, local food combines Hawaiian, American, Japanese, Chinese, Filipino and several other types and is (not surprisingly) eaten mainly by locals.

We often leave out restaurant hours of operation because they change so frequently that the information would be immediately out of date. (We do list them in our *Hawaii Revealed* app.) Most restaurants close around 9 p.m.

Lu'au, those giant outdoor Hawaiian parties, are described on page 290.

When a restaurant requires **resort wear**, that means collared shirts for men (though nice shorts are *usually* okay) and dressy sportswear or dresses for women.

Below are descriptions of various island foods. Not all are Hawaiian, but this might be helpful if you encounter dishes unfamiliar to you.

ISLAND FISH & SEAFOOD

'**Ahi**–Tuna; raw in sashimi or poke, also seared, blackened, baked or grilled; good in fish sandwiches. Try painting 'ahi steaks with mayonnaise, which *completely* burns off when BBQ'd but seals in the moisture. You end up tasting only the moist ocean steak. Most plentiful April through September.

Kampachi–In the wild these tasty but notoriously wormy fish are called kahala. Kampachi is farm-raised a mile offshore of the Kona airport and does not suffer from this problem.

Keahole Lobster–Maine lobster flown in and revived using cold water pumped from the deep ocean. Local Hawaiian spiny lobster (called "bugs" by lobster hunters) are quite good.

Mahimahi–Deep ocean fish also known as a dolphinfish; served at a lu'au; very common in restaurants. Sometimes tastes fishy (especially if frozen), which can be offset in the preparation.

Marlin–Tasty when smoked, otherwise can be tough; the Pacific Blue Marlin is available almost year round.

Monchong–Excellent tasting deepwater fish, available year round. Usually served marinated and grilled.

Onaga–Also known as a ruby snapper; excellent eating in many preparations.

Ono–(Wahoo); *awesome* eating fish and can be prepared many ways; most plentiful May through October. Ono is also the Hawaiian word for delicious.

Opah–(Moonfish); excellent eating in many different preparations; generally available April through August.

'Opakapaka–(Crimson snapper); great tasting fish generally cooked several ways. Common October through February.

'Opihi–Limpets found on ocean rocks. Eaten raw mixed with salt. Texture is similar to clams or mussels.

Poke–Fresh raw fish or octopus (tako) mixed with seaweed (limu), sesame seed and other seasonings and oil.

Shutome–Swordfish; dense meat that can be cooked several ways. Most plentiful March through July.

Walu–Also goes by other names such as butterfish and escolar. Be careful not to eat more than 6 ounces. The Hawaiian nickname for this oily fish is maku'u, which means—*ahem*, this is awkward—"uncontrollable bowel discharge." Eat too much, and you may find out why.

LU'AU FOODS

Chicken lu'au–Chicken cooked in coconut milk and taro leaves.

Haupia–Coconut custard.

Kalua pig–Pig cooked in an underground oven called an imu (hot rocks go *inside* the beast), shredded and mixed with Hawaiian sea salt. Outstanding!

Laulau–Pork, beef or fish wrapped in taro and ti leaves and steamed. (You don't eat the ti leaf wrapping.)

Lomi salmon–Chilled salad consisting of raw salted salmon, tomatoes and two kinds of onions.

Poi–Steamed taro root pounded into a paste. It's a starch that will take on the taste of other foods mixed with it. Best eaten with kalua pig or fish. Visitors are encouraged to try it so they can badmouth it with authority.

OTHER ISLAND FOODS

Apple bananas–A smaller, denser, smoother texture than regular (Cavendish) bananas. Most people mistakenly eat them unripe. You need to wait until the skin turns predominantly brown.

Barbecue sticks–Teriyaki-marinated pork, chicken or beef pieces barbecued and served on bamboo sticks.

Bento–Japanese box lunch.

Breadfruit–Melon-sized starchy fruit; served baked, deep fried, steamed, or boiled. Definitely an acquired taste.

Crackseed–Chinese-style, spicy preserved fruits and seeds. Li Hing Mui is one of the most popular flavors.

Dim Sum–Think tapas, Chinese-style. Small portion items served off a cart. It's intended to give you a huge variety of food during one meal.

Guava–Tart fruit whose inside is full of seeds, so it is rarely eaten raw. Usually prepared with lots of sugar, so it's used primarily for juice, jelly or jam.

Hawaiian supersweet corn–The finest corn you ever had, even raw. We'll lie, cheat, steal or maim to get it fresh.

Huli huli chicken–Hawaiian BBQ style.

Ka'u oranges–Grown on the Big Island. Usually, the uglier the orange, the better it tastes.

Kim chee–A Korean relish consisting of pickled cabbage, onions, radishes, garlic and chilies.

Kulolo–Steamed taro pudding.

Liliko'i–Passion fruit.

Loco moco–Rice, meat patty, egg and gravy. *Never* served as health food.

Lychee–A reddish, woody peel that is discarded for the sweet, white fruit inside. Be careful of the pit. Small seed (or chicken-tongue) lychees are so good, they should be illegal.

Macadamia nut–A large, round nut grown primarily on the Big Island.

Malasada–Portuguese donut that is dipped in sugar.

Manapua–Steamed or baked bun filled with meat.

Mango–Bright orange fruit with yellow pink skin. Distinct, tasty flavor.

Manju–Cookie filled with a sweet center.

Maui onions–Grown in Kula; sweet. Some people eat them like apples.

Musubi–Cold steamed rice, often with sliced Spam rolled in black seaweed.

Papaya–Melon-like, pear-shaped fruit with yellow skin best eaten chilled. Good at breakfast.

Pipi Kaula–Hawaiian-style beef jerky. Excellent when dipped in poi. (Even if you don't like poi, this combo works.)

Plate lunch–An island favorite as an inexpensive, filling lunch. Consists of "two-scoop rice," a scoop of macaroni salad and some type of meat, either beef, chicken or fish. Also called a Box Lunch. Great for take-out.

Portuguese sausage–Pork sausage, highly seasoned with red pepper.

Pupu–Appetizer, finger foods or snack.

Saimin–Thin Chinese noodles cooked in a Japanese-style chicken, pork or fish broth. Word is peculiar to Hawai'i. Local Japanese say the dish comes from China. Local Chinese say it comes from Japan.

Shave ice–A block of ice is "shaved" into a ball with flavored syrup poured over the top. Best served with ice cream on the bottom. Very delicious.

Smoothie–Usually papaya, mango, frozen passion fruit and frozen banana, but almost any fruit can be used to make this milkshake-like drink. Add milk for creaminess.

Taro chips–Sliced and deep-fried taro; resembles potato chips.

KAILUA-KONA AMERICAN

808 Grindz Café

75-5660 Kopiko St, Kailua-Kona • (808) 936-5909

ono Apparently the owners of this small breakfast diner haven't heard that food is supposed to cost more here in Hawai'i. (And don't *you* tell 'em.) For $8.08 (a nice homage to the state's area code) you get two eggs, toast, hash browns, bacon, Spam, and Vienna sausage. Not filling enough? The $20 *Breakfast for Champions* includes an 8-ounce steak with *four* choices of meat, three eggs, choice of starch and a waffle. An *outstanding* value and delicious as well. They also have yogurt, pancakes and plenty of menu items done in the loco moco-style. Hidden in the Kopiko Plaza. **$8–$21** for breakfast. Closed Mondays.

Beach Tree

72-100 Kaupulehu Dr, Kaupulehu
(808) 325-8000

ono Fantastic beachside setting with expansive ocean views at the Four Seasons Hualalai, 14 miles north of Kona. Mixed menu of gourmet pizza, sandwiches, burgers, a few grilled items, and salads at lunch. Dinner is steak, seafood and pasta. Lots of locally sourced ingredients. Impeccable service. **$20–$40** for lunch, **$20–$70** for dinner. They get an *ono* because of its great food and setting. But we're talking *painfully* expensive. Reservations for dinner. If you're after seafood and the above prices seem trivial, check out the Four Season's other restaurant, **'Ulu Ocean Grill & Sushi Lounge**.

Big Kahuna Beach Grill
75-5663 Palani Rd, Kailua-Kona • (808) 731-5055
A burger and seafood joint serving tasty smash burgers (a way of cooking so the patties are thin, juicy and flavorful), and some good combos like teriyaki and pineapple burgers, or Crankin', which comes with bacon and egg. They have pretty good seafood as well, but honestly, the burgers are more memorable. If you can get in at the right time, you'll have a lovely view of a four-way intersection from the second floor, but if you can ignore the cars, there are some not-bad views of the ocean beyond it. (Good thing the interior is nice.) Overall, the food here is decent, and the setting is acceptable. Expect to spend **$12–$16** for breakfast and **$16–$20** for lunch and dinner. Skip the cocktails here—they're pricey for what you get. Located on Alii Drive across from Kailua Pier.

Costco
73-5600 Maiau St, Honokohau • (808) 331-4800
ono You'd be surprised at how many people eat at the food stand at Costco. Their pizza is surprisingly good (they use pretty good ingredients, and the crust isn't bad), and it's *very* cheap. **$10** for a gigantic pizza. They also serve hot dogs, salads and a few other items. In the back of the store they have tasty whole rotisserie chickens for **$5**. You need to be a Costco member to get in. We gave them an *ono* because of the value—can't beat it. North Kona, see map on page 168.

Don The Beachcomber
75-5852 Alii Dr, Kailua-Kona • (808) 329-3111
If you remember the original Don the Beachcomber restaurant, you probably also remember the end of Prohibition.

This is the guy who claimed to have invented the mai tai in 1933. The theme has been revived here at the Royal Kona Resort, where commanding views of Kailua Bay and torches at night give it a nice ambiance. The food, however, is unremarkable at best and definitely overpriced. **$10–$18** for breakfast and **$17–$36** for lunch and dinner that features seafood. Personally, we prefer the killer bar location for a happy hour pupu and sunset cocktail instead of the restaurant. And yes, the original mai tais are good here.

Harbor House
74-425 Kealakehe Pkwy, Kailua-Kona
(808) 326-4166
ono Ask anyone who frequents Harbor House why they go, and they'll give you a one-word answer—*schooners!* Located at Honokohau Harbor 2 miles north of Kona overlooking the water and boats, they serve the coldest beer on the island in ultra-thick, 18-ounce frosted schooners for around $5–$6. (Oh, almost forgot, they serve food, too.) This is a popular place to stop after a fishing or scuba excursion. The food consists of average fish and chips, fried calamari, burgers and other assorted bar food. (Good fish sandwich, though.) We didn't give 'em an *ono because of the food;* it's just a great place to tip a cold one and watch the tranquil harbor waters while you go over your adventures of the day. If you sit near the bar, you may hear lots of watering hole talk. **$9–$16.** Head toward the harbor off Hwy 19 between mile markers 97 and 98 and turn right at the buildings. Closes around 7 p.m.; the schooners aren't as cold near closing time.

Huggo's
75-5828 Kahakai Rd, Kailua-Kona
(808) 329-1493
This one is frustrating. Their location *right*

next to Kailua Bay is hands down the best in town (they were grandfathered into regulations restricting oceanfront construction) and that alone should be enough to get them an *ono*. Gorgeous open-air views. But execution in the kitchen is spotty. Some dishes are good, but they seem to have trouble hitting the sweet spot—many tend to be either be bland or over-seasoned. Since it's so pricey and the view so important to the experience, consider them for an early dinner (**$15–$50**), because you're paying premium prices and getting a premium location but with unreliable food. Make a reservation if you want to get a coveted railing table. The adjacent **hBAR** lounge is a good place to enjoy a drink at sunset—open seating. Off Alii Drive, downtown Kona near the Royal Kona Resort. Their next door venue to the right is **Huggo's on the Rocks**, which has a large bar, sand-covered floor and cheaper food. Burgers, fish and chips, fish tacos and a few other items. Live music nightly. A much better value than Huggo's, but the table arrangements aren't as intimate with the ocean. **$17–$30**. Even though we can't give them an *ono* due to unreliability, it's almost worth the gamble to give them a try for the views.

Humpy's Big Island Ale House

75-5815 Alii Dr, Kailua-Kona • (808) 324-2337

A vast and varied menu of pub food on steroids. From pizzas to baked subs to local dishes to sandwiches and wraps, seafood and pork, burgers and more. You'd be hard pressed to walk away without finding something that grabs your attention. But we found the flavors to be so-so and the food greasy. (Even the seafood ain't great, and the ocean is *right there*.) We've also left the place still hungry—*not* what you expect from pub food. People watchers will like the downstairs level; ocean viewers will want the top. Both are accompanied

by traffic views and sounds. The menu reflects the Alaskan heritage of the founders with the use of halibut in the fish and chips. Avoid the garlic shrimp, especially if you've sampled the famous shrimp from trucks on O'ahu's north shore—this ain't in the same hemisphere. Big beer selection with 30 plus on tap, half locally crafted. **$9–$20** for breakfast, **$13–$20** for lunch and dinner plus a couple pricier items. In the Coconut Grove Market Place.

Island Lava Java

75-5801 Alii Dr, Kailua-Kona • (808) 327-2161

ono An awesome—and highly popular—place for breakfast. The coffee is pretty good (though sometimes not very hot), and the food is tasty and not too ridiculously priced for the location. (They're right across the street from the ocean with excellent views, and they always have a live musician in the morning softly playing classic Hawaiian melodies, so you ain't gonna get a bargain.) Above average baked goods and a large breakfast menu with generous portions. Their cinnamon rolls are obscene and utterly massive (big enough to use as a flotation device if you fall in the water), and they taste great. An easy recommendation, although the rolls don't usually come out of the oven until around 7:30 a.m. and service is sometimes attitudy. Good (though very pricey) fresh-squeezed to order juices, (our favorite being the pineapple). Get an outdoor table. Lunch is fairly well-prepared sandwiches, soups, salads and pizzas. Dinner adds meat and seafood. Great stop for an old school (not-too-sweet) mai tai. Alii Drive in Kona in Coconut Grove Market Place. **$10–$20** for breakfast, **$15–$27** for lunch, **$18–$40** for dinner.

Island Ono Loa Grill

75-5799 Alii Dr, Kailua-Kona • (808) 339-3037

Burgers, hot dogs and sandwiches. They

pride themselves on using local ingredients to give these classic all-American foods a Hawaiian twist. The burgers are pretty darn good (albeit greasy), but flavors resulting from some of the farther-out combos may be a bit too adventurous for some. Then again, maybe the idea of peanut butter on your hamburger appeals to you. Mostly indoor seating gives it a fast-food feel, but prices are higher than a hot dog justifies—even if it is served on a poppy seed bun. Do yourself a favor, and opt for the onion rings. Hidden in the Alii Sunset Plaza. **$11–$20.** Closed Wednesdays.

Jackie Rey's Ohana Grill
75-5995 Kuakini Hwy, Kailua-Kona
(808) 327-0209

ono The majority of customers are local, in part because it's not on touristy Alii Drive, but mostly because Jackie Rey's excels in every detail, from well-made drinks to decadent desserts. (Avoid the dessert drinks, though.) The appetizer portions are small but tasty and the dinner entrées—fish, steak, pasta and ribs—are attractively presented. The chef here definitely knows how to combine flavors, such as the kalua pork spring rolls. **$26–$48** for dinner. They have cheaper, but limited, happy hour entrées between 4–5 p.m. On Kuakini Highway across from Walua Road. They also have a location in Hilo on Keawe Street and Waianuenue Avenue.

Kona Canoe Club
75-5744 Alii Dr, Kailua-Kona • (808) 331-1155
Their sign reads, *Fish, Burgers and Grog.* And although we haven't found grog on the menu, they do make a powerful mai tai, if you're in the mood. It may not be world famous like they claim, but it may make you feel famous after just one. Great oceanside location, especially if you get a railing seat. Their mud pie, though, is truly great, as you calve it like your own personal iceberg. They're fussy about substitutions, and fries are extra charge with entrées. **$12–$50** for lunch and dinner. More if you get their *I-kid-you-not* **$300** *this-is-not-a misprint* wine cheeseburger that comes with a vintage bottle of Opus One or Joseph Phelps. With their other burgers fries are extra. We didn't have the nerve to order the wine cheeseburger, but fries *darned* well better be included. In the Kona Inn Shopping Village.

Kona Inn Restaurant
75-5744 Alii Dr, Kailua-Kona • (808) 329-4455
Mostly seafood (nice variety of fish) with steaks, soups, salads and sandwiches. At dinner, avoid the uncomfortable antique chairs in favor of the high-back wicker chairs. **$20–$60** for lunch and dinner. They've received an *ono* from us in the past, but our last couple visits have found the service and food noticeably lacking. Combine that with small portions at higher prices for a disappointing experience. The ambiance and setting are the saving grace here, plus their tasty mai tais. Just a strip of grass separates you from the ocean. Check out the ceiling fans—all connected by an old belt system. Some parents like to bring their keiki here so the munchkins can play on the grass while the grownups can dine and keep an eye on them. On the ocean side of Alii Drive in downtown Kona at the Kona Inn Shopping Village.

Laverne's
75-5819 Alii Dr, Kailua-Kona • (808) 331-2633
Sports bar liberally decorated with license plates, baseball memorabilia (Cubs fans will feel at home), surfboards, and a giant Elvis tiki. The view of the ocean is partially obstructed by power lines but not bad, and there is usually a nice

breeze coming off the ocean. So far we're feeling happy. But disinterested, inattentive servers is where the charm wears thin. Pizza, burgers, sandwiches and some local favorites. They really need to step it up in the kitchen—then we might enjoy this place. **$9–$20** for lunch and dinner. Breakfast on the weekends only.

Magics Beach Grill
77-6452 Alii Dr, Kailua-Kona • (808) 662-4427
Talk about beach*front*. This spot is directly on La'aloa Bay Beach Park, so close to the ocean your food might get a lil' extra salt from the nearby waves. We want to give this place an *ono* (the location definitely deserves one), but unfortunately, we find their menu hit and miss. Some items are delicious and keep us coming back (their fried 'ulu and Brussels are dream-worthy), but others strike us as strange or underwhelming. Go for dinner over lunch. The daytime sandwiches and salads aren't worth the dough, and the flavors can fall flat. Drinks fall on the sweet side but go well with the view and setting. (Have we mentioned how incredible it is?) Good deals during happy hour when there's a "Beach Shack" food truck outside the restaurant with a simpler menu. **$8–$17** for brunch only on Sundays—they close at 3 p.m. **$14–$40** for lunch. **$20–$40** for dinner.

Ohana Q
75-5742 Kuakini Hwy, Kailua-Kona
(808) 365-6171
ono A friendly BBQ spot with the usual wood-smoked offerings, and they do it well. You can get your meats on a sandwich, nachos or on their own plate, and when you take a bite, you'll feel the food melting in your mouth. Their open atmosphere has indoor and outdoor picnic table seating.

We recommend ordering the pork or brisket, but you really can't go wrong here. (Throw a dart and see where it goes—you'll be happy as long as it lands on the menu.) **$15–$22** for lunch and dinner. You'll find them right off the Kuakini Highway on the makai side. Closed Sunday.

Poi Dog Deli
75-1022 Henry St, Kailua-Kona • (808) 329-2917
Poi Dog Deli is a cool spot that can be tough to find (but we're convinced it's worth looking for). They have a variety of sandwiches, wraps and salads with a local twist. Try their Notorious P.I.G., which consists of smoked ham, pineapple and jalapeños, all grilled and served on sourdough bread, or (quietly) ask for a Weak Sauce P.I.G., which is just about the same thing without the peppers. They rotate their menu and frequently offer salad specials, and the new options are usually delightful and fresh. **$15–$20** for lunch and dinner (they close at 6 p.m.). On Henry Street, across from Denny's.

Quinn's Almost-by-the-Sea
75-5655 Palani Rd, Kailua-Kona • (808) 329-3822
ono Truth in advertising. You're close to the ocean but can't really see it. Lunch offers seafood, burgers and sandwiches. The fish sandwich is excellent, as are most seafood items. (Switch the mahimahi sandwich for ono or 'ahi—it's *mo bettah*.) For dinner, it's the same menu plus more steak and seafood. Service is family style and quicker at lunch time. Inside has a dive bar kind of feel. Consider the quasi-outdoor section for a nice lunch-time nautical, green ambiance. Most of the food is tastily prepared, but they do have off days. And when they are off, they are *really* off. We recommend lunch over the pricey dinner. **$9–$18** for lunch, **$9–$33** for dinner.

On Palani Road across from the King Kamehameha Kona Beach Hotel. Limited parking. Closed Wednesdays.

Sam Choy's Kai Lanai

78-6831 Alii Dr, Kailua-Kona • (808) 333-3434
Sam Choy is a giant presence in the food industry in Hawai'i with TV shows, books and restaurants. This location has an impressive view of Kona, looking down from the Keauhou Shopping Center over the Kona shoreline (try to ignore the roof of Longs Drugs). Sunsets from here are unbeatable. And the atmosphere is effective, wide open and feels roomy. As for the food: Sam is well known for his creativeness and flavor combinations, bringing a local and Asian twist...however, we suggest you skip eating here for now. The food is actually shockingly bleh. We wish, given their limited menu, they had chosen dishes that tasted...good. Have a piña colada and watch the sunset, then relocate to eat. **$14–$17** for lunch and dinner.

The Fish Hopper Seafood & Steaks

75-5683 Alii Dr, Kailua-Kona • (808) 326-2002
The food is hit or miss here (lately more hit than miss). Fish is what they do best (not surprisingly), but they also have tacos and sandwiches at lunch, and plenty of pasta and steak at dinner. Try the mac nut-crusted mahimahi, and definitely ask for the dessert tray—you can't go wrong with anything sweet here. Prices are pretty high, especially at dinner ($38 for ultimate seafood pasta is hard to swallow), but the view from across the seawall is one of the better first-floor views on Alii Drive. Some of their drinks, such as the Bucket of Fire, are downright amazing and the service is fast and friendly. **$8–$18** for breakfast, **$16–$22** for lunch, **$22–$50** (more if you order a platter for two) for dinner. Reservations

recommended. They also have some gluten-free options.

Tropics Tap House

78-6831 Alii Dr, Kailua-Kona • (808) 498-4507
We're *always* in the mood for greasy fried food and a sports game (any excuse for beer and onion rings), which is why we were particularly excited to sit down at one of the few *real* sports bars in the area. Stick with beer 'n' sports here. The food is pricey for the quality, and if you absolutely must eat, then you'll probably want to order something sports bar-esque: burgers, fries or jalapeño poppers. **$10–$30** for lunch and dinner. In Keauhou Shopping Center.

Ultimate Burger

74-5450 Makala Blvd, Kailua-Kona
(808) 329-2326

ono They raise lots of cattle on this island, but most burgers are made from frozen beef flown in from the mainland. Not this place. The hamburger is fresh and locally raised (which seems to have a...*beefier* flavor than standard beef). They also mix herbs into the meat, and results are wonderful. Patties are a third of a pound, and you can get one to four of them on a bun. (For the record, we can't visualize how someone could chow down the one-and-a-third-pound TKO burger.) The quality is excellent as are the tasty (but pricey) ultimate fries. Lines and waits can be long at peak hours. In the Kona Commons on Makala north of downtown Kona. **$7–$16** for lunch and dinner.

Willie's Hot Chicken

74-5599 Pawai Pl, Kailua-Kona • (808) 796-3088
This is a popular sports bar-themed restaurant in Kona with plenty of outdoor seating and live music on weekends. They offer hot chicken (a specialty dish from Nashville that consists of chicken slathered

in a spicy cayenne-based sauce), and they do a pretty good job of it considering you're a few time zones away from the source. Choose from seven spice levels, including the hottest "like lava" spice (which adds a $1 upcharge and is about as painful as you'd imagine). You can order the chicken as a hunk of meat, or get it in a sandwich or salad. Popular sides include mac 'n cheese, waffles and coleslaw. Overall, this is a pretty good spot to grab some chicken and other American staples. It's probably also worth mentioning that you can also order alcohol here, though they close disappointingly early to be considered a good nightlife option. **$10–$20** for lunch and dinner. Across the street from Kona Brew.

KAILUA-KONA CHINESE

Ocean Seafood

75-5626 Kuakini Hwy, Kailua-Kona
(808) 329-3055

Most of the offerings are the same beef, pork, chicken and vegetable dishes you'd expect to find elsewhere, with some seafood options like lobster and shrimp added to the mix. The $12 lunch special is a pretty good deal. Otherwise, it's **$12–$33** for lunch and dinner to order off the menu. In the King Kamehameha Mall in Kona. Closed Wednesday.

Royal Jade Garden (aka The Jade)

75-5595 Palani Rd, Kailua-Kona • (808) 326-7288
The best Chinese in Kona. No all-you-can-eat buffet, but the variety-plate portions are generous and you won't leave hungry. **$12–$22** for lunch and dinner, if you'd rather order off the menu, with most items priced on the lower end of the range. The usual dishes plus some less-common ones like honey glazed walnut shrimp. In the Lanihau Center. Closed Monday. See map on page 65.

KAILUA-KONA FRENCH

La Bourgogne French Restaurant

77-6400 Nalani St, Kailua-Kona • (808) 329-6711

ono Superb! This *tiny* restaurant on Hwy 11 between Keauhou and Kona serves delectable and well-conceived dishes, including lamb, duck, tender rabbit, tenderloin, lobster and even veal. Good and reasonably priced wine list. The atmosphere is intimate and the service attentive. Entrée prices are in a pretty narrow range. Dinner is **$46–$52**. The owners are exceedingly gracious with guests. Only ding: It's totally enclosed with no view, and the salads are a little simple for the price. Reservations recommended. Closed Sunday through Tuesday.

Peaberry & Galette Café

78-6831 Alii Dr, Kailua-Kona • (808) 322-6020

ono The food here is a bit on the pricey side for a coffeehouse, but the dessert crêpes are amazing (and we've tried 'em all). They're big enough to share, but we suggest getting one all to yourself. If you're looking for something more substantial to eat, the menu also includes sandwiches and several savory crêpes such as BLT, smoked salmon or grilled summer vegetables. But we find those kind of awkward—like trying to eat a poorly folded origami project. Stick to the dessert crêpes—you're on vacation, right? A very relaxing place. **$5–$15**. In the Keauhou Shopping Center (see map on page 67) to the left of the movie theater.

KAILUA-KONA INDIAN

Kamana Kitchen

75-5770 Alii Dr, Kailua-Kona • (808) 326-7888
This is pretty much the only Indian restaurant in the Kona area; fortunately,

it's a good one. Great range of regional cuisine, with plenty of vegetarian/vegan options. We especially enjoy the korma and vindaloo dishes (but watch out for that spice). **$14–$25** for lunch and dinner. In Waterfront Row, but only partial ocean view. See map on page 65. Closed between 3 p.m. and 5 p.m. daily. Their second location is in the Hilo Shopping Center (see map on page 112).

KAILUA-KONA ITALIAN

Bianelli's

78-6831 Alii Dr, Keauhou • (808) 322-0377
Their best item is the killer pesto and mac nut bread. For the pizza, opt for the 12-inch deep dish crust instead of the New York. Take out or snag an outdoor table. **$9–$17** for lunch and dinner. No desserts. In the Keauhou Shopping Center. Closed Sunday and Monday.

Kona Brewing Co. & Brewpub

74-5612 Pawai Pl, Kailua-Kona • (808) 334-2739
ONO A cool place to go for local beer and pretty good pizza. Thirteen or so different beers brewed on site, including varieties you can only get in Hawai'i and on tap. They range from the mild (Big Wave Golden Ale) to the not-so-mild (Pipeline Porter). Some beers are seasonal, so expect some new and interesting options. Most of the pizzas are delicious, but some inventive combinations for the more adventurous are a miss for us. If you'd like to try more than one variety of pie, tell 'em. They'll split the pizza however you like. (They offer helpful suggestions for which beer pairs well with the specialty pizzas.) Plenty of salad and sandwich options, too. Their Kilauea lava flow dessert is pretty criminal. The service could use a little improvement at times, and we wish they could do something about the flies

and gnats at the outside tables, but overall, this is a great place. **$11–$32** for lunch and dinner. At the end of Pawai Place off Kaiwi Street. See map on page 65. No reservations, and long waits are common because it's a popular place.

KAILUA-KONA JAPANESE

Hayashi's You Make the Roll

75-5725 Alii Dr, Kailua-Kona • (808) 326-1322
ONO Tasty and cheap, and as good as any place that charges twice as much. The sushi is made right before your eyes and tastes great. Just a few outdoor tables, but this is the place to get your sushi fix. **$5–$10** for lunch. Kona Marketplace Shopping Center off Alii Drive, way in the back. Closed Sundays.

Kenichi Pacific

78-6831 Alii Dr, Kailua-Kona • (808) 322-6400
ONO Very well-prepared sushi in a slightly ritzy atmosphere. In addition to the sushi, they also have other entrées under the fusion genre, such as steak, seafood and lamb. In fact, their mac nut-encrusted lamb is absolutely wonderful and unexpectedly un-Japanese. The attention to detail is obvious. The molten cake dessert is *ultra* rich chocolate. (Oh, yeah!) It ain't cheap here, and the service can be slow, but overall, it's a good choice. Happy Hour from 4:30–6 p.m. is good because all rolls ordered at the bar are 40–50% off. **$15–$45** for dinner. In the Keauhou Shopping Center at the south end of Alii Drive. Closed Monday.

Seiji's Sushi

75-5669 Alii Dr, Kailua-Kona • (808) 329-7278
ONO A small sushi, noodle and tempura joint tucked behind other shops along the north end of Alii Drive. Attentive service. Prices are very reasonable for a sushi place, although any time you

get involved with sushi, the bill can add up fast. Consider the chirashi bowl if you need something that sticks to your ribs. This is quality, no-frills sushi for a good price. **$14–$70** for dinner. BYOB. Reservations recommended. Closed Monday and Tuesday.

Sushi Shiono

75-5799 Alii Dr, Kailua-Kona • (808) 326-1696

ono Want to know where Japanese people go for sushi when they visit Kona? This is it. But even if you're not a sushi fiend, you'll find plenty of tasty options (such as the Japanese-style pork chop, Ton Katsu). If you are looking for the sushi experience, the Shiono Boat (three styles, starting at $70) has the chef choose their best options for the night and artfully serve it to you and your partner in a way that must be experienced to be appreciated. **$14–$45** for dinner (but the price can easily be more whenever sushi is involved). In the Alii Sunset Plaza. Closed Wednesday.

KAILUA-KONA LOCAL

Big Island Grill

75-5702 Kuakini Hwy, Kailua-Kona
(808) 326-1153

Popular with local residents and a bit loud with closely spaced tables and no-nonsense service, the food is hearty local-style with items such as chicken katsu or kalua pork and cabbage. A great choice for breakfast as well—the mac nut pancakes are very tasty as are the eggs Benedict. If you're feeling adventurous and hungry, try the Super Loco Moco. Portions are dependably generous, but it can take awhile to get your food and check. Desserts are big and deadly. (Excellent mud pie.) Breakfast is **$9–$18**, lunch is **$10–$22**. At the corner of Henry and Kuakini. Closed Sunday and Monday.

Da Poke Shack

76-6246 Alii Dr, Kailua-Kona • (808) 329-7653

Fresh-catch poke (pronounced *POE-kay*; raw, seasoned cubed fish), octopus, calamari and shrimp at this local deli counter-style eatery. Popular with island residents at lunch time, but the food can be a little bland and flavorless on off-days. Pick a side and two main dishes for the bowl; the plate is two sides and four main dishes. When picking, they recommend you mix a sweet and spicy option for balance. Price varies by item and weight, but expect to pay **$9–$17**. Located in the Kona Bali Kai condo complex. See map on page 67. Primarily takeout, but they have a couple of picnic tables by the parking lot. There can be a long wait during lunchtime.

Pine Tree Café

73-4038 Hulikoa Dr, Kailua-Kona
(808) 327-1234

Your options are limited out near the airport. This is probably your best bet. Reasonable prices and fairly good food. The menu is *huge* (except for the limited drink selection). Lots of burgers, most around $6, a good and exotic fried poke fish plate, saimin, and unusual items like the shrimp burger. Ambiance is classic strip mall, but the food is better than average and some of the daily specials (like the breakfast burrito) are just plain good. **$4–$15** for breakfast, **$5–$18** for lunch and dinner. Close to the airport near mile marker 95 on Hwy 19.

Umekes Fishmarket

74-5563 Kaiwi St, Kailua-Kona • (808) 238-0571

ono When it comes to the best poke, Umekes is the place locals rave about. The name is Hawaiian for *bowl* and usually consists of sushi-grade 'ahi tuna. (Although here you can also get beef, chicken, pork as well). The raw fish is seasoned and served on two scoops of rice with a side. Simple, satisfying and always fresh. Sides include pickled seaweed salad and lomi salmon. **$17–$25** for lunch and dinner.

KAILUA-KONA MEXICAN

El Maguey Mexican Restaurante
74-5563 Kaiwi St, Kailua-Kona • (808) 329-0636

oñô Located in an ugly part of town, dingy, slow, and at times it seems like the waitstaff is intentionally avoiding making eye contact. But *wow*, this is probably the best Mexican food on the island. The authentic salsa is runny and *very* hot, super good guacamole, large portion sizes, and items are so delicious that you will want to keep eating long past the point of being full. **$8–$17** with many items in the $12 range. At the corner of Kaiwi Street and Kuakini Highyway. See map on page 65. Family run and closed Sunday.

Killer Tacos
74-5483 Kaiwi St, Kailua-Kona • (808) 329-3335

oñô The kind of place you'd never find if someone didn't tell you about it. Tucked away in an industrial area, the name is spot on. (Well, we've never actually seen anyone drop dead here.) Killer tacos, killer burritos, killer portions and killer prices. Pretty deadly, huh? The most expensive thing is the $10 barnyard burrito. Put kalua pig or the spicy ground beef in your burrito, or bag one of the fish tacos with a taro tortilla for a little local fusion. The only thing that needs improving is the salsa—consider substituting it for hot sauce. Simple menu and the price is right. Near the highway, on Kaiwi, near Luhia Street. See map on page 65. **$5–$15** for lunch and dinner. Closed Sunday.

Los Habañeros
78-6831 Alii Dr, Kailua-Kona • (808) 324-4688
Here it's cheap Mexican food, nothing special, a (short) step above Taco Bell. With a name like Los Habañeros you'd expect the food to be bursting with flavor. Instead, it's incredibly bland unless you shower the food with salsa. Even then we've had saltine crackers with more flavor. In the Keauhou Shopping Center. **$7–$15** for lunch and early dinner. Closed Sunday.

Pancho & Lefty's
75-5725 Alii Dr, Kailua-Kona • (808) 326-2171
The menu is large and varied. The food here is filling (the nachos are hearty), and some items are more than acceptable. (Avoid the soggy chile rellenos.) You'd probably eat here again in a pinch…but you wouldn't recommend it to your friends. Mixed drinks here are tasty and fairly potent. **$9–$32** for lunch and dinner. Off Alii Drive and Kakina Road.

Patricio's Mexican Taqueria
73-4038 Hulikoa Dr, Kailua-Kona
(808) 334-1008
The main draw of this place is that it's right by the airport, so when you land, starving after a 12-hour flight and frantically type "FOOD" into your phone, it pops up immediately. Other than that, it's subpar Mexican food (or maybe we should say on-par, since this island doesn't offer much) with consistently grumpy service. **$7–$19** for lunch and dinner. On Hulikoa Drive south of the airport.

KAILUA-KONA THAI

Kona Taeng-On Thai Food
75-5744 Alii Dr, Kailua-Kona • (808) 329-1994
Sorry, but the food's not good enough to warrant these kind of prices. Good menu choices but uninspiring when prepared. Service is a little cranky, but if you ask for spicy, they will fully comply. You've got way better Thai choices in Kona. **$13–**

$32 for lunch and dinner. Upstairs on Alii Drive across from Kona Marketplace.

Krua Thai

75-5705 Kuakini Hwy, Kailua-Kona
(808) 327-5782

Close to the main visitor area of Kona but far from the ocean, meaning cheaper prices. The tradeoff is no view. Big menu with lots of seafood options. Ask them to hold the fish sauce in the green papaya salad. We haven't seen it crowded, so chances are you'll have some room to stretch after eating. Check out their lunch specials on weekdays for an extra good deal. We used to give them an *ono,* but food and service seems to have slipped. Some of the dishes are just plain mediocre. We love Thai food, so we have our fingers crossed that they'll get their groove back. **$9–$30** for lunch and dinner. Six levels of spice to choose from; it's $2 extra for extra Thai hot. Near the intersection of Henry. Closed Sunday and daily between 3 p.m. and 4:30 p.m.

Orchid Thai Cuisine

74-5563 Kaiwi St, Kailua-Kona • (808) 327-9437

ono Finding this one requires venturing to the industrial area, but the food is good and the atmosphere refined (although candles on the table would help—the restaurant can be dim at night). Lots of options to choose from. Super good chicken satay. Good curries. Service can be slow and is *not* warm and fuzzy, but overall this is a winner. BYOB if you want alcohol. **$12–$24** for lunch and dinner. Between Kuakini Hwy and Pawai Place. See map on page 65. Closed Sunday.

Original Thai

75-5629 Kuakini Hwy, Kailua-Kona
(808) 329-3459

We find it ironic that a place called Original Thai would plaster the definition of *original* all over their menu, claim that their food is

what original Thai tastes like, then serve burgers, wraps and coleslaw as well as Thai items. What's even more strange is that they do it so well. The larb wrap is bursting with goodness, and the burgers are made with curried meat. Even the fries and coleslaw have a hint of Thai. The curries are fantastic and come in big portions. A wonderful start is a cup of coconut milk soup. It's a shame that service can be snippy. In the Ilima Court Shopping Center. **$9–$34** for lunch and dinner. Closed Monday.

Royal Thai Café

78-6831 Alii Dr, Keauhou • (808) 322-8424

ono Much fancier than you'd expect given its strip mall location in the Keauhou Shopping Center on the far south end of Alii Drive. Every table is dressed with place settings and glass stemware, whether occupied or not. Every dish we've had here has been stellar and the prices are reasonable. Good lunch specials for $11. **$11–$27** for lunch, **$13–$27** for dinner. Closed Monday.

Thai Rin

75-5799 Alii Dr, Kailua-Kona • (808) 329-2929

Nice location on Alii Drive right across from the ocean. The curries are their weakest item—surprisingly bland and watery. They make a pretty good garlic eggplant, and the pad Thai is tasty, but overall, it's an underwhelming Thai experience. Impressively slow service; we suggest bringing a book to start...*and finish* while you wait for your check. In the Alii Sunset Plaza. **$11–$25** (more for the lobster combo) for lunch and dinner. Good lunch specials. Closed Tuesday.

KAILUA-KONA TREATS & COFFEE

Basik Café

75-5831 Kahakai Rd, Kailua-Kona • (808) 769-4068

They named it right. Pretty basic smoothies

and açai bowls, but there's nothing wrong with basic, right? **$7–$9** for a smoothie and **$11–$14** for a bowl of blended Brazilian superberries topped with other fruits and granola or nuts. The large bowl should be called "huge." Upstairs from Snorkel Bob's (near the Royal Kona Resort). See map on page 65. Cramped, but it has a few seats with a nice view of the water. Closed Sunday.

Green Flash Coffee
75-6000 Alii Dr, Kailua-Kona • (808) 329-4387

ONO What's the green flash? See page 61. This green flash is a convenient spot for anyone staying along Alii Drive south of the main tourist area to get coffee since you won't need to drill into town and find a place to park. They make serious drinks, like the Earthquake with Ghiradelli chocolate and four shots of espresso. Breakfast sandwiches, panini and baked goods available as well. The smoothies are also a good choice and use fresh fruit for an extra refreshing taste. **$5–$10**. In front of the Sea Village condos. See map on page 67. Closed weekends.

Hawaiian Ice Cones
75-5595 Palani Rd, Kailua-Kona • (808) 895-8390

ONO Kids will like the fun, colorful building and being able to choose from an almost infinite number of possible combinations of sugary flavors and candy toppings. Add ice cream on the bottom, and you have a *broke da mout* experience. **$3–$8**. Next to Longs Drugs in Lanihau Center off Palani Road in Kona.

HiCo
74-5599 Pawai Pl, Kailua-Kona • (808) 437-0033
A community coffee shop that hosts events like open mics, hip-hop nights and more. It's a favorite of Kona dwellers,

though the small space and limited seating means you'll probably be grabbing your drink to go during prime coffee hours. The menu includes exorbitantly priced specialty drinks and limited food options—some toasts can top $7. If the prices don't make you lose your appetite, you'll be rewarded with some very good flavors. This is a pretty good spot overall, and we can see why it has a dedicated community of regulars. **$10–$20** for breakfast, lunch and dinner. Open 6:30 a.m.–6 p.m. every day of the week (open later Wednesday through Saturday). Heading south on Hwy 19, take a right on Kaiwi Street, then a left on Pawai Place.

Kanaka Kava
75-5803 Alii Dr, Kailua-Kona • (808) 327-1660
Gee, we didn't know *where* to put this one. It's a kava bar, but you can also get traditional Hawaiian foods like 'opihi and poi. Kava (called awa in Hawai'i) is made from a root and tastes a little like woody water. It's a mild relaxant/pain killer. Polynesians have been using it for generations, and it has cultural importance here. When you get a bowl, you're supposed to gulp it down fast; don't sip. It may make your mouth tingle. Consider it once at least for the novelty. **$5** for a shell of kava, or order a bowl to pass around and share. Not much seating, but if you want to try traditional Hawaiian fare, this is where to go. **$5–$21** for lunch or dinner. On the back-side of Coconut Grove Market Place on Alii Drive.

Kona Coffee & Tea Company
74-5588 Palani Rd, Kailua-Kona • (808) 329-6577

ONO No Kona blends here, it's 100% Kona direct from the farm, as well as a small selection of baked goods. The white, open and airy architecture is inviting if you need a place to borrow WiFi during your trip, but if you are planning to set up shop and work for awhile, you might want to wear long sleeves—they keep the AC cranked real cold. They also have wine, beer and sake. **$3–$12**. Out front of the Kona Coast Shopping Center.

Kona Mountain Coffee
73-4038 Hulikoa Dr, Honokohau
(808) 329-5005

This place is filled with all kinds of home-made treats that look great…but taste mediocre. Stick with the coffee, which is pretty darn good and comes straight from the coffee farm; make your coffee "Mana Proof" if you want even *more* pep in your step. With a substantial selection of packaged treats, this is an option for picking up a few gifts (chocolate macadamia nuts, local honey, etc.) Close to the airport near mile marker 95 on Hwy 19. **$3–$6**. Closed Sunday.

Scandinavian Shave Ice
75-5699 Alii Dr, Kailua-Kona • (808) 326-2522

Located across from the south end of the Kailua Bay seawall, so lots of foot traffic. Bubble tea, ice cream, lots of toppings to choose from, quality is average. Prices range from **$5–$9** with jumbo shave ice at **$20** and it's *the size of a basketball*.

Tea-licious
75-159 Lunapule Rd, Kailua-Kona
(808) 209-8282

ONO A charming and intimate shop with more tea options than we knew existed. If tea isn't your cup of… that is, if it isn't your go-to beverage, they also have coffees plus a delicious breakfast and lunch menu as well as pastries you probably should stock up on. The owner is extremely friendly and welcoming. She seems to have collected a cult following of people who love both her teas *and* her warmth. It's a cozy shop with mismatched furniture, cups and decor. There's no WiFi, so it can feel like a pleasant time warp with people coming in, ordering a cup of tea and just chatting. If you really want to feel like royalty, call ahead and schedule a full tea party. **$3–$8** for breakfast, **$11–$27** for lunch. At the intersection of Lunapule and Walua. Closed Sundays. They close annually for a family vacation usually around end May to sometime in late June.

KAILUA-KONA VIETNAMESE

Ba-Le
74-5588 Palani Rd, Kailua-Kona • (808) 327-1212

ONO OK, so it's not really local. It's part of a chain of Vietnamese noodle shops with French bread sandwiches. But the food is good for the price. Those who aren't fond of Vietnamese flavors will probably like the sandwiches, beef stew or the roast beef croissant (when available). Lots of veggie items. **$7–$16** for lunch and dinner. In Kona Coast Shopping Center. Closed Sundays.

SOUTH OF KAILUA-KONA DINING

Big Jake's Island BBQ
83-5308 Mamalahoa Hwy, Honaunau
(808) 328-1227

ONO American—Yes, it's an easy miss. Yes, it's a dingy hole in the wall. Yes, you'll have to compete with the flies trying to land on your food. But the brisket here melts in your mouth, and the pulled chicken sandwich with their house-made BBQ sauce is so tasty we don't care about the limited seating next to the noisy highway. If you're a serious BBQ fan, this place is sure to please. Expect plastic baskets on picnic tables outside. **$13–$28** for lunch. On Hwy 11 next to the big meat smoker at mile marker 106. Hours and days can be inconsistent, so we suggest you call ahead.

Caffe Florian

81-6637 Mamalahoa Hwy, Kealakekua
(808) 238-0861

Treats—The focus is on panini (the Tuscan Chicken is delicious) as well as a large selection of baked desserts. 100% Kona coffee, free WiFi, distant ocean views from the back deck. The food is good and the atmosphere is comfortable. Breakfast and lunch, $7–$15. In Kealakekua near mile marker 112. Closed Saturday and Sunday.

Coffee Shack

83-5799 Mamalahoa Hwy, Honaunau
(808) 328-9555

ono **American**—A good place to stop (unless you want a *big* breakfast) on your way to the volcano—they open at 7:30 a.m. *Fantastic* view down the slopes of Mauna Loa overlooking Kealakekua and Honaunau—try to get a railing table and check out the gigantic avocado tree and the coffee trees below you. (It's nice to sit there drinking coffee grown from those very trees.) Tables are outdoors but covered. Nice selection of homemade baked goods and breads (when fresh, which is not a certainty), a small selection of breakfast items and a decent selection of sandwiches and pizzas (which are so-so) for lunch. Avoid the cinnamon rolls in favor of the chocolate cranberry mac nut bar. They're also known for their cheesecake, and we suggest you try a slice. $11-$18 for breakfast, a couple dollars more for lunch. Service is often slow. On ocean side of highway in Captain Cook between mile markers 109 and 108. Closed Wednesday.

Cultivate

79-7411 Mamalahoa Hwy, Kainaliu
(808) 461-3183

Vegan—We walked up to this vegan food window mentally prepared to have to stop for a second meal. Boy, were we wrong. These wraps (or salads) are *substantial*. Expect *big* flavors and *big* portions. Worth every penny, but we weren't overly crazy about the juices they offered. Foodwise, though, we especially like the Coconut BLT and Taste of Thai. Not much seating available (and it's all outdoors), but get the food to go and take it with you to watch the sunset. $9–$12 for anything off their small menu. Located in Kainaliu next to Donkey Balls. Open from 10 a.m.–4 p.m.

Gypsea Gelato

79-7491 Mamalahoa Hwy, Kealakekua
(808) 322-3233

ono **Treats**—Lots of very good, unique flavors made with local fruit, but try a sample spoon before committing to some of the perhaps-too-creative ones like Pele's Kiss, which is made with chocolate, cinnamon and hot pepper. They rotate over 90 different options (with a few standard favorites) so be adventurous and flexible. Small selection of baked goods at this location. Right off the mauka side of the highway near Amagaza Rd. $3–$7. They have a location on Alii Drive in Kailua-Kona and another in the Kings' Shops in the Waikoloa Beach Resort area.

Ka'aloa's Super J

83-5409 Mamalahoa Hwy, Captain Cook
(808) 328-9566

ono **Local**—An unassuming yellow building on the makai side of the highway above Kealakekua Bay. When you walk in, you might not be acknowledged. Don't take it personally; they're just relaxed. Once the grinding begins, you'll be happy you discovered the local flavors here. The plate lunches are a better value than the combo plates. Gotta try the lau lau (just don't eat the ti leaf wrapper). The kulolo makes a decent dessert. $7–$16 for lunch and dinner. In all, a good choice to grab local grinds. South of mile marker 107. Closed Sunday.

Kona Grill House

81-951 Halekii St, Kealakekua • (808) 323-3512

ono **American**—This place is having a bit of an identity crisis. It used to be Sun-dried Specialties, now it's Kona Grill House (and both names are still on the building). Doesn't matter what you call it—just call us next time you're goin'. Food is good, and you can find us regularly driving out of our way for their desserts (try the Key lime pie). They're known for their lobster crab cakes (called that because of the style, not because they actually contain any crab—just lobster). The seafood is fresh and the servings are generous. Nestled in a bit of a weird spot on Halekiʻi. **$10–$18** for lunch and dinner. Closed weekends.

Loko Wraps

82-6066 Hawaii Belt Rd, Captain Cook
(808) 895-3356

Mexican—Mexican meets local in this (usually) delicious mashup. Sometimes the flavors feel forced, but we like their lilikoʻi lani dressing. We prefer their wraps (it's what they're named for, after all) over the salads and sandwiches. We usually love jackfruit, but their barbecue version doesn't quite work for us. **$8–$25** for lunch and dinner. Located on the back side of Kealakekua Ranch Center. They have a second location in Kailua-Kona on Palani Road in Lanihau Center.

Manago

82-6155 Mamalahoa Hwy, Captain Cook
(808) 323-2642

ono **Local**—It's like eating in Grandma's kitchen. Ambiance is so homey, and this place never seems to change. They are famous across the island for their pork chops, which, we're happy to say, are *not* just like Mama used to make. (Hers were always so dry.) These are moist, fatty and flavorful. (They use an ancient, cast-iron pan and cook 2,000 pounds of chops a month.) They bring your sides at the very beginning, and you share them. They also have teri steak, butterfish, liver, etc. For dessert they feature…absolutely nothing. Pick up a Snickers bar in the lobby. South of Kona in Captain Cook off Hwy 11 at the Manago Hotel. Can't miss it. **$5–$10** for breakfast. **$11–$20** for lunch and dinner. Closed Mondays.

Teshima's Restaurant

79-7251 Hawaii Belt Rd, Kealakekua
(808) 322-9140

Japanese—A clean, friendly place with simple Japanese, American and local items, such as bento, teriyaki beef and fried fish. Some items are good (such as the sashimi), though other items, such as miso, saimin and the apple pie, might disappoint. This place is wildly popular with many local residents, but it has never really clicked with us. Off Hwy 11 in Honalo, just south of Kona. **$8–$26** for breakfast, lunch is **$11–$20**, dinner is **$11–$30**.

The HI Dive Bar

79-7460 Hawaii Belt Rd, Kealakekua
(808) 498-0993

American—An unabashed dive bar, and they really stick to that model. This is an eclectic place with a windowless sports bar on one side and an outdoor patio on the other. Our favorite parts of this place are the free skeeball game and the exit door. Our least favorite parts are…well, everything else. It often feels like you're interrupting the staff, and the food tastes about as good as moist cardboard. The bartender often serves as the cook (we assume)/microwaver, so service is slow and unfriendly. We recommend skipping this place, even if you're looking for a true dive bar with a bad attitude. If you wanna try it anyway, **$7–$20** for lunch and dinner. On Hwy 11, north of the town of Kealakekua.

KOHALA DINING

There are a lot of *ono* symbols in the Kohala dining section. That's no accident. If you're staying in Kohala, you'll find that the food choices are outstanding. That makes it difficult for us as reviewers. Normally, if we think a place is a dump, we say it's a dump. If the food or service is lousy, we say it's lousy. Unfortunately for us, most Kohala restaurants have great food and service and excellent atmosphere. This makes it hard to review without sounding like a bootlicking commercial for Kohala restaurants. The resorts go to great lengths (and expense) to feed you and keep you eating at the resort. The downside for you is that you can pay *dearly* for those *ono*s. Most of the restaurants here are pricey, and you'll find that eating in Kohala will cost you more than on any other part of the island. It wasn't our intention to gush over so many restaurants in Kohala, but we can't deny the fundamental quality of their offerings at these establishments.

Restaurants at the Four Seasons are in the Kona section since they are often frequented by people staying in Kona.

If you want to cook your own meals, you'll soon learn that there are no large grocery stores in this area, just a small upscale market in Queens' MarketPlace. You *will* find a big store, however, a few miles up the road in Waikoloa Village.

When we mention that a restaurant has lunch only, or breakfast and dinner only, you should take this with a grain of salt. Resorts are constantly rearranging these options. Also, you'll find the resorts mentioned are shown on the maps on page 57 and 154.

For simplicity, we are *excluding* restaurants in the northernmost part of Kohala (Hawi and Kapaʻau). They are described in *Dining Elsewhere* starting on page 284.

KOHALA AMERICAN

Brown's Beach House

1 N Kaniku Dr, Mauna Lani • (808) 887-7320

ono Elegant outdoor setting near the beach at the Fairmont Orchid. (Sometimes it gets too breezy.) Seafood is their best bet, which they do very well. They also have steak and chicken, even some vegan items. An easy recommend, but it's **$40–$80** for dinner. Make reservations and go before sunset to take advantage of the view—you're definitely paying for it.

Hawaii Calls

69-275 Waikoloa Beach Dr, Waikoloa (808) 886-8165

The menu tries to do a little of everything—a little steak, seafood, pasta, ribs and chicken. Service isn't as tight as other Kohala restaurants. The food's fairly bad for these prices with overcooked fish and embarrassingly small portions on some items. The open ambiance is a combination of tropical and modern and could use a bit more vision. There are sunset views, but it's fairly filtered through the pool area and lots of scenic palm trees. They also have a lounge that's available until later in the evening where they serve some great, creative cocktails. **$16–$30** for breakfast, **$15–$25** for lunch **$25–$40** for dinner. At the Waikoloa Beach Marriott.

Island Fish & Chips

69-250 Waikoloa Beach Dr, Waikoloa (808) 886-0005

They brag about using fresh fish at this stand, but we've seen frozen mahimahi used as the entrée, so be sure to ask what they have that day. Chips along with fried fish, fried shrimp, crab cakes or chicken and some sandwiches. It's a small operation and can take a while if anyone's in front of you. Mostly fried food with panko breading. Not bad, not great. The outdoor covered gazebo seating offers a decent view of the koi pond. In the Kings' Shops, Waikoloa. **$13–$15** for lunch and dinner.

Island Gourmet Markets

69-201 Waikoloa Beach Dr, Waikoloa
(808) 886-3577

ono Not actually a restaurant, it's the area's grocery store with an inventory chosen specifically with resort visitors in mind. They also have a deli that has some pretty good sandwiches, a soup bar, pizza, a wine bar, sushi and other items for reasonable prices. (Ahh… reasonable for *Kohala*, that is.) You can also pick up fresh fruits and cookables, and some of their specials, especially on wines, can be downright reasonable. **$7–$15**. In the Queens' MarketPlace.

Kamuela Provision Company

69-425 Waikoloa Beach Dr, Waikoloa
(808) 886-1234

ono Steak, seafood and a token veggie item at this Hilton Waikoloa Village restaurant. The views, especially from the outdoor tables, are fantastic. Inside you'll find an upscale yet casual decor. Dinner selections seem to change often enough that we won't recommend a particular dish. The desserts are very tasty. You may like the elevated outdoor oceanside tables for sunsets, lively indoor tables, or you may want to grab a cocktail at the other outdoor tables near the top of the pool waterfall. Food and service quality are high, but they do disappoint on occasion. Wine list is acceptable. **$42–$85** for dinner. Reservations recommended. Resort

wear with collared shirts required, but shorts are OK. Take the train *or boat* to the left from the lobby. In the Lagoon Tower of the resort.

Kohala Burger & Taco

61-3665 Akoni Pule Hwy, Kawaihae
(808) 880-1923

ono The name about covers it. This small burger joint keeps things simple and does it well. They really take pride in their food, and if something isn't right, they're quick to fix it. Burgers, hand-cut fries and good tacos. Add some killer milkshakes to the mix, and you have a great stop when you're cruising to Hawi or getting in from a morning boat trip. The space is tight, and the line to order at lunch makes things feel crowded. But they're pretty efficient, so don't turn away if it looks too busy. **$10–$20** for lunch. Adjacent to Kawaihae Harbor. The hours and open days are erratic, so check their website or be prepared to be flexible.

Kuleana Rum Shack

69-201 Waikloa Beach Dr, Waikoloa
(808) 238-0786

An upscale eatery in the Queens' MarketPlace that makes for a great spot—*to skip*. The food and drinks are expensive, and the portions are small, so we found ourselves wondering how many plates we would need to stop being hungry. (The answer was too many for our wallets to handle.) The location ain't much better, which is basically an upscale strip mall with no view. The cocktails may take the edge off the disappointment, but not by much, and even the happy hour (3–5 p.m.) doesn't live up to its name. There is one exception to the disappointment of this whole drab affair—there is a rum flight that lets you sip four rum options for about $12, and you get 10% off if you decide to buy a bottle, which is not a bad deal. It gets surprisingly busy here, and we've heard a few people say that reservations are "highly recommended." We highly recommend that you get a reservation anywhere else. **$25–$40** for lunch and dinner, plus whatever it costs you at the second restaurant to fill you up. Closed Monday and Tuesday.

Lava Lava Beach Club
69-1081 Kuualii Pl, Waikoloa • (808) 769-5282

ono With such a beautiful location right on 'Anaeho'omalu Beach, you're happy the moment you walk through the door. The ambiance is casual, and we love their open-air seating and live music. Choose the coconut mai tai over the regular, or try their cocktail sampler for a boozy appetizer. The menu isn't extensive, but what they lack in variety, they make up for in quality. Avoid the ribs, which can be overcooked. They do fish very well, and we love their salads. It ain't cheap, but with the incredible scenery (perfect for beachy sunset photo ops) and delicious food, we weren't even mad about it. From the highway, turn on Waikoloa Beach Road, left before the Marriott, park at the lot near the end of the road. An *ono* with qualifiers. Killer location and reasonably good food. But it's not the food you'll remember for years to come—it's the dreamy setting. That's why we chose this location for the opening chapter photo. They don't take reservations and waits can be long or futile. Lunch is **$15–$29**, dinner is **$26–$50**.

Manta
62-100 Mauna Kea Beach Dr, Kohala
(808) 882-5707

ono Views from here are soothing, looking obliquely down Mauna Kea Beach. Breakfast is a *hurt-me* **$39** buffet, which is awesome. (As it darned

well *better* be.) And if you decide to go off the menu, you're looking at items such as $19 pancakes and a $26 continental breakfast, so you might as well go for broke (literally). Dinner continues the expensive route, but you can still feel comfortable in walking shorts and a nice aloha shirt. Service is polished and what you'd expect from this kind of resort. If you eat here, come for the convenience (just a short stumble back to your hotel room) or for the impeccable sunset view. If you come just for the meal, you might be irritated at high prices for food that doesn't *quite* hit the mark. (Salads especially seem not up to scratch.) Be very specific about how you'd like your meat prepared. They're accommodating if you send anything back, but the rest of your table will be finishing when you get your new plate. Cocktails here are absolutely stellar, some of the best we've had on the island (and we've tried a lot for you). Consider the Spiced Coconut. **$37–$75** or more (especially when you add in the drinks) for dinner. At the Mauna Kea Beach Hotel.

Napua
68-1292 S Kaniku Dr, Mauna Lani
(808) 885-5910

ono This restaurant has an unreal location right next to the beach in Mauna Lani's Makaiwa Bay. The menu is pretty small with items such as fresh fish, steaks, ribs and maybe some seared 'ahi using all local ingredients. This is a good place to arrive early and have a cocktail, watching the beach before dinner. Good drinks here—gotta try the liliko'i margarita. The small lawn between you and the beach is a good place to park the kids while you watch 'em run around. **$24–$26** for lunch, **$44–$65** for dinner. While certainly not the best food on the island, and pricey, it's an *ono* for the cozy beachside experience. Parking can be confusing here. You'll need to use the intercom at the gate in order to have someone open it for you or park on South Pauoa Road and walk, depending on when you arrive.

Seafood Bar
61-3642 Kawaihae Rd, Kawaihae
(808) 880-9393

ono A cool tiki atmosphere featuring souped-up bar food with a local twist. Their poke burger is an easier way to try the dish if you've been hesitant. They also have a coconut shrimp sandwich (pretty good), 'ahi sashimi, etc. The lobster pot pie is more like a chowder, and it's a winner. At dinner add some short ribs, fresh fish, some steak and escargot. They seem to be catering to the watering hole crowd, so expect inexpensive well drinks, margaritas and mai tais as well as beer during happy hour. With the whimsical atmosphere (necessary, since the view out the windows is of industrial storage tanks) and prices in line with the product for this part of the island, it's an agreeable place for lunch or dinner, and we *kinda, sorta* figgered we'd give 'em an *ono*. **$13–$27** for lunch, **$13–$45** for dinner. On Hwy 270 before Kawaihae.

Tommy Bahama Restaurant
68-1330 Mauna Lani Dr, Mauna Lani
(808) 881-8686

ono If you've been to a Tommy Bahama restaurant before, you won't find any surprises here. Expect reliably good food and a high price tag. The open-air dining room takes advantage of the afternoon breezes. Being at the Shops at Mauna Lani, you're fairly removed from the ocean, but the sunset views can still be nice. (Just ignore the mall parking lot below you.) The menu is tiny for dinner

with fish, ribs and specials. Their fish tacos (for lunch) are well-executed, and they pour a consistently tasty mai tai. Happy hour (2–5 p.m. daily) brings good deals on drinks and a small selection of food for around $11. **$19–$24** for lunch, **$26–$50** for dinner. Upstairs from their retail store.

KOHALA ITALIAN

Romano's Macaroni Grill
69-201 Waikoloa Beach Dr, Waikoloa
(808) 443-5515

This is part of a chain of reliable Italian comfort food, and this location is no different. The food is tasty, portions generous, and the service is good. But the prices here are a bit different than you'll find elsewhere. While eating and looking at the menu, we went to Romano's website on our phone and found that prices here are *50% higher* than locations we looked at on the mainland. We know rent at the Queens' MarketPlace must be high, but *sheesh!* Except for the confiscatory prices, they'd probably get an *ono*. And when compared to others on the Kohala coast, maybe they're not that out of line. **$22–$40** for lunch and dinner.

KOHALA PACIFIC RIM

Roy's Waikoloa Bar & Grill
69-250 Waikoloa Beach Dr, Waikoloa
(808) 886-4321

ono Some people are born to do certain things. Roy Yamaguchi was born to run restaurants. This growing chain rarely fails to please. The food is delicious, well-conceived and nicely presented. Dishes range from spring roll appetizers, fish and beef. Specials abound and change nightly. The atmosphere is casual and somewhat noisy.

The service is efficient, sometimes bordering on pestering. Prices are reasonable *for what you get*. Entrées aren't huge, so consider the delectable appetizers. Reservations strongly recommended. (Ask for a table near the glass wall overlooking the golf course pond.) Their dark chocolate soufflé is legendary. Dinner is **$36–$60**. In the Kings' Shops in the Waikoloa Resort area near Hwy 19's mile marker 76.

KOHALA TREATS

Anuenue
61-3665 Akoni Pule Hwy, Kawaihae
Conveniently located in Kawaihae if you're heading along the shoreline up to Hawi. The shave ice is pretty good as is the ice cream. They also have some snack food that isn't overly compelling. Cash only. **$3–$5**.

WAIMEA DINING

Waimea is a cool place to eat—literally. Located up at the nippier 2,500-foot level, it's a nice place to dine when you're staying in the Kohala area and want to eat away from the resorts and enjoy the views along the way.

Big Island Brewhaus
64-1066 Mamalahoa Hwy, Waimea
(808) 887-1717

ono ☛ **Mexican**—This is what happens when the guy who started the Maui Brewing Company in 1997 buys a taco joint and starts brewing beer. With With 14 or so beers on tap, from the 9.3% Belgian-style Dark Abbey Ale to the easy drinking 4.5% Halfling IPA, be prepared to *suck 'em up*. The food is good, but it's the beer that you're probably here for. Mainly Mexican items (the restaurant used to be called Big Island

Brewhaus *& Tako*) plus burgers and a decent vegetarian and vegan menu. Mostly local ingredients. Try the Beer Float for a novel (but not so *ono*) experience. An easy place to recommend. **$8–$17** for lunch and dinner. On the corner of Mamalahoa Highway and Kamamalu in Waimea.

Hawaiian Style Café
65-1290 Kawaihae Rd, Waimea • (808) 885-4295

ono ☛ **Local**—Something of a Big Island institution, this is the kind of place you'll need to be taken out of in a wheelbarrow. Lots of greasy-spoon diner types of dishes, local favorites, and pancakes you could live under. Try to stick to the local fare, such as the loco moco (get the local style, which is fresh—the Angus beef is frozen), and look for the house specials (ask for the kalua hash crispy). They're best known for their breakfast, but their lunch is very popular, too. Check out their daily specials for some good deals. **$9–$18** for breakfast and **$10–$18** for lunch. The Waimea location on Restaurant Row is cash only, often has a wait, and closes by 1:30 p.m. (noon on Sun.). The Hilo location serves alcohol (great mai tai) and is open for dinner (same lunch menu) Tuesday through Saturday. Near Big Island Candies off Kekuanaoa Street.

Jade Palace Chinese Restaurant
65-1158 Mamalahoa Hwy, Waimea
(808) 887-1788

Chinese—Good Chinese food is hard to come by on this island. And you won't come by it here. But if your salt intake is too low, then this is your place. Our blood pressure kicks up a notch just thinking about their Mongolian beef. The hot and sour soup is neither hot nor sour—just bland. Even the tea seems weaker than usual. **$11–$26** for lunch and dinner. In the Waimea Center. You can do better.

James Angelo's Underground Pizza

64-974 Hawaii Belt Rd, Waimea • (808) 885-7888

Italian—It's about **$20** for a very large, New York-style pizza. Overall, a worthy place for a pizza fix. Across from Fish & Hog near Hwy 19's mile marker 56. Closed Monday, dinner only on Sunday. Cash only.

Liliko'i Café

67-1185 Mamalahoa Hwy, Waimea
(808) 887-1400

American—The kind of place you probably wouldn't find unless someone pointed it out. A simple menu in a bright, no frills café setting. Breakfast is a number of egg dishes, pancakes, crêpes and fresh fruits and juices. Lunch brings freshly made deli salads and soups, sandwiches, and hot entrées, such as meatloaf and vegetarian lasagna. Be careful with desserts like the liliko'i cheesecake and other desserts that beg you to make an entire meal of them. **$7–$14** for breakfast, **$11–$18** for lunch. Open till 4 p.m. Closed Sunday. On the back side of the Parker Ranch Center.

Merriman's

65-1227 Opelo Rd, Waimea • (808) 885-6822

ONO **American**—This is the best and most consistent food in Waimea. Peter Merriman is an excellent chef, and the recipes here are usually wonderful. Lunch includes fish tacos, salads, fish, burgers and sandwiches. The menu seems to change often, so we're nervous about recommending specific items. Dinner is three-course prix fixe menu with optional wine pairing for $52 more. They have an impressive wine list, but the markup seems pretty extreme. And although they are fairly knowledgeable with wines, their skills are more obvious with mixed drinks. If you're in Waimea and want a great meal, this is the place to go. **$10–$18** for brunch on Sundays only, **$14–$25** for lunch (except Fridays and Saturdays), **$95–$147** for three-course dinner. On Waimea's Restaurant Row. Reservations are strongly recommended. See map on page 137.

Pau Pizza & Provisions

65-1227 Opelo Rd, Waimea • (808) 885-6325

ONO **Italian**—A casual atmosphere with a straightforward menu of super-thin 18-inch(ish) pizzas, some sandwiches and salads. The pizza is outstanding. Meat lovers should consider the "whole hog" (which is great as pizza or a sandwich). Other items are similarly pleasing. Service is friendly and accommodating. They have a single breakfast item—a breakfast burrito (from **Taco Rosa**) for around $13. Prices in line with quality. **$13–$30** for lunch and dinner, $20–$30 for a whole pizza. In Waimea's Opelo Plaza. Closed Sundays.

Red Water Café

65-1299 Kawaihae Rd, Waimea • (808) 885-9299

ONO **American**—We don't really know how to categorize them. Creative entrées from different regions. Japan (sushi), America (steak), Hawai'i (Big Island seared 'ahi) and more. The food and music seem to reflect the owner's interests, which, fortunately, seem to coincide with ours. Ambiance is woody and eclectic. Portions are ample. The liliko'i curry dish rocks. If the special is filet, grab it. There's live music some nights. Don't let them seat you in the back area, if you can avoid it. Half portions available on entrées. For dessert, consider their Dark Side of the Moon (a flourless chocolate truffle torte). **$20–$50** (or more, if you go nuts on the sushi) for dinner. In Restaurant Row. Closed on Sundays and Mondays.

Sandwich Isle Bread Company

65-1158 Mamalahoa Hwy, Waimea
(808) 731-6712

Treats—Don't let the name fool you. They make much more than just bread. You'll find a variety of baked goods, including cookies, lilikoi bars, brownies, tarts and more. The shop itself ain't all that—it's a small grab'n'go place with no seating—but their treats are tasty, and it's a good choice if you're looking for something quick and easy to pick up before you head down the road. Pastries and bread are **$8–$12**. Located at the KTA Supermarket Shops in Waimea.

Taco Rosa

65-1227 Opelo Rd, Waimea • (808) 887-2802

ono 🍴 **Mexican**—Delicioso! Without a doubt, these are the best tacos we've had on island (and they're pretty high up there in the whole state of Hawai'i in general). Fresh corn tortillas are made *daily*, and we cannot begin to describe the satiating blend of flavors. (It's not an exaggeration to say that our mouths are watering as we write.) The small menu offers four taco options and simple sides like rice and beans, but don't let that discourage you. We tried everything (just for you), and each kind of taco took our wanderlusting tastebuds on a journey. It surprises us proud meat-lovers to say this out loud, but our favorite was the veggie taco. **$5–$15** for lunch and dinner. Located in the same building as **Pau Pizza** (which also sells their breakfast burritos). Closed Sundays and Mondays.

The Fish & The Hog

64-957 Mamalahoa Hwy, Waimea
(808) 885-6268

ono 🍴 **American**—Also known as Huli Sue's, they have a comfortable paniolo (Hawaiian cowboy) atmosphere that fits the area well. Expect to leave satiated even though some items are a miss. In general, stick with the fish but ditch the hog. They do burgers well, but the pulled pork is unremarkable unless you smother it in their house-made BBQ sauce. The brisket is dry on its own, but as the French dip it becomes a killer sandwich. They make one of the better lava flow cocktails you can find on the island, but avoid the mai tai at all costs—it tastes like it looks (alcoholic fruit punch). **$15–$30**. Avoid the liliko'i cheesecake dessert unless you like it real sour. Just across from mile marker 56 on Hwy 19.

Tropical Dreams Ice Cream

66-1250 Lalamilo Farm Rd, Waimea
(808) 885-8820

ono 🍴 **Treats**—This is the best ice cream that we've ever found in Hawai'i, and it's made on the island in Waimea. It's fairly easy to find island-wide at places that serve ice cream. If you see it, snag some. It's downright wicked. This location is off Mamalahoa Highway south of town does not do scoops. It's **$5** for 8 ounces and **$16** for a half gallon. Closed weekends.

Village Burger

67-1185 Mamalahoa Hwy, Waimea
(808) 885-7319

ono 🍴 **American**—Gourmet one-third-pound burgers made from locally raised beef, veggie mushroom burgers, and 'ahi. Quality is top-notch, and you can take your food to one of the food court tables or one of the few outdoor tables. Fries are extra, and the Parmesan fries are *outrageously* good. (Avoid the truffle fries.) They also make expensive but wicked shakes. **$10–$14** for lunch and early dinner (they close at 5 p.m.). In Parker Ranch Center.

Waimea Coffee Co.

65-1279 Kawaihae Rd, Waimea • (808) 885-8915
American—Waimea's best (and quintessential) coffee shop with a limited breakfast selection. For lunch they have some sandwiches and several salads. The coffee is good, and they'll usually have some interesting specialty drinks available. The service used to make you feel invisible, but recently it's been welcoming (although getting your order might take a while). Indoor and outdoor seating, free WiFi and a drive-thru window. They also have reasonably tasty baked goods, including their almond sticky bun. In Parker Square in Waimea. **$11–$16** for breakfast, **$10–$15** for lunch. Menu items are only served until 2 p.m.

Yong's Kal-Bi

65-1158 Mamalahoa Hwy, Waimea
(808) 885-8440

ono **Korean**—Korean food with a local twist. Good fried mandoo (Korean dumplings). Be brave when picking some of the odder items (but avoid the chicken katsu). If it's a cold Waimea day, consider the Youk Kae Jang, which is a pulled beef stew that has a striking resemblance to vegetable-beef soup found in mainland restaurants. **$11–$18** for lunch and dinner. In Waimea Center. Closed Sunday and Monday.

HILO AMERICAN

Coconut Grill

136 Banyan Way, Hilo • (808) 961-3330
This American-style diner is popular for breakfast but also has a range of Pacific Rim and local dishes available at lunch and dinner. Hit them up for happy hour to get some good deals on the pupus (we like the crab cakes). Burgers, sandwiches, salads and seafood are available for lunch while dinner brings a number of meats like prime rib, pork ribs and steak. They have four different menus for different times of day, and we'd probably just confuse you (or ourselves) trying to go through all of them. Just know, food is available and decent, nothing more. If you're staying here at the Hilo Seaside Hotel, it's convenient. Otherwise, there are more compelling dining choices in the area. Breakfast is **$8–$26**, lunch is **$17–$30**, Dinner is **$17–$60**. Next to the Ice Pond on Banyan Way.

Hilo Bay Café

123 Lihiwai St, Hilo • (808) 935-4939

ono You won't find oceanfront views in Hilo better than this. Even without ocean sunsets here on the *east* side, the bay is still primed for romantic dinners. The menu is a combination of American and Pacific Rim fare with sushi thrown in. Fresh flavors and nice presentation are found in both meals and cocktails, but they come together with mixed results—they do fish well, but some other entrées can be on the bland side (such as the mushroom curry pot pie.) Their creative mocktails are a refreshing choice for those who'd rather skip the booze. A nice range of burgers, salads and seafood is found throughout lunch and dinner menus, with steak, pasta and more seafood available at dinner. **$16–$22** for lunch, **$16–$42** for dinner. Adjacent to Queen Liliuokalani Gardens on Hilo Bay. Get reservations to secure the tables with the best views. Closed Sunday through Tuesday.

Hilo Burger Joint

776 Kilauea Ave, Hilo • (808) 935-8880

ono A likable place with a great selection of burgers using lots of unusual combinations, such as the nacho burger (nacho cheese, black beans, jalapeños, tortillas and sour cream on top), Peter Kim chee burgers, Greek burgers, etc. All one-third-pound patties from a local ranch. *Eh, no like beef?* (That's a local phrase we hope you never hear…) Anyway, they also have turkey, salmon and veggie patties. They have a full bar and 23 beers on tap for around $6 each and a good pupu menu. The atmosphere is a cross between a bar and a restaurant, and they even have some board games to amp up your meal. Service is friendly. Just south of Pauahi Street in Hilo. Parking can be a problem; check the side streets. **$11–$20** for lunch and dinner.

Island Naturals Market Deli
1221 Kilauea Ave, Hilo • (808) 935-5533

ono A local organic grocery chain with a small café. Menu changes daily but stresses vegan sandwiches and salads as well as smoothies for relatively cheap prices. Everything we've had there has tasted fresh and delicious. The Hilo location has the best selection, but don't stand there waiting to order like we did. Grab a card and write it down instead. At Kekuanaoa and Kilauea at the Hilo Center Shopping. (No, we didn't get those last two words mixed up. Someone *else* did.) **$5–$15**. They also have locations in Kailua-Kona and Pahoa.

Just Cruisin Coffee
835 Kilauea Ave, Hilo • (808) 934-7444

On the busy corner of Aupuni and Kilauea, this is a convenient spot for morning joe on the go. Limited assortment of breakfast bagels, muffins. Also lots of smoothies and blended coffee drinks. Hit the drive-thru or experience the charm inside and sit at one of the few scattered tables and use the free WiFi. The service is perky and friendly. They also have a limited food menu for lunch with cold sandwiches and salads. (Love the chicken mac nut pesto). Coffee and a tasty sausage, egg and

cheese bagel is about **$10**. Breakfast and lunch is **$5–$10**.

Ken's House of Pancakes
1730 Kamehameha Ave, Hilo • (808) 935-8711

ono A Hilo staple, they offer a vast menu that's hard to absorb. Service is sometimes unresponsive because the place can get crowded, but if you eat breakfast at the counter, it's fast and efficient. (Just when I need it, because I'm grumpy before my coffee.) Their corned beef hash loco moco is a delicious heart attack in a bowl. You ain't paying for gourmet here, and you won't get it. You *will* get pretty large portions of acceptable diner food at reasonable prices. That's why they eked out an *ono* from us in a moment of weakness, and it's for breakfast and lunch *only*. Breakfast is **$10–$23**, lunch and dinner are **$14–$32**. On Hwy 11 near Hwy 19.

Ola Brew
1177 Kilauea Ave, Hilo • (808) 731-0917

Ola Brew is a modern brewery in Hilo, complete with custom brews and tasty American fusion food. This is one of two locations on island, and in *our* humble opinion it's the better one. The Hilo brewery is large, open and almost feels food court-y (not necessarily in a bad way). We like the food here but are slightly confused about why the menus in each location are so darn different. They know their local audience, though, and do a good job, especially with their vegan and gluten-free options. **$15–$35** for lunch and dinner. On the corner of Kilauea Avenue and Kekuanaoa Street.

Pineapples Island Fresh Cuisine
332 Keawe St, Hilo • (808) 238-5324

ono This is what every restaurant in Hawai'i should be. Any time we sit down here, we get *incredibly* frustrated simply because we want to order *every*thing.

The menu is huge and still manages to be delicious. The teriyaki flank steak is popular (order it, and you'll understand why), as are the burgers and salads. You can't go wrong here. Order the Pineapple Pow with or without alcohol (we prefer *with*) for the quintessential island-drink Instagram shot. Only downside here is the traffic going by, and with no parking lot you might have to walk a little ways. But even with these setbacks, we don't think you'll mind too much. You'll be too busy scarfing. **$14–$40** for lunch and dinner. Closed Mondays. On the corner of Keawe and Mamo streets in Hilo.

Seaside Restaurant

1790 Kalanianaole Ave, Hilo • (808) 935-8825

A local institution. They built their reputation on freshwater fish raised right there in a large, serene pond, but they have mostly gravitated toward ocean fish because, we're told, "It's less work." If they didn't have the view of the pond, the atmosphere would be merely adequate and a bit loud. Service is friendly. The freshwater fish that they sometimes buy from others like aholehole (not pronounced the way you're *tempted* to pronounce it) is served head and all. Overall, the food's reasonable (love the butterfish, but you gotta be careful not to eat too much) but overpriced. Some tables include a show called *count how many skeeters the geckos can eat*. **$14–$39** for dinner. In east Hilo past Banyan Drive 2.5 miles east of Hwy 11. Reservations recommended. Closed Monday and Tuesday.

Sweet Cane Café

48 Kamana St, Hilo • (808) 934-0002

ono A primarily vegan spot that's easy to recommend (and it's nice that it's pretty healthy, too). We love their cold brew drinks. Try the cayenne-laced Wake Up Spice, which is tasty and has a bit of a kick to it, or the sweeter Macaccino. Their baked goods are just as good. (The sourdough bread especially gets an honorable mention.) Apart from their baked goods, you can find taro and black bean burgers, roasted veggie sandwiches, poke bowls (with taro instead of tuna) and a wide variety of salads. The food is an *ono* all around, and we frequently find ourselves ordering more than we can eat just so we can sample all the varieties of flavors. On Kamana Street around the corner from Ola Brew. **$10–$20** for breakfast and lunch.

The Booch Bar

110 Keawe St, Hilo • (808) 498-4779

ono Cute and colorful shop with a hippie vibe in downtown Hilo. They make their own kombucha (or "booch"—thus the name) and kombucha-infused cocktails. They also use a lot of fresh produce in their dishes (and you can really taste the difference). While they do have non-vegetarian options, they really emphasize vegetarian and vegan food here. We recommend the kimchi ceviche tostada and mushroom bibimbap. Overall, the food and drinks are very good, and this place is worth stopping by if you're looking for a bit of that hippie charm. **$14–$17** for breakfast, **$15–$20** for lunch and dinner. Open 8 a.m.–8 p.m., every day of the week. Located on Keawe Street, behind New Chiang Mai Thai Cuisine.

HILO ITALIAN

Café Pesto Hilo Bay

308 Kamehameha Ave, Hilo • (808) 969-6640

A reliable place, for the most part, to eat in downtown Hilo. They have fallen from an *ono* for being "good" rather than "great" of late. Nice salad selection, hot sandwiches and some good vegetarian offerings. Creative pizzas are often the daily specials and a good choice. Their pastas can be hit or miss. Consider the coconut-crusted calamari appetizer—you get chunks of calamari steak rather than rings. The lemonade is very tasty and is flavored with lemongrass, lime leaf and honey, giving it an extra tart kick with mellow sweetness. Dinner adds seafood and ribeye dishes that tend to be well executed on the plate but lack the big flavors you might be expecting. **$15–$30** for lunch, **$16–$40** for dinner.On Kamehameha between Mamo and Furneaux.

HILO JAPANESE

Miyo's
564 Hinano St, Hilo • (808) 935-2273

ono When most people think of Japanese food, they envision sushi or perhaps teppanyaki. But is this how people normally eat in their homes in Japan? Not really. *Miyo's Very Home Style Japanese Restaurant* is Japanese comfort food—an almost dizzying assortment of noodle dishes, rice dishes and bentos with fresh ingredients. Anything tempura here is very popular and tasty. They do seafood well and have a better selection at dinner. Some things are an acquired taste, such as the shabu shabu hot pot, which *sounds* good, but we found to be a bit bland. Lunch gets busy but gives the chance to see what the regulars like to order. **$9–$25** for lunch and dinner. On Hinano south of Hualani Street. Closed Sunday.

HILO LOCAL

Café 100
969 Kilauea Ave, Hilo • (808) 935-8683

ono Possibly Hilo's most popular eating establishment. This is the most successful local restaurant on the island. For nearly 70 years they've served cheap, tasty, artery-clogging food and are legendary for their loco mocos. (These consist of fried eggs over rice and Spam or a similar meat—if there *is* a similar meat—all smothered with brown gravy.) They have over a dozen varieties of loco moco, along with burgers, chili, stew, sandwiches and specials for as little as $4.50. We gave them an *ono* because this is quintessential local food. But if you're watching your cholesterol or fat intake, it'll rock your Richter scale like no other place. Grab your food at the window and eat at one of the outdoor tables. **$5–$12** for breakfast, **$5–$15** for lunch and dinner. On Kilauea near Mohouli in Hilo. Closed weekends.

Puka Puka Kitchen
270 Kamehameha Ave, Hilo • (808) 933-2121

Tasty entrées and stuffed pitas set in a tiny hole in the wall. (*Puka* is Hawaiian for "hole.") Food's good and the prices cheap. Even though the menu is short, it's hard to choose between the sautéed 'ahi, the locally raised lamb or the seafood platter. We're partial to the lamb, but they often run out, sometimes *very early*. Their 'Ahi Don is also pretty good. **$8–$20** for lunch and dinner (dinner only Tuesdays, Thursdays and Fridays). On the corner of Kamehameha and Furneaux in Hilo. Closed weekends. Hours and days can vary, so call ahead.

Suisan Fish Market
93 Lihiwai St, Hilo • (808) 935-9349

ono Primarily a wholesaler of various groceries, this is also one of the most accessible places to pick up fresh fish to prepare at home. They usually have 'ahi, mahimahi and ono available, and it is cool to just look at all they have displayed. They also make some killer poke and they're generous with the portions. (A two-choice poke bowl is enough for a couple to share). **$15–$21** for poke bowls, fresh fish is market price. Near the corner of Lihiwai and Banyan Drive, right on the water. A good place to grab fresh, local-style lunch after exploring Lili'uokalani Park. Closed Sunday.

HILO THAI

New Chiang Mai Thai Cuisine
110 Kalakaua St, Hilo • (808) 969-3777

The curries and pad thai are flavorful, but the heat index of the dishes can be erratic, and the service, though *sometimes* nice, can also be comically indifferent. (A fun game can be to *bet* on how many visits to the table it takes before your server utters a single word to you.) The non-Thai entrées aren't bad, but overall, the food is mediocre. That said, it's not too often we single out a Thai restaurant for dessert, but their honey banana (with ice cream) is excellent. They also have vegan ice cream with weird names like "not pecan butter". So what flavor is it? Lunch and dinner, both cost **$15–$22**. Dinner only on Sunday. Between Keawe and Kinoole streets in Hilo.

Sombat's Fresh Thai Cuisine
88 Kanoelehua Ave, Hilo • (808) 969-9336

ono *Very* good flavors and a real treat considering the prices. Don't neglect the wonderful green curry chicken—exceptionally good and complex flavors. Or the vegetables with oyster sauce. Or the *best* papaya salad we've ever had. The curries tend to be on the sweeter side, and you can definitely taste the fresh ingredients. It's BYOB, and they'll even give you a nice beer glass if you bring your own. Good quality and an obvious attempt to keep things healthy, growing most of their own herbs and

buying produce from local farmers. It's **$20–$31** for dinner. Next to Ken's House of Pancakes near the corner of Kamehameha and Hwy 11 in Hilo. Park around back. Closed Sunday. At press time they were only doing take out.

Tina's Garden Café
168 Kamehameha Ave, Hilo • (808) 935-1166

ono Amazing selection of dishes. This is the kind of place where people want to work just to be able to try everything. Interesting fusion of cuisine such as Thai pizzas and Thai burritos. Besides great flavors, the presentation here can be jaw-dropping. The Ocean in the Jungle curry dish, seafood served in a hollowed-out pineapple, is almost too gorgeous to eat. The Thai pizza is one of our favorites (not like any Thai pizza you've seen or tried before) and surprised us with how well the blending of cheese with curry works. All ingredients are organic and local when possible. Not to be overlooked, their teas and smoothies are also creative and delicious. Hot means hot here, and they make their own spices with Thai/Hawaiian chili peppers. In fact, most of the herbs come from their own garden. **$10–$25** for lunch and dinner with dinner. Wickedly easy to recommend. Closed Sunday. Kamehameha and Waianuenue. Take out only at press time.

HILO TREATS

Big Island Candies
585 Hinano St, Hilo • (808) 935-8890

Tasty but amazingly overpriced chocolates, cakes, cookies, nuts and candies. Some surprising flavor combinations. (Hawaiian red chili toffee actually works for us.) Fortunately, they have several samples scattered throughout the store. You can also look through the glass and watch the whole process. It's a tour bus magnet, so it's either packed inside or dead, depending on your timing. On Hinano Street off Kekuanaoa, east Hilo. **$9–$60.**

Two Ladies Kitchen
274 Kilauea Ave, Hilo • (808) 961-4766

ono These two ladies quit their day jobs to invest all their time into making mochi. It's a smooth, doughy dessert made from rice flour and traditionally stuffed with red bean paste. Here you'll find mochi stuffed with peanut butter, brownies, sweet potato or some confectionary morsel. Their best is the strawberry mochi, which cost **$3.25** each. (*Well worth it.*) You can get assortment packs of eight for about **$9–$30.** On Kilauea near Ponahawai in Hilo. Call ahead for special orders. Open 10 a.m.–4 p.m. Closed Sunday and Monday.

DINING IN PAHOA

Pahoa is the main place to eat when you're in lower Puna (meaning Kapoho to Kalapana). All the restaurants are on the main (and only) road going *through* town (not on the bypass). Most maps call it Government Main Road, but it's really Pahoa Village Road. Once in town you can't miss 'em.

Black Rock Café
15-2872 Government Main Rd, Pahoa
(808) 965-1177

American—A giant menu with burgers, and subs and local grinds at the low end, steak, seafood and frozen lobster tails at the high end with pizza in the middle, all in a diner-like atmosphere. Overall, the food is mostly fine, sometimes even good. Their biscuits and gravy is the best in Pahoa. (Of course, that's akin to having the greatest Mongolian food in all Ecuador.) The draft beer is embarrassingly cheap, and it's possible that fact colored our judgment; we almost gave 'em an *ono*. (But when the beer wore off, we got ahold of our senses.) The Bananas Foster is their best dessert. Service can be *slooow.* **$7–$12** for breakfast, **$8–$28** (more for lobster) for lunch and dinner.

Boogie Woogie Pizza
15-2937 Pahoa Village Rd, Pahoa
(808) 965-5575

Italian—New York style pizza with varying specials that make for pretty unbeatable deals. The food isn't great, but the prices are reasonable. Salads, spaghetti and smoothies make up the lunch and dinner menu, which will run you **$7–$10.** Pizza prices range **$9–$20,** depending on the size and toppings. On the main road in Pahoa.

Coco Cantina
15-2714 Pahoa Village Rd, Pahoa
(808) 731-4890

Mexican—A tidy Mexican restaurant in Pahoa. There's no view or romance, and honestly, the food ain't all that great either, but the staff is incredibly friendly, and they make a pretty good cocktail. It's not hard to find something that sounds good on the menu, but we learned pretty quickly that just because it sounds good doesn't mean it is good. The dishes we've tried consistently lack spice and aren't as flavorful as we were hoping, especially considering the price. Sure, it's nothing that a bit of hot sauce can't fix, but there are better places to satisfy your taste buds. If you plan on stopping by anyway, try to go for happy hour—the drinks make up for the food's shortcomings. **$15–$20** for lunch and dinner. Happy hour 3–5 p.m. weekdays. From Hwy 130, turn onto Keaau-Pahoa Road in Pahoa.

Kaleo's Bar & Grill
15-2969 Pahoa Village Rd, Pahoa
(808) 965-5600

ono American—In terms of ambiance and food, it's the nicest restaurant in Pahoa. The menu is all over the place, but we haven't found anything that wasn't good. From the black & blue burger to coconut chicken curry to seafood dynamite to fresh fish, preparation and ingredients are top-notch. (Great kalua pork won ton appetizer.) It can get loud inside (and outdoor tables have traffic noise and some irksome flies), but overall, you'll enjoy this place. Good wine list and excellent mai tais. On main road in Pahoa. **$12–$18** for lunch, **$12–$30** for dinner. Reservations recommended for dinner.

Ning's Thai Cuisine
15-2955 Pahoa Village Rd, Pahoa
(808) 965-7611

ono Thai—Great flavors, fun atmosphere and an easy *ono*. Too bad the rest of Pahoa can't look this good. Nice additions of avocado in a lot of dishes (best expressed in the avocado rolls). Consider the chiang mai salad with chicken for bright fresh flavors. They will crank up the spice level if you can handle it—ask for *Thai hot*. Their Thai tea with lemon is unique—no dairy, and the mint garnish and lime gives it a nice tang. **$15–$20** for lunch and dinner. Sundays is dinner only. In downtown Pahoa; can't miss it.

DINING NEAR HAWI

Bamboo Restaurant
55-3415 Akoni Pule Hwy, Hawi
(808) 889-5555

American—Located in an old, quaint dry goods building in Hawi with a quirky, tropical ambiance, they have an eclectic menu with uniquely prepared foods. You can get a good meal here if you're not on a budget. Lunch is fresh fish, BBQ pork sandwich (which is good), stir fry, burgers and sandwiches. At night add more steak, seafood and money. Prices at dinner are pretty high—especially the rack of ribs. Quality has improved of late, and they almost get an *ono* for lunch. They have a gallery inside the building offering all kinds of nice, locally carved wood and other products. Lunch and brunch on Sunday is **$12–$25**, dinner is **$17–$45**. Closed Mondays.

Gill's Lanai
54-3866 Akoni Pule Hwy, Kapaau
(808) 315-1542

American—A small shack with a few outdoor tables. Menu is fish tacos (avoid the "naked" preparation), hot dogs (reasonably priced and includes fries), fresh fish and chips and Hawaiian poke. Food's not stellar, but it's pretty cheap. **$8–$13** for lunch. On the mauka side of the Hwy on your way into Kapa'au. Closed Saturday–Monday.

King's View Café
54-3897 Akoni Pule Hwy, Kapaau
(808) 889-0099

ono American—On the makai side of the highway in Kapa'au, they have 7-, 12- and 16-inch pizzas, hot and cold sandwiches and some pretty big salads made from local greens along with cheap-tasting Roselani ice cream. There are some creative pizzas, and the personal size comes with a *small* salad for around $12. The food's pretty good, the pizza flavorful, and they use nice, fresh greens for the sandwiches and salads. Service can be *very* slow, even if no one is ahead of you. **$15–$25** for lunch and dinner. Across from the King Kamehameha statue.

DINING NEAR 'AKAKA FALLS

Mr. Ed's Bakery
28-1672 Old Mamalahoa Hwy, Honomu
(808) 963-5000
American—Mr. Ed's has a big selection of hit-or-miss baked goods. (Of course, of course.) **$3–$10**. But you can't help but be dazzled by their giant selection (well over a hundred) of locally made jams at $8.50–$10 each.

What's Shakin'
27-999 Mamalahoa Hwy, Pepeekeo
(808) 964-3080

ono ✏️ American—On the 4-mile Scenic Drive (between mile markers 7 and 11 on Hwy 19). This is a fantastic place to get outrageous smoothies. They also have a small lunch menu of rotating yet dependably tasty items, such as wraps and *super* fresh salads. They also have daily specials with seasonal and handmade ingredients. The smoothies, their signature items, often start with frozen bananas (instead of ice), and most, like the ginger twist, are wonderful. They also sell Tropical Dreams ice cream and some fruit. **$9–$14**. Closed Monday.

DINING NEAR LAUPAHOEHOE

Laupahoehoe is the tiny town north of Hilo and 'Akaka Falls before you get to Honoka'a.

Papa'aloa Country Store & Café
35-2032 Old Mamalahoa Hwy, Papaaloa
(808) 339-7614
American—This small, local grocer has plenty of great road snacks and beverages. They also have a café in the back that always has pizza and daily specials such as burgers and plate lunches, plus a small selection of pastries, burritos and loco moco for breakfast. The garlic fries will leave a taste in your mouth all day (in a good way). If you have a sweet tooth, be sure to check their baked goods, especially the mac-nut baklava. The bite-sized confections range from straight to chocolate to creative mixtures of local fruits, most $1–$3. **$6–$13** for breakfast, **$8–$27** for lunch and dinner. Down a road 0.3 mile past mile marker 24 on the ocean side of the highway. Closed Sunday.

DINING IN HONOKA'A

Café Il Mondo
45-3580 Mamane St, Honokaa • (808) 775-7711
Italian—Pizzas, calzones, lasagnas, salads and hot sandwiches. Lots of different coffee drinks. The pizza is pretty good (not great) with crunchy crust. The calzones are large and tasty. They have a fairly good meatball sandwich, or try their hearty lasagna. Service can be slow at times. On Hwy 240 in Honoka'a, ocean side. Their ambience is warm and inviting with lots of dark wood, stonework and a huge bar. **$15–$27** for lunch and early dinner. Closed Sundays and Mondays.

Gramma's Kitchen
45-3625 Mamane St, Honokaa • (808) 775-9943
American—A small, home-style diner that looks and feels like you've stepped back in time. (The owners did, in fact, have a '50s-style diner in Laupahoehoe for years.) The menu has plenty of the comfort food goodness of eggs, meat, potatoes and pancakes. A number of dishes draw on the owner's Portuguese roots and keep the menu interesting. Service can be loose, especially if they're busy. Portions are plentiful and the coffee weak (just like *my* grandma used to do). **$10–$18** for breakfast, **$9–$18** for lunch, **$10–$35** for dinner (Friday through Sunday only), which includes to-go, family-style meals. On the corner

of Mamane and Lehua. Closed Monday and Tuesday.

Tex Drive-In & Restaurant
45-690 Pakalana St, Honokaa • (808) 775-0598

ono **Local**—Every good restaurant does at least one thing well, and Tex is a perfect example. Most of the food is merely adequate fast food, such as burgers, teriyaki chicken, wraps, etc. for lunch and dinner, plus cheap (and it tastes that way) breakfasts. So why the *ono*? Because Tex *excels* at making the best malasadas (a Portuguese doughnut dipped in sugar) on the island, served fresh and warm throughout the day. The plain ones are delicious, but they also have them filled with Bavarian chocolate, tropical fruits, etc. We *never* hesitate to stop by when we're in the neighborhood. Located on Hwy 19 near Honoka'a and mile marker 43. Sometimes the wait (even if nobody is ahead of you) can be long. Don't overlook the drive-in window. **$8–$11** for breakfast (cheaper for the malasadas), **$7–$17** for lunch and dinner.

DINING NEAR KILAUEA VOLCANO

For such a small town, Volcano has a disproportionately high number of excellent restaurants (or maybe we just feel that way because hiking all day builds up an appetite). But nothing is cheap, so consider packing a picnic lunch.

Eagles Lighthouse Café
19-4005 Haunani Rd, Volcano • (808) 985-8587
Local—A hole in the wall with cheap food and local flavors. Just a few breakfast items—consider the breakfast bento with eggs, two meats and rice, or the croissant sandwich. This is our go-to choice when we just want to grab something hearty and get on down the road to the volcano without messing around. Lunch consists of random items such as spaghetti, chicken char sui, lau lau, pork with potatoes and sandwiches. Choices are limited, prices are cheap, and their main customer base is local residents. **$5–$8** for breakfast, **$11–$15** for lunch. At Haunani and Volcano roads in Volcano. Closed Sunday and Monday.

Kilauea Lodge & Restaurant
19-3948 Old Volcano Rd, Volcano
(808) 967-7366

ono **American**—This cozy restaurant in the sometimes chilly village of Volcano serves refined cuisine in a warm atmosphere. Dinner items such as steak, lamb, and chicken are expertly prepared and presented. Though they have fresh fish, we like to go here for a good red meat experience. We're seriously convinced they could make a mongoose appetizing. Expensive, but *very* good food in a comfortable environment. Lunch offers a pretty good variety with well-conceived sandwiches, salads and more. All the meals we've had are delicious, but you'll get the most out of the dinner menu. One of the best restaurants on the island. **$13–$20** for brunch, dinner is **$28–$45**. If there is a wait, enjoy coffee by the "International Fireplace." Closed Monday and Tuesday.

Koana
18-1325 Old Volcano Rd, Mountain View
(808) 209-4432

ono **Coffee**—An excellent little pourover coffee joint that takes great pride in their work (as they should—it's great). The staff is enthusiastic and will happily let you smell the coffee beans—which usually come with fun names like "Juicy IPA" or "Red Wine"—before choosing what you want to drink. Most drinks you see on the menu are flavorful and interesting, and the workers are happy to help you pick something good. Expect to spend **$5–$8** for a drink. They also serve some tasty chocolates (which are priced to reflect the quality). If you go for the chocolate, you can easily double or triple the cost. To get here, turn onto Old Volcano Road from Hwy 11. Closed Sunday and Monday.

'Ohelo Café
19-4005 Haunani Rd, Volcano • (808) 339-7865

ono **American**—Absolutely delicious. An easy and great choice. The kitchen is open so you can see the team of chefs at work, and you get the sense they really like cooking. The menu rotates, but whatever it is on the day you are there, it's going to be good. A typical night's offering may include ribs, rack of lamb, ribeye, wood-fired pizza or shrimp pasta alfredo. Prices aren't low but neither is the quality of the food (we love the thin crust pizzas). Don't be surprised to see the bartender use a blowtorch for the smoked rosemary. It's the kind of place that will make you *wish* you weren't full so you could keep on ordering. Hard to believe such unbelievable food comes from a place connected to a rural gas station convenience store, but Volcano is full of the unexpected. **$13–$59** for dinner. In Volcano Village, at the intersection of Old Volcano Road. Closed Tuesday and Wednesday.

Thai Thai Bistro & Bar
19-4084 Old Volcano Rd, Volcano
(808) 967-7969

ono **Thai**—Excellent menu of curries, soups, stir fry, noodle dishes and vegetarian items. It's noticeably overpriced, but the quality is top-notch, so consider it a splurge. They have good pad Thai. Curries are unusual and on the sweet side; curry lovers (like us) will either like the novelty (we do) or dislike the flavor. (Avoid the red.) Good (and generous) summer rolls.

If you like heat, they'll wound you here. Thai hot *means* Thai hot, so go milder unless you've got an asbestos-lined tongue. Our only concern is that the service can be uneven. Rushed at times, slow at others. If you catch 'em at the right pace, you'll like the place. Desserts are sparse—get the tapioca pudding. Decoration is beautiful and calming. **$16–$40** for lunch and dinner. In Volcano Village. Closed for one full month—sometimes longer—each year when the owners go back to Thailand. Closed Wednesday and Thursday.

The Rim at Volcano House
1 Crater Rim Dr, Volcano • (808) 930-6910

ono **American**—If you want to dine *inside* Hawai'i Volcanoes National Park, this is your only option. We gave them an *ono*, but that's owing almost entirely to the *absolutely incredible* view overlooking Kilauea Caldera. If the weather is good, you can see Halema'uma'u Crater in the distance. For dinner expect steak, seafood, chicken and pasta for **$25–$59**. Reservations recommended, especially if you want a window seat since it tends to get crowded come evening. Also located in Volcano House is **Uncle George's Lounge**, which serves breakfast (**$9–$13**), and lunch, which is mostly burgers, pasta and sandwiches for **$14–$23**. The view is the same, and there is usually less wait for a table.

Volcano's Lava Rock Café
19-3972 Old Volcano Hwy, Volcano
(808) 967-8526

Ameican—Cool lodge feel with diner-esque food. Solid selection of hearty burgers, sandwiches, chili, salads (try the liliko'i dressing), chicken fajitas (which you can avoid), fresh-tasting taco salad, stir fry and more. Many items are veggie with generous portions. (Good milkshakes.) Breakfast (Sundays only) items include some clever omelets and French toast with lilikoʻi butter. Lunch and dinner are pretty hit or miss—the sandwiches tend to be the safest bet. Skip dessert here. Service is so-so. An amazingly variable restaurant. You may get a good experience, or you may get ticked off. Feeling lucky? **$7–$11** for breakfast (Sundays only), **$11–$18** for lunch, **$11–$24** for dinner. Right in Volcano Village. No lunch or dinner on Sunday. Closed Monday.

DINING NEAR SOUTH POINT

Coffee Grinds

92-8674 Lotus Blossom Ln, Ocean View
(808) 939-7545

American—The best (and pretty much only) place for breakfast (and more importantly, coffee) near South Point. This place is a favorite for locals and is usually busy with regulars. The full order of the oven-baked skillet is filling and includes large chunks of fresh vegetables. Lighter options include bagels dressed up with hummus and sliced tomato. Soups, sandwiches and wraps also available. Everything tastes fresh and we like the friendly vibe. **$5–$14** for breakfast and lunch. In Ocean View, pull in at the gas station on the mauka side (mountain side) of Hwy 11 between mile markers 77 and 78.

DJ's Pizza & Bakeshop

92-8674 Lotus Blossom Ln, Ocean View
(808) 929-9800

Italian—If you pull in for gas on your way from one side of the island to the other, this might seem like an acceptable (and convenient) option for grabbing something to eat given the lack of restaurants in the area. The pizzas come out quick (in about 20 minutes), but the food is just OK. Don't worry—we got your back. **Ocean View Pizzeria** is in the next plaza over and much better. **$7–$20** for lunch and dinner. Closed Sunday and Monday.

Ka-Lae Garden

92-8395 Mamalahoa Hwy, Ocean View
(808) 494-7688

Thai—Their slogan should be "The best Thai food for miles!" It's certainly not the best on the island (their curries are a little watery), but it's nice to have a healthier dining option in the remote south island area, and the food is acceptable. In Ocean View. Lunch and early dinner. **$8–$13**. Closed Friday and Saturday.

Ocean View Pizzeria

525 Lotus Blossom Ln, Ocean View
(808) 929-9677

ONO **Italian**—Pizza, sandwiches, some baked goods and ice cream. The pizza is good for the area, but their hot deli sandwiches are the reason for the *ono.* (Your choices are meager around here unless you want to hit the grocery store.) In fact, both the pastrami and the Italian sausage Parmesan with marinara on garlic bread are delicious. In the big shopping center on the mauka side before mile marker 77. **$7–$23** for lunch and dinner.

DINING IN NAʻALEHU

Hana Hou Restaurant

95-1148 Naalehu Spur Rd, Naalehu
(808) 929-9717

ONO **American**—Naʻalehu is a pretty remote place on your way to the volcano, and it's surprising and gratifying to have good food in the middle of nowhere. We've seen them have off days, but not often. Breakfast includes egg dishes, breakfast burritos, home fries, pancakes, etc. Lunch and dinner include plate lunches, sandwiches (try the pastrami) and specials. Consider their tasty lilikoʻi lemonade. **$8–$12** for breakfast, **$10–$17** for lunch and dinner. Look for a sign on the ocean side shoulder of the road in Naʻalehu.

Honua's Coffee House

95-5587 Mamalahoa Hwy, Naalehu

Coffee—A laid-back sort of coffeehouse with a cool atmosphere, large murals and comfortable seating that feels more like a communal living room than a coffee shop. The offerings consist of smoothies, coffee and some baked goods, and while the menu won't knock your socks off, it's a good spot to swing by if you're looking for something quick. This place is easier to recommend than the nearby **Ka Lae Coffee**—mostly because they have similar offerings—but Honua's does them at a better price. **$8–$12**. In Na'alehu, along Mamalahoa Highway.

Ka Lae Coffee

95-5656 Hawaii Belt Rd, Naalehu

(646) 257-0339

American—Ka Lae Coffee is one of the few options for food in Na'alehu. Located directly across from the very popular Punalu'u Bake Shop (known for their malasadas and sweetbreads, but not their coffee), Ka Lae Coffee is a good spot with plenty of space and outdoor seating. You can expect good food and brews, but the prices might raise some eyebrows, especially considering the small portions. In this case, we think you're better off grabbing food from the bakery and then stopping by Ka Lae for your caffeine fix. **$10–$20** for breakfast and lunch. Open 8 a.m.–5 p.m., Monday through Saturday. To get here from the highway, head mauka on Kaalaiki Road after the Ace Hardware.

Punalu'u Bake Shop

95-5642 Mamalahoa Hwy, Naalehu

(866) 366-3501

ono American—A well known tour bus destination, their namesake sweetbread doesn't really work for us, but most of their other baked goods sure do, such as the *delicious* liliko'i-glazed Portuguese malasadas and the wonderful apple turnovers. They also have hot and cold sandwiches. Go somewhere else for coffee. On the highway; can't miss it. **$5–$11** for breakfast and lunch.

Shaka Restaurant

95-5673 Mamalahoa Hwy, Naalehu

(808) 929-7404

American—In Na'alehu, it's billed as "the most southern bar in the USA." Burgers, fried chicken, fish, loco moco. There ain't many options around here, but try *anywhere else* if you can. It's the kind of place that will leave you asking, "Can I get some food with this salt?" Bland food that tastes frozen and horrendous coffee. Bad food, bad service, bad idea. **$9–$15** for breakfast, **$11–$20** for lunch and **$11–$24** for dinner. Cash or Venmo only.

ISLAND NIGHTLIFE

Not in the same league as what you'll find in Honolulu or any other big city, but on the Big Island we don't exactly spend *all* of our evenings watching old reruns of *Gilligan's Island*. (Well…maybe Fridays.) There *is* life after sunset here.

Kona

Kona has the liveliest nightlife. Every Friday, the Entertainment section of the local newspaper, *West Hawai'i Today*, lists everything that's happening for the week ahead. Very handy. Much of the action takes place on Alii Drive. It's easy to walk downtown and check out what's shakin'. Directions to these places are in their reviews. For cocktails, the **Billfish Bar** (808-329-2911) at the Courtyard King Kamehameha Hotel is famed for their cheap drinks. **Don's Mai Tai Bar** (808-930-3286) at the Royal Kona Resort has a great happy hour. Most of their mai tais are excellent, especially the Original, Pele's Volcanic and the Don Jito. (That's just our hard work ethic shining through.) Service can be thin, but the location works. Nextdoor neighbors **Huggo's** (808-329-1493) and **Huggo's on the Rocks** (808-329-8711) are both great options. The first can be very romantic, and they often have live jazz. The second usually has a local guitarist. Avoid wearing heels here—the floor is covered in sand. If you're looking to dance, **Humpy's** (808-324-2337), **Laverne's** (808) 331-2633), and **Oceans Sports Bar & Grill** (808-327-9494)—all in the Coconut Grove Market Place—turn into a club scene at night, and get crowded when the cruise ship is in town. **Kona Brewing Co. & Brewpub** (808-334-2739) on Kuakini and Palani behind Kona Business Center is a good place for a cold, locally made beer. A dozen or so different brews and some wines. (No mixed drinks.)

The **Aloha Theatre** south of Kona up in Kainaliu often has fun local plays and concerts. Call 808-322-9924 for more information and a schedule of what's on.

Moviegoers will want to call **Keauhou Cinemas** (808-324-0172) or the **Makalapua Cinemas** (808-327-0444) in Kona to see what's playing.

Kohala

Nightlife is a resort affair (so to speak). Many of the mega-resorts have lounges. Good places to have a drink include **Kamuela Provision Company** (808-886-1234) at the Hilton Waikoloa Village, **Lava Lava Beach Club** (808-769-5282), **Kahakai Bar**, **Brown's Beach House** and **Luana Lounge** (808-885-2000) both at the Fairmont Orchid, and the **Beach Tree** (808-325-8000) at the Four Seasons.

Hilo

The **Hilo Burger Joint** (808-935-8880) at 776 Kilauea Ave. has some very good live music most nights, and their bartending skills tend to be pretty high. (Great burgers, too.) **Cronies Bar & Grill** (808-935-5158) at 11 Waianuenue is a pretty good sports bar with good beers, bar games and a young, lively atmosphere. Food is adequate.

LU'AU

We've all seen them in movies. People sit at a table with a mai tai in one hand and a plate of kalua pig in another. There's always a show where a fire dancer twirls a torch lit at both ends, and hula dancers bend and sway to the beat of the music. To be honest, that's not far from the truth. Lu'au can be a blast, and, if your time allows for one, they are highly recommended. The pig is *usually* baked all day in an underground pit called an imu, creating absolutely delicious results. Shows are usually exciting and fast-paced. Although lu'au on O'ahu can make you feel like cattle being led to slaughter, the lu'au on the Big Island are smaller, more intimate affairs of usually 100–200 people. Most lu'au include all you can eat and drink (including alcohol) for a set fee (except where noted below). If the punch they are serving doesn't satisfy you, they usually have an open bar to fill your needs.

Different resorts hold their lu'au on different nights. These change with the whims of the managers, so verify before making plans. Many lu'au advertise that they are rated number one. By whom? At any rate, this is what we thought of the choices within each area.

In Kona

Island Breeze Lu'au

75-5660 Palani Rd, Kailua-Kona • (808) 326-4969
Our current favorite in Kona is Island Breeze Lu'au at King Kamehameha's Kona Beach Hotel. The food is pretty good, and the bartender will happily pour some extra

rum in those candy-flavored mai tais. The show is well done and includes on-stage hula lessons for the brave. Check-in for the lu'au is on the opposite side of the hotel, but this will give you a chance to walk through and appreciate the art and artifacts that decorate the lobby. The "imu ceremony" is just two hotel cooks picking up the pig, but with a smaller crowd you may actually catch a glimpse of the whole thing. **$149** for adults, $75 for kids 4–12, keiki 3 and under are free. Parking is $5.

Royal Kona Lu'au

75-5852 Alii Dr, Kailua-Kona • (808) 672-2520
Our second choice in Kona is Royal Kona Lu'au. The food isn't very exciting, but it's not bad. Though they tell you to arrive at a certain time, ask what time they actually allow people in—otherwise be prepared for a long and slow-moving line. The show is presided over by a Hawaiian lounge lizard. It's a bigger area with more people (or at least more chairs) and it feels crowded. The free bar closes around 7 p.m. The imu ceremony, when they unearth the pig, is good, but it's hard to see through the crowd (and their phones). When you see the torch lighters, follow them to the pit right away and stand there so you can get a better view. The location is the real star here—*right* next to the water. Like the King Kamahameha, they erect a safety net for the fire knife dancer. Tables on the north (right) side are usually served last. **$131** for adults, $66 for kids 6–12, kids 5 and under are free. Parking is $5 for 3 hours.

In Kohala

Mauna Kea Lu'au

62-100 Mauna Kea Beach Dr, Kohala
(808) 882-5707
Probably the best lu'au on the island is at the Mauna Kea Beach Hotel. They have a good imu ceremony where they pull the pig from the ground. They handle serving the food well, and it's also pretty darn delicious. Checking in can be slightly confusing (make sure to give them your name as you head in), but once you're seated, you're free to head to the buffet, and getting seconds is easy. Drinks are ordered from your table, but only *one* is included with your entrance. The first half of the show is very strong and very Hawaiian, though the second half stalls a bit. Unfortunately, the stage is a little low, so those in back won't see as much. (And it can be pretty *loud* for those up front.) Overall, a pretty classy lu'au. **$160** for general seating, $110 for kids 5–12. An extra $20 gets you premium seating. They also have a show only option for $110, $84 for kids.

Sunset Lu'au

69-275 Waikoloa Beach Dr, Waikoloa
(808) 886-6789
Sunset Lu'au at Waikoloa Beach Marriott has mediocre food and a good show. They ask you to show up at 5 p.m., then make you wait an hour for no discernible reason before dining. After eating, it feels like another long wait before the show begins. If you don't have a food ticket in your hand, you *have* to go to the towel desk first. Although drinks are free, there may be three bartenders for 300 people, so expect long lines. The imu ceremony is pretty good; when the music stops, head to the right side of the stage to beat the crowd. Good show with talented performers. Located adjacent to the fishpond at 'Anaeho'omalu. **$140** for general seating, $70 for kids 6–12. $171 for premier seating (aka the first three rows), $102 for kids.

Legends of Hawai'i Lu'au

69-425 Waikoloa Beach Dr, Waikoloa
(808) 886-1234
Legends of Hawai'i Polynesian show is at the Hilton Waikoloa Village. Though

their ads show the stage with a sunset behind it, the actual seating is too low to see the sunset. On the upside they have an open bar, and the performance has improved a bit in quality from previous editions. **$146** for general seating, $79 for kids 5–12 and $23 for kids under 5. $173 for preferred access to the buffet, valet parking and front row seats, with kids $106, $23 for keiki under 5. Overall, a bit less compelling.

Paniolo Sunset BBQ Dinner

59-564 Kohala Mountain Rd, Waimea
(808) 430-6113

And finally, this isn't really a lu'au, but we didn't know where else to put it. Called Paniolo Sunset BBQ Dinner, this takes place on an 8,500-acre cattle ranch located at the 3,200-foot level of Kohala Mountain Road (250) with sweeping ocean sunset views. Instead of Polynesians dancing the hula, you'll hear a performer playing Charlie Daniels or Vince Gill, perhaps off-key, but he plays a mean fiddle. You'll also get a bit of line dancing, some stargazing, roping, branding of wood and fireside s'mores. The food is good and hearty—they do meat and 'taters well here. Drinks are beer, wine and soft drinks—no mixed drinks—and the adult beverages aren't included in the price. You won't leave hungry or thirsty. It cools off more here after sunset than it does at the shoreline, so a light jacket may help. And you are a long bus ride from Kona. Some may find the entertainment hokey, but this 3-hour event is family-run and done in earnest (although once the program is over, the tone changes a little and you may feel less wanted.) There are locals who attend the dinner annually, even though it hasn't changed much over the years...now that *says* somethin'. **$85.** Kids (6–12) are half price. Wednesdays only.

COCKTAIL & DINNER CRUISES

You've got a couple of options, both on the west side. One is a true dinner cruise, the other offers cocktails and light appetizers only.

Body Glove (808-326-7122) offers a 3-hour dinner cruise from Kailua Pier that heads to Kealakekua Bay. Along the way their impressively researched historical narration keeps things interesting. The food is very good, and their mai tais are better than we expected. (Only one free drink, then it's a cash bar.) You'll want to snag a table on the lower deck as soon as you board. (Preferable to the upper deck.) This is a well-oiled machine and one of the best dinner cruises we've seen. **$158.** ($94 for children ages 6–17, free under 5.)

In Kohala, **Ocean Sports** (808-886-6666) has a 65-foot catamaran called **Alala** that departs from Kawaihae Harbor. They use their smaller **Sea Smoke**, which leaves from 'Anaeho'omalu Bay, if they have 49 or fewer customers. The 2-hour cocktail cruise is relaxing, and the friendly crew is always asking if you want anything. They motorsail much of the time, and you can chill out on the trampolines if you like. (Outdoors is preferable because their old, hazy cabin windows make the interior less desirable.) Complimentary beer, wine and soft drinks and light snacks to eat for **$139.** ($70 for children ages 6–12, kids under 6 are free.) Prices include tax.

ISLAND DINING BEST BETS

Best Ambiance—Lava Lava Beach Club
Best Adventurous Burger—Hilo Burger Joint
Best Old School Mai Tai—Island Lava Java
Best Way to Feel Like You're on a Boat Without Being on a Boat—Harbor House
Best Tiny Restaurant—La Bourgogne

ABOUT THE AUTHOR

More than two decades ago, I bought a one-way ticket to the island of Kaua'i after another venture failed spectacularly. (That's a *really* good story…for another time.) I was devastated, broke, and working in the construction industry as an unskilled laborer just to survive, thinking that I had peaked at such a young age, and it was all downhill from there. But at least I was living in Hawai'i. I spent my free time exploring, but I got frustrated when weekend after weekend I couldn't find a particular beach I'd heard about that I wanted to go to. I looked at a couple of guidebooks, but they all referred to a road that hadn't existed in a long time. And I dreamed that maybe I could find a way to do it better.

Within days of of entertaining that dream, however, I had to return to the mainland due to the declining health of my mother, who passed away shortly thereafter.

It was while I was away that a plan emerged—I would return to Kaua'i and start writing guidebooks. There were just a few problems with this plan: I had no writing skills, I didn't know how a book was published, I wasn't good at photography, I didn't know how to use a computer, *and I had no money.*

So I spent a year on the mainland and applied for every credit card I could and tried to acquire the skills I would need to make my dream come true. Just when I was ready to return to the islands in 1992, I watched in horror as a category 4 hurricane smashed into Kaua'i, causing widespread devastation. I couldn't pick another island because Kaua'i was the one I knew, the island I had fallen in love with. Knowing that hurricanes clear out old growth, giving sunlight (and a chance) to encourage younger foliage, I figured that the same might be true in business. So with a huge stack of credit cards and two suitcases, I moved back to a ravaged island and got to work.

I completely covered one of the walls of my 290-square-foot rented room with highly detailed topographic maps of the island, so I could study them while drinking my morning coffee (gotta have coffee). This was before Google Earth, after all.

Over the next year, I spent my mornings exploring the island and checking out various visitor activities like helicopter rides and snorkel tours (which I did anonymously and paid for with my credit cards—*at 22% interest*). I'd review a restaurant at lunch, and then I'd spend my afternoons doing a hike or swimming a beach in multiple conditions to assess its safety, before returning to my room to have a simple dinner of canned chicken and rice (because it was so cheap), then worked into the evening making my own maps of the island. Before going to bed each night, I would read every book about Hawaiian history I could get my hands on.

The first edition of "the blue book" came out in March 1994. I paid to print the first 10,000 books (with cash advances from that stack of credit cards) and mailed free copies to newspapers for review. The first order was for only one case, but a year later a nationwide bookstore chain agreed to stock the book. It took off from there. Next came Big Island, then Maui and O'ahu. I packed up my equipment and lived for two years on each island researching, mapping, writing and photographing.

Today the *Revealed Series* is no longer a one-man show. I have an awesome team that has expanded over the years, but ultimately the books and the apps are an expression of what I think about Hawai'i and comes from the experience of actually *doing* all the things you'll read about. And our ability to keep current and find new things is greatly helped by feedback from our incredibly enthusiastic readers. Please keep it coming.

Once in a while, if you are *really* lucky in this life, you find the place and circumstance to which you belong. I hope you will fall in love with Hawai'i the way I did, and return often. But wherever you travel in life, take chances, embrace the uncertainty of outcome, go with an explorer's heart, and most importantly, share what you find with others.

—One lucky buggah, *Andrew Doughty*

INDEX

Dining Index on page 252.

INDEX

Dining Index on page 252.

INDEX

Dining Index on page 252.

INDEX

Dining Index on page 252.

Dining Index on page 252.

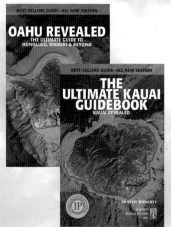